LSAT Hacks

Explanations for 10 Actual, Official LSAT Preptests, Volume V

LSATs 62-71

Volume I: Preptests 62-66

Graeme Blake

Blake Publications
Montreal, Canada

www.lsathacks.com

ISBN 13: 978-1-927997-06-2
ISBN 10: 1-927997-06-2

Testimonials

Self-study is my preferred way to prep, but I often felt myself missing a few questions each test. Especially for Logic Games, I wanted to see those key inferences which I just couldn't seem to spot on my own. That's where *LSAT Hacks* came in. These solutions have been a tremendous help for my prep, and in training myself to think the way an experienced test taker would.

- **Spencer B.**

Graeme paraphrases the question in plain terms, and walks through each step in obtaining the right answer in a very logical way. This book uses the same techniques as other guides, but its so much more consistent and concise! By the time you read through all the tests, you've gradually developed your eye for the questions. Using this book is a great way to test your mastery of techniques!

- **Sara L.**

Graeme's explanations have the most logical and understandable layout I've seen in an LSAT prep book. The explanations are straightforward and easy to understand, to the point where they make you smack your forehead and say 'of course!

- **Michelle V.**

"Graeme is someone who clearly demonstrates not only LSAT mastery, but the ability to explain it in a compelling manner. This book is an excellent addition to whatever arsenal you're amassing to tackle the LSAT."

- **J.Y. Ping, 7Sage LSAT,**
www.7Sage.com

I did not go through every single answer but rather used the explanations to see if they could explain why my answer was wrong and the other correct. I thought the breakdown of "Type", "Conclusion", "Reasoning" and "Analysis" was extremely useful in simplifying the question. As for quality of the explanations I'd give them a 10 out of 10.

- **Christian F.**

LSAT PrepTests come with answer keys, but it isn't sufficient to know whether or not you picked the credited choice to any given question. The key to making significant gains on this test is understanding the logic underlying the questions.

This is where Graeme's explanations really shine. You may wonder whether your reasoning for a specific question is sound. For the particularly challenging questions, you may be at a complete loss as to how they should be approached.

Having these questions explained by Graeme who scored a 177 on the test is akin to hiring an elite tutor at a fraction of the price. These straightforward explanations will help you improve your performance and, more fundamentally, enhance your overall grasp of the test content.

- **Morley Tatro, Cambridge LSAT,**
www.cambridgelsat.com

Through his conversational tone, helpful introductions, and general recommendations and tips, Graeme Blake has created an enormously helpful companion volume to *The Next Ten Actual Official LSATs*. He strikes a nice balance between providing the clarity and basic explanation of the questions that is needed for a beginner and describing the more complicated techniques that are necessary for a more advanced student.

Even though the subject matter can be quite dry, Graeme succeeds in making his explanations fun and lighthearted. This is crucial: studying for the LSAT is a daunting and arduous task. By injecting some humor and keeping a casual tone, the painful process of mastering the LSAT becomes a little less painful.

When you use *LSAT Hacks* in your studying, you will feel like you have a fun and knowledgeable tutor guiding you along the way.

- **Law Schuelke, LSAT Tutor,**
www.lawLSAT.com

Graeme's explanations are clear, concise and extremely helpful. They've seriously helped me increase my understanding of the LSAT material!

- Jason H.

Graeme's book brings a different view to demystifying the LSAT. The book not only explains the right and wrong answers, but teaches you how to read the reading comprehension and the logical reasoning questions. His technique to set up the games rule by rule help me not making any fatal mistakes in the set up. The strategies he teaches can be useful for someone starting as much as for someone wanting to perfect his strategies. Without his help my LSAT score would have been average, he brought my understanding of the LSAT and my score to a higher level even if english is not my mother tongue.

- Patrick Du.

This book is a must buy for any who are looking to pass or improve their LSAT, I highly recommend it.

- Patrick Da.

This book was really useful to help me understand the questions that I had more difficulty on. When I was not sure as to why the answer to a certain question was that one, the explanations helped me understand where and why I missed the right answer in the first place. I recommend this book to anyone who would like to better understand the mistakes they make.

- Pamela G.

Graeme's book is filled with thoughtful and helpful suggestions on how to strategize for the LSAT test. It is well-organized and provides concise explanations and is definitely a good companion for LSAT preparation.

- Lydia L.

The explanations are amazing, great job. I can hear your voice in my head as I read through the text.

- Shawn M.

LSAT Hacks, especially the logic games sections, was extremely helpful to my LSAT preparation.

The one downside to self study is that sometimes we do not know why we got a question wrong and thus find it hard to move forward. Graeme's book fixes that; it offers explanations and allows you to see where you went wrong. This is an extremely helpful tool and I'd recommend it to anybody that's looking for an additional study supplement.

- Joseph C.

Regardless of how well you're scoring on the LSAT, this book is very helpful. I used it for LR and RC. It breaks down and analyzes each question without the distraction of classification and complicated methods you'll find in some strategy books. Instead of using step-by-step procedures for each question, the analyses focus on using basic critical thinking skills and common sense that point your intuition in the right direction. Even for questions you're getting right, it still helps reinforce the correct thought process. A must-have companion for reviewing prep tests.

- Christine Y.

Take a thorough mastery of the test, an easygoing demeanor, and a genuine desire to help, and you've got a solid resource for fine-tuning your approach when you're tirelessly plowing through test after test. Written from the perspective of a test-taker, this book should help guide your entire thought process for each question, start to finish.

- Yoni Stratievsky, Harvard Ready,
www.harvardready.com

This LSAT guide is the best tool I could have when preparing for the LSAT. Not only does Graeme do a great job of explaining the sections as a whole, he also offers brilliant explanations for each question. He takes the time to explain why an answer is wrong, which is far more helpful when trying to form a studying pattern.

- Amelia F.

Explanations for 10 Actual, Official LSAT Preptests
Volume I: Preptests 62-66
Table Of Contents

Introduction

The LSAT is a hard test.

The only people who take the LSAT are smart people who did well in University. The LSAT takes the very best students, and forces them to compete.

If the test's difficulty shocked you, this is why. The LSAT is a test designed to be hard for smart people.

That's the bad news. But there's hope. The LSAT is a *standardized* test. It has patterns. It can be learned.

To get better, you have to review your mistakes. Many students write tests and move on, without fully understanding their mistakes.

This is understandable. The LSAC doesn't publish official explanations for most tests. It's hard to be sure why you were wrong.

That's where this book comes in. It's a companion for LSAT Preptests 62-71. This volume covers 62-66.

This book lets you see where you went wrong. It has a full walk through of each question and of every answer choice. You can use this book to fix your mistakes, and make sure you understand *everything*.

By getting this book, you've shown that you're serious about beating this test. I sincerely hope it helps you get the score you want.

There are a few things that I'd like to highlight.

Logical Reasoning: It can be hard to identify conclusions in LR. You don't get feedback on whether you identified the conclusion correctly.

This book gives you that feedback. I've identified the conclusion and the reasoning for each argument. Try to find these on your own beforehand, and make sure they match mine.

Logic Games: Do the game on your own before looking at my explanation. You can't think about a game unless you're familiar with the rules. Once you read my explanations, draw my diagrams yourself on a sheet of paper. You'll understand them much better by recopying them.

Reading Comprehension: You should form a mental map of the passage. This helps you locate details quickly. Make a 1-2 line summary of each paragraph (it can be a mental summary).

I've written my own summaries for each passage. They show the minimum amount of information that you should know after reading a passage, without looking back.

I've included line references in my explanations. You do not need to check these each time. They're only there in case you aren't sure where something is.

Do these three things, and you can answer most Reading Comprehension questions with ease.:

1. Know the point of the passage.
2. Understand the passage, in broad terms. Reread anything you don't understand.
3. Know where to find details. That's the point of the paragraph summaries. I usually do mine in my head, and they're shorter than what I've written.

Review This Book

Before we start, I'd like to ask you a favor. I'm an independent LSAT instructor. I don't have a marketing budget.

But I do my best to make good guides to the LSAT. If you agree, I would love it if you took two minutes to write a review on amazon.com

People judge a book by its reviews. So if you like this guide you can help others discover it. I'd be very grateful.

Good luck!

Graeme

p.s. I'm a real person, and I want to know how the LSAT goes and what you think of this book. Send me an email at graeme@lsathacks.com!

p.p.s. For more books, check out the further reading section at the back. I'm also offering a free half hour LSAT lesson if you fill out a survey.

How To Use This Book

The word "Hacks" in the title is meant in the sense used by the tech world and Lifehacker: "solving a problem" or "finding a better way".

The LSAT can be beaten, but you need a good method. My goal is for you to use this book to understand your mistakes and master the LSAT.

This book is *not* a replacement for practicing LSAT questions on your own.

You have to try the questions by yourself first. When you review, try to see why you were wrong *before* you look at my explanations.

Active review will teach you to fix your own mistakes. The explanations are there for when you have difficulty solving on a question on your own or when you want another perspective on a question.

When you *do* use the explanations, have the question on hand. These explanations are not meant to be read alone. You should use them to help you think about the questions more deeply.

Most of the logical reasoning explanations are pretty straightforward. Necessary assumption questions are often an exception, so I want to give you some guidance to help you interpret the explanations.

The easiest way to test the right answer on a necessary assumption question is to "negate" it.

You negate a statement by making it false, in the slightest possible way. For example, the negation of "The Yankees will win all their games" is "The Yankees will *not* win all their games (they will lose at least one)."

You *don't* have to say that the Yankees will lose *every* game. That goes too far.

If the negation of an answer choice proves the conclusion wrong, then that answer is *necessary* to the argument, and it's the correct answer.

Often, I negate the answer choices when explaining necessary assumption questions, so just keep in mind why they're negated.

Logic games also deserve special mention.

Diagramming is a special symbolic language that you have to get comfortable with to succeed.

If you just *look* at my diagrams without making them yourself, you may find it hard to follow along. You can only learn a language by using it yourself.

So you will learn *much* more if you draw the diagrams on your own. Once you've seen how I do a setup, try to do it again by yourself.

With constant practice, you *will* get better at diagramming, and soon it will come naturally.

But you must try on your own. Draw the diagrams.

Note that when you draw your own diagrams, you don't have to copy every detail from mine. For example, I often leave off the numbers when I do linear games. I've included them in the book, because they make it easier for you to follow along.

But under timed conditions, I leave out many details so that I can draw diagrams faster. If you practice making drawings with fewer details, they become just as easy to understand.

Keep diagrams as minimal as possible.

If you simply don't *like* the way I draw a certain rule type, then you can substitute in your own style of diagram. Lots of people succeed using different styles of drawing.

Just make sure your replacement is easy to draw consistently, and that the logical effect is the same. I've chosen these diagrams because they are clear, they're easy to draw, and they *keep you from forgetting rules.*

I've included line references to justify Reading Comprehension Answers. Use these only in case you're unsure about an explanation. You don't have to go back to the passage for every line reference.

Short Guide to Logical Reasoning

LR Question Types

Must be True: The correct answer is true.

Most Strongly Supported: The correct answer is probably true.

Strengthen/Weaken: The answer is correct if it even slightly strengthens/weakens the argument.

Parallel Reasoning: The correct answer will mirror the argument's structure exactly. It is often useful to diagram these questions (but not always).

Sufficient Assumption: The correct answer will prove the conclusion. It's often useful to diagram sufficient assumption questions. For example:

The conclusion is: A → D

There is a gap between premises and conclusion:

A B → C → D **missing link:** A → B or ~~B~~ → ~~A~~

A → B → C D **missing link:** C → D or ~~D~~ → ~~C~~

A → B C → D **missing link:** B → C or ~~C~~ → ~~B~~

The right answer will provide the missing link.

Necessary Assumption: The correct answer will be essential to the argument's conclusion. Use the negation technique: If the correct answer is false (negated), then the argument falls apart.
The negation of hot is "not hot" rather than cold.

Point at Issue: Point at Issue questions require two things. **1.** The two speakers must express an opinion on something. **2.** They must disagree about it.

Flawed Reasoning: The correct answer will be a description of a reasoning error made in the argument. It will often be worded very abstractly.

Practice understanding the answers, right and wrong. Flawed Reasoning answers are very abstract, but they all mean something. Think of examples to make them concrete and easier to understand.

Basic Logic

Take the phrase: "All cats have tails."

"Cats" is the sufficient condition. Knowing that something is a cat is "sufficient" for us to say that it has a tail. "Tails" is a necessary condition, because you can't be a cat without a tail. You can draw this sentence as C → T

The **contrapositive** is a correct logical deduction, and reads "anything without a tail is not a cat." You can draw this as ~~T~~ → ~~C~~. Notice that the terms are reversed, and negated.

Incorrect Reversal: "Anything with a tail is a cat." This is a common logical error on the LSAT.

T → C (Wrong! Dogs have tails and aren't cats.)

Incorrect Negation: "If it is not a cat, it doesn't have a tail." This is another common error.

~~C~~ → ~~T~~ (Wrong! Dogs aren't cats, but have tails.)

General Advice: Always remember what you are looking for on each question. The correct answer on a strengthen question would be incorrect on a weaken question.

Watch out for subtle shifts in emphasis between the stimulus and the incorrect answer choices. An example would be the difference between "how things are" and "how things should be."

Justify your answers. If you're tempted to choose an answer choice that says something like the sentence below, then be sure you can fill in the blank:

Answer Choice Says: "The politician attacked his opponents' characters",

Fill In The Blank: "The politician said _________ about his opponents' characters."

If you cannot say what the attack was, you can't pick that answer. This applies to many things. You must be able to show that the stimulus supports your idea.

A Few Logic Games Tips

Rule 1: When following along with my explanations....draw the diagrams yourself, too!

This book will be much more useful if you try the games by yourself first. You must think through games on your own, and no book will do that for you. You must have your mind in a game to solve it.

Use the explanations when you find a game you can't understand on your own, or when you want to know how to solve a game more efficiently.

Some of the solutions may seem impossible to get on your own. It's a matter of practice. When you learn how to solve one game efficiently, solving other games becomes easier too.

Try to do the following when you solve games:

Work With What Is Definite: Focus on what must be true. Don't figure out every possibility.

Draw Your Deductions: Unsuccessful students often make the same deductions as successful students. But the unsuccessful students forget their deductions, 15 seconds later! I watch this happen.

Draw your deductions, or you'll forget them. Don't be arrogant and think this doesn't happen to you. It would happen to *me* if I didn't draw my deductions.

Draw Clear Diagrams: Many students waste time looking back and forth between confusing pictures. They've done everything right, but can't figure out their own drawings!

You should be able to figure out your drawings 3 weeks later. If you can't, then they aren't clear enough. I'm serious: look back at your old drawings. Can you understand them? If not, you need a more consistent, cleaner system.

Draw Local Rules: When a question gives you a new rule (a local rule), draw it. Then look for deductions by combining the new rule with your existing rules. Then double-check what you're being asked and see if your deduction is the right answer. This works 90% of the time for local rule questions. And it's fast.

If you don't think you have time to draw diagrams for each question, practice drawing them faster. It's a learnable skill, and it pays off.

Try To Eliminate a Few Easy Answer Choices First: You'll see examples in the explanations that show how certain deductions will quickly get rid of 1-3 answer choices on many questions. This saves time for harder answer choices and it frees up mental space.

You don't have to try the answer choices in order, without thinking about them first.

Split Games Into Two Scenarios When Appropriate: If a rule only allows something to be one of two ways (e.g. F is in 1 or 7), then draw two diagrams: one with F in 1, and one with F in 7. This leads to extra deductions surprisingly often. And it always makes the game easier to visualize.

Combine Rules To Make Deductions: Look for variables that appear in multiple rules. These can often be combined. Sometimes there are no deductions, but it's a crime not to look for them.

Reread The Rules: Once you've made your diagram, reread the rules. This lets you catch any mistakes, which are fatal. It doesn't take very long, and it helps you get more familiar with the rules.

Draw Rules Directly On The Diagram: Mental space is limited. Three rules are much harder to remember than two. When possible, draw rules on the diagram so you don't have to remember them.

Memorize Your Rules: You should memorize every rule you can't draw on the diagram. It doesn't take long, you'll go faster, and you'll make fewer mistakes. Try it, it's not that hard.

If you spend 30 seconds doing this, you'll often save a minute by going through the game faster.

You should also make a numbered list of rules that aren't on the diagram, in case you need to check them.

Preptest 62
Section I – Reading Comprehension
Passage 1 – Earthquake Lichenometry
Questions 1–8

Paragraph Summaries

1. Radio-carbon dating is the traditional method of dating past earthquakes.
2. Lichens grow at a constant rate, and they grow on rocks exposed by earthquakes. Geologists are now using lichens to date past earthquakes.
3. Lichenometry is more accurate, but only for the past 500 years. Weather must be taken into account.

Analysis

This is a detail-heavy passage. It's not an argument. Instead, it's a scientific discussion of the advantages and disadvantages of lichenometry.

You shouldn't try to memorize all the details on a passage like this, but you should know roughly where they are. For example, if a question asks about how lichenometry works, that's the second paragraph. If it asks when to use lichenometry, that's the third paragraph.

You should retain a few key points as well. The summaries I wrote above are what I remember from each paragraph. I know more than that of course, but I know the details I wrote especially well.

If you had trouble *understanding* this passage, then I recommend you go to the library, and get 20-30 back issues of the Economist. Then read their science section. Each issue has 2-3 pages of science.

The Economist's science section is very well written. It doesn't dumb down the science, but it's written at a level that an intelligent non-scientist can understand. If you read many of these articles, you'll develop a base of general scientific knowledge that will serve you well on all science passages.

The gist of this passage is that when there's an earthquake, rock is exposed. The largest amounts of rock are exposed at the center of the quake. When rock is exposed, lichen grows on it. And lichen grows at the same speed, for a very long time.

So you can identify when and where an earthquake happened by studying lichen. It's generally quite accurate, though there are a few factors that affect lichen growth (lines 54-58), so these must be accounted for.

Radio-carbon dating is the traditional approach, but the third paragraph explains that it can be inaccurate in some circumstances. I didn't memorize the specifics, I just made sure I knew where they are in case a question asks about them.

Note that lichenometry is *new*. It has some advantages, but the passage is not saying that we should get rid of radiocarbon dating and only use lichenometry. We have know idea if many scientists use lichenometry. Perhaps only its inventors, Bull and Brandon, use it.

Question 1

DISCUSSION: Main idea questions first of all have to be true. You can eliminate answers that contradict the passage.

All of the wrong answers either contradict the passage or aren't supported by it.

A. CORRECT. Lines 15-16 support this. Lichenometry is a *new* method. The passage describes the advantages of lichenometry, but that's it. This is a better answer than D.
B. The emphasis of the passage is not on lichenometry's limitations. And we don't know if it's more accurate than *all* other methods. It certainly isn't more accurate for earthquakes older than 500 years (lines 53-54)
C. The passage never mentions "most seismologists". We only know Bull and Brandon (line 15) are using lichenometry.
D. This is a bit strong. The passage never says that lichenometry has "revolutionized" the study of earthquakes. And we don't know if it's "easily applied". You have to go look at lichen on rocks, and carefully consider weather factors.
E. This is false. Line 54 says that lichenometry is only useful for earthquakes up to 500 years old.

Question 2

DISCUSSION: Remember, the right answer will actually be answered by the passage. If you can't find a line answering the question, you haven't got the right answer.

A. This isn't addressed.
B. Lines 43-45 mention radiation, but they don't say how it is measured.
C. CORRECT. Lines 57-58 say that shade and wind make lichen grow faster.
D. Line 54 says we should use lichenometry for earthquakes less than 500 years old, but the passage never says what the oldest earthquake dated by lichenometry is.
E. The passage never mentions other uses for radiocarbon dating.

Question 3

DISCUSSION: The rate of growth is a constant 9.5 mm per century. This is useful because it lets us measure how long lichen has been growing. For example, 95 mm of lichen would be 1000 years old.

Read the lines above and below lines 29-30 to get the full context.

A. The growth rate isn't relevant to how fast lichen establish themselves. There's a difference between *starting* to grow, and growing.
B. The passage doesn't say that 9.5 mm per year is a slow speed.
C. Environmental conditions are only mentioned on lines 54-58.
D. The passage never says why lichenometry doesn't work well for earthquakes older than 500 years.
E. **CORRECT.** This is the best explanation. The author just wants to illustrate how fast lichen grows.

Question 4

DISCUSSION: The right answer will have a line supporting it. If you can't find the line, you probably don't have the right answer.

You can quickly find lines if you know the structure of the passage. Always try to know roughly what information each paragraph has.

A. The passage never mentions predicting future earthquakes.
B. **CORRECT.** Paragraph 1 says radiocarbon dating is used to date samples from trenches along visible fault lines (line 3). So it's unlikely radiocarbon dating is useful if there are no fault lines.
C. The passage never said "these are the only two methods". There could be others.
D. We have no idea. We know radiocarbon dating is not good for 300 years ago (lines 45-48) and lichenometry is not useful for more than 500 years ago (line 54). But 400 years ago? We have no idea. This answer is just trying to confuse you by throwing in a random date we know nothing about.
E. Lines 54-58 say we can correct for factors that change lichen growth rates. This answer contradicts the passage. Presumably, factors affecting growth rate are not a deal-breaker.

Question 5

DISCUSSION: The first paragraph describes radiocarbon dating, the traditional method of dating earthquakes.

This sets the stage for discussing the advantages and disadvantages of lichenometry.

Most of the wrong answers contradict the passage or receive no support.

A. Radiocarbon dating is well known, but the passage doesn't examine it on a step by step basis.
B. CORRECT. Radiocarbon dating is the established procedure. Lichenometry is then described (paragraph 2) and compared (paragraph 3).
C. The passage never says radiocarbon dating is outdated. Lichenometry is new. Only time will tell if it's ultimately better than radiocarbon dating.
D. There's no other traditional process. Lichenometry is a *new* process. (lines 15-16)
E. The passage never says that radiocarbon dating has led to errors. We know it's inaccurate in the past 300 years (lines 45-47), but that doesn't mean there are errors. Scientists may have avoided it for earthquakes dating from the past 300 years because they knew of the inaccuracies.

Question 6

DISCUSSION: You should always reread the lines in question. Line 50-58 discuss the limits of lichenometry:

- It should be used for earthquakes less than 500 years old.
- Sites should avoid snow avalanches.
- Shade and wind must be factored in.

Bull and Brandon are assuming that those things can be done. Especially the last one. It seems hard to factor in shade and wind. It's hard to say what shade and wind were like over a few hundred years.

This question is very much like a LR necessary assumption question. You can negate the answers.

A. Bull and Brandon aren't assuming anything about earthquakes older than 500 years. They say lichenometry is best used only for recent quakes.
Negation: Lichenometry is not the best method for earthquakes older than 500 years.
B. Radiation relates to radiocarbon dating (lines 43-45). This isn't relevant to lichenometry.
C. This would *weaken* the argument if true.
Negation: Lichens can grow in many places.
D. This would *weaken* the argument if true. Bull and Brandon say to *avoid* snow avalanches, so it would be better if lichenometry could be used on mountains that don't have avalanches.
E. CORRECT. This is necessary. If we can't determine how shade and wind affect growth, then we can't factor them in. See lines 57-58.
Negation: The extent to which shade and wind affect lichen growth cannot be determined.

Question 7

DISCUSSION: The problems of radiocarbon dating are discussed in the the third paragraph. Radiation intensity has changed over the years, and this reduces accuracy. See lines 40-48.

A. The first paragraph mentions radiocarbon dating uses "wood or other organic materials". It never says that multiple types of materials are a problem.

B. This would be in paragraph 1. That paragraph talks about getting material from shifted sediments. But paragraph 1 never talks about variable amounts being a problem.

C. Tempting, but there are two problems:
1. The passage never says that some fault lines aren't visible.
2. The passage only says that seismologists *usually* dig along visible fault lines (lines 2-3). Maybe radiocarbon dating can also be used on non-visible fault lines.

D. **CORRECT.** See lines 40-48. They describe this problem directly.

E. This sounds right, but it's referring to the wrong thing. Lines 44-45 say that the amount of radiation striking the upper atmosphere *varies*. The passage doesn't say that radiation may have *never* struck the upper atmosphere.

Question 8

DISCUSSION: We know lichenometry is useful under the following conditions:

- Mountain rocks less than 500 years old.
- Sites should avoid snow avalanches.
- Shade and wind must be factored in.

A. Too old. We should only use lichenometry for sites up to 500 years old. Also, we don't know if there are mountain rockfalls near this river.

B. Same as A. Also, there are no rocks here.

C. Lichenometry is useful for *mountain rocks*. There are no mountain rocks at the shore. Also, an "ancient beach" is probably older than 500 years.

D. **CORRECT.** This has the right factors. It's in a mountain. And rocks are being exposed. So we can measure how much lichen has grown over the past five centuries. We can figure out when the glacier retreated by checking when lichen started growing – that's the date rocks were first exposed.

E. The timeframe is right. But lichenometry is for mountain rocks. We don't know if this is in a valley. Also, lichenometry isn't useful for identifying rainfall. Instead, rainfall is a confounding factor that must be accounted for.

Passage 2 – Medical Illustrations
Questions 9–14

Paragraph Summaries

1. Some argue against custom illustrations for trials – medical textbooks are adequate.
2. Some say medical illustrations misrepresent facts. But illustrations need to be vouched by a medical expert.
3. Courtroom medical illustrations are designed to be neutral. They also leave out details that are irrelevant to the case, making them easier to understand.
4. Many physical conditions can only be described in hard-to-understand technical terms. Medical illustrations allow juries to visualize the explanations provided by experts.

Analysis

This passage is an argument. The author thinks that custom medical illustrations are useful in trials. The author first presents the opposing view, then rebuts it.

The opposing view has two main arguments:

1. Medical textbook illustrations are adequate.
2. Custom illustrations are biased.

Lines 36-49 show that custom illustrations are more useful than medical textbooks. Custom illustrations remove unnecessary details, so they are considerably easier to understand.

There are actually two criticisms about potential bias of custom illustrations. The first is blatant. In the second paragraph, the author presents the idea that corrupt illustrators will misrepresent the body. Lines 25-29 show this isn't likely because illustrations must be approved by medical experts.

The second criticism is more subtle. It's in lines 30-34. The worry is that there may be subtle bias in custom illustrations through the use of color and emphasis.

The rest of the third paragraph rebuts this idea. The author says that professional illustrators avoid unnecessary color and other unnecessary details in order to clarify diagrams and avoid bias. Medical textbook illustrations, by contrast, have much color and additional detail, which may confuse the jury and also bias them.

The final paragraph describes an additional advantage of custom illustrations: they make it easier to visualize and understand complex technical descriptions.

Note that the author does not think medical experts are doing anything wrong when they testify. It is legitimately difficult to describe complex anatomy without confusing non-experts. The author doesn't think experts need to do a better job of speaking about anatomy. Instead, they think custom medical illustrations are a useful aid to medical experts that help clarify what they say.

Note: I'll repeat the advice I gave for Passage 1. If you had trouble *understanding* this passage, then I recommend you go to the library, and get 20-30 back issues of the Economist. Then read their science section. Each issue has 2-3 pages of science.

The Economist's science section is very well written. It doesn't dumb down the science, but it's written at a level that an intelligent non-scientist can understand. If you read many of these articles, you'll develop a base of general scientific knowledge that will serve you well on all science passages.

Question 9

DISCUSSION: Custom made illustrations do the following:

- They are visual aids (paragraph 4)
- They remove unnecessary detail (lines 36-49)
- They are produced for a non-expert audience – judges and juries. (lines 41-42)
- The custom illustrations accompany and clarify oral testimony (paragraph 4)
- They are custom made for the situation at hand.

A. CORRECT. This matches several of the factors. A schematic is:

* Custom made
* A visual aid
* Accompanying an oral presentation

Schematics probably also remove unnecessary detail, since the engineer is producing them to help their presentation. We don't know if the audience is non-expert, but you don't have to match all factors.

B. Road maps *are* simplified, but avoiding verbal instructions is wrong. In a trial you get a diagram AND verbal instructions.

C. Medical illustrations are useful to clarify legal testimony. Here the illustrations are used for investigation.

D. Custom illustrations aren't reproductions of textbooks. They are *simplified* diagrams. It sounds like this painting is an exact copy.

E. Preliminary sketches are for the artist's own use, and they probably aren't simplified. Custom medical illustrations are for others, and they are simplified.

Question 10

DISCUSSION: On this type of question, you're looking for a line that supports the right answer. If you can't find a line supporting the answer, you're likely to make a mistake.

A. Line 36 says that it's custom illustrations that often avoid color.

B. The author says *custom illustrations* can't be admitted without expert testimony (line 29). But established medical textbooks might be admitted without further testimony. We don't know.

C. We have no idea. The passage never says what kind of illustrators draw medical textbooks.

D. Lines 16-20 describe this view, but they only say *some* lawyers hold it. We don't know if *most* lawyers believe this. If most lawyers thought custom illustrations were misleading, then custom illustrations probably wouldn't be used.

E. CORRECT. See lines 41-46. Custom illustrations remove detail to avoid confusing judges and juries.

Question 11

DISCUSSION: Lines 28-29 say that custom medical illustrations are only admissible if an expert says they are accurate.

A. I almost chose this. But medical experts don't say whether illustrations are *admissible*. Judges say what's admissible. Medical experts only say if the diagrams are accurate. Read lines 28-29 carefully.
B. Nonsense. Custom illustrations are designed to be easy to understand, and to avoid bias (see lines 33-36). So the author doesn't think medical experts need to correct any bias.
C. Actually, it's the other way around. The fourth paragraph says that medical illustrations help judges and juries understand medical experts. Without diagrams, expert testimony is confusing.
D. This sounds like lines 28-29. But the passage never says medical experts advise attorneys on which diagrams are useful. The passage only says they advise whether diagrams are *accurate.* That's why E is right and this answer is wrong.
E. **CORRECT.** See lines 28-29. They say this directly.

Question 12

DISCUSSION: The third paragraph discusses the differences between medical textbooks and custom illustrations. You should look there to justify answers.

A. Both illustrations are accurate. The difference is that custom illustrations remove unnecessary detail.
Note: You may think that custom illustrations are inaccurate because they remove detail. But textbook illustrations remove some detail too. The only exact model of a human arm (for example) is a real-life human arm. Any illustration is a simplification.
B. This sounds like lines 35-36. But the author didn't say that custom illustrations *always* remove color.
C. Nonsense. Line 34 says that custom illustrations aim for accuracy.
D. **CORRECT.** Lines 36-46 say this directly. Custom illustrations remove unnecessary detail.
E. This is backwards. Nonmedical audiences find *custom illustrations* easier to understand. See lines 41-45.

Question 13

DISCUSSION: The author thinks that medical experts are reliable (lines 28-29) but confusing (lines 55-59) without diagrams.

The author has a neutral attitude towards experts. He doesn't think they should change. I doubt the authors thinks experts *can* change. You can't describe technical details of the body without technical words.

But such testimony will be hard to understand without a diagram to clarify it.

A. The author isn't "skeptical" of testimony. The author plainly states that testimony is confusing. That's more than skeptical. And the author proposes a solution: custom images. Skeptics rarely propose action, instead they sow doubt.
B. This is tempting. The author did say that medical experts are hard to understand. But the problem isn't their communications skills. The problem is that it's very, very hard to describe technical details to an everyday audience.
C. **CORRECT.** Lines 28-29 suggest that the author accepts that medical experts give good testimony. Lines 55-59 show that testimony is hard to understand without diagrams.
D. The author did say that medical experts can overwhelm juries. But the author didn't say that medical experts *try* to overwhelm juries.
E. The author said medical terminology is confusing. But the author didn't say medical experts should stop using it. The author appears to admit that describing the human body requires technical language.

Question 14

DISCUSSION: This is a very tricky question. I was stuck between B and C, until I realized I had misunderstood the 3rd paragraph.

In the second paragraph, the author claims that custom illustrations will be technically accurate. In the 3rd paragraph, he raises a subtler criticism: maybe custom images are biased, even if they're technically accurate. Lines 33-36 directly rebut this attack.

Then the paragraph talks about medical textbook illustrations. Why? In light of question 14, I now think they're describing medical textbook images to show that the high level of detail in medical textbooks may actually introduce bias using color, detail, emphasis, etc.

Whereas custom images are made solely for the purpose of clarifying the issue at hand. They are less likely to bias judges and juries.

A. Careful. A "greater" use. The author didn't say we should use more custom images than we do right now. Instead, they're defending our current usage.
B. **CORRECT.** See the explanation above.
C. I was very tempted by this. The 3rd paragraph does help show that images from medical textbooks are not well suited to the classroom. But....that's not the *purpose* of the 3rd paragraph. The purpose of the 3rd paragraph is to show that custom illustrations are not biased, including when compared to medical textbook illustrations.
D. Nonsense. The third paragraph is an argument. Notice the word "but" in line 33.
E. Not quite. The third paragraph does do this, but it's not the *purpose*. Notice the word "but" in line 33. The author is disagreeing with lines 30-33, and giving their opinion in lines 33-49. The 3rd paragraph not mere description. It is an argument.

Did you pick this answer because it was true? That's not what you're supposed to be looking for.

Passage 3 – Dental Caries (comparative)
Questions 15–21

Paragraph Summaries

Passage A

1. Tooth decay lets us know when a population started agriculture.
2. Carbohydrates lead to more caries. Carbohydrates come from agriculture.
3. Some non-agricultural populations ate foods that decayed teeth.

Passage B

1. Researchers found 2,000 years worth of skeletons in Thailand. Over the 2,000 years, the prehistoric people gradually switched from hunter-gathering to agriculture.
2. Agriculture causes caries. There is more sticky-starch, and less fiber.
3. Over time, the diet had rice and yams. Both are carbs, so in theory they cause caries.
4. Yet caries didn't go up. They may have eaten more rice, which is less cariogenic.

Analysis

There is *one* word in this passage you must understand: caries.

I doubt you've heard it before, unless you went to dental school. Most people read these passage with no idea what "caries" means. So every five lines the passage throws them a word they don't understand, and they get very confused.

This is the wrong way. When you see a word you don't know, AND that word seems important, stop! Read around the word for context. Try to understand it.

In this case, the passage actually defines caries for you. Look at line 1: "dental caries (decay)". Let's turn this into a simpler word. In three steps, I'm starting with the original term, then substituting words you know.

1. Dental caries
2. Dental decay
3. Tooth decay

So "caries" in this passage = tooth decay. Every time you read the word "caries", you should replace it with "tooth decay".

Both passages are *much* easier if you understand this. Passage A says "Agriculture and carbs cause tooth decay, though tooth decay can happen without agriculture."

Passage B says "One example in Thailand shows that additional carbs don't always lead to tooth decay".

Simple, right? I don't memorize all the details in these passages. For example, paragraph 2 in passage A has the evidence of tooth decay in agricultural populations. If a question asks, I know to look there. But I don't retain all the information.

Likewise, paragraph 2 of passage B has technical information on how carbs can cause tooth decay. Great! If a question asks, lets look there. Otherwise, who cares.

I do retain a few details. I remember fiber is protective somehow, but can be bad. If a question asked about it, I would reread that section to learn the rest. I know *where* the passage talks about fiber, and that's the important part.

Have a look at the paragraph summaries I made of both passages, above. That's about all you have to know and understand. If you're still confused about the passage, I recommend you reread it while keeping in mind that caries = tooth decay.

Tooth wear is not caries. Tooth wear is only mentioned in paragraph 2 of passage B. It's caused by fiber, and it can be helpful in *preventing* caries.

Note: I'll repeat the advice I gave for Passage 1. If you had trouble *understanding* this passage, then I recommend you go to the library, and get 20-30 back issues of the Economist. Then read their science section. Each issue has 2-3 pages of science.

The Economist's science section is very well written. It doesn't dumb down the science, but it's written at a level that an intelligent non-scientist can understand. If you read many of these articles, you'll develop a base of general scientific knowledge that will serve you well on all science passages.

Question 15

DISCUSSION: This is a bit of a hard question. I had to check a few of the answers against the passage. I found B and C tempting, but they both contain terms that don't match the passages.

A. CORRECT. See lines 3-5 in passage A, and 36-38 in passage B.
I don't love this answer, because I'm not sure passage B is "primarily concerned" with the agricultural record. They seem more specifically concerned with the tooth health of the Ban Chiang populations. But passage B is at least concerned with the development of agriculture in that population, so this is the best answer.

B. "Overall health" is why this is wrong. Both passages were only concerned with tooth decay.

C. "Strictly agricultural societies" is why this is wrong. Passage A talks about tooth decay in nonagricultural populations (paragraph 3) and passage B says the Ban Chiang groups were not entirely agricultural – they ate some wild foods (lines 54-54).

D. Neither passage mentions the first agricultural society. Passage B, in particular, only talks about Thailand.

E. This is a general answer. Neither passage talks about hunter-gatherer carbohydrate availability in general.

Question 16

DISCUSSION: You should reread the last paragraph of passage A. It discussed societies that:

- Weren't agricultural
- Had lots of caries

A. Lines 28-31 show that the groups in passage A *did* eat cariogenic foods.
B. **CORRECT.** The groups in passage A were nonagricultural (line 25). Nonagricultural means they didn't cultivate foods. Whereas the Ban Chiang groups were agricultural (line 38).
C. There are two problems with this. First, passage B doesn't say that the Ban Chiang groups *primarily* ate carbohydrates. They had a "varied diet" (line 55). Second, we don't know that the groups in passage A avoided carbohydrates. In particular, tubers are carbohydrates – tubers are mentioned in line 31.
D. "Tooth wear" is only mentioned in lines 44-50. It's not the same things as caries. In fact, tooth wear can help prevent caries (lines 47-48).
In the last paragraph of passage A, only caries are mentioned.
In other words, this answer is talking about the wrong thing! Tooth wear never occurs in passage A. RC answers do this a lot.
E. Line 27 says one of the groups in passage A *did* eat a highly processed diet.

Question 17

DISCUSSION: As with most RC questions, the wrong answers either have no support from the passage, or they contradict the passage.

If you find wrong answers tempting, you don't know the passage well enough, and you need to learn to check the passage faster to disprove answers.

A. **CORRECT.** Read lines 47-50. They say that tooth wear from fiber helps prevent decay, but too much fiber exposes pulp and causes decay.
B. The passage never says whether agriculture leads to more or less fiber.
C. This contradicts lines 47-48. Some fiber can be helpful for health by providing tooth wear.
D. Line 46 says fiber *removes* fissures.
E. Nonsense. This answer just takes two unrelated terms from the passage ("sticky carbs" and "fiber") and combines them. The passage never mentioned a relationship between these terms.

Question 18

DISCUSSION: Passage B is a bit less clear for the purposes of this question. It never explicitly says agriculture leads to carbs. But it's implied by the statements that agriculture leads to caries, carbs cause caries (lines 43-45) and that the Ban Chiang groups cultivated carbs.

A. Careful. The passage don't say that highly process = carbohydrates. You can process non-carbohydrates as well.
B. **CORRECT.** Both passages say this. Passage A says that agriculture leads to carbs (lines 1-3) and agriculture is linked to caries (lines 20-22). Passage B says that caries are rare in pre-agricultural populations (lines 39-42) and that cultivated foods (rice and yams) are carbs (lines 55-56).
C. Passage A never mentions fiber and grit.
D. "Tooth wear" is only mentioned in paragraph 2 of passage B. Tooth wear refers to fiber and grit smoothing away fissures in tooth surfaces. It's not the same thing as tooth decay.
E. Neither passage mentions overall human health.

Question 19

DISCUSSION: The wrong answers either contradict the passage, aren't mentioned in the passages, or are insane (answer A).

The right answer is found in both passages. Most RC questions really are as simple as that: if you know the passage, you know the answer.

A. The author of passage B, in particular, might not agree with this. The Ban Chiang groups seem to have surprised researchers because they did *not* get more caries.
Also, you should interpret answers literally. This answer would mean all populations, including our own, would constantly be having more tooth decay. That's crazy.
B. Nonsense. If tooth decay were hard to detect, then we couldn't effectively study tooth decay in past populations.
C. "More prevalent" means more common. The authors *disagree* with this.
D. **CORRECT.** Both authors agree. The last paragraph of passage A supports this, and so do lines 58-60 in passage B. The Early group had more decay even though the Ban Chiang groups became more agricultural over time (lines 36-38).
E. Passage A never mentions tooth wear! Only passage B mentions it, in lines 44-50.

Question 20

DISCUSSION: The right answer is a little tricky to justify. You have to use common sense. This is a misunderstood issue on the LSAT. A lot of people think you can't use outside knowledge.

But outside knowledge is allowed, even *encouraged.* You just have to use it in the right way. You can only assume things that *no one would disagree with.* You're supposed to assume the knowledge of a well informed person. For example, someone who knows about tubers knows they're carbs. Since this is true in real life, it's a fact you can use.

What you *can't* use as outside knowledge are opinions that people might disagree with, such as "taxes are good/bad".

A. The passages never explicitly mention wild carbohydrates, so there is no comparison.
B. Assuming acorn flour is a carbohydrate, passage A *contradicts* this answer. See line 27. Passage B never mentions processed carbohydrates.
C. **CORRECT.** Passage B says this directly. See lines 66-68.
Passage A is a bit less supported. You have to read between the lines. There are two lines that support this. First, lines 8-10 say that carbohydrates' texture and composition affect caries. This likely means: "Carbohydrates have different textures. Carbohydrate texture tends to promote caries, but some textures do this more than others." After all, you know from common knowledge that carb textures differ.

Second, line 31 says that tubers are a highly cariogenic wild food. Again, it's common knowledge that tubers are carbohydrates. No well informed person would disagree with this. Lines 29-31 say that wild plants "included several cariogenic foods". This implies that some wild foods (plants) are not cariogenic. An it is common knowledge that most wild plants are carbs. So some carbs are not cariogenic.
D. Only passage B mentioned fiber.
E. Neither passage says that carbohydrates change if they're cultivated.

Question 21

DISCUSSION: The generalization in passage A is that more agriculture leads to more tooth decay, in general.

The Ban Chiang are a counterexample. The early, less agricultural Ban Chiang groups had more tooth decay (lines 58-60).

A. No, see the explanation above.
B. No, see the explanation above.
C. The Ban Chiang are definitely relevant. The generalization is talking about all populations. The Ban Chiang increased their use of agriculture, so according to the generalization they should have had more tooth decay.
D. **CORRECT.** The Ban Chiang don't fit with the generalization. They had less tooth decay as their agriculture increased.
E. You can't disprove a generalization with a single example. A generalization is just a tendency. If I say "Americans tend to be nice", you can only disprove that by showing "No, most americans are mean". A single mean American doesn't disprove the generalization.

Passage 4 – Jewett
Questions 22–27

Paragraph Summaries

1. Sarah Orne Jewett's novels are superficially similar to domestic novels. But her work is secular and doesn't focus on children.
2. Domestic novels were also religious works and instructions on how to run a home. Sarah Orne Jewett wrote books that were only novels.
3. By Jewett's time, fiction had become pure art. So Jewett's work should be seen differently than domestic novels even though they are superficially similar.

Analysis

This passage is a bit dull, but I don't think it's difficult to understand. The passage is an argument. It's responding to a theory: some say Sarah Orne Jewett's wrote domestic novels.

The author disagrees. They show that despite superficial similarities, Jewett wrote for art's sake. I actually don't know what to say about this passage beyond what I wrote in the paragraph summaries: I don't think there's much more to it.

Incidentally, I have a theory for why the LSAT has reading comprehension passages about obscure literary topics: no one knows about them. Very, very few people have pre-existing knowledge about Sarah Orne Jewett or domestic novelists.

And yet, there is a large existing body of scholarship about this and most other literary topics. So it's easy for the LSAC to find a scholarly article or book to summarize. If you look at the end of preptest 62, you'll see that this passage was adapted from:

Richard H. Brodhead, *Cultures of Letters: Scenes of Reading and Writing in Nineteenth-Century America*. © 2003 by the University of Chicago.

In other words, an entire book was written on this topic. And likely there are many other books and articles discussing Sarah Orne Jewett. So it's easy to adapt material into rigorous, technical arguments.

This passage takes place against the backdrop of a changing society. The passage implies that in the 1850s, women's place was in the home. Domestic novels served several purposes (lines 28-34):

- Entertainment (they were novels, after all)
- Piety (this means being religious)
- Domestic instruction (how to be a good wife and mother)

The books were set in the home, and their main subject matter was children and how to raise them. (lines 10-13).

Jewett's work was pure art. By the late 19th century the novel had emerged as a genre unto itself. (line 44-51). Jewett's novels were meant to be read for their own sake. They had no goals beyond that. In particular, Jewett's novels weren't religious and they didn't tell you how to raise kids (lines 13-19).

The author's argument is: despite superficial similarities in setting, Jewett's work is not like the domestic novels.

Question 22

DISCUSSION: The passage doesn't quite answer the question in answer D, but it at least hints at an answer. This is just a "most helps" question.

From the context of the whole passage, we know that Jewett's idea of fiction influenced the type of books she wrote. Her books were secular and artistic.

A. The passage never mentions men.
B. The passage never says if some domestic novels stayed popular after the 1860's.
C. The author actually implies that migration to the cities was *not* as significant as you might think: see lines 20-25. In any case, we don't know *how* urban migration changed fiction.
D. CORRECT. In lines 49-51, the author says Jewett viewed her novels as ends in themselves. This probably explains why Jewett's work wasn't religious and wasn't intended to instruct people on how to live.
E. The passage never says where Jewett lived.

Question 23

DISCUSSION: The author spends the entire passage arguing against this recent position. The argument starts on line 7. The "but" indicates disagreement. Line 13 continues with disagreement: the words "by contrast" means the author disagrees with the "recent criticism" in lines 1-7.

Lines 49-53 state the author's thesis fully: Jewett and the domestic novelists shouldn't be placed in the same category.

However, the author does make some concession to the recent criticism. Lines 4-7 say that "Her work does resemble....". So the author thinks the recent criticism is not completely insane: it's at least based in real evidence.

A. The author disagrees with the recent criticism. See lines 49-53.
B. The author disagrees with the recent criticism. See lines 49-53.
C. CORRECT. At first I thought this was too wishy-washy. But I reread the first paragraph and decided that it's a fair characterization. The "reasonable evidence" is the similarity in setting between Jewett's work and the domestic novels. Ultimately, the author thinks the recent criticism is wrong, but it's not entirely without evidence.
D. The author does think the recent criticism is "questionable". But not because of any "currently dominant literary aesthetic". I have no idea what that refers to – the author doesn't discuss current literature.
E. This goes too far. Lines 4-7 show that the recent criticism has *some* support. The author disagrees with the criticism, but they admit there is at least a little bit of evidence for that view.

Question 24

DISCUSSION: Keep reading line 30.
It says "a continuum that also included....piety and domestic instructions....goal of promoting morality and religious belief".

In other words, apart from entertainment, the domestic novels were supposed to help you be a good mother and a good Christian.

Fiction as continuum means there was no clear dividing line between novel; religious book and household manual.

A. The passage never mentions earlier times. It says the domestic novel was from the mid-nineteenth century (lines 28-29) and it doesn't say that any earlier novels had similar goals.
B. **CORRECT.** The domestic novels were fiction, religious work and instruction manuals all rolled into one.
C. "Serial" means publishing a part of book in a magazine, usually on a weekly basis. For example, Charles Dickens' novels were published piece by piece.
So, this answer has *nothing* to do with the passage. We have no idea how domestic novels were published.
D. Rubbish. Read line 30 and the surrounding lines carefully. Nothing they say has anything to do with the evolution of fiction.
E. Nonsense. The only reason this answer is tempting is because continuity sounds like continuum. If you thought this was tempting, you completely failed to understand the use of the word "continuum". Go reread lines 25-35.

Some people in the 19th century might have thought domestic fiction promoted cohesiveness. But you're not looking for what might be true. You're looking for *why* the author used the word "continuum".

Question 25

DISCUSSION: The author first introduces the opposing view, in lines 1-7. Then the rest of the passage is spent arguing against this opposing view.

The conclusion is in lines 49-53: Jewett was not like the domestic novelists.

As usual, most of the wrong answers contradict the passage or mention things that never appeared in the passage.

A. What? The author doesn't redefine anything. They're arguing against recent criticism which is attempting to redefine Jewett's role.
I have no idea what "several historical categories refers to". We only know about the domestic novelists and Jewett.
B. What style of writing? Jewett is the "one writer", but the author only tells us that she is *not* a domestic novelist. She's not part of any category or style.
C. What group of writers? The author is arguing that Jewett is *not* part of a group.
D. The author didn't say that Jewett is *better* than the domestic novelists. The author just said that Jewett is different.
E. **CORRECT.** The author says that Jewett wasn't a domestic novelist. The "alternate view" is that Jewett wrote to make art.

Question 26

DISCUSSION: The second paragraph starts with a hypothesis: maybe changes such as urbanization or secularization caused the differences between Jewett and the domestic novelists.

The "but" on line 24 shows the author does not agree with this theory. The rest of the paragraph explains that the differences are more likely due to different ideas of the role of art.

Domestic novels were intended as instruction manuals as well as fiction. Jewett wrote for art's sake.

A. What the devil does this refer to? The 2nd paragraph never talks about risking the "unity" of our conception of domestic novels by trying to explain them.

B. The author didn't show that the two explanations are *incompatible*. They even said the first theory may be partially correct (line 24).

C. First, there are only two hypotheses. Second, the author didn't say all explanations were the same. They clearly prefer their own explanation, starting on line 24.

D. This is completely different from the 2nd paragraph. I've written an example below that fits with what this answer says. Beyond that, I can't "explain" how this answer is wrong except to say that it didn't happen! Not even close.
Example of answer: We could classify all domestic novels are helpful or not helpful. Alternatively, we could classify them as dull or not dull.
Some say neither classification is useful: we shouldn't classify at all.
Start of next paragraph: But I reject that counterargument. If we didn't classify novels, what could we write about?

E. CORRECT. The different explanatory hypotheses are factors such as urbanization or secularization (lines 20-24). The mildly approving comment is in lines 24-25 ("may help to explain"). The other explanation is 26-28: a different conception of fiction explains the differences. The rest of the paragraph gives evidence for this conception.

Question 27

DISCUSSION: Many of the wrong answers talk about things that weren't mentioned in the passage. Some wrong answers even contradict the passage.

Don't fall for traps. The wrong answers usually choose a term from the passage, and then use that term in the wrong context. This makes the answer seem familiar even though they're completely irrelevant.

Check your answer against the passage to make sure you're not being fooled.

A. We don't know why Jewett didn't write about children. Secular, artistic novels are sometimes about children.
The reason this is wrong is that the passage never says Jewett was "unwilling" to write about children.

B. The passage didn't say if Jewett's work was urban or rural. This answer just throw in terms that were mentioned on line 23.

C. CORRECT. Jewett didn't have to focus on religion and maternity because she was part of a movement that saw the novel as art. There was no obligation to any goals outside of the work itself. See lines 44-49.

D. The passage never said why Jewett wrote about women.

E. The passage didn't say Jewett was *unable* to feature children. The passage just said she *didn't*.

Section II – Logical Reasoning

Question 1

QUESTION TYPE: Principle

FACTS:

1. Children were taught the word "stairs" by walking up and down stairs.
2. Later, the same children saw a person climbing a ladder. They called the ladder stairs.

ANALYSIS: There's not much to be done on a question like this. I did prephrase a couple of ideas. Maybe the answer will be "children take a word to have a broad meaning".

A. The object was "stairs". The children did see the object – they climbed up and down stairs.
B. The object was "stairs". The children *were* shown how stairs are used. Yet the children did not learn the correct meaning of stairs.
C. We have no way of knowing this. "Earlier" implies a comparison, but we only know about one group of children.
D. **CORRECT.** This is the best answer. The object was "stairs". Ladders are similar to stairs, and the children applied the meaning of stairs to the ladder.
E. "Best learn" implies a comparison, but the stimulus only showed us one situation. Also, we don't know whether other objects were present.

Question 2

QUESTION TYPE: Strengthen

CONCLUSION: Genetics are probably the cause of long life.

REASONING: Many people who live to the age of 100 lead "unhealthy" lives. They smoke, drink, eat fat and don't exercise.

ANALYSIS: This argument hasn't given us any reason to expect genetics is the cause. It's presented a paradox (unhealthy habits + long lives) but then said genetics is the solution without any direct evidence in favor of genetics. We can strengthen this argument by providing actual evidence that genetics is the cause.

All of the wrong answers use "some". This is a very vague word, and you must take it at its weakest. If an answer says "some Americans are jerks" you should take that to mean there's one surly guy named Bob in Arkansas, and every other American is very friendly.

A. This weakens the argument that genetics are the cause. This answer shows that one negative behavior cancels another negative behavior.
B. Take "some" to mean "one person". The argument isn't affected if *one* person doesn't smoke or drink, but does eat fatty food.
C. This is identical to B. It just switches the terms around. The argument didn't differentiate between the bad habits.
D. Take "some" to mean "one person". This means that one person who does not live to 100 is also unhealthy. Who cares about one person?
E. **CORRECT.** Your siblings (brothers and sisters) are genetically related to you. If the siblings of very old people also live a long time, this supports the idea that the cause is genetics. The stimulus had a total lack of evidence that genetics was the cause – this answer gives us actual support.

Question 3

QUESTION TYPE: Strengthen

CONCLUSION: M will probably be capsules.

REASONING: M couldn't be a tablet or a softgel. Medicines with an unpleasant taste are usually tablets, softgels, or capsules.

ANALYSIS: The argument uses process of elimination. For medicines with an unpleasant taste, there are usually three possibilities. The argument eliminates two of them.

So far, so good, but there's a big flaw....The argument didn't say that M has an unpleasant taste! Process of elimination only works if we know M is within the right category!

A. This weakens the argument. It shows there's another possibility for M, apart from capsules.
B. CORRECT. This tells us M is within the right category. Therefore the argument's process of elimination is relevant.
C. Who cares? The argument already eliminated the possibility of soft-gels. This answer just jumbles together two terms from the stimulus in an attempt to confuse you.
D. We don't care about "most" medications. We care about M. And the stimulus says that M's company doesn't have soft-gel technology.
E. The stimulus didn't say whether medication M has an unpleasant taste, and the argument wasn't about how to make M taste more pleasant.

Question 4

QUESTION TYPE: Paradox

PARADOX: Analysts predict that Morris will own the *Daily,* even though the majority shareholder refuses to sell.

ANALYSIS: The question stem reads like a strengthen question, but this is really a paradox.

Use your common sense for this question. The majority refuses to sell. So Morris can't buy the shares. Unless the majority is somehow *forced* to sell. I saw that was the only possibility, and looked for it in the answers.

A. Who cares about other newspapers. We only care about the *Daily.*
B. The stimulus said that Azedcorp has refused to sell. Presumably a high price won't sway them. Also, this offer was in the past, and the stimulus says that Azedcorp refused all offers.
C. It doesn't matter who is buying. Azedcorp has refused to sell.
D. That's great for Morris. But there can only be *one* majority owner. Currently, Azedcorp has a majority. Morris therefore needs at least some of Azedcorp's shares to form a majority.
E. CORRECT. If Azedcorp is *forced* to sell its shares, then Morris will be able to buy them.

Question 5

QUESTION TYPE: Flawed Reasoning

CONCLUSION: If we eliminate household lead, we'll get rid of childhood lead poisoning.

REASONING: Household lead is one cause of childhood lead poisoning.

ANALYSIS: This argument gives us *one* cause of lead poisoning. It then incorrectly assumes that household lead is the *only* cause of lead poisoning.

But maybe there's lead in the air, lead in the ground, lead in pipes etc.

A. We have no reason to doubt the statistics. This is only a flaw if we have a reason.
Example of flaw: This survey of four households indicates that 25% of them have lead.

B. This answer is circular reasoning. That wasn't in the argument.
Example of flaw: Getting rid of household lead will end lead poisoning because getting rid of household lead will end lead poisoning.

C. **CORRECT.** The argument didn't rule out other causes of lead poisoning.

D. The argument didn't say we *should* eliminate lead in houses, or that it's economical to do so. The argument is just talking about what would happen *if* we eliminate lead.
Example of flaw: *If* we spent $1 trillion per child we'll eliminate lead poisoning. So we *can* eliminate lead poisoning.

E. The argument didn't do this. Something can only be a flaw if it happens!
Example of flaw: 200 homes have lead. So 200 homes are poisoning children.

Question 6

QUESTION TYPE: Must be True

FACTS:

1. Soft drinks don't list exact caffeine content.
2. Listing exact caffeine content would make it easier to limit caffeine.
3. Many people would limit their caffeine if it became easier, thus improving their health.

ANALYSIS: The facts combine nicely:

List caffeine → easier to limit → many will do so → benefit health

---

A. **CORRECT.** This follows from combining all the facts. Exact caffeine content lets more people limit caffeine, which will improve their health.

B. This isn't supported. Listing caffeine content will help some people limit their intake, but there may be other people who can limit caffeine even without labels.

C. The stimulus talked about *limiting* caffeine. This answer talks about *elimination*. You don't need exact caffeine content to eliminate caffeine – you just can stop drinking caffeinated beverages.

D. Same as C. You don't need exact caffeine content to eliminate caffeine. You just need to know what products have any caffeine at all, so you can avoid those products entirely.

E. Why would some people be worse off from labels? The stimulus only talked about people improving their health from labels.

Question 7

QUESTION TYPE: Flawed Parallel Reasoning

CONCLUSION: MacNeil can't afford any piece of art.

REASONING: MacNeil can't afford to buy the entire collection.

ANALYSIS: What a silly argument. There might be a $5 painting in the collection. Anyone could afford that.

This is a whole-to-part flaw. It takes the property of the whole collection (expensive) and assumes every part of the collection has that property.

Note that a part-to-whole flaw is different. Flawed reasoning question often use part-to-whole and whole-to-part, and you must judge which way the flaw goes. Some answer choices will use the wrong direction.

A. This is a part-to-whole flaw. That's a different flaw.
B. This is a good whole-to-part argument. If the council voted *unanimously,* then every councillor did vote for the plan.
C. **CORRECT.** This is a whole-to-part flaw. You can have a long paragraph made up of short sentences.
D. This is a part-to-whole flaw. That's a different flaw.
E. This is a part-to-whole flaw. That's a different flaw.

Question 8

QUESTION TYPE: Flawed Reasoning

CONCLUSION: A catastrophe is unlikely during the entire journey.

REASONING: A catastrophe is unlikely during any individual stage of the journey.

ANALYSIS: This argument makes a part-to-whole flaw. There could be 1,000 stages of the journey. A small likelihood of catastrophe at each individual stage could add up to great danger.

Hopefully this analogous argument makes it easier to see the flaw: "If you speed through city streets while drunk, an accident is unlikely on any given stretch of road. So you're not likely to have an accident at any point while drunk driving."

B, C and D are practically the same answer. They simply don't happen in the stimulus. An answer has to happen for it to be a flaw.

A. **CORRECT.** The evidence is about the stages (the parts of the journey). The conclusion is about the whole journey.
B. The conclusion didn't say a catastrophe was impossible.
Example of flaw: A catastrophe is unlikely. So traveling to Mars is 100% safe, accidents are impossible.
C. This is almost exactly the same as B. The argument didn't say that the trip would definitely work.
Example of flaw: The trip will probably be safe. So it will be.
D. The same as B and C. The argument didn't say this!
Example of flaw: This rocket has a 1% chance of reaching Mars. So it *will* reach Mars, we're 100% certain.
E. A conclusion can be right even if the evidence is wrong. This is a common flaw on the LSAT, but it doesn't happen here.
Example of flaw: Critics said a Mars journey is dangerous, but their evidence is flawed. So traveling to Mars is certainly safe.

Question 9

QUESTION TYPE: Sufficient Assumption

CONCLUSION: Retrospective studies aren't reliable ways to learn about humans' present characteristics.

REASONING: Retrospective studies depend on human subjects' own reports.

ANALYSIS: You must prove the conclusion is true. You only have one piece of evidence. You can prove the conclusion by adding a premise that says "if the evidence is true, the conclusion is true". So you're looking for something that says any study based on subjective reports is useless.

Here's a diagram of the evidence and the conclusion:

Subjective Unreliable

There's no link between them. So here's the new premise we need:

Subjective → Unreliable

The answers are really dense. You need to focus, and keep in mind what you're looking for. Skip answers that aren't talking about the right thing, and be ruthless in your search for the right sufficient condition.

A. What a wishy-washy answer. This can't prove anything. I think it's safe to say that "may depend at least in part" has never been a sufficient condition on the LSAT. We're looking for something *definite* that proves the conclusion.
B. This says "if there are no correlations, the study can't work". This answer is a total red herring. Correlations were never mentioned.
C. **CORRECT.** Retrospective studies depend on subjective reports. If the subjective reports are unreliable, then the studies will be unreliable.
D. This answer adds a sufficient condition for a study being reliable. We need a sufficient condition for a study *not* being reliable.
E. This just tells us that studies must use subjective reports. This doesn't tell us the studies are unreliable.

Question 10

QUESTION TYPE: Identify the Conclusion

CONCLUSION: The additional airplane space will be used for seating.

REASONING: We're making new, larger passenger planes which will have extra space. And we'll soon have more air passengers. Airports won't able to handle the number of normal sized jets required to carry those passengers.

ANALYSIS: The word "however" almost always indicates a conclusion. This argument has the following structure:

1. Fact.
2. Conclusion, arguing fact is wrong.
3. Evidence supporting the conclusion.

A. This is something that the argument argues will not happen.
B. **CORRECT.** The word "however" indicates this is the conclusion.
C. This is evidence that supports the conclusion. If there are more passengers, the extra space in planes will probably be used for seats.
D. This is evidence to support the conclusion. We can't accommodate extra passengers by flying more planes. Each plane will need more seats.
E. This isn't even in the stimulus. We have no idea if this is true. It's certainly not the conclusion.

Question 11

QUESTION TYPE: Flawed Reasoning

CONCLUSION: ~~Athlete's foot cured~~ → ~~Received medication M~~

REASONING: Athlete's foot cured → Received medication M

ANALYSIS: The reporter's evidence showed that medication M is a *necessary* condition for being cured.

The reporter then incorrectly concludes that medication M is a sufficient condition. In technical terms, the reporter has incorrectly negated the premise.

The reporter ignores the possibility that medication M cures some but not all cases of athlete's foot.

Whenever you see a "flawed reasoning" question that uses conditional logic, it's virtually certain that the author will mix up sufficient and necessary. You should only give an answer serious consideration if it mentions sufficient and necessary conditions, as the correct answer does here.

A. **CORRECT.** This says that the reporter mixed up sufficient and necessary conditions. That is the flaw. We know medication M is necessary for a cure, but that doesn't mean it's sufficient.
B. The reporter said "anyone in the study". She wasn't talking about the population as a whole.
C. Same as B. The reporter was only talking about those in the study. She wasn't talking about the whole population.
D. The scientist already eliminate this possibility. They said that medication M was a necessary condition for a cure, and the reporter didn't say otherwise.
E. This answer refers to the population at large. The reporter was only talking about the study.
The reporter didn't say that in the whole world there's no subgroup that will only be cured if they *don't* take the medicine.

Question 12

QUESTION TYPE: Necessary Assumption

CONCLUSION: Plesiosauromorphs probably hunted with long distance chases.

REASONING: Plesiosaurmorphs had long, thin fins. These are like the wings of birds that fly long distances.

ANALYSIS: This is a weak argument. The author has just shown that Plesiosaurmorphs had fins that look like wings. But there are at least two necessary assumptions:

1. Because fins look like wings, they serve the same function as wings.
2. Because plesiosauromorphs can travel long distances, they hunt over long distances.

A. It doesn't matter *why* birds and reptiles have similarities.
Negation: Birds and reptiles share features for random reasons that have nothing to do with common ancestors.
B. It doesn't matter what kinds of fins other reptiles had. We only care what plesiosauromorphs did with their fins.
C. This is a sufficient assumption. We're looking for a necessary assumption. The negation of this answer doesn't wreck the argument.
Negation: A gigantic marine mammal might be able to meet its calorie requirements whether or not it hunted over long distances.
D. "Most" is a terrible choice for necessary assumption answers. Negating from "most" to "half" is almost never significant.
Negation: Only half of marine mammals that chase prey over long distances are specialized for long-distance swimming.
E. **CORRECT.** If fin *shapes* and wing shapes don't produce the same effects, then the evidence is worthless.
Negation: Fin shape doesn't affect the way an animal swims in the same way that wing shape affects how birds fly.

Question 13

QUESTION TYPE: Principle

PRINCIPLE: Screensavers waste money, even though they save electricity and prevent damage. Employees waste time playing with screensavers.

ANALYSIS: What a funny little argument. Who plays with screensavers these days? This was something people did in the 1990's though.

The principle can abstractly be summarized as: A plan can have a good result in one area, but have a bad overall result due to side-effects.

A. There are no side-effects here. And not getting the cheapest package might be ok, if students are satisfied.

B. The stimulus wasn't talking about up-front costs vs. long run savings. All of the costs and benefits of screensavers are long-term.

C. This isn't necessarily a reason not to order pizza. You don't have to cook pizza that you order in, even if you have to wait a bit longer. You can just order in advance.
So this is wrong because the stimulus described a mistake, while it's not clear that ordering pizza is a mistake.

D. CORRECT. This matches the stimulus. The security system has a small, known benefit (less theft), but the overall effect is negative due to side effects (loss of goodwill).

E. This is similar to B in that it compares up front costs to ongoing costs. The stimulus didn't talk about the upfront costs of screensavers. All of the costs + benefits were ongoing.

Question 14

QUESTION TYPE: Method of Reasoning

CONCLUSION: It is wrong to say that rap is individualistic and non-traditional.

REASONING: Rap musicians don't follow their individual desires; they meet public expectations. And the themes and styles of rap have become a type of tradition.

ANALYSIS: You should first look at the conclusion the student is disagreeing with. The professor's conclusion has two parts:

1. Rap is individual.
2. Rap isn't traditional.

The student offers evidence to disprove each point. The student does *not* contradict any of the professor's evidence. Instead, they bring up new facts that add context to the professor's argument.

A. The student didn't challenge either of the professor's premises. Instead, they offered us new evidence that directly contradicts the conclusion.

B. CORRECT. The additional observations are evidence that provide context, showing the professor's conclusion to be wrong.

C. The professor *doesn't* generalize from rap music to all music. I have no idea what this answer is referring to.

D. The music student didn't do this.
Example of answer: Learning rap isn't formal in the same way an instrument is, but it's still formal in a different way.

E. The student didn't challenge the professor's evidence.
Example of answer: It's not true that rap musicians can work alone. They need sound technicians and backup singers.

Question 15

QUESTION TYPE: Sufficient Assumption

CONCLUSION: Smith doesn't understand her own words.

REASONING: If Smith is right, we should only be able to understand an author's meaning if we understand their social circumstances.

ANALYSIS: Smith gave exactly one conditional premise. I'll draw that premise and its contrapositive:

Understand meaning → Know social circumstances

~~Know social circumstances~~ → ~~Understand meaning~~

The speakers wants to prove that Smith doesn't understand her own words. So use the contrapositive above: if Smith doesn't know her social circumstances, then she can't understand her own meaning.

All of the wrong answers are nonsense. Three of them talk about "intended" meaning, which wasn't mentioned in the stimulus. The other answer talks about a theory lacking insight. But the stimulus was about lacking insight *into social circumstances.*

Don't choose nonsense answers that have nothing to do with the stimulus.

- **A.** The argument didn't talk about "intended" meaning. This answer is just gibberish.
- **B.** **CORRECT.** See the analysis above. This answer provides the sufficient condition of the conditional statement, which lets us prove the necessary condition, which is the conclusion.
- **C.** The argument didn't talk about intended meaning. Like A, this answer is total nonsense.
- **D.** This just jumbles together random words from the stimulus. The stimulus talked about lacking insight *into social circumstances*. The stimulus didn't talk about *theories* lacking insight.
- **E.** Another nonsense answer. The stimulus didn't talk about intended meaning!

Question 16

QUESTION TYPE: Strengthen

CONCLUSION: Snoring can damage your throat.

REASONING: There's a correlation between snoring and throat damage.

ANALYSIS: Correlations can't prove anything. Whenever there's a correlation, there are four possibilities:

1. Snoring causes throat damage.
2. Throat damage causes snoring.
3. A third factor causes both.
4. It's a coincidence.

If an argument uses a correlation to prove causation, you can strengthen the argument by eliminating one of the other possibilities.

Throat surgery is mentioned in a couple of answers. But it's irrelevant. The conclusion is about snoring in the general population, not just those who had surgery. Surgery is only mentioned because it's what let us discover abnormalities.

- **A.** This weakens the argument by showing that the study's data may be flawed.
- **B.** It doesn't matter why patients had surgery. Surgery is just how we established there was throat damage.
- **C.** This is a common wrong answer. Studies don't need to use subjects of the same age/weight etc. The study is about snoring in the general population, so the argument is *stronger* if the study used subjects from the general population.
- **D.** Throat surgery doesn't matter. Throat surgery is the reason we discovered abnormalities, but the argument is about the abnormalities in the whole population, even those who don't have surgery.
- **E.** **CORRECT.** This answer eliminates the second possibility from my list above. This strengthens the conclusion that the first possibility is correct.

Question 17

QUESTION TYPE: Sufficient Assumption

CONCLUSION: You shouldn't give up health for money.

REASONING: Without health, you can't have happiness.

ANALYSIS: This argument appeals to our common sense. Everyone wants happiness, so this argument seems self-evident. But this is the LSAT, and you can't make assumptions like that. Common sense can let you make predictions, but you can't use it to prove an argument correct if the question says the argument is not correct.

Maybe wealth is worth having even if you're horribly unhappy. To prove the argument correct you must eliminate this possibility and say that money is only worth having if you can also be happy.

A. CORRECT. If this is true, then you shouldn't sacrifice your health for money.
B. This doesn't help the argument. If this is true then maybe you can be happy with just money.
C. This weakens the argument. We're trying to prove that we *shouldn't* sacrifice health. This shows that health isn't valuable in itself.
D. The argument is *only* talking about the kind of wealth that destroys happiness. So we already know this answer is true – it can't prove the argument.
E. This doesn't tell us to seek health instead of wealth. We're not looking for something that tells us what is likely to lead to happiness. We need an answer that tells us *never* to seek wealth if it makes us unhappy.

Did you choose this because you thought it was true? That's not what you're supposed to be looking for.

Question 18

QUESTION TYPE: Principle

PRINCIPLES: Vanessa wants all programming to be done in pairs.

Jo thinks the most productive programmers should be allowed to work alone.

ANALYSIS: You're looking for something that *violates* one of the two principles. It's easy to violate Vanessa's principle: if even a single programmer works alone, that violates her principle.

Jo's principle is harder to violate. She says *the most productive* programmers should be allowed to work alone. Jo doesn't say whether any other programmers must work alone.

A. This matches Vanessa's principle. And Jo was only talking about the most productive programmers, so this doesn't violate her principle.
B. Same as A.
C. Same as A and B.
D. CORRECT. This matches Vanessa's principle. This violates Jo's principle: Yolanda is the most productive programmer, so Jo would say she should be allowed to work alone.
E. Same as A, B and C.

Question 19

QUESTION TYPE: Must be True

FACTS:

1. Pet store (Most)→ has birds
2. Has birds (Most) → Has fish
3. Fish and ~~Birds~~ → Gerbils
4. Contrapositive: ~~Gerbils~~ → NOT(Fish and ~~Birds~~)

ANALYSIS: First, you can't combine "most" statements with anything. You can only combine "most" statements with the sufficient condition of a conditional statement.

Second, let's talk about contrapositives. Normally, you would draw a contrapositive by negating both statements, and changing "and" to "or", like this:

~~Gerbils~~ →~~Fish~~ or Birds

You probably drew that, but still struggled. The diagramming method above is just a trick to get you to the right place. But it's better to know what a contrapositive *really* is.

Contrapositives are really just "not that", whatever that is. The negation of something is just "not that thing". This gets complicated with compound conditions (e.g. this AND that). There are four possibilities with any compound statement. Let's use tropical fish and exotic birds as an example:

1. Fish and birds
2. ~~Fish~~ and birds
3. Fish and ~~birds~~
4. ~~Fish~~ and ~~birds~~

The sufficient condition in the stimulus is the third one. So the contrapositive is "not the third one". So numbers 1, 2 and 4 are all included in the contrapositive.

"NOT(Fish and ~~Birds~~)" capture this idea better than "~~Fish~~ or Birds". Both statements actually mean "any of 1, 2 or 4", but the first one is much clearer. And the correct answer, D, is phrased in the form of "NOT(Fish and ~~Birds~~)".

A. We only know that independently owned pet stores don't sell gerbils. This answer says "most". The fact about gerbils doesn't connect with any "most" statements.

B. We only know that no *independently* owned pet stores sell gerbils. This answer talks about *all* pet stores. The bird and fish part is wrong too: it should have said "no pet stores....sell tropical fish *but not* exotic birds". That's what we can conclude about a pet store that doesn't sell gerbils.

C. We don't even know if any independently owned pet stores *do* sell gerbils. The question gives us a sufficient condition for a store to sell gerbils, but it doesn't tell us whether any pet stores do meet that sufficient condition.

D. **CORRECT.** This is the contrapositive of the conditional statement from the stimulus. If a pet store "sells tropical fish but not exotic birds" then it sell gerbils.
So if a pet store *doesn't* sell gerbils, then it doesn't "sell tropical fish and not exotic birds".
Note: And = But
See the analysis section above for more detail.

E. We have no idea. We know that independent pet stores don't sell gerbils. That just means they can't "sell tropical fish but not exotic birds".
As long as they don't do that, they could sell:
1. Tropical fish and exotic birds
2. No tropical fish and no exotic birds
3. No tropical fish, and exotic birds

This answer is too restricted. It excludes the third possibility.

Question 20

QUESTION TYPE: Paradox

PARADOX: The stars are older than the universe, which can't be true. If the new calculations are right, the stars are further away and intrinsically brighter than we thought.

ANALYSIS: This situation isn't really a "paradox", but I've kept the same name for the question type.

According to our old calculations, the stars are older than the universe. This is obviously impossible. The astronomer says the new calculations indicate the stars are younger, thus resolving the paradox. We have to explain how the new information means the stars are younger. We know two new things about the stars:

1. They are further away than we thought.
2. They are brighter than we thought.

One of these facts must show that the stars are not as old as we thought. That's the only way that this new information can prove the stars aren't older than the universe.

A. Useless. This has nothing to do with the astronomer's calculations. We're trying to explain how the calculations show the stars are younger than we thought.
B. It doesn't matter how old the universe is. However old it is, we want explain why the stars are *less* old.
C. **CORRECT.** The astronomer found that the stars are brighter than we thought. So this answer shows that the stars are also younger than we thought.
D. Tempting, but useless. This answer refers to the wrong concept. We're still on earth. The stars *appear* just as bright as they always have. The astronomer's calculations show that the stars are *actually* brighter than we thought. Intrinsic brightness refers to how bright stars really are, not how bright them appear to be.
E. So what? We're trying to explain how old the stars are. It doesn't matter if we can see more stars. Whoop-dee-do. This has nothing to do with the astronomer's findings.

Question 21

QUESTION TYPE: Most Strongly Supported

FACTS:

1. Large nurseries (most) → sell mainly to commercial growers AND sell with disease free guarantee
2. Johnson received diseased raspberries.

ANALYSIS: This question is testing how precisely you read. It's also testing how well you understand "most" statements.

There's not much you can do with "most statements". You can only read them left to right. You can't take a contrapositive of a "most" statement, and you can't join them with anything except a conditional statement. * (see note)

So *if* Wally's is a large nursery, then we know something. Otherwise, we don't know anything.

It doesn't matter if Johnson is commercial. It doesn't matter if the plants were guaranteed. Those are "necessary" conditions of the most statement. Knowing those doesn't tell us anything, because you can't read "most" statement backwards or take contrapositives.

This understanding of "most" statements eliminates answers A–D. Only E tells us that Wally's is a large nursery.

Note that we don't know whether Wally's guarantees its plants. We just know the plants were diseased. So *if* they were guaranteed, *then* they weren't as they were guaranteed to be.

* (Note: There's one exception. If we know "most americans are women" and "most americans wear hats" then we can conclude "at least some women wear hats". That's because the two majorities of americans must overlap. This doesn't occur in the question. I'm only mentioning it for the sake of completeness.)

A. It doesn't matter whether Johnson is a commercial grower. That's on the right hand side of the "most" statement. Right hand side conditions don't tell you anything.

B. This is a weird answer. It's trying to link the two conditions of the "most" statement. It negates the guarantee condition then tries to negate the commercial grower condition.
You *can't* do this with most statements! There are no links between the right hand conditions, and negating the right hand condition has no effect. There's *very* little you can do with "most" statements.

C. You can't take a contrapositive of a "most" statement. That's what this answer does. It reverses the "most" statement and negates it.

D. We can't *ever* conclude that Wally's is probably not a large nursery. You can't ever negate the left hand condition of a "most" statement.
This answer is trying to do that, because it negates one of the right hand conditions (the guarantee). But you can't do this.
The commercial grower thing is also wrong; being a commercial grower is not a sufficient condition for anything.

E. CORRECT. If Wally's is large, then they probably guarantee their plants. Probably = most large nurseries.
The plants were diseased. So if there was a guarantee, then the plants weren't as guaranteed.

Question 22

QUESTION TYPE: Weaken

CONCLUSION: We should try the plan.

REASONING: The plan might work.

ANALYSIS: This is not a good argument. The drug company manager has only talked about the benefits of the marketing plan: it *might* save the product.

But any action has downsides too. Maybe the marketing plan is really expensive. Or maybe it will distract from the company's other products.

To make this a good argument, the manager would have to show the downsides as well as the benefits of the plan.

Since we're trying to weaken the plan, we should show that it has downsides. And we need specific information about the new drug or about marketing. Most of the wrong answers just give us context that doesn't apply to the situation.

A. This strengthens the idea that we should try to save the product. But we're trying to *weaken* the argument.

B. This is useless information. Many new products fail. Many succeed. Who cares? This answer doesn't tell us what will happen to *this* product if we run a marketing campaign.

C. This is useless. The marketing plan has some chance of succeeding, so the statement in this answer doesn't apply.

D. CORRECT. This shows there is a downside to the marketing plan. We don't know if the plan will succeed, so it's not a good idea to risk the company's other products.

E. Great! This means the company has lots of money. This doesn't tell us whether or not the company should try to save the new product with a marketing plan.

Question 23

QUESTION TYPE: Principle

CONCLUSION: TMD hasn't been shown to be acceptable.

REASONING: Some of the population eats far more peaches and thus far more TMD than the national average. We have no research on consumption of this level of TMD.

ANALYSIS: The advocate has shown that we don't know if TMD is harmful to certain segments of the population. So we need a principle that says we shouldn't do something unless we know it's safe. Or that we shouldn't do something that may harm a segment of the population.

A. This sounds good, but look at what it's concluding: be cautious in assessing a pesticide's risk. That's *not* what the advocate is recommending. She says we shouldn't use TMD on peaches. That's a different recommendation.

B. Nonsense. The sufficient condition here is knowing that a majority of the population is likely to ingest TMD. But the stimulus said a majority of the population *doesn't* eat peaches. And the advocate didn't say that TMD use is likely unacceptable. She said it *is* unacceptable.

C. **CORRECT.** You can draw this statement and its contrapositive:
Acceptable → intended purpose AND shown no harm
~~Shown no harm~~ OR ~~intended purpose~~ → ~~acceptable~~
The advocate says we haven't shown there is no harm to children. The contrapositive above shows that lets us conclude "not acceptable".

D. The stimulus said that average doses *are* low and average doses *have* been proven to be safe. So this answer doesn't tell us we have any special obligation to children. Besides, children were just an example. The main point was that some people eat more peaches than average. We should protect all of them, not just children.

E. The argument mentioned one "measure to protect the population from harm": restricting pesticides. The stimulus never said this leads to a greater harm.

Question 24

QUESTION TYPE: Must be False

FACTS:

1. The law is supposed to protect employees from secondhand smoke.
2. The law doesn't cover homes.

ANALYSIS: Before looking at the answers, play around with the two statements from the stimulus. How could they overlap?

Employees, and homes. What if there are employees in homes? This new law couldn't protect those employees.

Remember, you're trying to find a statement that must be *false*.

A. We have no idea if legislators intended to ban smoking in homes. So we can't say if this is true or false.

B. We don't know if supporters think the law will be effective or not. We can't say if this is true or false.

C. We don't know. The stimulus only mentioned workplaces and homes. We don't know if the law also cover smoking in parks, public squares, etc.

D. The stimulus didn't mention "most people". So we have no idea what they think.

E. **CORRECT.** This can't be true. The law can't ban smoking in homes. So any household employees are out of luck.

Question 25

QUESTION TYPE: Necessary Assumption

CONCLUSION: We should raise tuition.

REASONING: Low tuition *might* be the cause of our problems.

ANALYSIS: The president gets ahead of himself. He says that low tuition *might* be the cause of the problem. By the end of the argument he's convinced himself that low tuition *is* the cause of the problem.

For the negations, I haven't used a narrow, grammatical approach. A negation is really just "anything the statement says is false." Take a look at what I did with answers D and E, for example. Those are negations, but it's obvious they cause no harm to the argument.

A. CORRECT. The negation of this answer destroys the argument.
Negation: The low tuition explanation *doesn't* apply in this case.

B. We're not concerned about actual quality. We're concerned with what parents *think* determines quality.
Negation: Quality doesn't depend on tuition.

C. The president didn't say that tuition is sufficient. He said we *need* to raise tuition. That's a necessary condition. The president doesn't need to assume that raising tuition is also a sufficient condition.
Negation: An increase in tuition might not lead to a larger applicant pool.

D. Tempting, but it doesn't matter if there are additional explanations. Those explanations could be wrong. It only matters if the president's explanation applies.
Negation: There exists another, really stupid explanation for low enrollment: Evil clowns are frightening away prospective students.

E. The president is talking about the overall level of tuition. It doesn't matter if it's gone up a bit. It only matters how high tuition is compared to other universities.
Negation: Tuition has increased $1 in recent years.

Question 26

QUESTION TYPE: Principle

CONCLUSION: We shouldn't let private companies supply water.

REASONING: We need clean water for health. Private companies exist for profit, not health.

ANALYSIS: This isn't a good argument. It's possible that a company might seek profits yet also promote health. We need a principle that shows that a company can't promote health if it seeks profit.

A. I can see how this is tempting. Governments aren't supplying clean water in the areas of the world we're talking about. So this answer proves we shouldn't let private companies do it either. But, we're trying to support the *reasoning* in this argument. The conclusion was that private companies should *never* supply water, because their purpose is profit. This answer only proves the conclusion on a technicality. And further, it allows that private companies could supply water if governments did too. The stimulus is more strict: private companies should never supply water.

B. Private companies *are* willing to supply water, so this explanation doesn't apply.

C. The stimulus never said that private companies are *unable* to supply water. The worry is that private companies might skimp on water delivery even if they are "able" to provide clean water.

D. This is completely off base. Here's a situation where it would apply:
"John punched James in the mouth. This knocked out a diseased tooth, thus improving James' health"
The principle in this answer shows that even though John *did* improve James' health, he didn't necessarily *intend* to do it.
The principle is *true,* but it has nothing at all to do with the situation in the stimulus.

E. CORRECT. Water is necessary for health. So this answer tells us not to let someone supply water unless health is their main purpose. And private companies don't have health as their main purpose.

Section III – Logic Games

Game 1 – Appointments

Questions 1–6

Setup

This is, at first glance, a linear game where you just list the rules and apply them. But by drawing the rules on the diagram and making a couple of deductions, you can figure many things out up front.

First, let's draw rules one and two. Water is before landscaping, and power is before gas and satellite:

W — L

```
  G
P<
  S
```

Next, draw rules three and four directly on the diagram. Gas, satellite and telephone can't go second or third, and telephone can't go sixth:

1	2	3	4	5	6
	~~G~~	~~G~~			~~T~~
	~~S~~	~~S~~			
	~~T~~	~~T~~			

Many people stop here. But with so many restrictions, we should see if there are other restrictions we can add to the diagram.

For instance, gas and satellite can't go first (rule 2). Since there are so many gas/satellite restrictions, you should draw that on the diagram:

1	2	3	4	5	6
~~G~~	~~G~~	~~G~~			~~T~~
~~S~~	~~S~~	~~S~~			
	~~T~~	~~T~~			

Next, let's see who can't go last, since it also has a restriction. Power can't, because power is before gas/satellite. And water can't, because water is before landscaping:

1	2	3	4	5	6
~~G~~	~~G~~	~~G~~			~~T~~
~~S~~	~~S~~	~~S~~			~~W~~
	~~T~~	~~T~~			~~P~~

TWP can't go last....so only gas, satellite and landscaping can go last. This is an important deduction! And gas/satellite must take up two of the last three spaces.

I'd like to have a better sense of who can go where. If you just think about a deduction but don't write it down, it's easy to forget.

I divided the diagram into two. Gas and satellite are always 4-6. Water is always 1-3, because it's before landscaping. G/S already take up two of the three final spaces, so there's no room for G, S and W – L:

W | G, S

1	2	3	4	5	6
~~G~~	~~G~~	~~G~~			~~T~~
~~S~~	~~S~~	~~S~~			~~W~~
	~~T~~	~~T~~			~~P~~

This way, it's easy to see who must go 1-3 and who must go 4-6.

(Note: Landscaping doesn't have to go 4-6. You just can't put water 4-6, because landscaping is after water.)

Now we're set. You do need to remember the first two rules to use this diagram properly, of course.

Note that I only drew the final diagram as my main diagram. For individual questions, I drew this diagram:

___ ___ ___ ___ ___ ___

It has no detail. I look down to the main diagram to see detail and fill in the local diagrams. I keep my main diagram near the questions so I can easily look down at it.

In these explanations, I include details on all the local diagrams, for clarity. But my local diagrams are rather more minimal.

Main Diagram

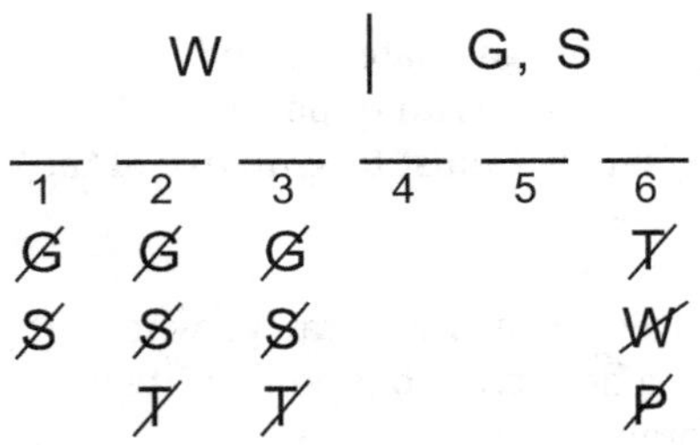

W | G, S

1	2	3	4	5	6
~~G~~	~~G~~	~~G~~			~~T~~
~~S~~	~~S~~	~~S~~			~~W~~
	~~T~~	~~T~~			~~P~~

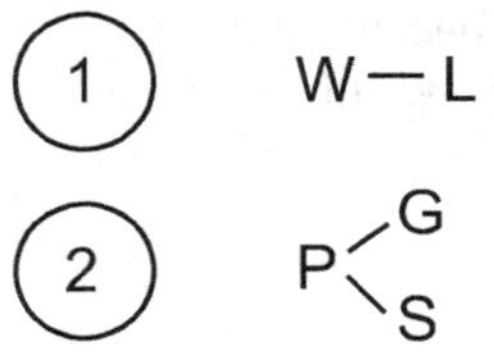

(1) W — L

(2) P < G, S

Question 1

For acceptable order questions, go through the rules and use them to eliminate answers one by one.

Rule 1 eliminates **C.** Water needs to be before landscaping.

Rule 2 eliminates **A.** Power has to be before gas.

Rule 3 eliminates **E.** Telephone can't be second.

Rule 4 eliminates **B.** Telephone can't be last.

D is **CORRECT.** It violates no rules.

Question 2

This question adds a new rule: gas, satellite and telephone can't be fourth. This really restricts the game. Here's the new diagram:

1	2	3	4	5	6
~~G~~	~~G~~	~~G~~	~~G~~		~~T~~
~~S~~	~~S~~	~~S~~	~~S~~		~~W~~
	~~T~~	~~T~~	~~T~~		~~P~~

Now gas and satellite can only go fourth and fifth!

				G/S	S/G
1	2	3	4	5	6
~~G~~	~~G~~	~~G~~	~~G~~		~~T~~
~~S~~	~~S~~	~~S~~	~~S~~		~~W~~
	~~T~~	~~T~~	~~T~~		~~P~~

That also leaves only space one for telephone:

T				G/S	S/G
1	2	3	4	5	6
~~G~~	~~G~~	~~G~~	~~G~~		~~T~~
~~S~~	~~S~~	~~S~~	~~S~~		~~W~~
	~~T~~	~~T~~	~~T~~		~~P~~

This leaves water, landscaping and power to go in 2-4:

W — L , P

T				G/S	S/G
1	2	3	4	5	6
~~G~~	~~G~~	~~G~~			~~T~~
~~S~~	~~S~~	~~S~~			~~W~~
	~~T~~	~~T~~			~~P~~

D is **CORRECT.** The other answers could be true but don't have to be.

Question 3

The diagram from question 2 disproves **A** and **B:**

W — L , P

T				G/S	S/G
1	2	3	4	5	6
~~G~~	~~G~~	~~G~~			~~T~~
~~S~~	~~S~~	~~S~~			~~W~~
	~~T~~	~~T~~			~~P~~

C and **D** both said the telephone must go early. So I made a scenario putting telephone as far back as I could. This scenario disproves both **C** and **D:**

P	W	L	G	T	S
1	2	3	4	5	6
~~G~~	~~G~~	~~G~~			~~T~~
~~S~~	~~S~~	~~S~~			~~W~~
	~~T~~	~~T~~			~~P~~

E is **CORRECT.** We saw this in the setup. Water has to be earlier than gas and satellite.

The reason is that gas and satellite already take up 2/3 spaces in the back half. That means there's only one space open after gas, at most.

Since landscaping goes after water (rule 1) that means we would need *two* open spaces to place water after gas.

W — L (above space 6)

			G	S	
1	2	3	4	5	6
~~G~~	~~G~~	~~G~~			~~T~~
~~S~~	~~S~~	~~S~~			~~W~~
	~~T~~	~~T~~			~~P~~

This diagram shows water won't fit.

Question 4

In the setup, we saw that gas and landscaping must take up two of the three spaces in 4-6. That's because gas and satellite can't go first, second or third (rules 2 and 3).

Since these answers show the last three spaces, at least two of the variables must be gas and satellite.

E is **CORRECT.** It's missing satellite.

Question 5

Gas and satellite are already restricted to days 4-6. This question further restricts them to only spaces 4 and 5:

G S (4, 5, reversible)

1: not G, not S
2: not G, not S, not T
3: not G, not S, not T
6: not T, not W, not P

I prefer to draw them with a loop to show they are reversible. This is the fastest way I know of doing this.

Now, in the setup we saw that only gas, satellite and landscaping can go last. This question further restricts gas and satellite from going last, so only landscaping is left:

G S (4, 5, reversible), L (6)

1: not G, not S
2: not G, not S, not T
3: not G, not S, not T
6: not T, not W, not P

You can fill in the rest of the diagram for fun, should only take you three seconds if you know the game. Telephone must go first, and power and water are in the two remaining spaces:

P, W

T _ _ G S L
1 2 3 4 5 6

However, landscaping = last was the first major deduction, and the first major deduction is usually the answer. So whenever you find a major deduction, you should check the answers to see if it is there.

It is. **B** is **CORRECT.** The diagram shows that the other answers don't have to be true. They all deal with reversible variables. (P, W is another way of drawing reversible variables, once there are already some restrictions on the board).

Question 6

Everyone hates rule substitution questions. But I actually don't think they're that hard. You have to ask the right questions:

1. Does this new rule add the same restrictions?
2. Does it allow everything that used to be allowed?

Most of the wrong answers add weird new restrictions. You can use your past scenarios to eliminate answers. If an answer contradicts a past, working scenario, then that answer is WRONG!

LSAT answers are worthless. Don't give them the time of day. They're 80% likely to be wrong. Approach them looking for reasons to disprove them.

Now, we're looking for something that makes telephone "not last".

A seems to add the correct restriction. If telephone is before gas or satellite, it's not last. Let's come back to this.

B and **D** add weird new restrictions that weren't in the original setup. Telephone doesn't need to be directly in front of gas or satellite. This scenario from question two disproves both answers:

W — L, P

T				G/S	S/G
1	2	3	4	5	6
~~G~~	~~G~~	~~G~~			~~T~~
~~S~~	~~S~~	~~S~~			~~W~~
	~~T~~	~~T~~			~~P~~

This diagram from question three disproves **C.** The telephone doesn't have to go before landscaping:

P	W	L	G	T	S
1	2	3	4	5	6
~~G~~	~~G~~	~~G~~			~~T~~
~~S~~	~~S~~	~~S~~			~~W~~
	~~T~~	~~T~~			~~P~~

This diagram from question five disproves **E.** Gas or satellite don't have to go last:

P, W

T			G	S	L
1	2	3	4	5	6
~~G~~	~~G~~	~~G~~			~~T~~
~~S~~	~~S~~	~~S~~			~~W~~
	~~T~~	~~T~~			~~P~~

That leaves **A.** It's **CORRECT.** Since we thought **A** was right, and we eliminated the other answers, we can be very sure it's right.

Just for fun, I'll prove conclusively that **A** is true. We saw in the setup that Gas and Satellite had to be in spaces 4-6. So if something goes *after* gas and satellite, it must go last.

Therefore, saying that "T can't go last" is the same as saying that "T must go before gas and satellite".

Game 2 – Stained Glass
Questions 7–13

Setup

This game is rather unique, I can't think of any others like it. You have to choose colors for stained glass windows, in three groups.

One very important point: the order of the windows *doesn't matter*. There is no difference between window 1 and window 3. This lets you be flexible in your diagrams.

For instance, I drew the first rule directly on the diagram:

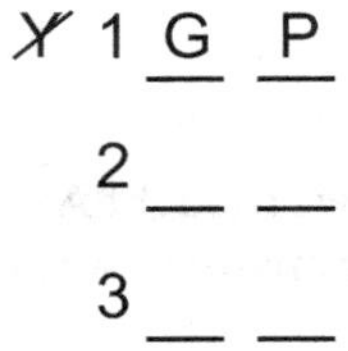

```
Y̸ 1 G  P
  2 __ __
  3 __ __
```

Rule one says there's exactly one GP. You can draw them in any group, because *group order doesn't matter*. I chose group one.

Note that I've also drawn "not Y" beside this group. That comes from rule three, we'll get to that soon.

Next, there are exactly two roses. I recommend just memorizing this rule. There's no good way to draw it, and you'll go faster if you know it cold.

I did draw one rose by itself as a reminder. Since there are two roses, at least one of the non-GP groups has a rose. This is an optional addition:

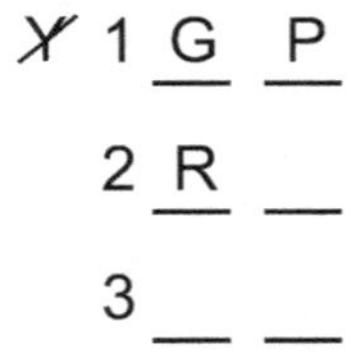

```
Y̸ 1 G  P
  2 R  __
  3 __ __
```

You should combined rules three and four. Both rules mention orange. You can almost always combine rules that mention the same variable. They say:

- If you have yellow, you don't have green or orange.
- If you're missing orange, you have purple.

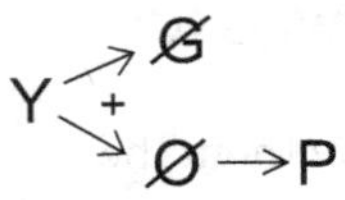

```
   ↗ G̸
Y   +
   ↘ Ø → P
```

You should always draw the contrapositive of any conditional diagrams, especially if they combine multiple statements:

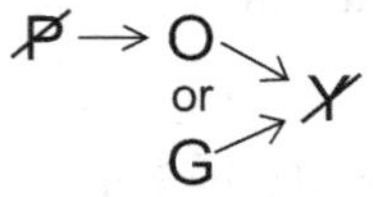

```
P̸ → O ↘
    or   Y̸
    G ↗
```

Note that yellow always leads to purple. So there's always at least one YP in the game. It's also important to note that yellow can't go with green or orange. That's why I drew "not Y" beside GP on the main diagram.

The relationship between orange and purple (rule 4) is a bit special. Most students find this type of rule confusing, so the LSAT tests it mercilessly. If you can wrap your head around this kind of rule, you'll do much better on in-out games.

So, the fourth rule says that if we *don't* have *purple,* we *do* have orange. The contrapositive is that if we *don't* have orange, we *do* have purple.

This means we always have at least one of purple or orange. In every window. This is crucial: remember this as a separate deduction.

Now, the part that people find confusing: orange and purple can both be in the same group. There's no rule that says *if* you have orange, *then* you don't have purple.

So if you're missing one of O and P, you need the other. But you can have both O and P. Another way to think about it is that you need "purple or orange" and "or" is inclusive on the LSAT. "Inclusive" means that "or" includes the possibility of both.

Technically this is already covered in the conditional diagrams I drew earlier, but it's something that most people miss if they just look at the diagram. The games test kind of rule so much that you need to be aware of it as a separate deduction. Think of it as "at least one and maybe both".

Another way to think about this game is that there's a minimum number of variables that you *must* place:

- GP
- Two R's (in separate groups)
- At least one O (every variable need to be used)
- YP

You've got to fit those into the three groups. And YP can't go with GP, or with O. This is hard to do. Whenever a question has you place some of these variables, you should ask yourself what's left and where they can't go.

It's worth thinking about numbers. For instance, green, orange and yellow cannot be in all three groups. That's because yellow can't go with green and orange. Two questions test this deduction (11 and 12).

Note: There are a couple other rules. Every window needs at least two colors, and every color needs to be used at least once. You should just memorize these. I drew two spaces for every window, which helps me remember that. If those spaces were "only two", I would have drawn a vertical line indicating those spaces were closed off.

Main Diagram

Y̸ 1 G P

2 R __

3 __ __

(1) G̸P̸

(2) R, R

(3) Y → G̸ + O̸ → P

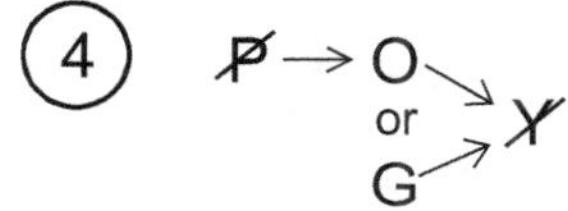

I said in the setup that every window needs either orange or purple. If you *ever* find yourself forgetting this deduction, then you should draw a note, like this. Remember that "or" includes the possibility of "and":

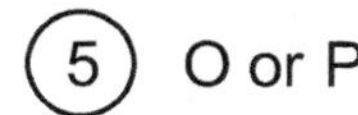

It may also be useful to list the elements that need to be used at least once:

- GP
- Two R's (in separate groups)
- At least one O (every variable need to be used)
- YP

Note: There are a couple other rules. Every window needs at least two colors, and every color needs to be used at least once. You should just memorize these. I drew two spaces for every window, which helps me remember that. If those spaces were "only two", I would have drawn a vertical line indicating those spaces were closed off.

Question 7

For acceptable order questions, go through the rules and use them to eliminate answers one by one.

Rule 1 eliminates **C.** There can only be one window with green and purple.

Rule 2 eliminates **E.** There must be two windows with rose glass.

Rule 3 eliminates **D.** Yellow and orange can't go together.

Rule 4 eliminates **A.** Every window needs at least one of orange or purple. Window 2 has neither.

B is **CORRECT.** It violates no rules.

Question 8

This question is asking what cannot be the complete combination of colors.

The only way to solve this question is by finding a rule violation. The rule violation has to be within a single window, because that's all the answers show.

Only rules three and four can lead to rule violations within a single window. Here are the two possible violations:

1. Yellow with either orange or green (rule 3).
2. A window without orange or purple (rule 4).

None of the answers violate rule 3. **C** violates rule 4. **C** is **CORRECT.**

Many people choose **D.** If you did this, you need to review the rule about purple and orange. Here was the form:

~~A~~ → B
~~B~~ → A

This form means that you need at least one of A or B. But you could have both! You can only read diagrams left to right. The diagrams don't say that if you have A you can't have B.

I'll give an example with parents. Suppose I say "if you're a parent, you have a boy or a girl". Here's that rule in the same format:

~~boy~~ → girl
~~girl~~ → boy

If you have no boy, you have a girl. But everyone know parents can have both boys and girls.

So remember: if the sufficient condition is negated and the necessary is normal, it means "you need at least one and could have both".

Question 9

This question says that two windows have exactly two colors of glass. It seems like a hard question, so I skipped it at first. I eliminated two answers, then left it and came back after the final question.

I do this sometimes on "brute force" questions. I can disprove answers faster once I've finished other questions and developed a better sense of the game.

A and **D** were the two answers I eliminated. Both violate rule 4: every window needs at least one of purple or orange.

The only way I know how to choose between the remaining answers is to make scenarios to disprove or prove those answers.

Note: The vertical lines in these scenarios indicate the group is full. Remember, the question says that two of the groups only have two. And the letters mentioned in the answer are a *complete* list of what's in that window.

This scenario proves that **B** is **CORRECT.**

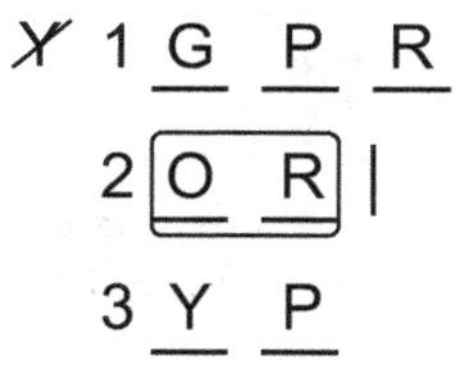

```
Y 1 G P R
  2 [O R] |
  3 Y P
```

This is what I drew to eliminate **C:**

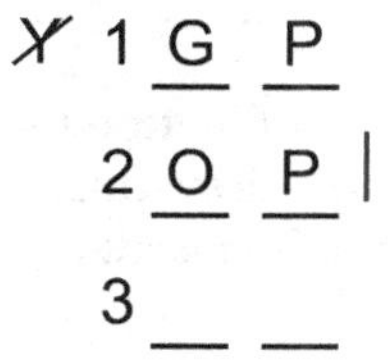

```
Y 1 G P
  2 O P |
  3 _ _
```

I've placed GP (which is always in one group) and OP (which is in the answer) fills window two. Now we have two groups left to place:

YP
Two R's

YP can't go with either green or orange, so they must go in group three. That leaves us no space to put both R's, since this question says two windows must have only two colors.

I drew the incomplete diagram above to show you what I *actually* drew to eliminate this question.

E has the exact same problem. Here's green and orange in the second group:

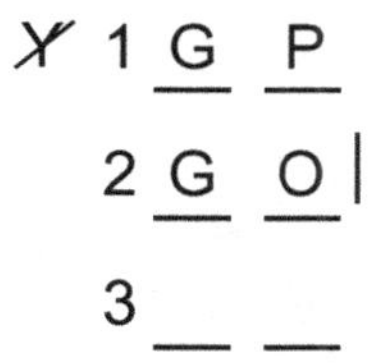

```
Y 1 G P
  2 G O |
  3 _ _
```

Once again, there's no space to put YP and both R's without having more than two colors in two groups.

If you have trouble following either of those eliminations, draw the diagrams yourself, and try to place YP and both R's while keeping in mind the new rule for this question.

Question 10

This question says that the complete combination in one window is purple, rose and orange. I drew this, with a vertical line indicating the group is closed:

~~Y~~ 1 G P
2 P R O |
3 _ _

I added the rule to the main diagram. The main diagram includes GP, because of rule 1. It's in window one because the order of windows doesn't matter. Reread the setup if you don't remember why I've drawn things this way.

Now, who do we still have to place? YP and one R. YP can't go with green or orange, so they must go in window three:

~~Y~~ 1 G P
2 P R O |
3 Y P

So now there's one more rose to place. It could go with GP or YP.

Also, you *can* put an orange in the first window, though you don't have to. This proves **B CORRECT.** One window could be green, purple and orange. Here's the full scenario:

~~Y~~ 1 G P O
2 P R O |
3 Y P R

Remember, this is a *could* be true question. **B** is right because it's possible.

None of the other answers work. They don't fit in any of the three windows.

Question 11

The question says orange glass is used more than green glass. We know two things:

1. Green glass is used once already.
2. Orange glass can't be in every window, because orange and yellow can't go together.

This means that orange is used twice, and green is used once. We can also say that yellow is used separately from orange. Here's what we get when we draw that:

~~Y~~ 1 G P O
2 O _
3 Y P

(remember, window order *does not matter*. This diagram would be the same with YP in 2 and O in 3.)

We still have to place the two roses. But let's use this diagram to eliminate answers. Remember that these answers are talking about the *complete* combination.

A seems possible. We'll leave it for now.

None of **B-E** work. Window one has the only green. And that window has GPO. None of the answers list GPO, so they're all wrong.

A is **CORRECT.** This diagram proves it works:

~~Y~~ 1 G P O R
2 O P
3 Y P R

There's no reason you can't put purple with orange.

Question 12

Almost all of the colors have restrictions. This prevents them from going in all three windows, since every color must be used once.

- Green and orange block yellow. They're out.
- Likewise, yellow is out. It blocks green and orange.
- Rose can't go in three windows because rule 2 says it can't.

That leaves purple. **C** is **CORRECT.**

Question 13

This question is a bit hard. You need to do some up front thinking. But then the most important thing is drawing. There's actually very little room for thought on logic games, apart from deciding what to start drawing.

The question says no windows have both rose and orange. And there are two oranges. So that fills all three groups.

That's interesting. Let's look at the base diagram again. GP is there because of rule 1:

~~Y~~ 1 G P

2 __ __

3 __ __

We have to place two Rs and an O, across all three groups. This means there are only two scenarios: GP is either with one of the Rs, or with an O.

Let's try putting one of the Rs with GP. We'll place O in two (remember, window order doesn't matter – O could equally go in 3).

Why start with GP and R? It doesn't really matter. The main thing is to make a working scenario. If you make a working scenario, you can do two things:

1. You can eliminate answers that don't have to be true in the scenario.
2. You can see if there's another scenario. Then look for what must be true in both scenarios.

Now, if orange is in 2, rose is in windows 1 and 3.

```
Y 1 G P R
  2 O _
  3 R _
```

Next, we need to place YP. YP can't go with green or orange, so it must go with R in group 3:

```
Y 1 G P R
  2 O _
  3 R Y P
```

Finally, every window needs two colors, so one of P/G needs to go with O in group 2:

```
Y 1 G P R
  2 O P/G
  3 R Y P
```

This scenario eliminates answers **A-D**. None of those answers need to be true, because they're not true or not necessarily true in this scenario. And **E** does have to be true in this scenario. So **E** is **CORRECT.**

Technically, we've just proven that **A-D** don't have to be true. We can't be 100% certain that **E** has to be true. Maybe there's another possible scenario where it isn't true. Maybe we've made a mistake.

This is unlikely, but if you want to be extra sure, you can draw a second scenario to check whether yellow, purple and rose must go together in that scenario. The other scenario will place O with GP, and R in the other two groups. Here's the other one I drew:

```
Y 1 G P O
  2 R P
  3 Y P R
```

This scenario still has YPR, so **E** is definitely true.

I recommend practicing making scenarios constantly. The more you do it, the faster you'll get, and the better you'll become at seeing how variables interact.

For instance, the *reason* YPR must go together is that O and the two R's must go in different groups.

YP must go in one group. Since they can't go with O, then they must go with R. No one else can go with YPR, since G can't go with Y.

If that didn't make sense, I recommend trying to draw it, and make a scenario that obeys the rules and doesn't use YPR (it won't work). That's really the only way to understand these restrictions.

Game 3 – Management Skills
Questions 14–18

Setup

This is a hard game. There are lots of elements to keep track of. It's easy to get paralyzed.

On logic games, you have to trust that the game is easier than it looks. There's always an easy way. On this game, if you just draw new diagrams for each question and go one step at a time, the game will lead you to the right answer.

The key to logic games is trying things, rather than thinking. But trying things in a methodical way, where you look for deductions and what *must* be true. Don't just draw things that *could* be true.

On to the setup. I looked at the first question and drew this. The first question often shows you the best way to diagram a game, though I don't always follow it:

```
F __ __
G __ __
H __ __
I __ __
L __ __
```

Each talk has up to two people. But there are only eight people to place in this game, so two spaces will be empty.

I drew the first two rules directly on the diagram. Quigley doesn't attend Feedback or Handling People. And Rivera doesn't attend Goal Sharing or Handling People:

```
    Q̸ F __ __
    R̸ G __ __
R̸ H̸ H __ __
       I __ __
       L __ __
```

The last three rules can't be put on the diagram, and they can't be combined. So I numbered them 1, 2, 3 and made a list. A numbered list makes it easy to see all the rules at a glance:

(1) ~~ST~~

(2) $T_1 \rightarrow TQ$

(3) $R_1 \rightarrow RS$

The final two rules are most important. There is always a TQ to place, and always an RS to place. And they have to be the first T, and the first R. And there are many places where Q and R can't go. So TQ and RS are *restricted*. You should always look for the most restricted elements.

Oddly, the rule that S and T can't go together never came up when I solved this game. That happens sometimes.

There's one small deduction you can add to the main diagram. The first T can't go in F. This is because Q goes with the first T and Q can't go in F.

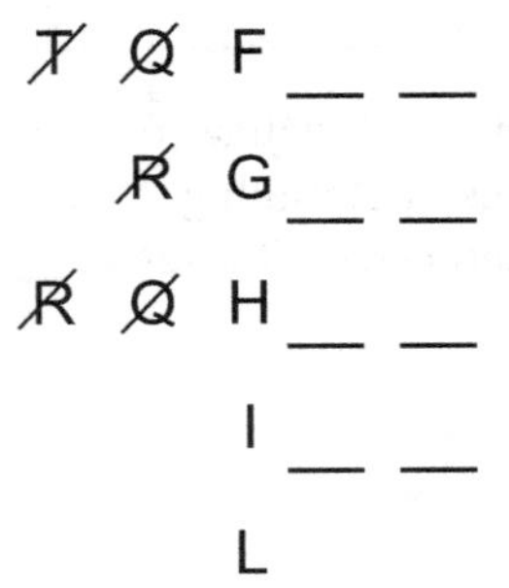

Note: I thought it might be the case that RS has to go in F. But I tried this, and it's not true. That's because there are ten spaces but only eight variables. So it's pretty easy to avoid the restrictions. Most of the questions add artificial restrictions which tie things down.

Main Diagram

T Q F __ __

R G __ __

R Q H __ __

I __ __

L __ __

(1) ST

(2) $T_1 \rightarrow TQ$

(3) $R_1 \rightarrow RS$

Question 14

For acceptable order questions, go through the rules and use them to eliminate answers one by one.

Rule 1 eliminates nothing.

Rule 2 eliminates **B.** Riviera can't attend Handling People.

Rule 3 eliminates **A.** Spivey and Tran can't go together.

Rule 4 eliminates **D.** Quigley has to attend Tran's first talk.

Rule 5 eliminates **E.** Spivey has to attend Riviera's first talk.

C is **CORRECT.** It violates no rules.

Question 15

This question says that no Softcorp employees attend Handling People. That's interesting, because normally there are two extra spaces in this game. But for this question, *every* remaining space has to be filled.

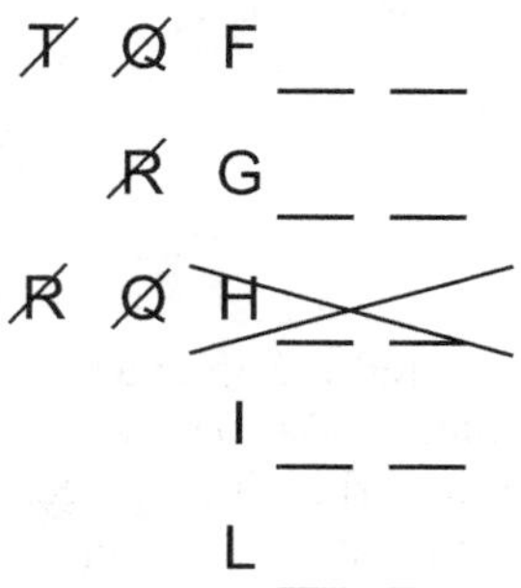

You should think about how to place TQ and RS. They're the most restricted elements. And TQ is the hardest to place, because neither T nor Q can go in Feedback.

Now, think about the two things I've said so far:

1. RS and TQ are the most restricted
2. *Every* space has to be filled.
3. TQ can't go in F.
4. There are only four variables: TQRS

If TQ can't go in F, and every space has to be filled, then RS must go in F:

T̸ Q̸ F R S
R̸ G _ _
R̸ Q̸ ~~H~~
I _ _
L _ _

This may seem like a hard deduction. On logic games, you must always think through consequences. If TQ can't go in a place, then who *can* go there? In this case, since only RS are left, we know exactly who *must* go in F.

This means that **A** is **CORRECT.**

Many people choose **D.** But Tran doesn't have to attend goal sharing. This diagram proves it:

T̸ Q̸ F R S
R̸ G Q S
R̸ Q̸ ~~H~~
I T Q
L T R

B is another popular choice. This diagram proves that R doesn't have to attend leadership.

T̸ Q̸ F R S
R̸ G T Q
R̸ Q̸ ~~H~~
I Q R
L T S

This diagram also eliminates **C** and **E.** Note that the fact that RS go in feedback is enough to prove **A** correct. But on review or in case of doubt it's worth making diagrams to disprove the other answers. The more diagrams you make, the faster you will get at making them.

Question 16

I used elimination for this question.

B is wrong because rule two says that R can't attend Goal Sharing.

C is wrong because it's missing Feedback. The diagram from question 15 shows that R can attend F.

D is wrong because it's missing information overload. The correct answer from the first question shows that R can attend information overload.

Only **A** and **E** are left. Can R attend leadership?

I looked at the correct answer to the first question, and I saw that no rule prevents you from switching S and R between Information Overload and Leadership.

So R can attend Leadership and **A** is **CORRECT.** Remember, if something isn't explicitly forbidden by the rules, then it's allowed.

Question 17

First you should draw the new rule. Q is the only person attending leadership:

```
T̸ Q̸ F __ __
  R̸ G __ __
R̸ Q̸ H __ __
     I __ __
     L Q |
```

Next, ask yourself what rules affect Q. Rule 4 does:

- We need to place TQ somewhere.
- It must be the first T.

Q can only attend Goal Sharing and Information Overload. But information overload won't work, because there's nowhere for the second T to go. So TQ must go in Goal Sharing:

```
T̸ Q̸ F __ __
  R̸ G T  Q |
R̸ Q̸ H __ __
     I __ __
     L Q |
```

Next, think about the other restricted variable: RS. This must be the first R. Information overload doesn't work for the first R, because there's no place to put the second R. And since Goal Sharing is full, the first R must go in Feedback:

```
T̸ Q̸ F R  S |
  R̸ G T  Q |
R̸ Q̸ H __ __
     I R  __
     L Q |
```

The second R goes in information overload. I drew that too. Now, who's left? We need to place one T, and one S. They can go in either Handling People or Information Overload:

```
T̸ Q̸ F R  S |
  R̸ G T  Q |
R̸ Q̸ H __ __     S , T
     I R  __
     L Q |
```

Note that *both* S and T could be in Handling People. Either way, this diagram proves that S could attend Handling People, so **D** is **CORRECT.** All the other answers contradict the diagram.

Question 18

Your first step should be to draw the new rule. R is the only one attending Information Overload:

```
T̸ Q̸ F __ __
   R̸ G __ __
R̸ Q̸ H __ __
     I R |
     L __ __
```

This must be the second R, because the first R is RS. So the next step is to think about where to place RS. It can't go in Leadership; RS is the *first* R. And we know R can't go in Goal Sharing or Handling people. So RS must go in Feedback:

```
T̸ Q̸ F R S |
   R̸ G __ __
R̸ Q̸ H __ __
     I R |
     L __ __
```

Next, think about where to place TQ, the other restricted element. This is the first T, so TQ can't go in leadership. And Q can't go in handling people. So TQ must go in Goal Sharing:

```
T̸ Q̸ F R S |
   R̸ G I Q |
R̸ Q̸ H __ __
     I R |
     L __ __
```

Finally, the second Q must go in Leadership. There's one S and one T left to place. They can go in Handling People or Leadership. Note that they could *both* go in handling people.

```
T̸ Q̸ F R S |
   R̸ G T Q
R̸ Q̸ H __ __   S, T
     I R |
     L Q __
```

E is **CORRECT.** Tran doesn't have to attend handling people.

Game 4 – Six Witnesses
Questions 19–23

Setup

I found the first three questions easy, and the last two questions hard. I drew a lot of diagrams to eliminate answers on the final two questions.

The key to drawing diagrams quickly is to have a ready list of the rules you can refer to. Any diagram that doesn't violate a rule is legal. I find most students are way too hesitant when drawing "could be true" diagrams. Usually the problem is that they don't know the rules and they don't have a clear list.

I couldn't make any upfront deductions on this game. Instead I just drew the rules. I did draw the third rule second. This makes for easier scanning, because the first and third rules are similar:

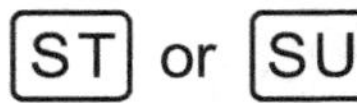

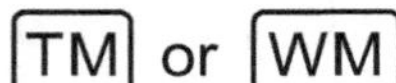

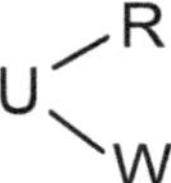

Note that the or's are exclusive. I just committed this to memory.

Main Diagram

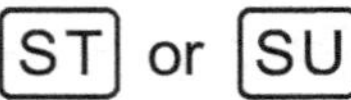

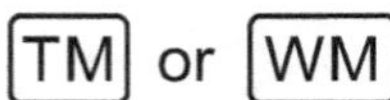

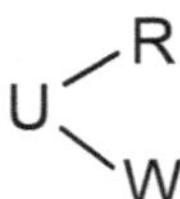

Note: The or's are exclusive. I just committed this to memory.

Question 19

For acceptable order questions, go through the rules and use them to eliminate answers one by one.

Rule 1 eliminates **D.** Sanderson needs to be before Tannenbaum or Ujemori.

Rule 2 eliminates **A** and **E.** Ujemori needs to be before Ramirez and Wong.

Rule 3 eliminates **C.** Tannenbaum or Wong must be before Mangione.

B is **CORRECT.** It violates no rules.

Question 20

When a question gives you a new rule, the first thing you should do is draw it:

```
T
__ __ __ __ __ __
1  2  3  4  5  6
```

Don't skip this step. It seems trivial, but it's far easier to make the next deduction if you have something on paper.

Once you draw the new rule, see what rules it affects. T is mentioned in the first rule: we need ST or SU. We can't have ST on this question, so we need SU.

This in turn connects with the third rule: SU is before R and W:

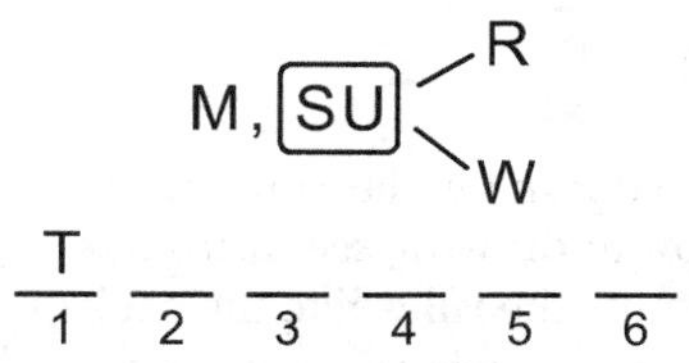

```
          / R
M, [SU] <
          \ W
T
__ __ __ __ __ __
1  2  3  4  5  6
```

I drew them floating above the diagram. I also drew the one remaining variable, M. The comma indicates that M could go before or after SU and the rest.

Now, we can use this diagram to eliminate wrong answers.

Ramirez has so be after T, S and U, so **A** is wrong.

Wong has to be after T, S and U, so **B** is wrong.

Sanderson has to be before U, R and W. S can go third at latest. So **C** is wrong.

Ujemori has to be before R and W, so they can't go fifth. So **D** is wrong.

This diagram proves that **E** is **CORRECT:**

```
T  S  U  R  W  M
1  2  3  4  5  6
```

Question 21

This question gives us a new rule. First, draw that: Sanderson is fifth.

```
             S
__ __ __ __ __ __
1  2  3  4  5  6
```

Next, see which rules are affected. The first rule says we need ST or SU. When I was doing this game, I drew both possibilities. When I did that, I realized the SU is impossible here, because R and W must be after U.

So T is sixth:

```
             S  T
__ __ __ __ __ __
1  2  3  4  5  6
```

Next, we need TM or WM. We can't have TM on this question, since T is last. We need WM. This modifies our remaining rule:

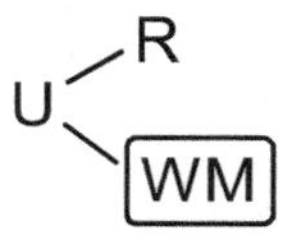

```
  / R
U <
  \ [WM]
```

Every variable is after U. So U has to be first. **A** is **CORRECT.**

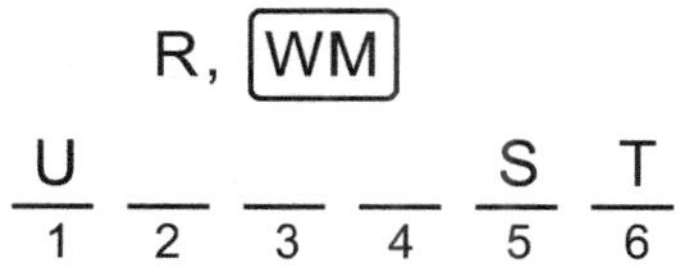

```
   R, [WM]
U           S  T
__ __ __ __ __ __
1  2  3  4  5  6
```

Question 22

There's no easy way through this question. You just have to brute force it.

That's what *I* thought at first, anyway. But I realized there was a better way. Remember, on this game there are four special configurations:

- ST
- SU
- TM
- WM

Reversing one of those is difficult. And we're looking for an answer that *can't* be true. So why not look for an answer that reverses one of them?

That's **A,** which is **CORRECT.** It reverses TM to MT. If you don't have TM, you need WM. And you need SU since you can't have ST.

So we would have WMT. And SU would have to go before them, because U is before W. There's no space:

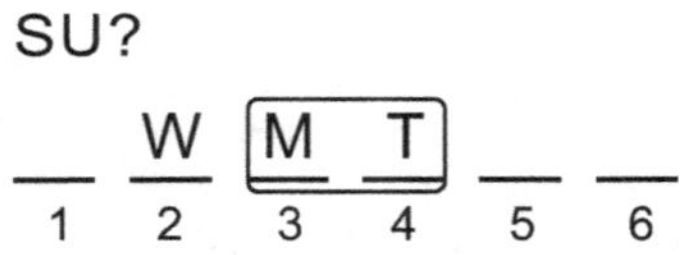

SU?

_	W	[M	T]	_	_
1	2	3	4	5	6

These diagrams prove that **B–E** are possible:

B

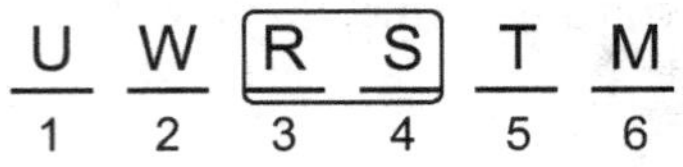

U	W	[R	S]	T	M
1	2	3	4	5	6

C

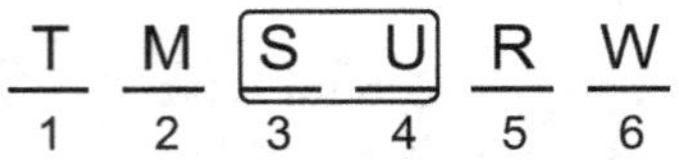

T	M	[S	U]	R	W
1	2	3	4	5	6

D

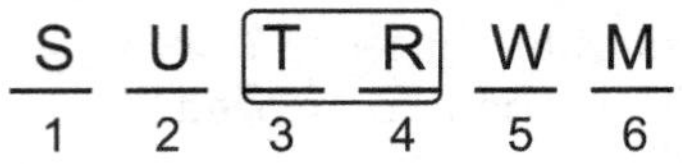

S	U	[T	R]	W	M
1	2	3	4	5	6

E

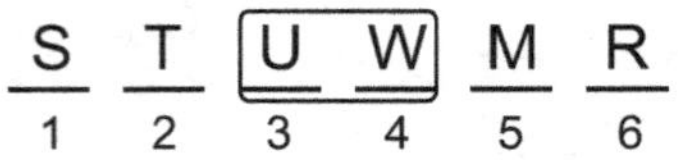

S	T	[U	W]	M	R
1	2	3	4	5	6

Remember, if a scenario doesn't violate any rules, it's correct. If you're slow at drawing scenarios like these, practice! If you know the rules like the back of your hand you can draw a scenario to disprove an answer in about 5-10 seconds.

Question 23

This is very similar to question 22. I thought I had to brute force it. But then I remembered the four special configurations:

- ST
- SU
- TM
- WM

Answers **C** and **D** reverse one of these configurations. Reversing a special configuration makes it harder to obey the rules.

I drew **C** first, but it was possible:

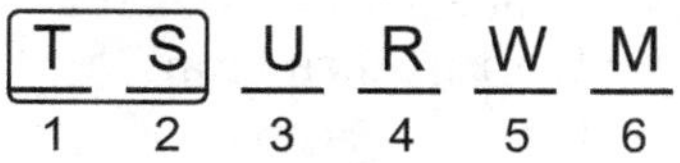

[T	S]	U	R	W	M
1	2	3	4	5	6

D doesn't work, so it's **CORRECT.** If you draw UT first, then there's no way to do ST or SU:

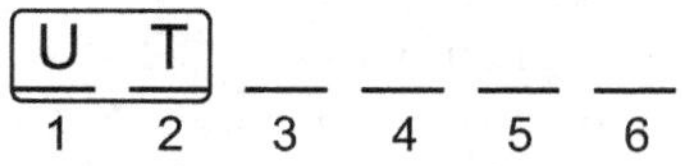

[U	T]	_	_	_	_
1	2	3	4	5	6

I'll repeat the rationale for trying **C** and **D** first. We need ST or SU. So taking two of those letters and putting them out of order (UT) greatly restricts our options for placing ST or SU.

These diagrams prove that **A, B** and **E** are possible:

A

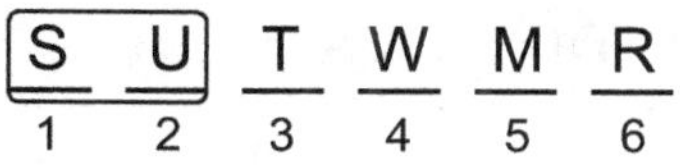

[S	U]	T	W	M	R
1	2	3	4	5	6

B

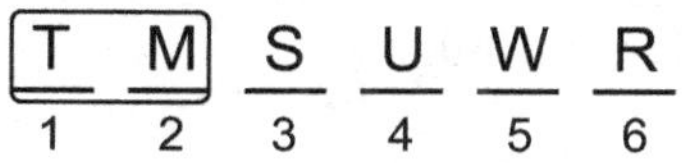

[T	M]	S	U	W	R
1	2	3	4	5	6

E

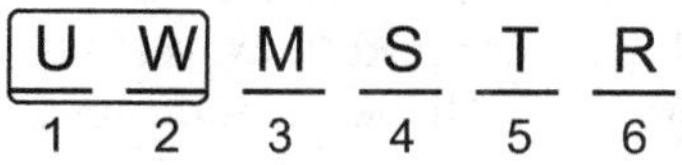

[U	W]	M	S	T	R
1	2	3	4	5	6

Note that **A** and **B** use SU and TM. Those are two of the four special configurations. So these answers make it *easier* to satisfy the rules. They were poor candidates.

Section IV – Logical Reasoning

Question 1

QUESTION TYPE: Identify the Conclusion

CONCLUSION: It is wrong to say that reef fish are colorful because reefs are colorful.

REASONING: Reefs aren't colorful.

ANALYSIS: This is a dense stimulus that hides a very short argument. Notice the word "however" at the start of the third sentence. "However" indicates the conclusion.

The conclusion says that "this suggestion" is wrong. So you have to read back to see what the suggestion is: the idea was the reefs are colorful, and therefore reef fish are colorful for camouflage.

A. The conclusion is that the hypothesis in this answer is wrong.
B. This is a true statement, but it's not the conclusion. The conclusion is that the colorful camouflage statement is wrong.
C. **CORRECT.** Read the third sentence, starting with "however". This is the conclusion.
D. This is evidence supporting the conclusion. Colorful fish aren't camouflaging themselves in reefs.
E. This is evidence that supports the conclusion. The conclusion is that fish aren't camouflaging themselves.

Question 2

QUESTION TYPE: Principle

CONCLUSION: The survey is ambiguous.

REASONING: The survey question was ambiguous.

ANALYSIS: This is sort of like a must be true question. We want a statement supported by the information in the argument.

You might have been unsure why the question was ambiguous. It's because "influence objects with your thoughts" doesn't necessarily mean telekinesis. If I think about picking up a coffee cup, then I can influence the movements of the coffee cup by actually picking it up.

A. The survey didn't use an uncontroversial statement. It used a statement that could be *interpreted* as being uncontroversial.
B. This is too broad. We know that *one* statement had multiple interpretations. We can't conclude that *all* statements have multiple interpretations.
C. We have no support for this. We only know about one survey which had a badly phrased question. We have no idea how people respond to well phrased questions.
D. **CORRECT.** This has the most support. We know of one survey with a poorly phrased, ambiguous question. That survey lead to ambiguous responses. This is a weak answer, but it's the best one.
E. Nonsense. We know of *one* statement about psychic phenomena that can be naturalistic. But some statements about psychic phenomena couldn't be naturalistic. For example: "Some people have magic, psychic powers that defy the laws of nature". There's no naturalistic interpretation for that statement.

Question 3

QUESTION TYPE: Strengthen

CONCLUSION: Perfect pitch is genetic.

REASONING: You're more likely to have perfect pitch if you're related to someone who has it.

ANALYSIS: There's a big flaw in this argument. It ignores that entire families can be musical and that music can be taught.

If one of your parents has perfect pitch, they may teach you perfect pitch. So in this case the cause is upbringing, not genetics.

We can strengthen the argument by eliminating this cause.

A. CORRECT. This strengthens the argument by eliminating education/upbringing as a cause. If we didn't know this, then it's possible your relatives teach you perfect pitch.
B. It doesn't matter if researchers have perfect pitch. It only matters if they can identify perfect pitch.
C. This isn't relevant. The stimulus never talked about choosing music as a career. We only care if someone *has* perfect pitch – it doesn't matter if they use it.
D. This *weakens* the argument. It shows that upbringing may be the cause, not genetics.
E. This weakens the argument by showing that genetics may not be the only cause.

Question 4

QUESTION TYPE: Role in Argument

CONCLUSION: The predator was chasing the grazing dinosaur, and the predator attacked shortly afterwards.

REASONING: The predator was probably matching the stride of the grazing dinosaur. Modern predators match strides just before they attack.

ANALYSIS: This is an argument by analogy. I'll summarize it in parts:

1. Predator dinosaur was matching stride.
2. Modern predators do this just before attacking.
3. Conclusion: Predator dinosaur was about to attack.

The question is asking about the first part. That statement is evidence that helps show the predator was about to attack.

A. This is false. The statement *is* evidence for the conclusion. The matching stride is why we conclude the predator was about to attack.
B. This didn't happen. If you picked this, you fundamentally misunderstood the argument. Reread it, and see the analysis section above.
C. CORRECT. The analogy is the lions. This evidence from modern predators shows that the predator was about to attack, since the predator was also matching stride.
D. The author doesn't mention any possible objections.
E. The final sentence is the conclusion. It starts with "this suggests" which typically indicates the author's opinion.

Question 5

QUESTION TYPE: Weaken

CONCLUSION: Sunscreen isn't likely to reduce skin cancer.

REASONING: Skin cancer has grown even though more people are using sunscreen.

ANALYSIS: This is a bad argument. People might be using sunscreen *because* they're out in the sun. Sunscreen could *reduce* their risk of skin cancer, even if it can't totally offset the increased exposure.

I checked the answers, and noticed that my prephrase wasn't there. Who cares? It *could* have been the answer, but I didn't get attached to it. Prephrasing is extremely valuable, but don't get stuck on a single explanation.

The correct answer weakens the argument by pointing out that cancer takes decades to develop. So the current cancers developed before sunscreen use was common, and sunscreen might still be effective.

Small public service announcement: sunscreens focus on SPF, which is UVB. But UVA is the main cause of melanoma. Check whether your sunscreen blocks both UVA and UVB.

A. It's not clear why the most expensive brand matters.
B. **CORRECT.** This shows that current skin cancer had its origins a long time ago, before the recent increase in sunscreen use.
C. It's good that sunscreens are based on research. But this can't weaken the *fact* that cancer rates are increasing.
D. This doesn't tell us anything about sunscreen.
E. I can see how this is tempting. This would be the right answer, *if* the argument had said:

"Sunscreen doesn't help. Those who use sunscreen are just as likely to get cancer."

Then this answer would show that the cancer group had a higher risk, and sunscreen may have lowered their risk.
But the argument was different! It said we have more cancer even though we use more sunscreen. So the question is: why hasn't increased sunscreen use reduced cancer on average? If sunscreen was protective we would expect rates to go down if more people use it.

Question 6

QUESTION TYPE: Must be True

FACTS:

1. fewer than 50 for hire AND more than 25% duplicate → ~~funding~~
2. Contrapositive: Funding → ~~Fewer than 50 for hire~~ OR ~~more than 25% duplicate~~
3. Area studies duplicates more than 25%
4. Area studies will get funding.

ANALYSIS: We know area studies will get funding. Look at the contrapositive diagram I drew above. We know at least one of the necessary conditions must be true as well.

We know that area studies does duplicate more than 25%. So that means it's the other necessary condition that's true: There must be more than 50 people available for hire (i.e. ~~Fewer than 50 for hire~~)

Must be true questions are often very formulaic. You absolutely should figure this one out before you look at the answers.

A. CORRECT. See the explanation above.

B. This answer contradicts the second-to-last sentence. We know that area studies *will* duplicate more than 25% of the material.

C. This is a nonsense answer. It strings together relevant words in a way that makes no sense. We know that duplication is a factor that *prevents* funding. This answer is saying that duplication is necessary for funding. That's ridiculous.

D. This is an incorrect reversal. Area studies could be a really, really big department. So it could duplicate 25% of anthropology, but perhaps anthropology only duplicates 10% of area studies.

E. If this were true, then area studies couldn't get funded. The stimulus says that having fewer than 50 people for hire is a factor in *preventing* funding. Reread the first sentence if you picked this.

Question 7

QUESTION TYPE: Paradox

PARADOX: Over three decades, the average beak size of wild birds shrunk. The average beak size of the captive birds stayed the same.

ANALYSIS: On paradox questions, open your mind and think about the situation. What are differences between wild and caged birds?

- Wild birds eat by themselves. Captive birds eat the food they're given.
- Wild birds have to worry about predators.

I can think of other differences, but those two differences are the ones that seem relevant to beak sizes. Maybe food for wild birds has shrunk. Or maybe smaller beaks are needed to deal with a new predator.

After taking the time to form hypotheses, I immediately saw that C was the correct answer. Before thinking hard about any answer, I looked over all of them quickly to check if the prephrase was there.

A. This isn't relevant. The stimulus was talking about the *change* in beak size over three decades. The captive population was captured three decades ago, and then observed. Starting beak size doesn't matter – only *change* does.

B. Same as A.

C. CORRECT. This shows that the wild population faced selective pressure. More small beaked birds survived. Captive birds faced no such selective pressure.

D. Body size doesn't matter. I'm sure you've seen toucans, which have massive beaks but small bodies.

E. So? This doesn't tell us whether the researcher measured the beaks of captive birds more than once. We need a *difference* between the two populations.

Question 8

QUESTION TYPE: Most Strongly Supported

FACTS:

1. All cultures use storytelling.
2. Common themes appear in many diverse cultures.

ANALYSIS: Remember, this is a "most strongly supported" question. You're not looking for an answer that's 100% true, with no exceptions. You're just looking for something that is probably true, based on the stimulus.

We know storytelling seems to be common to all cultures.

The evidence about creation myths being widespread is also strong, but not as strong. The study examined narratives from different times and places. (e.g. ancient Rome, modern china, medieval Russia) and found similar themes. This suggests those themes are universal – and that's enough for a MSS question.

A. We know cultures have common themes. We don't know if this is due to borrowing, or because people think alike across cultures.
B. We have no idea what storytellers think. They aren't mentioned.
C. **CORRECT.** This is fairly well supported by the fact that the diverse cultures in the study all have similar themes.
D. This we don't know. We know that storytelling has been important in all cultures. But we don't know whether it is more or less important in modern cultures.
E. Storytellers aren't mentioned. We have no idea what motivates them, or whether this lets us understand cultures.

Question 9

QUESTION TYPE: Flawed Parallel Reasoning

CONCLUSION: Jackie's first child probably wasn't born before the due date.

REASONING: 1st child born before due (most)→ second child born before due.

Jackie's second child wasn't born before due.

ANALYSIS: "Likely" is a synonym for most. So this argument gives us a "most" statement, then tries to take the contrapositive. But you *can't* take the contrapositive of a "most" statement the way you can for a conditional statement. That's because there can always be exceptions to a "most" statement.
(A conditional statement is one where the sufficient condition *always* leads to the necessary condition)

The answers are a bit technical. I'll give examples.
Take this statement: Cat → has tail

Incorrect reversal: tail → cat
Incorrect negation: ~~cat~~ → ~~tail~~
contrapositive (correct) ~~tail~~ → ~~cat~~

Now, this argument uses a "most" statement. You can't do *any* of these with a most statement. Even contrapositives. This argument is wrong because it tries to reverse and negate a "most" statement. You need to find the answer that does the same thing.

A. This incorrectly negates a "most" statement. That's not the same as trying to take the contrapositive of a "most" statement.
B. This incorrectly reverses a "most" statement. That's not the same thing as trying to take the contrapositive of a "most" statement.
C. **CORRECT.** This reverses the terms of a "most" statement, and negates those terms. This is the same error as the stimulus – you can't take the contrapositive of a "most" statement.
D. This is a good argument. Unlike all the other answers, this one has a conditional statement. In *every* case where a business is likely to fail, people won't invest.
E. This incorrectly reverses a conditional statement and adds a "probably".

Question 10

QUESTION TYPE: Flawed Reasoning

CONCLUSION: It is likely that primitive life has evolved on Europa.

REASONING: A necessary condition for life exists on Europa. (liquid water)

ANALYSIS: Necessary conditions don't tell you *anything!* Here are some necessary conditions for going to law school:

- Being human
- Applying to law school
- Breathing
- Knowing how to read

Those are not very useful necessary conditions! Telling me that a candidate fulfills them doesn't help prove the candidate will go to law school.

Likewise, knowing that there is water on Europa doesn't tell us life occurred. We need a *sufficient* condition or a statement of probability in order to have evidence life occurred. At the very least we should rule out all other necessary conditions.

A. Actually, this is true. If a condition is necessary for life, then life couldn't evolve without it. This is not a flaw!

B. **CORRECT.** Water is *one* necessary condition for life. But there could be 1,000 other necessary conditions. The author incorrectly assumes water is the *only* necessary condition.

C. Rubbish. The argument didn't do this! There's no distinction between life being present on Europa and life evolving on Europa. And "if but only if" is just thrown in because it's confusing.
Answers have to prove they're right. Don't give nonsensical answers the time of day.

D. The argument didn't overlook this possibility! It said "life *as we know it*" could only evolve with liquid water. The author wasn't talking about water being a necessary condition for all life.

E. The author didn't do this! They said the data "strongly suggest" that liquid water is present. And then their conclusion appropriately only says "likely". So the author isn't saying water is *definitely* present and life *definitely* evolved.

Question 11

QUESTION TYPE: Most Strongly Supported

FACTS:

1. Antibiotics will produce resistant bacteria, unless the antibiotics can eliminate the bacteria entirely.
2. Bacteria X can't be eliminated by any single anti-biotic.

ANALYSIS: On "most strongly supported" questions, it's important not to assume more than the question tells you.

We can conclude exactly *one* thing from the facts above: If any *single* existing anti-biotic is used against bacteria X, then bacteria X will develop resistance.

We *don't* know whether bacteria X can be eliminated. Maybe a combination of drugs can eliminate it. We also don't know what future antibiotics will be able to do.

A. We don't know. Maybe future antibiotics will be able to deal with bacteria X.

B. **CORRECT.** This is true, because none of the antibiotics on the market can eliminate bacteria X by itself.

C. Careful....there might be other ways of eliminating bacteria, apart from antibiotics. Maybe quarantines and good hygiene can eliminate bacteria X.

D. The stimulus only talked about greater resistance – it didn't mention virulence. Virulence is how strong a bacteria is. This answer has no support at all from the stimulus.

E. We don't know if any antibiotics have been used against bacteria X. This answer has no support.

Question 12

QUESTION TYPE: Identify the Conclusion

CONCLUSION: The criticism is insincere. (note: "the criticism" is that ideas are muddled)

REASONING: Any successful political idea must be clear.

ANALYSIS: This is actually a really bad argument. The author ignores the possibility that many political ideas are really unclear and thus will never be realized.

But our job is to find the conclusion, not critique the argument. Look to the word "however". It almost always indicates the conclusion. The second sentence says "such criticism, however, is misguided".

So the conclusion is that the criticism is wrong. You just to read the first sentence to see what "the criticism" is. The author is concluding that it's wrong to say that political ideas are muddled.

A. Read more carefully. The author said that people who *criticize* political agendas *for being* incomprehensible are insincere.
B. The second sentence is the conclusion, it says "however". Furthermore, the ideas described in this answer simply doesn't appear in the argument, even as premises. This is a total nonsense answer.
C. What rubbish is this? The argument didn't *say* any of this. It can't be the conclusion. If you can find this in the argument, I'll pay you $1000. Answers have to prove they're right. Don't give nonsense answers the time of day.
D. CORRECT. The second sentence is the conclusion. It says "such criticism" is insincere. "The criticism" is criticism of ideas for being incomprehensible.
E. This isn't even true. This answer mixes up the last sentence. The last sentence says that political agendas must be able to be understood. But this answer says that political agendas must be *impossible* to misunderstand. That's crazy.

Question 13

QUESTION TYPE: Flawed Reasoning

CONCLUSION: Organic factors aren't evenly distributed.

REASONING: Mental illness symptoms vary around the world. Organic factors cause mental illness.

ANALYSIS: I couldn't prephrase this one. I just looked through the answers quickly, and eliminated those that didn't seem correct. I then returned to the answer that remained (C). On flaw questions, you're looking for two things:

1. The answer actually happened. Almost all flaw answer choices don't occur in the stimulus.
2. The answer is actually a flaw. For example, answer A may have happened, but it's not an error.

As for the stimulus itself, I don't have much commentary. The main thing I took from it is that mental illnesses vary around the world, and that the author thinks that this means organic factors vary.

A. This isn't a flaw. From context, the author appears to be talking about all mental illnesses.
B. The stimulus didn't talk about nutrient deficiencies! This answer used that word because you've probably only heard deficiency refer to food. They know you well and they trapped you! "Deficiency" can refer to many things. The stimulus was about the brain being short of certain compounds. Not necessarily due to diet.
C. CORRECT. This is a flaw. Cultures have many differences around the world. This can change how symptoms appear. In that case, the same organic compounds might be deficient around the world. But how people react to deficiencies would change due to culture.
D. The argument didn't do this! An answer can't be a flaw unless it happens.
Example of flaw: Well, his brain chemistry changed in a really, really insignificant way, so obviously his mental condition will change.
E. The argument didn't say this. Whether or not this is a flaw, it didn't happen in the argument.

Question 14

QUESTION TYPE: Weaken

CONCLUSION: Privatizing parks would probably be good for park visitors.

REASONING: Privatizing telecommunications was good for telephone customers.

ANALYSIS: This is an argument by analogy. Any analogy is vulnerable to differences between the two situations. Maybe national parks aren't like telephones.

So look for an answer that points out a factor that makes parks not like telephones.

A. This answer talks about whether politicians *will* privatize parks. That doesn't matter. The argument was about what would happen *if* parks were privatized.
B. This is tempting. Maybe privatizing was a bad idea because it was bad for workers. But the conclusion isn't about whether privatization is a good idea *in general*. The question is: will privatization help *visitors*?
C. It doesn't matter if people know about the proposals. It only matters how the proposals will affect them.
D. This sounds tempting, but it doesn't contradict the conclusion. The conclusion is that park visitors would benefit. This answer suggests that park visitors would, in fact, benefit to some extent. The conclusion didn't say how much benefit there must be – even a tiny bit works.
E. **CORRECT.** Competition was the reason that privatization produced low prices. If parks don't have competition, then maybe there will be no benefit for consumers.

Question 15

QUESTION TYPE: Principle

CONCLUSION: Counterfeit diamonds should be worth as much as real diamonds. (assuming we can't tell them apart)

REASONING: A counterfeit should give people as much aesthetic pleasure as a real diamond.

ANALYSIS: This argument is assuming that aesthetic pleasure is the only reason to buy a diamond. But there may be other reasons:

- Exclusivity
- Durability

I can't think of any others. But those are real things consumers care about. We can strengthen the argument by showing that they don't matter, and that only aesthetic value matters.

A. This is a stupid answer. You have to take LSAT answers literally. This answer means that jewel collectors should collect nothing but the best jewels. This has nothing to do with diamonds. Instead, it means jewelers shouldn't sell rings that cost $500/$1000/$2000. Instead, they should sell only the most valuable jewels: $1,000,000/$2,000,000/$500,000,000
B. Market demand wasn't mentioned. We have no idea if there's market demand for aesthetics.
C. The question is not whether everyone receives the same aesthetic pleasure. It's instead whether someone will receive *less* aesthetic pleasure from a counterfeit than they would have received from a real diamond.
D. **CORRECT.** Counterfeits provide as much aesthetic pleasure as real diamonds. According to this answer, we should therefore value them equally.
E. We're trying to prove that jewelers *should* buy counterfeit jewels. This answer adds a necessary condition to buying counterfeit jewels. A necessary condition can only help prove when we *should not* buy counterfeits.

Question 16

QUESTION TYPE: Sufficient Assumption

CONCLUSION: More etching tools are used for engraving than are not used for engraving.

REASONING: All pin tipped tools are used for engraving. Some bladed tools are used for engraving and some are not. All etching tools are pin tipped or bladed.

Note: This situation may be confusing. I've drawn a diagram to illustrate this question. The key to this question is we don't know how many bladed tools are used for engraving and how many aren't:

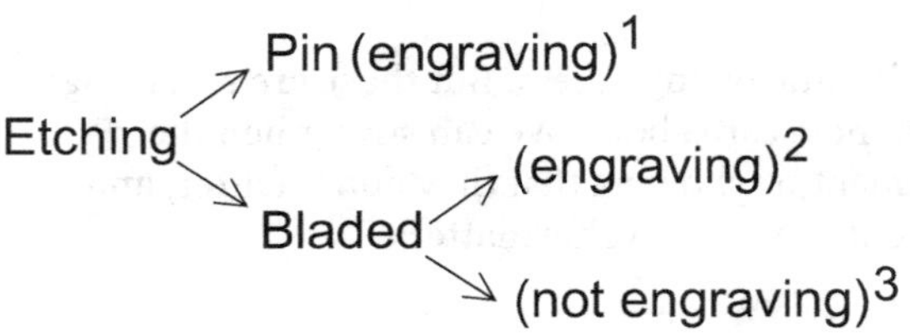

So category 3 (bladed, not engraving) could be enormous. Way bigger than categories 1 + 2.

ANALYSIS: This argument ignores quantities. There could be three types of pin tipped tool, and 3,000,000 types of bladed tools. And maybe only 2 bladed tools are used for engraving. That would mean 5 tools are used for engraving and 2,999,998 are not.

We need to eliminate this possibility. For instance, by saying there are equal numbers of pin tipped and bladed tools, or more pin tipped tools.

A. This tells us that there are no chiseling tools used for engraving (for example). And no hammering tools used for engraving. So what? The conclusion is only about etching tools. Etching tools are only pin tipped or bladed

B. **CORRECT.** This equalized the numbers of both tools. It makes it mathematically certain that most etching tools are used for engraving. Let's say there are 8 pin tipped tools and 8 bladed tools. Then at least nine would be used for engraving: 8 pin tipped, and at least one bladed.

C. This answer isn't a sufficient assumption. It just tells us a useless fact about pin tipped and bladed tools. Look at my example in the analysis section. I was already assuming the two categories didn't overlap, yet the conclusion wasn't true in my example.

D. This *weakens* the argument! We want to prove that etching tools *are* used for engraving.

E. We actually already knew this. Pin tipped tools are all used for engraving, and pin tipped tools are the only etching tools that aren't bladed.

Question 17

QUESTION TYPE: Paradox – Exception

PARADOX: Beta-carotene in foods was associated with less cancer and heart disease. Beta-carotene supplements had no such association.

ANALYSIS: Your main job on "EXCEPT" question is not to forget that they're "EXCEPT" questions.

Beyond that, just open your mind to ways that the paradox could be resolved. What are differences between foods and supplements? Here are some I brainstormed:

- Supplements are synthetic
- Supplements have the wrong dose
- Supplements don't absorb well
- There are other compounds in foods that help

I don't know if these will all be in the answers. But I think I'll go through the answers faster for having taken a few seconds to think about possibilities.

Here's a tip for prephrasing. I often here students say "I can't prephrase!". Pretend someone was paying you $50 if you could think of an explanation. Or $50 to find a reason an argument was wrong. You'd think a bit harder then, wouldn't you?

A. This is my third explanation from the analysis section.
B. This is something I didn't think of, but it's a relevant difference between the two studies. The supplement study only lasted 12 years.
C. This is my fourth explanation from the analysis section.
D. **CORRECT.** This actually shows the study was well performed. You're *supposed* to have a control group that takes a placebo.
E. This is a complex answer, but it says: if you eat beta-carotene, you smoke less. And we know from outside knowledge that smoking causes cancer and heart disease. So this shows an alternate cause: less smoking in the beta-carotene group.
(You can assume facts that *no one* would disagree with. That's called a "warranted assumption".)

Question 18

QUESTION TYPE: Sufficient Assumption

CONCLUSION: We won't know if there are aliens outside our solar system unless the aliens are as smart as us.

REASONING:

1. We can't send spaceships to aliens.
2. If aliens were to send us messages, they'd have to be at least as smart as us.

ANALYSIS: I simplified the language in the conclusion/reasoning to make the argument clearer.

Now, you first must find the flaw, so your job is to imagine an alternate possibility. Pretend someone is paying you $50 to spot the flaw in this argument. Is there *any* other way we could figure out aliens exist, even if we can't travel to them or receive messages?

Well, what about a telescope? There are other ways to discover what's in the universe. The argument's flaw is assuming that the two possibilities it gave are the *only* two possibilities for discovering aliens.

This is a sufficient assumption question, so you must prove this argument correct. The argument works if you assume that there are *no* other ways to discover the aliens. Then the argument will be correct. (This almost is a necessary assumption question)

Note that the argument is only talking about aliens outside the solar system. Note also that diagrams are not useful on this question, so I haven't drawn any.

A. The argument is talking about aliens *outside* the solar system. This answer is irrelevant.

B. The argument wasn't saying that aliens *will* communicate with us if they're as intelligent as us. The argument is saying that the only way we could *possibly* discover aliens is if they communicated with us.

C. The stimulus already said we can't send spaceships to planets outside our solar system. Since the conclusion is only about aliens on planets outside the solar system, this answer doesn't help.

D. **CORRECT.** This says that there are only two possibilities for discovering aliens:
1. We send a spaceship.
2. They communicate with us.
The argument already eliminated the first possibility. And the second possibility only works if aliens are as smart as us. So this answer proves that the only way we'll discover aliens outside our solar system is if they're at least as smart as us.

E. This gets things backwards. The argument didn't say that we'd definitely hear from aliens if they were at least as smart as us. It said that we'd *only* hear from aliens if they were at least as smart as us.
So this answer adds nothing. We're trying to prove that sentient aliens are the *only* possibility for communication. So we need to show there are no other possibilities. Whether or not aliens actually *do* or *can* communicate with us doesn't matter.

Question 19

QUESTION TYPE: Flawed Reasoning

CONCLUSION: Slipped or bulging disks can't lead to back pain.

REASONING: Some people with no back pain have slipped or bulging disks.

ANALYSIS: The LSAT often treats causes as absolute. Either something always leads to an effect, or it never does.

That's not how things work in real life, and this question acknowledges that. Maybe slipped disks cause back pain 30% of the time.

So they haven't caused pain to those in the study, but they might cause pain to other people. Something can occasionally be a cause even if it isn't always a cause.

A. This says something might be a sufficient condition even if it's not necessary. But slipped disks aren't sufficient or necessary, so this answer is irrelevant.

B. **CORRECT.** Something can be a cause even if it isn't a sufficient cause. Slipped and bulged disks may cause pain in some other cases.

C. This is different.
Example of flaw: The lights work when there is no hurricane, so clearly they'll work when there is a hurricane.

D. The doctor didn't say that half of the population has slipped or bulged disks. Something can't be a flaw unless it happens.

E. This is different. This says that slipped disks may be correlated with pain even if they're not the *cause* of pain.

Question 20

QUESTION TYPE: Principle – Strengthen

CONCLUSION: The manufacturer is at least partially responsible for the illnesses caused by substance T.

REASONING: The manufacturer didn't know substance T was harmful, but it could have investigated the safety of substance T.

ANALYSIS: You may have already thought this was a good argument. Shouldn't companies investigate the safety of substances they use? Well, that's a *principle* you're using to judge the situation. On most principle questions, you just have to say "the company was wrong not to do the thing they didn't do". This is the difference between "is" and "ought". The company didn't investigate – that's a statement of fact. The company *should* have investigated – that's a moral principle.

(The right answer is slightly different. It says you should be held accountable if the harm could have been prevented. And the manufacturer could have prevented the harm by investigating.)

Remember, you want to *prove the manufacturer responsible*. You want a *sufficient condition* for proving guilt. No wrong answer provides a sufficient condition for guilt.

A. The argument isn't talking about compensation. It's talking about who is guilty.
B. This adds a *necessary* condition for holding the manufacturer responsible. Necessary conditions *never* help prove an argument. They make it *harder* to hold someone responsible – there are now more conditions to fulfill.
C. The manufacturer wasn't aware of the health risks, so this doesn't help.
D. This doesn't help us prove that the manufacturer was responsible. It just tells us a factor that *isn't* relevant in determining responsibility.
E. **CORRECT.** The illnesses were definitely preventable – the manufacturer could have investigated the health effects of substance T. This proves that the manufacturer was responsible.

Question 21

QUESTION TYPE: Method of Reasoning

CONCLUSION: Phoenix will almost certainly get the contract.

REASONING: The contract will almost certainly go to Phoenix or Cartwright. But Cartwright won't get it.

ANALYSIS: This is a fairly good argument. It shows that one of two possibilities will probably happen, then it eliminates one possibility.

The main difficulty on these questions is understanding what the heck the answers mean. Rather than "explain" why the answers are wrong, I've given an example of what each one would look like. The "reason" they're wrong is that they didn't happen in the stimulus.

A. **CORRECT.** This is exactly what the argument does. The argument ruled out Cartwright, and Phoenix is the only plausible alternative.
B. This is a different situation.
Example of answer: Bob and Suzy are applying to law school. I heard that Bob will definitely get in. So Suzy won't get in.
C. This is a different situation.
Example of answer: You say that Smith will definitely be elected president. But it's possible he will be struck by lightning. So it's not inevitable.
D. This is a different situation.
Example of answer: Phoenix and Cartwright have always gotten the contract in the past. So one of them will probably get the next contract.
E. This is a different situation.
Example of answer: 42% of men will die of lung cancer. So you, John, have a 42% chance of dying of lung cancer even though you don't smoke.

Question 22

QUESTION TYPE: Strengthen

CONCLUSION: Exposure to germs makes you less likely to get allergies.

REASONING: Children with many siblings have fewer allergies.

ANALYSIS: This argument has established a possible cause. But they've only shown a correlation.

We can strengthen the idea that germ exposure reduces allergies either by eliminating alternatives or by showing that germ exposure works in another context (i.e. not in families).

A. This sounds good, but it's not very compelling. A century is a long time. There may have been other factors that caused allergies to increase. Also, notice that this answer didn't tell us what has happened in countries where the average number of children did *not* decrease. Maybe those countries also have an increase in allergies! We would need to know that allergies increased *faster* in countries with *larger* declines in the number of average children per family.
B. This *weakens* the argument. It shows an alternate cause for the lower number of allergies in large families.
C. This is just a couple of useless facts about allergies and germs. We're trying to *explain* the rate of allergies. We're not trying to decide if germs are a good thing.
D. This doesn't tell us anything about small families vs. large families. And it slightly weakens the argument by presenting an alternate cause for allergies: genetics.
E. **CORRECT.** Daycare has lots of children, and therefore germs. This is a warranted assumption from outside knowledge – no one would disagree with it. So this answer supports the idea that germ exposure reduces allergies.

Question 23

QUESTION TYPE: Necessary Assumption

CONCLUSION: Some early Hollywood films won't be preserved.

REASONING: We can't transfer all films from their original material to acetate.

ANALYSIS: This argument makes a whole-to-part flaw. It's true that we can't save *all* films. But that doesn't mean we can't save all *old Hollywood films*. For example, we could focus on preserving old Hollywood films, and save those films. Or maybe they've already been preserved. The argument has to assume that neither of these two things is possible.

I've taken a bit of liberty on negations. Most people try to use a really technical grammatical approach. It works, but it's not the best way to do it. With negations, you're just trying to prove the idea false, in the least useful way possible. If you can imagine a situation where the answer is true, but the situation doesn't hurt the argument, then the answer isn't necessary.

A. This is a good example of how useless some assumptions are. If you negate this in the slightest way possible, it's really, really useless.
Negation: One new technology will be developed in the year 2542. The technology won't work.
B. The argument wasn't even talking about cost.
Negation: There is one cheaper method. But it really sucks – it destroys 89% of the films it tries to preserve.
C. Close, but "many" is vague enough that this isn't truly necessary. The negation doesn't wreck the argument.
Negation: Many films have been transferred, but thousands remain. Too many to save.
D. **CORRECT.** The negation of this destroys the argument.
Negation: No early Hollywood films exist only in their original material.
E. This is just a random fact. We're concerned with saving *all* early Hollywood films, so it doesn't matter which ones are most likely to be lost. One is too many.

Question 24

QUESTION TYPE: Complete the Argument

CONCLUSION: The conclusion will probably be that the weather doesn't affect arthritis pain.

REASONING: Arthritis sufferers who thought the weather affected their pain gave completely different start times for their pain during the same weather conditions. There was no correlation between weather and pain.

ANALYSIS: The study is leading toward a conclusion. The researchers failed to find any correlation between pain and weather. And when people said weather caused pain, they all gave different start times for their pain.

In short, the study found no evidence that weather causes pain, and plenty of evidence that weather does not cause pain. The conclusion will likely be that the correlation doesn't exist.

A. The researchers found *no* correlation between weather and pain. So it's unlikely the study would conclude that weather actually was the cause.

B. This might be true, in a narrow technical sense. Arthritis sufferers think that weather affects the intensity of their pain.
But it's not the conclusion of the argument. The entire argument is leading towards the idea that arthritis sufferers are imagining the correlation between weather and pain. All the evidence showed the arthritis sufferer's were making things up.
You're looking for the conclusion, not something that is true!

C. CORRECT. The researchers found no correlation. And there wasn't any consistency in how long it took for weather to "cause" pain.

D. The entire argument is leading towards the conclusion that there is no such thing as weather-caused arthritis pain.

E. What an odd answer. The study has investigated the correlation, and found none. Scientific investigation is clearly possible. Sometimes the result of scientific investigation is to *disprove* ideas.

Question 25

QUESTION TYPE: Parallel Reasoning

CONCLUSION: If you want a job, you should move to a high tech city.

REASONING:

1. (B) Healthy economy (most) → (C) job openings
2. (A) High tech (most) → (B) healthy economy

ANALYSIS: This is not a good argument. It incorrectly joins two "most" statements. You can't connect "most" statements. I've drawn, A, B and C to clarify the structure. Premises:

B (most) → C
A (most) → B

Conclusion: If you want A, you should do C.

You need to parallel that argument. So find an answer with two "most" statements that share a term. Then the conclusion should parallel the one I wrote above.

Note: Probably, likely, usually etc. are all synonyms for "most".

A. Here, the two "most" statement don't share any term. We know antique dealers authenticate the age, but we don't know if they generally have old antiques.

B. Authenticated (most) → most to sell
Most valuable (most)→ authenticated
The two bits of evidence work, but the conclusion doesn't work. It should have said "if you're looking for those dealers who have the most to sell, you should buy from those who have the most valuable antiques".

C. CORRECT.
(B) Authenticated (most) → (C) valuable
(A) Antique dealer (most) → (B) authenticated
Conclusion: If you want A, you should go to C
This argument parallels the structure exactly.

D. This has a "many" statement. We're looking for two "mosts", so that's an instant eliminate.

E. Same as D, this only has one "most" statement.

Question 26

QUESTION TYPE: Paradox – Exception

PARADOX: Older people are more likely to be malnourished than to be below the poverty line. Younger people are more likely to fall below the poverty line than to be malnourished.

ANALYSIS: You can't really prephrase this type of question. Instead, just remember what you're looking for. You're looking for something that explains the *difference* between the two groups.

Note that we don't know how many people under 65 are poor. We just know that more of them are malnourished than poor. Here are some possible numbers for those under 65:

1. Malnourished: 97% Poor: 99%
2. Malnourished: 3% Poor: 73%
3. Malnourished: 17% Poor: 43%
4. Malnourished 1% Poor: 2%

In each case, their poverty rate is higher than the malnourishment rate. That's *all* we know. We have no idea if younger people are more/less poor than older people, or more/less malnourished.

A. This explains the higher malnutrition rate in older people: their malnutrition goes untreated.
B. This is a relevant difference. Older people have deficiencies caused by medications.
C. This also explains malnutrition. You need to eat to get nutrients.
D. **CORRECT.** See the analysis section. It actually doesn't matter how many younger people fall into poverty, as long as fewer of them fall into malnutrition.
E. This also gives a relevant difference. You need digestion to get nutrients.

Preptest 63
Section I - Logical Reasoning

Question 1

QUESTION TYPE: Complete the Argument

CONCLUSION: Backyard gardeners should grow stinging nettles beside their potato plants.

REASONING: Stinging nettles attract insects that eat the harmful pests that attack potatoes. It is true that stinging nettles also attract aphids (many species of which attack potatoes), but that's fine because ________. (fill in the blank)

ANALYSIS: The only logical way to end this argument would be to show that the aphids either cause no or little harm. The correct answer shows that only some species of aphids attack potatoes and stinging nettles don't attract those aphids.

A. This doesn't explain why aphids aren't a problem.
B. That's good for the stinging nettle plants. But the stimulus warned that the aphids could harm the potatoes.
C. CORRECT. Here we go. Some aphids harm potatoes. But the aphids attracted by stinging nettles don't harm potatoes, so everything is fine.
D. This isn't nearly as strong as C. Aphids could still potentially cause a lot of damage even if they cause less damage than other organisms.
E. The conclusion is only about gardeners who want to increase yields of potato plants. It doesn't matter how other plants are affected.

Question 2

QUESTION TYPE: Weaken

CONCLUSION: Jocko purposefully avoided making noise to prevent the other chimpanzees from taking his banana.

REASONING: Jocko was given a single banana when he kept silent. When he was given many bananas he made a lot of "food barks" and the other chimpanzees came to get the bananas.

ANALYSIS: To weaken this we need to give an alternate explanation for Jocko's silence. The correct answer shows that chimps will never make noise when give only a small quantity of food. This could be why Jocko stayed silent: if he had been given a large quantity then maybe he would still have barked and lost everything.

The wrong answers are all consistent with the idea that Jocko had learned to keep his mouth shut.

A. If so, then presumably bananas are among a chimpanzee's favorite foods: Jocko did make food barks when he got a larger amount of bananas. This doesn't explain why he didn't bark at a single banana.
B. CORRECT. This provides an alternate explanation: chimpanzees never make food barks if they're given only a small quantity of food (such as a single banana.)
C. This could explain why the other chimpanzees stole the bananas. It doesn't tell us why Jocko kept silent.
D. This could explain the initial food barks. But it doesn't provide an alternate explanation for Jocko's silence when he got a single banana.
E. This would explain why Jocko got so excited and why the other chimps stole the bananas. But it also strengthens the idea that Jocko stayed silent to prevent the loss of his banana.

Question 3

QUESTION TYPE: Flawed Reasoning

CONCLUSION: The survey indicates that publishers are mistaken about the interests of the public.

REASONING: Publishing is full of trashy gossip stories. A survey of journalism students said they wanted to see more serious journalism and less trashy gossip.

ANALYSIS: This is a classic case of sample bias. Journalism students are likely to have different taste in news articles compared to the public at large. The public may love celebrity gossip even if journalism students hate it.

A. The stimulus didn't try to find out why publishers were mistaken. It didn't try to explain any cause or effect.
B. This is a different error. An example would be: I drop and break a glass. You assume that I must have meant to do it and that it wasn't an accident.
C. **CORRECT.** Journalism students pay a lot of attention to the news. They likely have very different views from the public.
D. This would have been the case if the stimulus had said that the publishers were: "stupid jerks who can't read." (for example) The argument doesn't insult the publishers personally.
E. The conclusion does not say that the public definitely hates gossip. It just says that the evidence from the survey "indicates" (suggests) that the publishers are wrong.

Question 4

QUESTION TYPE: Paradox

PARADOX: Bug zappers are great for getting rid of flying insects in an area. But pest control experts generally say we shouldn't use bug zappers.

ANALYSIS: Normally it wouldn't be a problem to use bug zappers combined with sprays, even if the bug zappers didn't work very well. But the pest control experts are implying that bug zappers are actually harmful. So even if you had no other methods of pest control, you *still* shouldn't use bug zappers.

That's unusual. The right answer choice (D) explains how bug zappers can actually make things worse.

B doesn't work because it doesn't show there is any harm to using a bug zapper.

A. The pest control experts haven't said if birds are a good or a bad idea. This solution doesn't explain why a bug zapper wouldn't also work, and work better.
B. This doesn't explain why we shouldn't use bug zappers in combination with some other method. The pest control experts seem to indicate that bug zappers are actually harmful.
C. Of course. Bug zappers have a different purpose than normal outdoor lights: they use a lot of electricity zapping bugs. This doesn't explain anything.
D. **CORRECT.** Here we go. Want to kill all the friendly, helpful insects and let the harmful ones take over? Get a bug zapper.
E. That's nice. This (slightly) supports the idea that sprays are a good idea. But it doesn't tell us why zappers are a bad idea.

Question 5

QUESTION TYPE: Necessary Assumption

CONCLUSION: Rocks in a Japanese garden should look different from each other.

REASONING: Japanese gardens should be in harmony with nature. Rocks found in nature look different from each other.

ANALYSIS: The argument is assuming that only something that imitates nature can be in harmony with nature.

A. It isn't necessary that the selection of rocks obeys every key value. It's only necessary that the selection obeys the key value of harmony with nature.
B. CORRECT. If imitation of nature doesn't improve harmony with nature then we have no reason to imitate nature in our Japanese gardens.
C. There could be other criteria. It's only necessary that harmony with nature is a criterion for selecting rocks.
D. This doesn't matter. Presumably making a garden is not "natural." But we can still try to keep our garden in harmony with nature.
E. It isn't necessary that each component is varied. There might be some aspects of nature that don't vary: in that case we should do the same in our gardens.

Question 6

QUESTION TYPE: Must be True

FACTS:

1. Small experimental vacuum tubes can operate in high heat that would cause semi-conductors to fail.
2. It would be nice if (for digital circuits) we could have a component that does everything a semi-conductor does but that also resists heat better.
3. Vacuum tubes don't have the same current capacity as semi-conductors.

ANALYSIS: This supports the idea that vacuum tubes can't replace semi-conductors in digital circuitry. They lack the necessary current capacity.

A. CORRECT. Their heat resistance is nice, but any semi-conductor replacement would have to do other things too, like have a good current capacity.
B. Hard to say. Vacuum tubes might have some other massive flaw compared to semi-conductors.
C. This is basically the same answer choice as B, worded differently. There could be some other huge problem with vacuum tubes. Maybe they don't do anything that semi-conductors can do, apart from resisting heat.
D. We have no clue. We don't even know what vacuum tubes and semiconductors do. Maybe semi-conductors are terrible for most things that aren't digital circuitry.
E. We have no idea. The stimulus didn't tell us anything else about what vacuum tubes can and can't do.

Question 7

QUESTION TYPE: Weaken – Exception

CONCLUSION: The Ebola virus caused the plague in Athens in 430 B.C.

REASONING: The plague in Athens caused hiccups. The only disease that we know of that causes hiccups is the Ebola virus. The ancient plague shared some other symptoms with Ebola.

ANALYSIS: The fact that the two diseases shared symptoms doesn't tell us much. Lots of diseases share symptoms.

The fact that both diseases caused hiccups sounds like stronger evidence, but it's possible that there is more than one disease that causes hiccups. We just may not have discovered that other disease.

It may be that the other disease caused the plague, but then it disappeared over time. That would explain why we don't know of it. Or maybe the other virus is so uncommon now that we haven't re-discovered it.

A. This shows that the diseases may have been different. If they were the same then we wouldn't expect different symptoms.
B. CORRECT. Not everyone has to experience all symptoms of a disease. One common symptom of Ebola and the Athenian plague was: death. It doesn't matter that not everybody died, as long as some people died. Same with hiccups.
C. This makes it difficult to see how the Ebola virus could have spread to Athens.
D. Contagiousness is a major difference between diseases. This supports the idea that another disease caused the Athenian plague.
E. This is a big difference between the two diseases.

Question 8

QUESTION TYPE: Identify The Conclusion

CONCLUSION: The article was wrong to criticize environmentalists.

REASONING: Studies show that wolf populations have stayed the same. This might seem to indicate that hunters aren't killing too many wolves. But environmentalists have been adding new wolves to the island's wolf population for decades.

ANALYSIS: When trying to identify a conclusion, ask yourself: Why are they telling me this? What's their point?

The point is that the article was wrong and unjustified. The rest of the information supports that conclusion.

It's a good argument. The only reason wolf populations haven't been dropping is that environmentalists have been replacing the wolves.

A. This is a fact that supports the conclusion that the article was wrong.
B. This is actually false, according to the letter. Hunters kill more wolves. Environmentalists make up for it by introducing new wolves.
C. The letter isn't telling us how to solve the problem. It's just complaining that the article was wrong when it claimed there was no problem.
D. The studies weren't flawed; they were just cited out of context by the article. So the article was wrong. That's the main conclusion.
E. CORRECT. This is a long and fancy of saying that the article was unjustified.

Question 9

QUESTION TYPE: Must be True

FACTS:

1. For several decades microchip computing speed has doubled every 18 months.
2. This was done by doubling the number of transistors.
3. From the mid 1990s to the early 2000s the cost of producing a microchip has also doubled every time the speed has doubled.

ANALYSIS: This is a reference to Moore's Law.

We're told that it was the doubling of transistors that doubled the speed. Since the price doubles whenever the speed doubles then the price must double when transistors double, too. (Because doubling transistors doubles speed)

Doubling transistors → doubling speed → doubling cost

(The logical chain above only applies to the mid 1990's to the next decade)

A. We know that transistors are one way to double the speed. But there might be other ways.
B. This is actually false. The cost of microchips frequently doubled during this period. That likely increased retail prices.
C. Prices did increase. But that doesn't mean that no efforts were made to control prices. Prices might have been even higher otherwise.
D. CORRECT. Yup. During that period prices doubled whenever speed doubled.
E. Who knows? Prior to the mid 1990s we actually were able to double the speed without doubling the price. Maybe we can do it again.

Question 10

QUESTION TYPE: Sufficient Assumption

CONCLUSION: Ms. Sandstrom should pay for the damage if she could have reasonably expected that the column would lead to the damage.

REASONING: Sandstrom's newspaper led to damage on the Mendels' farm.

ANALYSIS: Don't bring your outside assumptions about the legal system to this question. The stimulus doesn't tell us that we have any system set up to make people pay for the damage they cause.

The correct answer tells us that there is such a system and that people in Ms. Sandstrom's position should pay.

The wrong answers don't tell us whether anyone should ever pay for anything.

A. CORRECT. The argument doesn't mention when and if anyone needs to pay damages. This clears that up and tells us that people should pay for damages they should have expected.
B. This tells us that we should pay for damages "only if." That's a necessary condition: it tells us when we shouldn't pay for damages. It doesn't tell us when we should pay for damages, if at all.
C. This doesn't tell us that Ms. Sandstrom should pay. The stimulus doesn't even say if we have a legal system that covers this sort of thing.
D. This doesn't tell us Sandstrom should pay.
E. But why should she pay? There's nothing here that tells us she has a legal or moral obligation.

Question 11

QUESTION TYPE: Strengthen

CONCLUSION: The University revoked Meyer's PhD.

REASONING: The University found that Meyer had committed scientific fraud by falsifying data. They also found that he had not falsified data for his PhD.

ANALYSIS: The information in this stimulus is a bit confused. I'll make a summary:

1. Meyer's employer (not the university) found that he had committed scientific fraud.
2. The university confirmed that Meyer had committed fraud.
3. The university investigated whether Meyer had also committed scientific fraud during his thesis.
4. They concluded he had not.
5. They took away the PhD anyway.

We don't know why the university took away Meyer's PhD, since he didn't commit fraud while getting it. The correct answer says that the University should take away someone's PhD if they commit any scientific fraud, during or after the PhD. Meyer did commit fraud, so away goes his PhD.

A. The University did not find any evidence that Meyer committed fraud while working on his PhD. The fraud they did find occurred afterwards.
B. The University isn't trying to decide whether to admit Meyer. They already admitted him and gave him a PhD.
C. We don't even know where Meyer was working. It sounds like "his employer" was someone else apart from the University. The University verified the employer's finding. Then the University took away his PhD. They didn't "dismiss" him.
D. CORRECT. Here we go. Meyer did commit scientific fraud even if he didn't commit fraud while working on his PhD. So the university was right to revoke his PhD.
E. This doesn't tell us when someone should lose their PhD.

Question 12

QUESTION TYPE: Most Strongly Supported

FACTS:

1. Kickboxing aerobics is highly risky, compared to many forms of exercise. (Kickboxing may be less risky than some other forms of exercise of course)
2. Overextending during kicks can cause injuries.
3. If beginners try to match the kicks of experienced practitioners then the beginners are very likely to injure themselves.

ANALYSIS: This question is a good example of statements that sound definite but are actually quite limited. Here's a short list of stuff we don't know:

- How dangerous aerobic kickboxing actually is? We only know how dangerous it is *compared to sports*.
- How many sports are more dangerous than aerobic kickboxing?
- How many ways you can injure yourself doing aerobic kickboxing.
- How many people try to imitate the kicks of skilled practitioners?

On the LSAT, don't go beyond what the stimulus tells you. It's often very specific and unfounded assumptions are dangerous. The only thing we can say is supported by this stimulus is that beginners should not imitate kicks if they are likely to overextend.

A. Who knows? The sport is highly risky. Skilled practitioners may get hurt too.
B. CORRECT. We know it is very likely that beginners will injure themselves if they do this.
C. We only know that imitating kicks is one way to hurt yourself. But the sport is highly risky. There might be many other ways to get hurt.
D. We don't know. We know kickboxing aerobics is riskier than "many" forms of exercise. But that could just mean it is riskier than walking, bicycling and jogging. It could be that other types of aerobics are also extremely risky.
E. It could be that most beginners are smart and don't try to imitate kicks until they learn the ropes.

Question 13

QUESTION TYPE: Identify The Conclusion

CONCLUSION: The trial was worthwhile even if the penalty won't do much to affect the company's behavior.

REASONING: We learned about the company's practices. Now competitors and potential rivals know. This knowledge will force the company to be less unfair.

ANALYSIS: The main idea is that it was worthwhile to have a trial even though the penalty itself won't have much of an impact.

A. We don't know if this is true. Maybe no one would have noticed the trial if there was no conviction. This certainly isn't the conclusion.
B. This is information that supports the conclusion that the trial was worthwhile.
C. This is just information. The main conclusion is that the trial was worthwhile despite the fact that the penalty won't have much impact.
D. CORRECT. Yup. The trial was worthwhile because the information release will probably reduce the company's unfair behavior.
E. We don't even know if this was true. The information release seems to have been the best part of the trial.

Question 14

QUESTION TYPE: Point at Issue

ARGUMENTS: Waller argues that if anyone really had ESP then it would be easy for them to convince the public that they had such powers. Since that hasn't happened, ESP must not exist.

Chin argues that it is impossible to convince all skeptics. As long as the elite are skeptical then the general public will remain skeptical too.

ANALYSIS: The hardest part about this question is realizing that Chin does not say whether or not he thinks ESP is real. He just thinks that the fact that the public does not believe in ESP does not necessarily mean that ESP does not exist.

In other words, Chin thinks ESP could exist, even if the public doesn't believe in ESP.

A. Chin doesn't say that ESP is necessarily real. He just argues that if it *were* real it still might be difficult for people to convince the public that they had ESP.
B. Waller doesn't claim that literally *every* skeptic could be convinced. He just thinks that the general public (e.g. most people) could be convinced. The earth is a big place, and it's hard to imagine convincing every single human that ESP exists.
C. Waller thinks that skeptics have a strong case. Chin doesn't say whether he believes in ESP.
D. CORRECT. Waller thinks that lack of belief is good evidence that no ESP exists. Chin believes that it isn't: the lack of belief could be caused by elite skepticism.
E. They both agree that the general public tends not to believe in ESP.

Question 15

QUESTION TYPE: Principle – Strengthen

CONCLUSION: Hagerle should apologize to the counselor too.

REASONING: Hagerle sincerely apologized to the physician for having lied to her.

ANALYSIS: We don't actually know if Hagerle ought to have apologized to the physician. This rules out answer choice B.

A. We don't know if Hagerle can sincerely apologize to the counselor.
B. This is very tempting. But we don't actually know if Hagerle owed the doctor an apology.
C. CORRECT. Hagerle already did sincerely apologize to the Doctor. So they must apologize to the counselor as well, according to this principle.
D. We don't know if Hagerle is capable of sincerely apologizing to the counselor.
E. This tells us when someone should not apologize. We need to figure out when they *should* apologize.

Question 16

QUESTION TYPE: Strengthen

CONCLUSION: The next census (which counts all residents regardless of age) will show that Weston's population has declined since ten years ago.

REASONING: Ten year records from the post office and driver's license bureaus show that more households have left Weston than have entered it.

ANALYSIS: There are a few problems with the argument. One problem is that "household" can mean one person or ten people. It depends on family size.

The other problem is that post offices and drivers bureaus may not accurately track all residents. Not everyone gets a new drivers license when they move.

A. This is pretty vague: many people could be 1,000 or 100,000 people. Further, if they move in and out they'll have no net effect on the population.
B. It doesn't really matter what happened during the past century. Trends can reverse themselves.
C. This would weaken the argument. It shows that the population is unnaturally low.
D. CORRECT. This shows that the households that left were large and the ones that stayed were small. This increases the likely population loss.
E. This tells us something about each group but it doesn't tell us how big each group is. Further, the census measures the entire population and not just adults.

Question 17

QUESTION TYPE: Method of Reasoning

CONCLUSION: People shouldn't necessarily get rid of the tendency to make mistakes about how happy a future event will make them.

REASONING: Everyone sees certain things wrong (such as parallel lines) but it would be a mistake to get a surgeon to fix that.

ANALYSIS: This is an interesting argument. It's saying that if we share an error with the entire population then we should not get rid of that error.

A. There was no such event mentioned. The stimulus is just describing how people tend to perceive things.
B. The argument is not undermining any "theory." It's just pointing out that there might be good reason not to alter our perceptions.
C. **CORRECT.** This is an argument by analogy. We see things wrong and we perceive the future wrong. Since it would be a mistake to fix our vision then by analogy it might also be a mistake to fix our perception.
D. The argument is saying that change is not reasonable.
E. Actually the stimulus uses a particular situation (not fixing eyesight) to argue against a general course of action (not changing your perceptions.) There are many different ways we could try to change how we perceive the future.

Question 18

QUESTION TYPE: Principle – Strengthen

PRINCIPLE: An opinion in an art catalogue is misleading if the opinion was a deliberate attempt to mislead bidders.

APPLICATION: Healy's did say that all descriptions were opinions. And the opinion was incorrect.

(What we are missing is something that tells us the opinion was deliberately designed to mislead.)

ANALYSIS: We need something that tells us about Healy's motives for writing the opinion. It's the only missing piece of the principle.

The correct answer doesn't say they hoped to mislead, but it strongly implies the opinion was included only for profit and therefore may have been knowingly misleading.

A. This tells us what consequences the incorrect opinion could have had for bidders. It doesn't tell us why Healy's gave an incorrect opinion.
B. This tells us that the bidders were skeptical. It doesn't tell us why Healy's mis-described the vase.
C. This shows that the opinion went against that policy. But it's not clear if this was a mistake or a deliberate attempt to mislead.
D. "Some" is very vague and could mean just a single employee. For examples, this answer could mean that *the janitor* has a strong opinion about whether descriptions should be certified. This answer doesn't tell us whether the description was intended to mislead.
E. **CORRECT.** This shows that Healy's was only interested in profit. It doesn't tell us that they knew they were lying; we don't know if Healy's knew the vase was a modern reproduction. But this shows sloppiness at the least and misrepresentation at worst. It's the strongest answer choice.

Question 19

QUESTION TYPE: Necessary Assumption

CONCLUSION: DNA testing shows that Neanderthals and humans did not interbreed.

REASONING: The DNA of contemporary (current) humans is very different from Neanderthal DNA.

ANALYSIS: This argument is assuming that human DNA has not changed significantly since the time the Neanderthals existed. It's possible that early humans interbred with Neanderthals but we have lost those genes since that time.

A. This would be a necessary assumption for anyone arguing that the two species interbred. But this argument is arguing that no breeding happened.
B. This would weaken the argument. The argument is stronger if DNA testing of remains is very reliable.
C. **CORRECT.** If the DNA of prehistoric homo sapiens was significantly more similar then perhaps the two species did interbreed. Then we could have lost that similarity over time and erased the evidence.
D. This would be helpful to the argument but it isn't necessary. Species don't breed merely because they are near one another.
E. This answer weakens the argument if true. The argument is concluding there was no interbreeding. This answer says that even the *slightest* similarity means there was interbreeding. Humans and Neanderthals probably have *some* similarity, even though are DNA is significantly different.

Question 20

QUESTION TYPE: Must be True

FACTS:

1. More consumers downtown means more profits for downtown businesses.
2. A decreased cost of living downtown means that more consumers will live there.
3. The profits of downtown business will not increase unless congestion decreases.

ANALYSIS: This is counterintuitive. We're told profits can't increase unless congestion decreases. But that just means less congestion is a necessary condition for increased profits. We can reword statement three as:

"If profits increase then congestion will decrease." It's odd, but logically true based on the stimulus.

We can combine all three statements.

Decreased cost of living → More consumers → More profits → less congestion

Logically, that does work. Lower cost of living and more people lead to less congestion. More consumers lead to more profits, always. And if profits go up then congestion goes down...somehow.

So answer choice B is correct even though it doesn't mention congestion.

A. We don't know. We only know that downtown traffic can prevent an increase in profits.
B. **CORRECT.** The first two sentences tell us this. Lower cost of living equals more consumers. More consumers lead to more profits. It's the first three statements in the logical chain above.
C. Same as A. We only know that traffic is somehow related to profits. We don't know if it is related to cost of living.
D. Same as A and C. We have no idea if or how traffic congestion is related to cost of living.
E. This mixes things up. The number of consumers present increases profits. But increased profits might not draw in more consumers.

Question 21

QUESTION TYPE: Parallel Reasoning

CONCLUSION: Any domestic long distance phone call that does not cost 15 cents per minute costs 10 cents per minute.

REASONING: If a domestic phone call is placed between 9–5 then it costs 15 cents. Any other domestic long distance call costs 10 cents.

ANALYSIS: This is a good argument. There are only two types of phone calls: 15 cent and 10 cent calls. So if one doesn't cost 15 cents then it must cost 10 cents.

The structure is: If it isn't one then it must be the other.

The answer choices all use similar words but have different structures. If a class has lab work, it will be in a lab. Otherwise it will be in a normal class.

To properly match the "if not one then the other" structure, the correct answer must say that if the class isn't in one room then it is in the nother.

A. This is close, but the conclusion should have said the class will be conducted in a normal classroom.
B. This should conclude that a class will be held in a lab if it isn't in a normal classroom.
C. This does not match the structure, which was: If not one, then it must be the other.
D. This should have said that if it was in a lab then it wouldn't be in a normal classroom. Using "extensive lab work" as the sufficient condition introduces a new element into the structure.
E. **CORRECT.** Here we go. If it isn't in one (a normal classroom) then it is in the other (a lab)

Question 22

QUESTION TYPE: Principle – Strengthen

CONCLUSION: The first child was wrong to push the second child, assuming the first child intended to harm the second child.

REASONING: The first child pushed the second child from behind. The first child understands the difference between right and wrong.

ANALYSIS: We need a principle that actually tells us that it's wrong to push someone, if:

1. You intend harm, and
2. You know the difference between right and wrong.

Answer B does that.

A. This tells us a necessary condition for an action being wrong. We need something that is sufficient to tell us an action is wrong.
B. **CORRECT.** Here we go. The kid did understand the difference between right and wrong. So if he intended to hurt the second child then his action was wrong.
C. We're trying to *prove* that the action was wrong....we don't know if it is yet. This answer talks about actions we *already* know are wrong.
D. This sets the bar too low. The stimulus didn't say the act would be wrong if the child "didn't think" about whether the act would injure the other child. It said the act had to be actually intended to harm.
E. The child did understand the difference between right and wrong. This is irrelevant.

Question 23

QUESTION TYPE: Flawed Reasoning

CONCLUSION: Some makes of car must be more common in some regions versus other regions.

[the researcher is assuming that people see their own car more frequently in their own regions because more people buy that car in that region. That explains the inaccurate estimate]

REASONING: Car owners overestimate how common their cars are.

ANALYSIS: The researcher has identified one possible explanation for the research findings.

But it's possible that people simply overestimate how popular their own cars are (without reference to other cars in the region.) People tend to like the things they buy. So perhaps they assume that many other people also buy the cars they bought.

Or maybe people just have trouble conceptualizing the enormity of the car market.

Who knows? There are many different possible explanations supported by this evidence.

A. Actually, the argument assumes that people didn't know the real statistics about cars. Otherwise they might have answered the questionnaire correctly.
B. CORRECT. The evidence provides support for the conclusion but that evidence also supports other, competing conclusions.
C. It wouldn't matter if test subjects came from different regions. According to the argument they all should overestimate their own car's prevalence based on regional differences.
D. There isn't a "set" of premises. There is just one: cars owners overestimate how common their cars are.
E. Actually, the statistical generalization was intended. The survey was meant to find out car owners' estimates of nationwide car ownership. These surveys are generally extrapolated nationally.

Question 24

QUESTION TYPE: Flawed Parallel Reasoning

CONCLUSION: Most parking citations are issued to students.

REASONING: In university towns, more parking citations are issued during the school year.

ANALYSIS: This is a terrible argument. It doesn't tell us how many extra citations are earned by students. It could be a very small number. Most students don't have cars.

E.g. Suppose typical parking citations are 200 per month and they are 220 per month when the students are there. That hardly supports the idea that "most" citations go to students.

The structure is the following: more of event Y happens when X is present. So X must account for most cases of event Y.

A. This is close but not quite the same. It doesn't say sales go up when more children are present. It says sales go up when there is a higher ratio of children. Very similar structure, but slightly different. E is better.
B. This is a bad argument, but only because some plants are naturally more green than others. It doesn't compare two situations or claim that one plant gets most of the sunlight.
C. This isn't a good argument, but only because studying is not enough to make someone "studious." Studious means someone who studies quite a lot, whereas most students may just study a bit. This is a different error from the stimulus: if studying meant studious then this would be a good argument.
D. This is a bad argument. It's assuming that variety equals quantity. But this doesn't make an error with most.
E. CORRECT. Here we go. When X (other people's children) are present then more of Y (snacks being given out.) happens. That does not mean that most snacks go to other people's children. One's own children probably eat most of the snacks, because they are at home most often.

Question 25

QUESTION TYPE: Flawed Reasoning

CONCLUSION: Only harsh criticism will cause change.

Change → Harsh criticism

REASONING: Change → motive
Harsh criticism → unpleasant → motive

ANALYSIS: The author has shown that harsh criticism is sufficient to provide a motive for change. And having a motive is a necessary condition for change.

But the author then assumes that harsh criticism is *necessary* for a motive. This is reversing sufficient and necessary. Any "flawed reasoning" question that uses conditional logic will probably mix up sufficient and necessary.

A. CORRECT. Bingo. A polite request can often also change behavior, for example. Harsh criticism isn't necessary, even if it can occasionally work.
B. This isn't a problem. The counselor's conclusion only addresses whether or not criticism will work as a means of changing behavior.
C. The counselor only said that change requires a motive. He didn't say that harsh criticism will work every time.
D. The counselor only talks about a motive for changing. He doesn't mention a motive for avoiding change.
E. The counselor technically didn't refute any argument. He just said that the people mentioned in the first sentence should consider his argument.

Section II - Logic Games

Game 1 - Trial and Appellate Courts

Questions 1-5

Setup

This is one of the easiest logic games I've ever seen. If you redo this, you should aim not just to get everything right, but to be able to solve it in four minutes or less.

Here's how I drew the trial and appellate courts:

```
A ___ ___ ___
T ___ ___ ___ ___ ___ ___
```

The first and second rules are easy. You just place Li on the appellate court, and place Kurtz on the trial court:

```
A _L_ ___ ___
T _K_ ___ ___ ___ ___ ___
```

The third rule says that Hamidi and Perkins can't go on the same court. You might be tempted to draw that rule separately. That would be a mistake. You should always draw rules directly on the diagram, if possible. Watch what happens when you draw the third rule directly on the diagram:

```
A _L_ _H/P_ ___
T _K_ _P/H_ ___ ___ ___ ___
```

Now it's obvious that the appellate court only has one space open. This is the key to solving the game *very* quickly. This deduction can save you 2-3 minutes on this game, which will leave you extra time for the hard games.

Finally, you should think about who's left to place. J, M and O have no rules. I drew these at the upper right of the diagram. This way, they were always in my mind.

```
                          J , M , O
A _L_ _H/P_ ___
T _K_ _P/H_ ___ ___ ___ ___
```

Main Diagram

```
                          J , M , O
A _L_ _H/P_ ___
T _K_ _P/H_ ___ ___ ___ ___
```

Question 1

For list questions, go through the rules and use them to eliminate answers one by one.

Rule 1 eliminates **A.** Li must be on the appellate court.

Rule 2 eliminates **C.** Kurtz must be on the trial court.

Rule 3 eliminates **B** and **D.** Hamidi and Perkins can't be on the same court.

E is **CORRECT.** It violates no rules.

Question 2

Questions 2, 3 and 4 deal with the fact that there's only one space open on the appellate court. I looked for this rule violation first.

B is **CORRECT.** If McDonnell and Ortiz are both on the trial court, then there are four people on the trial court: L, one of H/P, M and O.

If you think any of the other answers also can't work, you've likely got one of the rules wrong. Go back over the setup to see what you're missing.

Question 3

There's only one space open on the appellate court. So Jefferson and McDonnell can't both go there.

A is **CORRECT.**

Question 4

If Ortiz is placed on the appellate court, the appellate court is full. Thus, Jefferson and McDonnell must go on the trial court.

A <u>L</u> <u>H/P</u> <u>O</u>

T <u>K</u> <u>P/H</u> <u>J</u> <u>M</u> ___ ___

C is **CORRECT.**

Question 5

The only hard question on this game. Remember, four answers are wrong. You shouldn't treat them as if they're good answers! They're almost certainly wrong. The answers have to *prove* themselves to you before you take them seriously.

You're looking for a rule which will have:

1. The same restrictions as the original rule.
2. No additional restrictions.

The original rule was simply: Hamidi and Perkins can't be together, on either court. Let's evaluate the answers from this perspective.

A: What about the trial court? This answer lets H and P be together on the trial court.
B: This answer lets H and P be together on the trial court.
C: Jefferson can go on either court. So using this answer, Jefferson could go on the appellate court, and Hamidi and Perkins could be together on the trial court.
D: What happens if Hamidi is not appointed to the same court as Li? In that case, this rule allows Hamidi and Perkins to be together.

Those answers are useless. They were put there to distract you and prevent you from looking at answer **E.**

Let's talk about *how* you can replace a rule. You can't just reword a rule. That would be the same rule. Instead, you have to use some other factors already present in the game to achieve the same effect.

The game places Li in the appellate court, and Kurtz in the trial court. So, we can say that Li *is* the appellate court and Kurtz *is* the trial court. By which I mean: anyone placed with Li is on the appellate court. Anyone placed with Kurtz is on the trial court.

E talks about "three of Hamadi, Kurtz, Li and Perkins". Li and Kurtz are already separate. So three of those four must either be:

Hamadi, Perkins and Li, or
Hamadi, Perkins and Kurtz

Those are the two possibilities rule three originally prevented. So answer **E** is **CORRECT,** it achieves the same effect as the original rule.

Game 2 - Skydiving
Questions 6-10

Setup

This is an interesting game. You could solve it effectively by making a list of rules and applying them to every question. But you can solve it even faster by making two main scenarios.

Let's look at the fourth rule first. It's the most complicated. Pei is after one of Obha or Larue, but not after both.

The LSAC has been including this type of rule more and more on modern sequencing games. It's confusing the first time you read it. What this rule is *really* saying is that Pei is in the *middle* of Obha and Larua, in either order. Like this:

O—P—L

L—P—O

Now, Larue was mentioned in the second rule as well. Anytime a game mentions a variable in two rules, there's usually a way to combine those rules.

First, let's draw the second rule. There are two possibilities: Larue goes first or last. Whenever there are only two possibilities, you should split the diagram:

L̲ _ _ _ _ _

_ _ _ _ _ L̲

How do we combine the rules? Look at both diagrams. The placement of Larue determines the order for Pei and Ohba in each scenario. If Larue is first, then we get P – O. If Larue is last, then we get O - P.

P—O

L̲ _ _ _ _ _

O—P

_ _ _ _ _ L̲

I've drawn P – O and O – P floating above the diagram. This is a reminder of what order the members must be in, in each diagram. There's no sense making a deduction then not drawing it. This way you can never forget the order of L, P and O in each scenario.

Next, let's add the third rule. Weiss and Zacny can't be last. This only affects the first scenario, since L is last in the second scenario:

P—O

L̲ _ _ _ _ _

(last space: ~~W~~ ~~Z~~)

O—P

_ _ _ _ _ L̲

Finally, Treviño is before Weiss. That's just a simple ordering rule, drawn like this:

T—W

However, I prefer to place that rule directly on the diagram, along with the remaining variables. When you see everything together, you can make deductions and form scenarios:

```
   P—O, T—W, Z
L  __ __ __ __ __
                 W̶
                 Z̶
   O—P, T—W, Z
__ __ __ __ __ L
```

Now we can see everything at once. The commas indicate there's no ordering rule. So in the second diagram, Zacny could go first, second, third.... anywhere but last.

These two scenarios let you visualize *all* the possibilities without getting sucked into drawing endless "could be true" scenarios.

But we're not done. Notice that the first scenario is more restricted than the second scenario. Weiss and Zacny can't go last. Whenever a space has restrictions, you should see who can go there.

Not Weiss and Zacny, due to the third rule.
Not Treviño, because Weiss is after Treviño.
Not Pei, because Obha is after Pei.
Not Larue, because Larue is first in scenario one.

Only Obha can go last in scenario 1!

```
   P, T—W, Z
L  __ __ __ __ O
   T—W, O—P, Z
__ __ __ __ __ L
```

This is the final diagram I used to solve this game. I had never seen this game before, and I did it in five and a half minutes. Such a diagram is far *faster* than the normal approach of making a list of rules and applying them.

(On some games I do make a list of rules and apply them, because it's not possible to make a diagram like this.)

I recommend you print a fresh copy of this game, and draw this diagram on the page. Then solve the questions. Do this before you look at the explanations. I want you to practice visualizing scenarios using this kind of diagram.

Main Diagram

```
   P, T—W, Z
L  __ __ __ __ O
   T—W, O—P, Z
__ __ __ __ __ L
```

Question 6

For list questions, go through the rules and use them to eliminate answers one by one.

Rule 1 eliminates **C.** Treviño must be before Weiss.

Rule 2 eliminates **E.** Larue has to be first or last.

Rule 3 eliminates **A.** Weiss can't be last.

Rule 4 eliminates **D.** Pei has to be between Ohba and Larue.

B is **CORRECT.** It violates no rules.

Question 7

Here are the two scenarios again:

```
     P, T—W, Z
L  __  __  __  __  O

     T—W, O—P, Z
__  __  __  __  __  L
```

I looked at these diagrams to eliminate answers. Remember, if an answer doesn't *have* to be true, then it's not right.

A doesn't have to be true in the second scenario. Larue is last.

B doesn't have to be true in the first scenario. Obha is last.

C doesn't have to be true in either scenario. We can place Pei fifth. The commas indicate that Pei can go anywhere in the open spaces, as long Pei is in between Obha and Larue.

E doesn't have to be true. We can place Weiss fifth in either scenario. Though I've drawn Zacny after Weiss, the commas indicate that they're interchangeable.

D is **CORRECT.** Weiss is always after Treviño. And in both scenarios there's someone after Weiss: Ohba or Larue. That makes at least two people after Treviño.

Question 8

Larue is last in the second scenario. Here's that scenario again:

```
     T—W, O—P, Z
__  __  __  __  __  L
```

Remember, you're looking for something that *can't* be true.

I disproved the wrong answers by rearranging the variables in my mind. For instance, in **A,** I saw that nothing stopped my from placing Treviño and Weiss fourth and fifth, like this:

```
   O—P, Z
__  __  __  T  W  L
```

I recommend you practice shuffling variables around like that, mentally. It's a very fast method. I only drew this diagram so I could have something to show you. I wouldn't draw it under timed conditions. I'd do everything mentally.

Here's the diagram again for the remaining answers. That most recent diagram was just to prove A:

```
     T—W, O—P, Z
__  __  __  __  __  L
```

B is possible. T – W can be placed third and fourth.

C is not possible. Obha goes before Pei, so Obha is fourth at latest in this scenario. **C** is **CORRECT.**

D and **E** are possible. There's nothing stopping Pei or Zacny from going fifth.

Question 9

When a question gives you a new rule, you should draw the new rule. Here are both scenarios, with Zacny immediately after Weiss:

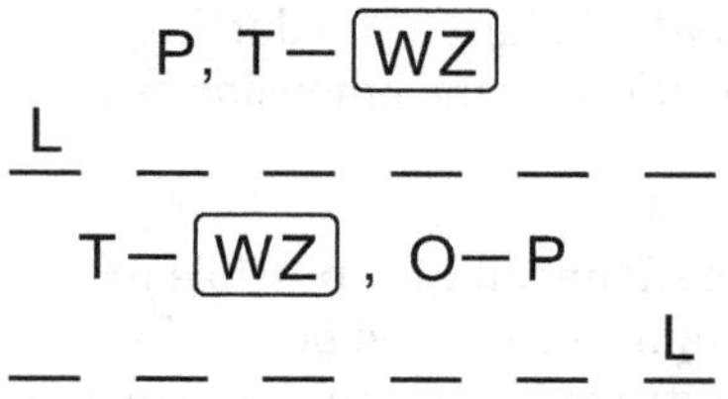

```
    P, T—[WZ]
L
_  _  _  _  _  _

  T—[WZ] , O—P
                L
_  _  _  _  _  _
```

Now you can use the same approach of visualizing the scenarios using these two diagrams. If an answer is possible, it's wrong.

A is possible in the first scenario. Larue is first in that scenario.

B is possible in the first scenario. Just put Pei second and Treviño third.

C is possible in the second scenario. Just put T – WZ in the first three spaces.

E is possible in the first scenario. Put Zacny fourth and Pei fifth.

(Note that most of these are possible in either scenario. I'm not trying to prove *all* the possibilities. I'm just trying to prove the answers *are* possible somewhere, and therefore wrong.)

D is **CORRECT.** In this scenario, Pei can only go second, third or fifth. I recommend trying a couple of sketches using the diagram above if you have any doubts on this point.

Question 10

This question places Treviño after Larue. That means we're in the first scenario, since Larue is last in the second scenario.

Here's the first scenario, with Treviño directly after Larue:

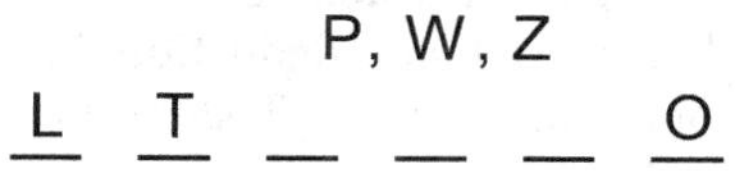

```
          P, W, Z
L  T  _  _  _  O
_  _              _
```

You're looking for an answer that can't be true.

A is **CORRECT.** In the first scenario, Obha is last.

All of the other answers are possible. There are now no restrictions on where Pei, Weiss and Zacny can go. Any of them can go third, fourth or fifth.

Game 3 - Vehicle Servicing
Questions 11-17

Setup

I made almost no deductions on the setup when I first did this. But as I was going through the questions, I saw I had missed a major deduction. I'll first show you the standard setup, then I'll show you how to make the deduction.

(I still did fine on this game. I figured out the deduction on the first question where it was useful, and so I was able to use the deduction on all the questions where it mattered.)

Here's the standard setup. I combined rules one and two:

V – R – H – __

We don't know *who* is after H, but someone is, so you should draw that.

The third rule, I drew as an "Or" statement. This is an exclusive or, unlike most "Or's" on the LSAT. Since both "Or's" in this game are exclusive, I just memorized that detail.

[PV] or [PS]

The fourth rule is very common on modern linear games. Most students just draw this:

S – P or S – L

This is incomplete. The rule says "but not both". If the sedan is before the pickup, then it can't be before the limousine. That means the sedan is after the limousine. Likewise, if the sedan is before the limousine, then it can't be before the pickup, so the sedan is after the pickup. Here's the full rule:

L – S – P or P – S – L

Always draw the full rule.

Now, the three diagrams I've drawn above are enough to solve the game. It's what I drew when I first did this game – *but* I made a big deduction on question 14: only the pickup or the limousine can go last.

I'll explain how I figured that out. It's possible to make this deduction upfront. You can do this by looking at the most restricted space. In this case, the last space is very restricted.

- The van and the roadster can't go last, because they're before the hatchback.
- The first rule says the hatchback can't go last.
- The sedan can't go last, because it's in between the pickup and the limousine.

You can draw these restrictions as "not" rules under the final space:

M	Tu	W	Th	F	S
					~~V~~ ~~R~~ ~~H~~ ~~S~~

That's four variables that can't go last. So only the limousine and the pickup can go last. You can turn this into two diagrams:

P – S

M	Tu	W	Th	F	S
					L

L – S

M	Tu	W	Th	F	S
					P

Remember, the order has to be P – S – L or L – S – P. Having P or L last determines the order of this group in both diagrams. I've drawn this.

We know that the pickup needs to be beside either the sedan or the van. In the second scenario, only the sedan can go fifth. That's because the van is before the roadster and the hatchback. (You can't deduce anything new in the first scenario):

```
        P—S
                        L
___ ___ ___ ___ ___ ___
 M   Tu  W   Th  F   S

        L
                    S   P
___ ___ ___ ___ ___ ___
 M   Tu  W   Th  F   S
```

Next, you should draw the remaining variables on each diagram. This helps to visualize possibilities:

```
P—S, V—R—H
                        L
___ ___ ___ ___ ___ ___
 M   Tu  W   Th  F   S

V—R—H, L
                    S   P
___ ___ ___ ___ ___ ___
 M   Tu  W   Th  F   S
```

The commas indicate that variables are interchangeable. For instance, P – S could go before V – R – H in the first scenario, or after, or in between.

In the initial setup, I drew V – R – H – ___. I haven't drawn a space after H here because the rule just says H can't go last, and both diagrams now have someone last. So the first rule is automatically fulfilled in both diagrams.

Only the third rule isn't on the diagram now. That still applies to the first scenario. I drew it up and right as a reminder:

```
P—S, V—R—H                  ( PV or PS )
                        L
___ ___ ___ ___ ___ ___
 M   Tu  W   Th  F   S

V—R—H, L
                    S   P
___ ___ ___ ___ ___ ___
 M   Tu  W   Th  F   S
```

This is *exactly* what my diagram looked like the second time I did the game. It was much faster. I recommend you try this game with both the rules based approach and the scenario based approach. Personally, I find the scenarios *much* faster, but I don't always see them up front.

Main Diagram

In the setup, I showed two ways to do this diagram. The first way is the rules based setup. The second splits the game into two scenarios, because only L and P can go last.

See the setup section for a walkthrough of how to get the two scenarios.

```
(1)   V—R—H—___

(2)   PV  or  PS

(3)   L—S—P   or   P—S—L
```

OR

```
P—S, V—R—H                  ( PV or PS )
                        L
___ ___ ___ ___ ___ ___
 M   Tu  W   Th  F   S

V—R—H, L
                    S   P
___ ___ ___ ___ ___ ___
 M   Tu  W   Th  F   S
```

Question 11

For list questions, go through the rules and use them to eliminate answers one by one.

Rule 1 eliminates **C.** The hatchback can't be last.

Rule 2 eliminates **A.** The van has to be before the hatchback.

Rule 3 eliminates **D.** The pickup needs to be beside the sedan or the limousine.

Rule 4 eliminates **E.** The sedan needs to be between the limousine and the pickup.

B is **CORRECT.** It violates no rules.

Question 12

This question asks who can't go Thursday. Thursday is closer to the end. We should look for people who are hard to place near the end. Check the rules and see who has to be placed earlier.

V – R – H – ___

The van needs three people after it. It can go Wednesday at the latest. **E** is **CORRECT.**

Question 13

This question says that the pickup and the limousine can't be placed Monday. Whenever a question placed restrictions on a spot, you should check what *other* restrictions exist.

Who else can't go Monday? Not the sedan, the sedan must go between the pickup and the limousine.

Not the roadster and the hatchback, they must go after the van (rule 1). So none of the pickup, the limousine, the sedan the roadster or the hatchback can go last on this question:

__ __ __ __ __ __
M Tu W Th F S
~~P~~
~~L~~
~~S~~
~~R~~
~~H~~

Only the van can go Monday! **C** is **CORRECT.**

Question 14

Remember the deduction from the setup: only the pickup and the limousine can go last. This question says the limousine can't go Saturday, so that means the pickup goes saturday:

__ __ __ __ __ P
M Tu W Th F S

The third rule says that either the sedan or the van is beside the pickup. In this scenario is has to be the sedan, since the van must go before the roadster and the hatchback (rule 2):

__ __ __ __ S P
M Tu W Th F S

Once you make a deduction like this, check to see if it answers the question. **E** is **CORRECT.** The sedan can't go Wednesday, because the sedan must go Friday.

Now, for the other answers. Here's a diagram showing all the possibilities when SP and 5 and 6:

V–R–H, L
__ __ __ __ S P
M Tu W Th F S

The order as I've drawn it disproves **B** and **C.** Just lower the variables into the spaces they're hovering above.

The comma indicates L could go before V – R – H. If you put LVRH in 1-4, then this disproves **A** and **C.**

Question 15

Remember the deduction from the setup: only the pickup and the limousine can go last. This question places the sedan before the pickup. Therefore the order is L – S – P (rule 4) and the pickup must be last:

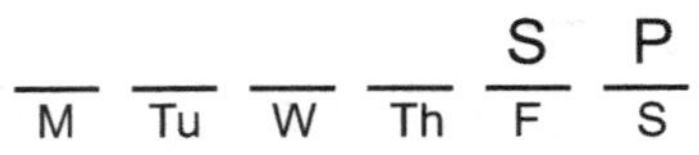

				S	P
M	Tu	W	Th	F	S

The sedan goes friday because the pickup needs the sedan or the van beside it. And the van can't go Friday, because it's before the roadster and the hatchback.

(So far, this is exactly the same as question 14)

Now that you have this diagram, you should use it to eliminate answers. I'm going to eliminate the easy ones first.

B is wrong because the sedan is Friday, not Wednesday.

D is wrong. The hatchback can't go Friday because the sedan is already there.

E is wrong. The limousine can't go Saturday because the pickup is already there.

That leaves **A** and **C.** You should always try and eliminate the answer with the most restrictions.

The van has more restrictions than the limousine, so let's try **C.** But, this doesn't work; it turns out the van can't go Wednesday. Only Thursday is left open after the van, but both the roadster and the hatchback must come after the van.

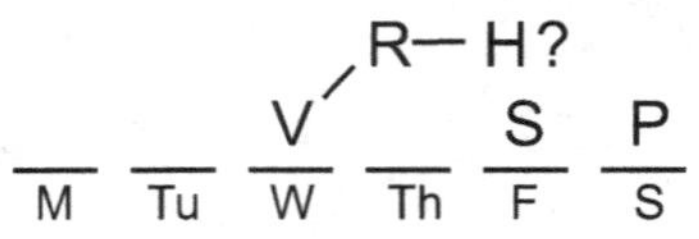

R– H?

		V		S	P
M	Tu	W	Th	F	S

A is **CORRECT.** The limousine can go Wednesday. This diagram proves it:

V	R	L	H	S	P
M	Tu	W	Th	F	S

Question 16

The limousine is mentioned in rule four: the order of the three variables is either L – S – P or P – S – L

This question places the limousine last, so the order must be P – S – L.

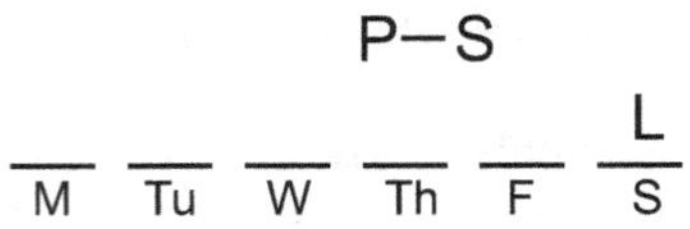

P–S

					L
M	Tu	W	Th	F	S

Once you make a deduction, check the answers to see if it's there. It is: **B** is **CORRECT.**

If you make a prephrase and you find it in the answers, you can be very sure it's right. Especially if it's based on a deduction linked to the local rule.

Whereas if you approach the answers not knowing the answer, you have to be skeptical of every answer, because they may be traps.

Question 17

I used the deduction from the setup for this one: either the pickup or the limousine has to be last.

I'll repeat that, it's extremely important. **Either the pickup or the limousine must be last.** See the setup section for how to reach that deduction.

Also, the sedan has to be in between the pickup and the limousine. These two facts eliminated three answers.

Remember, the answers are telling us who's in Tuesday, Wednesday and Friday. Thursday is skipped:

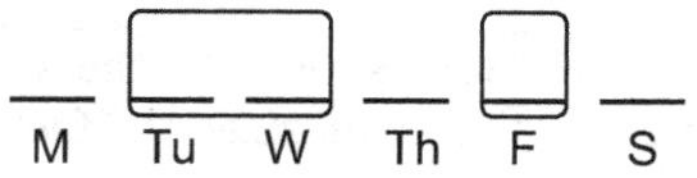

M	Tu	W	Th	F	S
__	[__	__]	__	[__]	__

A is wrong because either the pickup or the limousine needs to be last.

C is wrong because the sedan has to be in between the limo and the pickup. But since one of P or L must go last, the pickup. That means the sedan is not in the middle:

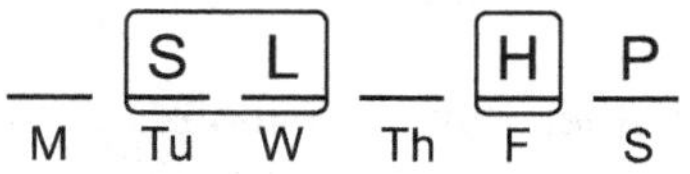

M	Tu	W	Th	F	S
__	[S	L]	__	[H]	P

E is wrong because the limousine and the pickup would be beside each other. Either the limousine or the pickup must go last. Since this question place the limousine Friday, then the pickup would go saturday. There's no space for the sedan to go between them:

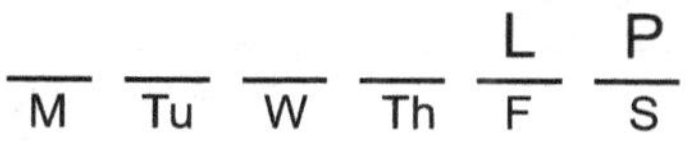

M	Tu	W	Th	F	S
__	__	__	__	L	P

Note that I eliminated those answers without drawing diagrams. I'm including them only so this explanation is easier to follow.

Now only **B** and **D** are left. I did draw diagrams to test these.

This diagram shows that **B** is **CORRECT.** It violates no rules:

M	Tu	W	Th	F	S
V	[P]	[R]	S	[H]	L

This diagram shows that **D** doesn't work. there's no space for R to go after V:

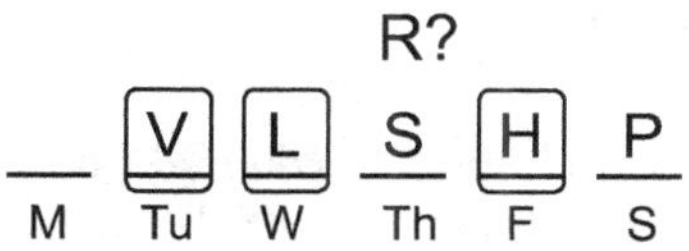

M	Tu	W	Th	F	S
			R?		
__	[V]	[L]	S	[H]	P

The sedan has to go Thursday because the sedan must go between the limousine and the pickup.

Game 4 - Colored Balls
Questions 18-23

Setup

This is a linear game, but it says the balls are above/ below each other. So here's how most people draw this game:

6 __
5 __
4 __
3 __
2 __
1 __

But here's how you've drawn dozens of games that are very much like this one:

__ __ __ __ __ __
1 2 3 4 5 6

Why would you totally switch the way you make a diagram, just because the setup says above/below? None of the questions use "above/below". They just use the normal numbers you've seen on dozens of other linear games.

Draw this one left-to-right, like the rest.

The rules themselves are nothing special. I couldn't combine them. Here's how I drew the three rules:

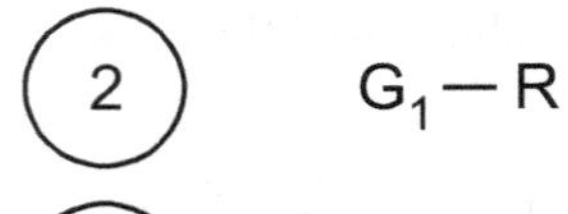

(3) $\boxed{WG}_1$

Rules two and three are both "at least one", so the '1' in both rules is a reminder. I just memorized the fact that it was "at least one" and not "only one".

(The "at least one" is implied by "there is a". Unless a rule specifies "only one", the rule means "at least one".)

The first rule is the one worth thinking about. There are more red balls than white balls. The possibilities are rather limited. If there are two white balls, there are three red balls, and one green ball.

If there is one white ball, then things are more flexible. There could be as many as four red balls, and at least one green ball. Or there could also be as many as three green balls, and only two red balls.

The other two rules you simply have to memorize. This game is a lot faster if you always remember that there's a green ball before any red balls, and that there's at least one white directly before a green.

Main Diagram

(1) R > W

(2) G_1 — R

(3) $\boxed{WG}_1$

Question 18

If there are two white balls, then there must be three red balls (rule 1) and one green ball – you always need a green ball.

Since there's only one green ball, there must be a white ball directly in front of it (rule 2). And this WG pair must be in front of all red balls (rule 3):

$\boxed{WG}$ — R

There is a second white ball. This is the only ball that can go in front of the WG pair. So green can go second or third:

W	G				
1	2	3	4	5	6

W	W	G			
1	2	3	4	5	6

B is **CORRECT.**

Question 19

Whenever a question gives you a new rule, you should draw it. There are green balls in boxes five and six:

_	_	_	_	G	G
1	2	3	4	5	6

Now, let's think about the other elements we need:

- A green before the reds (rule 3)
- A white directly before one of the greens (rule 2)

That's four letters. There are two left. Rule one says we need more reds than white, so the other two balls must be red. So here's what's left to place: W, G, R, R

Let's see what happens if we put white in four:

_	_	_	W	G	G
1	2	3	4	5	6

We have a green and two reds left. They must go like this:

G	R	R	W	G	G
1	2	3	4	5	6

There's a second scenario, where the WG block is first:

W	G	R	R	G	G
1	2	3	4	5	6

Next, look through the answers to see which one of them is possible in one of the two scenarios.

C is **CORRECT.** It's possible in the second scenario.

Question 20

This is a tricky question. I skipped it the first time I did it. I was then able to use scenarios from later questions to eliminate some answers.

Note: This question is asking if a ball cannot be the *only one of its kind,* and in the listed space. So if a ball *can* be the only one of its kind, in the listed space, that answer is wrong. For example: if there is a scenario with only one white ball, and that white ball is in spot 3, that scenario eliminates **B.**

This scenario from question 19 eliminates **C:**

G	R	R	W	G	G
1	2	3	4	5	6

This scenario from question 23 eliminates **D:**

G	R	R	R	W	G
1	2	3	4	5	6

In question 18, we saw a scenario with two white balls, three red balls and one green ball. We were able to place Green 2nd or 3rd, and it was the only green. This eliminates **A** and **B:**

W	G	_	_	_	_
1	2	3	4	5	6

W	W	G	_	_	_
1	2	3	4	5	6

(There are no other greens. That's why I haven't bothered to fill out the rest of the scenarios. In a timed situation, I just looked back at the diagram I drew for question 18 and said "ok, this eliminates A, there is only one green, etc.")

Sometimes it makes sense to do questions out of order. Thanks to elimination from other questions, we disproved all the wrong answers.

E is **CORRECT.** Process of elimination is enough, but I'll explain why it's right using logic. If the sixth spot is red, it isn't unique. There are always multiple reds.

If the sixth spot is white, it isn't unique. There must be another white before a green, somewhere (rule 3). If the sixth spot it green, it isn't unique. There must be a green before the reds too (rule 2).

Question 21

A is **CORRECT.** I'll prove it must be true. Green must be before red. And there are always at least two reds. If there are three or more reds, we can't put green fourth. Green would go third at earliest.

So let's try with just two reds. We could put them in five and six, and put a green in four:

```
__  __  __  G  R  R
1   2   3   4  5  6
```

So far so good – but what color are the other balls? We can only have one white ball, because we need more red balls than white balls. So the other balls must be green. Here's one example:

```
W  G  G  G  R  R
1  2  3  4  5  6
```

With so many greens, there's no way to avoid putting them earlier than four!

My scenario above disproves **B** and **C.**

This scenario disproves **D** and **E.**

```
G  R  R  R  W  G
1  2  3  4  5  6
```

Remember, you can do anything as long as the rules don't specifically ban it.

Question 22

This question says red balls are in boxes two and three. You should draw that, then apply the rules. Green has to come before red (rule 2), so green goes first:

```
G  R  R  __  __  __
1  2  3  4   5   6
```

Next, think about who's left to place. We need a WG block. The third variable will be red or green. It can't be white, because we need more reds than white:

```
            R/G, [WG]
G  R  R  __  __  __
1  2  3  4   5   6
```

This diagram disproves **A** and **B.**

D and **E** don't fit. **C** is **CORRECT.** The fourth ball can definitely be green.

Question 23

This question says that balls 2, 3 and 4 are the same color as each other.

That can only be green or red. We can't have three whites, because there must be more red than white (rule 1).

I made both diagrams (red and green):

	R	R	R		
1	2	3	4	5	6

	G	G	G		
1	2	3	4	5	6

Let's apply the rules. There must be a green before the reds. And there are at least two reds. In the first diagram, that means we need to put green first. In the second diagram, that means we need to put two reds in 5-6.

G	R	R	R		
1	2	3	4	5	6

	G	G	G	R	R
1	2	3	4	5	6

Next, we to place a WG block (rule 3). In the first diagram, only 5-6 has space. In the second diagram, we can put a white in spot 1:

G	R	R	R	W	G
1	2	3	4	5	6

W	G	G	G	R	R
1	2	3	4	5	6

D is **CORRECT.** In both diagrams it must be true that there's only one white.

Section III - Logical Reasoning

Question 1

QUESTION TYPE: Role in Argument

CONCLUSION: Acme Engines should be held liable.

REASONING: Acme claims there was nothing wrong with knee level switches. Yet its new locomotives did not have knee level switches. It cost $500,000 to move the switches, so it's more likely that the switches were unsafe.

ANALYSIS: This isn't a bulletproof argument, but it's common in legal cases. Civil legal cases generally have to be proven only based on a standard of "more likely than not." So an argument doesn't have to be 100% certain for damages to be awarded.

The fact that Acme spent $500,000 is meant to show that changing the switch was a serious issue. The high price indicates the company didn't move the switches purely for convenience. Therefore the switch may have been done for safety reasons.

A. The argument didn't claim that the engineer had no fault. It just claimed that Acme was responsible. More than one group can be responsible for something.
B. If the older locomotives had been remodeled then the engineer wouldn't have accidentally hit the switch with his knee.
C. Not quite. The changes only affected new cars. The changes can't explain why a crash occurred in the old cars.
D. The argument used this evidence to show that the switches were hazardous. Otherwise, why would the company have spent $500,000 replacing them?
E. CORRECT. If the company spent a lot of money moving some of the switches then they likely realized there was a risk of an accident.

Question 2

QUESTION TYPE: Flawed Reasoning

CONCLUSION: The artist says that almost everyone in the country wants to be an artist.

REASONING: Almost everyone the artist knows wants to be an artist.

ANALYSIS: This is a terrible argument. Artists tend to be friends with other artists. Engineers tend to be friends with engineers. And so on. The artist is working from a very unrepresentative sample.

If you want to find out what the whole country believes then you shouldn't just ask your friends. Your friends probably have opinions similar to yours.

A. This isn't circular reasoning. The artist's evidence about the whole country is (poorly) supported by their evidence about their friends.
B. Not quite. The artist is assuming that what is true of their friends must be true of the whole country.
C. The artist only mentions what they think their friends want to do for a job. They haven't said any beliefs are widely held.
D. CORRECT. The artist should interview people they aren't friends with. It's highly unlikely everyone wants to be an artist and much more likely that the artist's friends are an unrepresentative sample.
E. Actually the distinction is clear: someone can want to be an artist while working as a dishwasher. Yet they aspire to actually make a living from their art.

Question 3

QUESTION TYPE: Most Strongly Supported

FACTS:

1. The Dvorak keyboard is much faster.
2. But there are many costs to switching. These costs would outweigh the eventual increase in typing speed.

ANALYSIS: It's clear that we would be better off if we could use the Dvorak keyboard without having to deal with transition costs. But we can't. If we switch, then there will be many disadvantages while we get used to the new system. The fact that QWERTY came first means that we should stick with the current system and avoid the transition costs.

A. As far as we can tell, the Dvorak keyboard is accurate. The problem is the costs of switching.
B. We have no idea what "usually" happens; we only know about keyboards. And with keyboards, people settled on a less efficient standard.
C. People don't stick with current standards because they're afraid of change. They stick with current standards because the transition costs would outweigh the benefits.
D. Same as C. Emotions have nothing to do with it. It simply isn't rational to switch: the transition costs are simply too high.
E. CORRECT. If we had no keyboards and had to choose then we would choose the Dvorak. But we are already using the QWERTY keyboard, so there are high transition costs. We are stuck with QWERTY.

Question 4

QUESTION TYPE: Point at Issue

ARGUMENTS: Sam thinks that we should let mountain lions eat bighorn sheep. Both species are endangered but we shouldn't mess with nature.

Meli thinks we should ensure that the bighorn survives even if it means killing mountain lions.

ANALYSIS: They disagree on whether they should "let nature take its course." Sam thinks we should do nothing and Meli thinks we should limit the mountain lion population.

Neither of them says for sure whether the sheep will go extinct if nothing is done.

A. CORRECT. Right. Sam thinks there should be no intervention. Meli thinks that we should intervene.
B. Neither of them is certain if all of the sheep will die if they don't intervene.
C. Sam doesn't say how easy either option would be. He's only clear on what we should do: nothing.
D. Meli seems to think that there wouldn't be an extinction of mountain lions. Sam doesn't say what he thinks would happen.
E. Sam isn't certain whether the sheep will die. He says he "hopes" that they will survive. Similarly, Meli doesn't say that sheep are certain to die if we don't act. But by acting we can "ensure" the survival of the sheep.

Question 5

QUESTION TYPE: Must be True

CONCLUSION: We shouldn't push very young children into rigorous study [in an effort to make the nation more competitive].

REASONING: Curricula for young children must meet their developmental needs. Rigorous work can make young children burn out. It's unfair to children to make them work so hard and it might work against us. Rigorous study can be appropriate for secondary students.

ANALYSIS: Process of elimination works well on this question. A and B are about the high school curriculum and we have very little info about that. C is about the requirements for competitiveness: we don't know much about that either. Lastly, E contradicts the argument's assertion that rigorous study could actually hurt us in the long run.

Only D is left. This answer is hard to be sure about, so it's worth checking the stimulus to find the key term "developmental needs" and refresh your memory on how it was relevant.

A. We don't know. Maybe the secondary school curriculum is already rigorous enough.
B. Same as A. We have no idea if the secondary school curriculum is good or bad.
C. Hard to say. Maybe we have such an advantage that we could be competitive even if we fail to meet the developmental needs of some students.
D. CORRECT. We know that curricula for very young students must address their needs. But a rigorous curriculum could burn them out. So a rigorous curriculum doesn't meet the needs of young students.
E. The argument actually argues that a very rigorous curriculum could reduce our competitiveness by burning out young students.

Question 6

QUESTION TYPE: Necessary Assumption

CONCLUSION: It is likely that the best drivers with a supervisor on-board are also the best drivers in normal conditions.

REASONING: All drivers are evaluated by supervisors and every driver is affected by their supervisor's presence.

ANALYSIS: This is a bad argument. Many people react in different ways to the same situation. Some drivers might be very stressed by having their supervisor present. Some drivers might perform better because they want to show off. Some drivers might become nervous wrecks and crash their bus. Who knows?

The argument is assuming that all drivers react in a similar manner.

A. It's only necessary that the chosen method is fair. There could be other methods.
B. The argument would still be fine if the supervisors were merely competent experts.
C. This would be helpful, but it's not necessary. The argument would still be fine if this were only true of 49% of drivers (49% is not most.)
D. CORRECT. Here we go. If this isn't true and all drivers are affected differently then the evaluations won't be fair. Some drivers will perform poorly despite the fact that they are good drivers when no supervisor is watching.
E. This isn't necessary. It's up to the supervisors to judge the drivers' performance.

Question 7

QUESTION TYPE: Most Strongly Supported

FACTS:

1. Economic growth accelerates demand for new technologies.
2. Few businesses supply those technologies while many businesses want to buy them.
3. Increased technological change can cause suppliers of technologies to fail.

ANALYSIS: Rapid change can doom many companies, even high tech companies. You may be very good at building a new technology. But if conditions change then maybe no one will want to buy your product anymore. If you don't adapt fast enough then you may go out of business.

A. Hard to say. It could be that some businesses are even more likely to prosper. The stimulus hasn't told us about prospects for all other businesses.
B. CORRECT. Economic growth causes demand for new technology to rise. That can presumably lead to accelerated technological change. That can cause failure amongst businesses that supply new technologies.
C. Hard to say. Economic growth causes demand for technology. We don't know if the reverse occurs.
D. Not quite. It is businesses that sell new technologies that are more likely to prosper.
E. We only know that some business can fail: a few businesses that supply technology. We don't know if overall business failures are increased. Technological change might make some other businesses less likely to fail.

Question 8

QUESTION TYPE: Paradox

PARADOX: Air conditioning use during a heat wave threatens to cause blackouts. Residents have been asked to cut back on air conditioner usage to help with the blackouts. But blackouts will probably happen anyway even if they do cut back.

ANALYSIS: If air conditioners are the problem then we need to figure out why shutting off residential air conditioners won't help.

The right answer explains that businesses and factories also use air conditioners. Those are likely to be important to the success of the business and they are less likely to be shut off. The authorities were only asking residents to shut off their systems.

A. Of course air conditioners aren't the only things that use electricity. But it's specifically *extra* air conditioner use that has overloaded the system and added extra demand. If consumers cut A/C use then why doesn't power consumption drop to normal? We're not told that anything else is using more power than normal.
B. CORRECT. Here we go. Factories and businesses aren't likely to cut back on air conditioning: otherwise they might lose customers and/or their factory machines factory machines might break from overheating.
C. That's nice. But the authorities didn't propose this solution, and it doesn't seem likely to work in the short term. This does nothing to explain why a voluntary cutback of A/C use couldn't also work.
D. This is very tempting. But the stimulus says the blackout will happen even if the residents do cut back.
E. Excellent. But the stimulus says we should expect blackouts until the heat wave ends. This doesn't help explain why.

Question 9

QUESTION TYPE: Weaken

CONCLUSION: Expensive long-term relaxation training is unnecessary for most people.

REASONING: Symptoms of anxiety generally decrease to normal at the end of the time it takes to complete the short course. This is true whether someone is taking the long training or the short training.

ANALYSIS: The argument is only looking at short term results. It should really compare how the two groups do after a few years. We want anxiety levels to stay low for a long time.

The right answer tells us that patients who only receive short term treatment are more likely to relapse.

A. This would be an argument against both types of treatment.
B. This isn't a problem if the more experienced practitioner can get better results. The only reason cost is mentioned is because results for short and long term seem to be the same. Why pay more for the same thing?
C. **CORRECT.** Here we go. Short terms works....at first. But then you are more likely to have a relapse and have to complete expensive training again.
D. If this is equally true of both types of treatment then this doesn't really change anything.
E. This could explain why short term relaxation works. It doesn't weaken the argument though.

Question 10

QUESTION TYPE: Identify The Conclusion

CONCLUSION: The accusation [that advertising turns people's wants into perceived needs] rests on a fuzzy distinction.

REASONING: It's not possible to know whether we really need something or whether we only want it.

ANALYSIS: This is an OK argument. It's quite plausible that there is no way to distinguish wants and needs. It's correct in pointing out that the critics' argument needs more definition.

Words like "however" often indicate the conclusion. They always indicate the author's opinion. She disagrees with the sentence before "however". In this case, the final sentence supports her statement after "however".

A. **CORRECT.** It's a fuzzy distinction because it's impossible to say what a need is and what a want is.
B. This is the claim that the stimulus argues against.
C. The argument doesn't go this far. It just says that the argument used to attack advertising is flawed. The editorial might still believe that advertising is wrong, but for a different reason.
D. Not quite. The problem is that the critics don't realize it's sometimes hard to say what is essential to our happiness and what isn't.
E. The editorial didn't say that critics *often* use fuzzy distinctions. It just said they're using one in this specific case.

Question 11

QUESTION TYPE: Necessary Assumption

CONCLUSION: People who rely on the web to diagnose their medical conditions are likely to do themselves more harm than good.

REASONING: People who look for medical info on the web often can't tell what is scientific and what is quackery (nonsense). A lot of the quackery is attractive because it is more clearly written than scientific papers.

ANALYSIS: The argument is assuming that people will often hurt themselves if they rely on quackery. But this doesn't have to be the case. Maybe quackery is harmless or occasionally beneficial.

A. This isn't necessary. It's only necessary that when they do try to diagnose themselves, they hurt themselves more often than not.
Negation: Most of the time, people browsing the web for medical information aren't trying to diagnose themselves.

B. **CORRECT.** If people are not more likely to do themselves more harm than good even if they look at quackery then this argument isn't much good.

C. This isn't necessary. The argument would actually be slightly strengthened if some of these people hurt themselves too.

D. This would be helpful to the argument, because it would mean that people might assume that quackery is scientific. But it doesn't need to be true.
Negation: Few people who browse the web assume information is not scientifically valid unless it is clearly written.

E. This isn't necessary. The argument is fine if some people manage to harm themselves despite looking only at scientific literature.
Negation: People attempting to diagnose themselves may hurt themselves even if they only use scientific literature.

Question 12

QUESTION TYPE: Paradox

PARADOX: Adults toss children balls slowly, since children have low coordination. But children are actually better at catching balls if they are thrown quickly.

ANALYSIS: The right answer shows us that a fast moving ball is perceived as a threat and triggers a more effective part of the child's brain. This makes sense to anyone who's ever performed well in a dangerous situation yet is clumsy in everyday life.

A. **CORRECT.** The self-defense part of the brain is likely to be more effective than the part of the brain that merely attempts to catch a slow ball. Without self-defense reflexes you would get seriously hurt; even children have these reflexes. Throwing the ball quickly triggers self-defense instincts.

B. If a slow ball is less likely to get obscured then it should be easier to catch.

C. This tells us about *adults*. We need to explain the strange facts about *children*.

D. This tells us how well children can throw balls. We're trying to explain something about how they can catch them.

E. This is to be expected. But it's still strange that children are better at catching a faster ball than a slower ball, up to a point. This fails to explain that.

Question 13

QUESTION TYPE: Most Strongly Supported

FACTS:

1. An fMRI contains information that a patient might want to keep private.
2. So does a genetic profile.
3. An fMRI of a skull can allow us to identify the patient's face.
4. A genetic profile can be linked to a patient only by looking at labels or records.

ANALYSIS: It's fairly strongly supported that an fMRI allows identification to be done in a different way than by using a genetic profile. We're told clearly that genetic profiles can only ID a patient through labels and records, not pictures.

A. We're not told anything about fMRI labeling.
B. **CORRECT.** An fMRI can identify a patient by creating their picture from a skull shape. Weird. You can't do that with a genetic profile. The only way to identify a genetic profile is through labeling.
C. We have no idea. Maybe the privacy controls on genetic profiles are quite good despite how easy it could be to match the profiles to patients in theory.
D. We don't know. If this were true then there might not be any reason to do fMRIs.
E. We're not told what patients think. I don't imagine most people realize they can be identified with an image of their skull.

Question 14

QUESTION TYPE: Flawed Reasoning

CONCLUSION: The abandoned shoe factory would be a better shelter site than the courthouse.

REASONING: The councilor's opponents have provided no evidence that the courthouse would be better.

ANALYSIS: The councilor commits the same flaw he accuses his opponents of committing: he provides no evidence that the shoe factory is a better site for a shelter.

A. Close, but not quite. The counselor didn't say there was no evidence against his claim. He said there was no evidence for the opposing claim.
B. **CORRECT.** Lack of evidence for one claim does not mean we should accept the other claim if that claim also has no evidence.
C. The councilor didn't say anything personal about his opponents. He made a statement of fact: they hadn't provided any evidence.
D. The councilor did not say anything about how scary homeless people would be if they were sheltered at the courthouse (for example).
E. Other councilors do actually hold the position that the shelter should be at the courthouse.

Question 15

QUESTION TYPE: Necessary Assumption

CONCLUSION: It was misleading for James to say that the chair of the anthropology department endorsed his proposal.

REASONING: The chair has said she would support the proposal, but only if the draft would include all of the recommendations that James would make to the Core Curriculum Committee.

ANALYSIS: The argument is assuming that James added recommendations beyond those that were already in the draft he showed the chair. If James didn't add anything to his draft then James did in fact have the chair's support.

A. The argument is not about whether James' recommendations will be implemented. It's about whether James' statement was *misleading*.
B. This is beside the point. Whether or not the chair would approve of other recommendations, she wanted to know about them beforehand. She wanted to avoid surprises, most likely.
C. This could be why James told the committee that he had the chair's support. But this isn't a necessary assumption; the argument wouldn't fail if this answer were false.
D. If James didn't think this then the proposal is stronger.
E. **CORRECT.** If the draft proposal *did* include all of the recommendations then James had the chair's support and everything was fine.

Question 16

QUESTION TYPE: Weaken

CONCLUSION: Travaillier must be planning to enlarge its customer base [to include people who would travel by bus.]

REASONING: It looks like Travaillier is planning to expand into bus services. It currently focuses on air travel and its existing customers don't care about buses.

ANALYSIS: We're looking to weaken the idea that Travaillier is looking for new customers. A-D don't even touch on this point. Remember what you're looking for; most LSAT questions aren't nearly as hard as they seem.

There's no reason to think that Travaillier couldn't try to change the preferences of its existing customers.

A. This doesn't mean that Travaillier won't try again. But if anything, this strengthens the argument.
B. This doesn't mean Travaillier won't or shouldn't try.
C. This is pretty vague. At least one could just mean one. That doesn't tell us much.
D. This could be bad news for Travaillier but it doesn't help us weaken the idea that Travaillier is looking for new customers.
E. **CORRECT.** If Travaillier listens to its consultants then it might be trying to expand by trying to change the preferences of existing customers. This weakens the idea that Travaillier is looking for new customers.

Question 17

QUESTION TYPE: Sufficient Assumption

CONCLUSION: Traditional classroom teaching is ineffective because it is not a social process.

REASONING: Only social processes can develop students' insights.

ANALYSIS: The last sentence is just fluff. It's important to figure out which parts of the stimulus are directly involved in the reasoning and which parts are just fluff. This lets you quickly eliminate answers B, C and E.

You can draw the premises, and the conclusion the argument is aiming at. This lets you spot the gap:

Traditional → not social → not insight   not effective

There is a gap between insight and effectiveness. We need to say either [effective → insight] or [not insight → not effective]. Answer choice D makes this link. If students don't have insights then teaching is ineffective.

Answer choice A is close, but it's backwards. The correct answer needs to let us conclude "education ineffective." A only lets us say "if education is ineffective, then..." It's a necessary condition, but we need a sufficient condition.

- **A.** This gets it backwards. We need to show insight is a *necessary* condition for effectiveness. Answer choice D puts these in the right order.
- **B.** This doesn't help us conclude that education is ineffective.
- **C.** Traditional classroom are rigid and artificial. So this answer shows that traditional classrooms are not social process.
  Great, but....the argument already told us that! It's in the first sentence. This is a trap answer.
- **D. CORRECT.** Classroom education doesn't lead to the development of insight. So according to this answer choice it must be ineffective.
- **E.** Who cares? The conclusion isn't about whether non-traditional classrooms would work.

Question 18

QUESTION TYPE: Flawed Reasoning

CONCLUSION: You'll be healthier if you avoid dairy.

REASONING: You'll get fewer heart attacks if you avoid fat. You're likely to eat less fat if you avoid dairy.

ANALYSIS: This is a bad argument. We only know that avoiding dairy can lead to some reduction in heart disease risk. But the professor did not prove that dairy products have no benefits for health. Health includes a lot of important things besides lack of heart attacks.

So even if we protect ourselves from heart attacks we might risk other problems by avoiding dairy.

- **A. CORRECT.** Dairy might protect your health in other ways (calcium?) even if it slightly raises the risk of heart attack.
- **B.** The argument didn't claim that avoiding dairy is the only way to avoid heart attacks.
- **C.** The argument did not say that we *should* avoid dairy. It was just attempting to make a factual statement about what would happen if we chose to eliminate dairy. Maybe dairy's milky goodness is worth the risk of a heart attack.
- **D.** The evidence is definitely relevant. Dairy has fat, and fat can lead to heart disease (which is part of health.)
- **E.** The professor did not claim that we could avoid heart disease with any certainty. Avoiding dairy merely lets us *reduce* our risk.

Question 19

QUESTION TYPE: Method of Reasoning

CONCLUSION: Similarly, any history book gives a distorted view of the past.

REASONING: One cannot understand one's environment based on a single momentary perception. A glimpse of your environment gives you only a momentary perspective. And a history book will inevitably reflect the biases and prejudices of the author.

ANALYSIS: There are two arguments. We're meant to understand that the first argument is correct. The second argument is supported by the fact that it is similar to the first argument.

It's not a great argument, but that's the structure.

A. The author thinks that both pieces of reasoning mentioned are correct.
B. The argument didn't mention what would happen if either conclusion were false.
C. **CORRECT.** The second argument resembles the first. If the first is good then presumably that helps make the case for the second. Bias is like a fragmentary glimpse: you only get part of the picture.
D. Nope. What group of characteristics would that be? The stimulus didn't mention anything like this.
E. There are actually two types of human cognition (thinking) mentioned: brief glimpses of a moment and personal bias. They're two very different phenomena.

Question 20

QUESTION TYPE: Parallel Reasoning

CONCLUSION: Any future proposal by the citizen's league will probably be passed as well.

REASONING: Most of the proposals to date have been passed.

ANALYSIS: This is not really a good argument. It's true that most past proposals were successful. But the argument gives us no reason to assume this trend will continue in the future.

If the argument had said *all* past proposals were successful, therefore future proposals *probably* will be passed, it would be a better argument. "Probably" technically only means "greater than 50% chance of occurring."

So the structure is: something was likely, so it will continue to be likely. The reason this is weak is because "most" could be as low as 50.1%, and it's hard to guarantee that the percent of proposals won't drop to "not most" in the future (50%).

A. This changes the structure. The argument should have said "thus, in future years most of the awards will continue to go to academic biologists."
B. Trees and tree species are different things. There could be thousands of tree species with a handful of trees, and then one extremely common deciduous species with 95% of the trees. That way most species wouldn't be deciduous even if most trees were. Either way, this doesn't match the structure of the stimulus.
C. We have no idea. Maybe "sympathy for the local farmers" is pretty low down the list of issues the newspaper cares about in an editor and the candidate will be hired anyway.
D. Who knows? Maybe the people who resend entries are simply idiots and they'll send in their applications late again.
E. **CORRECT.** This has the same flawed structure. It's true that most stone artifacts have been domestic tools. But that doesn't mean most of the remaining artifacts are domestic stone tools. (Probably = most).

Question 21

QUESTION TYPE: Strengthen

CONCLUSION: Much of the data on the effects of the weed-killer are probably misleading.

REASONING: The effectiveness of the weed-killer depends on local soil conditions.

ANALYSIS: The stimulus doesn't tell us anything about the data. If the studies accurately measure the soil conditions in the real world then they will be valuable. If they don't measure conditions in the real world then they won't be valuable. Simple as that.

Any answer choice that doesn't mention data quality is wrong.

Don't get distracted by the fancy language at the start. It's just saying that the weed killer sometimes works and sometimes doesn't. It can vary with soil conditions.

A. This tells us absolutely nothing about data quality. The conclusion is only about data quality.
B. **CORRECT.** Bingo. Soil conditions in the real world generally don't have the weed-killer molecules present in equal quantities. So the data is misleading.
C. This tells us that in most areas the weed-killer will be effective. But we don't know if the research studies have taken this fact into account. So this doesn't tell us if the research is useful or not.
D. This shows that the data is likely to represent real world conditions. It weakens the argument.
E. This is true. But it doesn't tell us how much of the data makes this error. This answer choice leaves open the possibility that most data is accurate.

Question 22

QUESTION TYPE: Principle

PRINCIPLES:
To receive the award (Franklin):

Exemplary records AND beyond call AND saved life → receive award

To be sure of not receiving an award (Penn):

~~Exemplary record~~ → ~~Award~~

ANALYSIS: You must be *very* precise on principle questions. You're looking for a very specific outcome. Figure the conditions that will guarantee that outcome for Franklin and Penn, then look for the answer that has those conditions.

Ruthlessly eliminate answers that are missing the conditions. For example, I first eliminated any answer that didn't say Penn lacked an exemplary record. That's the *only* way to disqualify Penn from an award.

A. **CORRECT.** Yup. They both went beyond what could reasonably be expected and saved someone's life. That is a sufficient condition for receiving an award if you have an exemplary record. So this gets an award for Franklin. Penn is denied an award because an exemplary record is a necessary condition.
B. This doesn't let us deny the award to Penn, because he has an exemplary record.
C. If Franklin doesn't have an exemplary record then she can't get an award.
D. We don't know if either of them have exemplary records. So it's impossible to know whether we can give Franklin an award or deny one to Penn.
E. If Penn has an exemplary record, we can't be sure it's correct to deny him an award. And we're not told if Franklin saved a life on those same occasions when she went above and beyond what was reasonably expected of her.

Question 23

QUESTION TYPE: Principle – Strengthen

CONCLUSION: Everyone should be allowed to choose the people they want to associate with.

REASONING: It is easier to enjoy life if you can have your lifestyle choices accepted by others. It's easier to get lifestyle choices accepted if you can choose your friends.

ANALYSIS: The argument is in favor of letting people choose their own associates. Among other things, it would make enjoying life easier.

The right answer supports this by showing that any freedom that makes enjoying life easier should be supported.

A. It would be possible to allow the freedom to make lifestyle choices but forbid the freedom to choose your associates. It will be a bit more difficult to live an enjoyable life...but you will still have the freedom to make lifestyle choices.
B. Who knows? The stimulus just claims that we should have the freedom to associate with those who share our beliefs. But maybe not everyone actually ought to *exercise* that freedom.
C. CORRECT. The freedom to choose your associates will make it easier to enjoy life. Therefore, according to this answer, no one should be denied that freedom.
D. The stimulus is not just talking about people who depend on having friends and associates that will accept their personal beliefs. It's also talking about people who would simply have an easier time enjoying life if they could choose associates who accept their beliefs.
E. The stimulus is concluding that we should have the right to choose our associates: period. It shouldn't matter whether we actually improve our life by doing so.

Question 24

QUESTION TYPE: Sufficient Assumption

CONCLUSION: Some older people can lower their blood pressure by drinking milk.

REASONING: Lack of calcium often causes the rise in blood pressure associated with aging. One glass of milk per day has enough calcium to make up for a deficiency. But the deficiency is often caused by a lack of vitamin D that is needed to absorb calcium.

ANALYSIS: This is a bad argument. It presents a problem: we can't use calcium without enough vitamin D. But then the solution only mentions adding more calcium, and doesn't address the vitamin D problem.

The correct answer solves this by showing that milk has enough vitamin D to allow calcium absorption.

A. CORRECT. This does it. Milk not only provides enough calcium but also the vitamin D to absorb it.
B. This shows that milk merely isn't harmful. But we're trying to conclude that it will actually *improve* blood pressure.
C. Same as B. This shows that milk doesn't do damage. But we need to know if it can help.
D. That's good. But it doesn't tell us how milk helps.
E. Yikes. You'd better get some vitamin D. Unfortunately, this doesn't tell us if milk has vitamin D.

Question 25

QUESTION TYPE: Flawed Parallel Reasoning

CONCLUSION: Each person should be taxed solely in proportion to their income.

REASONING: Each person's contribution should be based on how well society serves that individual's interests. Wealth is the most objective way to determine how well society serves someone.

ANALYSIS: This argument switches terms. Wealth is how much money and capital you have. Income is how much money you're earning.

You'd be fine with having an income of zero if you have two billion dollars in the bank. So if wealth is the most objective measure, taxing income will miss the mark. We should tax people directly on wealth. The right answer must make a similar concept shift.

A. CORRECT. Speed is how fast a car can go. Acceleration is how quickly a car can speed up. Those are different. A car could accelerate very quickly but have a low top speed. This is the same concept shift error from the stimulus. It matches the difference between an absolute amount of something (wealth/speed) and how quickly you gain that it (income/acceleration).

B. We should be granted autonomy in proportion to maturity. Giving "complete" autonomy to those at a high school level is too much – "high school student" definitely isn't the highest level of maturity. This answer doesn't match the concept shift from the stimulus.

C. This has similar language to the stimulus but it doesn't make the same mistake. The mistake here is assuming that corporations get *more* subsidies just because they get *some* subsidies. The argument didn't what subsidies citizens get.

D. This doesn't make the error from the stimulus, but it is a bad argument. We should be taxing incomes themselves, not the activities. Taxing the activities will probably reduce them.

E. This is a bad argument, but it doesn't make the total amount/speed of gain concept shift from the stimulus. The reason this argument is bad is that there could be people *outside* hospitals with more serious health needs.

Question 26

QUESTION TYPE: Paradox

PARADOX: About half of the town thinks the mayor is unethical. Yet about 52% support him, and that hasn't changed since the allegations of unethical behavior.

ANALYSIS: People often have fixed opinions about politicians. If I told you something new about George Bush or Barack Obama, chances are very low that it would change your opinion. It is very hard to change anyone's opinion on something they consider important.

So it could be the case that 48% (about half the town) of people thought that Mayor Walker wasn't a good mayor. When they heard about the ethics violations, they added that to the list of things they hate about him.

Meanwhile, the other 52% like him. They liked him before the story about ethics violations and they still like him afterwards. They may not even believe the accusations of ethical violations.

People can be stuck in their ways.

A. CORRECT. The ethics violations are a red herring: they didn't change anyone's opinion, for good or ill.

B. This doesn't explain why people's opinion of Walker didn't change.

C. This doesn't explain why the other 80% of people did not change their minds.

D. The anti-corruption groups don't seem to have had much impact. This explains nothing.

E. Nonetheless, about half of the people think the mayor was guilty of ethics violations. The question is: why didn't his popularity sink?

Section IV - Reading Comprehension

Passage 1 - Alaskan Traditions

Questions 1-7

Paragraph Summaries

1. Alaska hasn't defined 'tradition', which causes problems.
2. The law has considered tradition to be a long standing process, regular and continuous.
3. Laws banned the use of sea otter pelts. This meant that sea otter pelts hadn't been used by natives 'within living memory'
4. Courts found that 'within living memory' was too restrictive, especially when natives were legally banned from exercising certain traditions.

Analysis

This passage is both a discussion of tradition in Alaska, and an argument. The author clearly believes that tradition has been defined too narrowly. See lines 10-12 and lines 17-20.

The central dilemma in the example given is that Natives were banned from using sea otter pelts. So by law, they couldn't continue to exercise certain traditions. This meant that there had been no use of seal otter pelts 'within living memory'.

There are two laws. The fur seal treaty of 1910 banned the hunting of sea otters. This stopped Alaska Natives from exercising their tradition.

The Marine Mammal Protection Act of 1972 allowed natives to hunt protected animals, if they were being hunted to make "traditional" articles.

You may see the problem. By 1972, many traditions had died out, thanks to the 1910 treaty. So if courts defined a tradition as something continuous, then natives could not start making things from sea otter pelts again.

Initially, the courts applied this narrow view of tradition. But the fourth paragraphs explains that now courts take a broader view. Sea otter pelts qualify for the exemption under the 1972 law, because natives had a longstanding tradition of using sea otters, and the tradition only died out because natives were forcibly prevented from continuing to hunt sea otters.

It's not clear whether natives could restart exercising a tradition if they had stopped doing it voluntarily. This distinction isn't tested in the questions.

The main point of the passage is not the sea otter pelts. They're an example supporting the broader point: the concept of tradition has some flaws in the way it's often defined.

The Russians come up in a few answers. We know that sea otter hunting by Alaska Natives was common before the Russian occupation in the late 1700s. That's *all* we know. We don't know if Russians stopped sea otter hunting, or if any Russians hunted otters.

Question 1

DISCUSSION: Main point questions must pass two hurdles:

1. Is the answer even true, according to the passage?
2. Does the answer describe the main point?

Most answers fails the first test. The second test often means that the answer should refer to every paragraph, but in some cases the main point only covers one paragraph. You have to ask yourself "why is the author telling me this?"

In this case, the author uses two legal cases to argue that the definition of "tradition" is too restrictive.

A. CORRECT. This is the best answer. It alludes to the general discussion of tradition in the first two paragraphs, and the specific application to sea otter pelts in paragraphs 3 and 4.

B. This only describes paragraphs 3 and 4. Paragraphs 1 and 2 applied to tradition generally, not just sea otter pelts. The sea otter cases are just an example illustrating the argument.

C. The passage didn't mention a wave of lawsuits. This answer doesn't pass the truth test.

D. Legal "terms", plural? The passage is only about one term: tradition.

E. This is way too broad. Lines 4-7 tell us that state and federal laws use tradition, but we don't know if state laws are being challenged. The passage is about how to define tradition, not about legal challenges in general, or vague "concerns". The natives have a very specific concern: tradition is defined wrong.

Question 2

DISCUSSION: To answer this question, you should reread lines 46-57. It doesn't take that long to reread lines you've already read; you'll go much faster the second time.

The judges think the view of tradition is strained because it excludes real traditions that were forcibly stopped, and it allows traditions that only existed for a short time (lines 54-57).

In other words, the legal definition of "traditional" is not how most people understand the word "traditional". You have to read in between the lines a bit to see the judge's point, but it's pretty clear from context.

A. We don't care how Alaska Natives define the *word* traditional. It's an English word. The judges are deciding how the word should be defined in English. Once we know what the word means, *then* we concern ourselves with whether Alaska Natives consider their activities to be a tradition.

B. Tempting, but the judges don't mention dictionaries. They seem to refer to common understanding of the word traditional.

C. CORRECT. The judges are appealing to the common understanding of the word traditional. Most people would not consider that the native tradition stopped existing just because a law prevented them from exercising their tradition.

D. Actually, the judges ruled that native activities *were* traditional. The AWS had labelled the activities "not traditional", that's why they were prosecuting Alaska Natives.

E. This simply isn't mentioned in lines 45-57. I can't explain that why it's wrong, because it didn't happen.

Question 3

DISCUSSION: This is in the fourth paragraph. The 1991 case is the one that ruled in favor of allowing Alaska Natives to continue their traditional use of sea otter pelts.

The judges heard testimonials describing the tradition (lines 41-45) and determined that the government's definition of traditional was too narrow (lines 45-57).

A. The fourth paragraph doesn't mention "long-standing". This term was only mentioned in the second paragraph.

B. The court ruled that "within living memory" was not the right standard to use in determining what is traditional, particularly when Alaska Natives had been banned from exercising their tradition. The definition of "within living memory" was not at issue.

C. The intent of the regulations was never mentioned.

D. It's not even clear if the Fur Seal Treaty is still in effect. The fourth paragraph doesn't mention any interpretations of this treaty.

E. **CORRECT.** The historical facts are that Alaska Natives had made many uses of sea otters prior to the occupation of Alaska by the Russians (lines 41-45).

Question 4

DISCUSSION: The 1986 case was the one that ruled the government was *correct* to ban the use of sea otter pelts.

So the 1986 court must have believed that the "in living memory" standard was correct.

A. There was no compromise in 1986. The court ruled that the AWS was entirely correct to prosecute the natives.

B. **CORRECT.** "Continuity and regularity" is mentioned in paragraph two, and line 34 then specifies that AWS interpreted "continuity and regularity" to mean "within living memory".

Because the court agreed with the AWS, they must have agreed that using sea otter pelts was not a continual and regular tradition.

C. Most people would not say that traditional means "within living memory". The court in 1986 defied common understanding of the word traditional.

D. Actually, the court did not think "traditional" applied to the age-old activity of sea otter pelt usage, because there was a gap in the tradition. Further, the court didn't indicate that tradition should refer to any recent activities.

E. The court in 1986 didn't reflect the concerns of Alaska Natives. It said their activities were not traditional.

Question 5

DISCUSSION: There will always be a line in the passage that directly supports the right answer on this type of question. Find it.

A. CORRECT. Lines 21-24. The 1910 treaty banned sea otter hunting. This ban continued until 1972, when there was an exemption for traditional activities.
B. If sea otter pelts were specifically exempted by law, then the government would not have prosecuted people for using sea otter pelts.
C. Lines 40-45 say that Alaska Natives made use of sea otters before the Russian occupation. We don't know what happened after the occupation.
D. The passage never mentions sea otter population levels.
E. The passage never mentions which animals were most commonly hunted.

Question 6

DISCUSSION: The Fur Seal Treaty of 1910 prevented Alaska Natives from hunting sea otters. This broke their tradition.

This had the effect that the tradition was not exercised "within living memory", and thus the Federal government didn't grant Alaska Natives an exemption to hunt sea otters under the 1972 MMPA.

A. We don't know why the Fur Seal treaty banned the sea otter hunt. It may not have been for ecological reasons.
B. We're not told if other animals were affected, apart from sea otters.
C. The passage never says that the Fur Seal Treaty is well known, or that it is required as a precedent for hunting bans.
Also, laws don't require precedents. *Judgements* require precedents. A hunting ban is a law, not a judgement. This answer just throws in an irrelevant legal word.
D. The passage never mentions Russian hunters.
E. CORRECT. This is a weirdly worded answer. But it's true that the Fur Seal Treaty helps explain why Alaska Natives didn't have a right to their tradition for many decades: The Fur Seal Treaty banned sea otter hunting.

If the Fur Seal Treaty had never existed, then it wouldn't have been clear why Alaska Natives had stopped making things from sea otter pelts. The court upheld the tradition partly because the natives had been prevented from exercising it (lines 49-54).

Question 7

DISCUSSION: For this question, you should think about *why* the court ruled in favor of the Alaska Natives:

- The natives had a long tradition of using sea otter pelts (lines 41-45).
- The natives had only stopped this tradition because the law forbid them to hunt sea otters (lines 49-54).

The correct answer should match both of those factors.

A. Several millennia is a long time. Too long. It's like if Italians wanted to have gladiator fights to the death because of "tradition".
B. This answer doesn't indicate whether these handicrafts are traditional.
C. **CORRECT.** In the passage, the Alaska Natives were prevented from exercising their tradition due to a factor beyond their control: the law. Here, the tradition was also ended due to an outside factor: industrial development.
D. This sounds like a rare tradition. It's not likely to receive legal protection.
E. This sounds like the tradition is dying out by itself. In the passage, the tradition only died because the law banned it.

Passage 2 - Kate Chopin
Questions 8-15

Paragraph Summaries

1. Chopin grew up with sentimental novelists. She instead took the local colorists as her model.
2. The local colorists mythologized the dying world of "women's culture".
3. Chopin used the conventions of local color to describe extreme psychological states without drama.
4. Later, Chopin took a more impressionistic approach to writing.

Analysis

This passage is not an argument. Instead, it's a description of a specific author: Kate Chopin. The passage traces her career and stylistic influences.

On a passage like this, it's important to keep track of every major group.

Women's culture: The old domestic world of women, from a time when women's major life goal was marrying well. The garden, the house, and domestic tools were the common features of women's lives.

Local Color: By the 1870s, "women's culture" was beginning to disappear as women sought lives outside the home. The local colorists were nostalgic about this dying world, and they invested elements of "women's culture" with mythic significance.

Early Kate Chopin: This is in the third paragraph. Kate Chopin wasn't a local colorist. But she used the styles of local color to tell dramatic stories without melodrama.

The passage isn't very clear about this phase of Chopin's career, or how local color lets you tell a story without drama. But what I wrote is all you need to know.

Late Kate Chopin/Impressionism/New Women: These novels were not straightforward narratives. Instead, the writers tried to explore female consciousness.

For example, a book might look at *how* a woman feels and thinks, rather than a story which brings her from event to event.

There's no overall argument to understand in this passage. Instead, you should have an understanding of the elements I wrote about above, and where to find them. When a question asks about a specific detail, you should know where to find it in the passage.

The Awakening is the product of this later period in Chopin's life. By this point she had moved past the local colorists and on to Impressionism.

The questions are mostly about details. You don't need to memorize all the details in a passage, but you should retain them. If a passage mentions a detail, you ought to be able to recall it or remember where it was talked about, then check the passage to confirm.

Several of the questions also test whether you *understood* what you read. For example, question 10 uses the word "strong" yet the passage uses the word "crisp" to describe plots. If you understood the passage, you'd recognize those refer to the same thing. Likewise, Chopin's writing "avoided the excesses of sentimental novels" by telling "melodramatic tales in an uninflected manner". The answers variously describe this as "dispassionate" or "detached", which mean the same thing.

You may not know words like "uninflected", but from context you should be able to figure them out. Don't rush through the passage. The LSAT is merciless: If you don't understand what you read, it will burn you.

Read a second or even a third time, until you understand. The second read is much faster. You'll get more questions right, and more quickly, if you understand.

Question 8

DISCUSSION: The point of this passage is to describe Kate Chopin's style and her influences.

All of the wrong answers are not only not the main point; they are false! The passage contradicts every wrong answer.

A. This answer is total nonsense. The New Women are in the *fourth* paragraph. Chopin used the techniques of the local colorists in the *third* paragraph. And nowhere does Chopin try to recapture the atmosphere of the novels of her youth.

B. CORRECT. The best answer: this covers every paragraph. Chopin had three sets of influences. She moved through them to reach the style she used in *The Awakening*.

C. Lines 52-53 say that Chopin "embraced this impressionistic approach" in *The Awakening*. The book was part of a literary movement, and thus clearly *was* like other novels.

D. The third paragraph talks about how Chopin *did* use the conventions of the local colorists. This answer choice is totally false.

E. Lines 31-32 say that Chopin *did* use the conventions of the local colorists.

Question 9

DISCUSSION: The question is asking about Chopin's opinion, not the author's opinion. Chopin rarely expresses her opinion, so most of the wrong answers can be eliminated because they are not things Chopin talks about.

Lines 38-40 answer this question: Chopin "didn't share the local colorists nostalgia for the past." This is the only direct opinion of Chopin's about the local colorists.

Lines 22-28 describe the local colorists' nostalgia.

A. CORRECT. By the 1870s and 1880s, women's culture was in decline. The local colorists were fascinated with the objects of the former women's culture, and the local colorists invested these objects with mythic significance. (lines 22-28).
Chopin did not agree with this nostalgia (lines 38-40).

B. *Chopin* was the one who described scenes dispassionately. See paragraph three.

C. The local colorists were an inspiration for Chopin, but not necessarily for the New Women. The fourth paragraph doesn't say who inspired the New Women.
Also, we're looking for *Chopin's opinion,* not what is true in the passage.

D. Lines 16-20 say that the local colorists were able to move through these new worlds as artists. It sounds like the local colorists were able to explore these new worlds.
Also, we're looking for *Chopin's opinion,* not what is true in the passage.

E. The third paragraph describes how Chopin used the conventions of the local colorists to describe scenes with scientific detachment. So Chopin would disagree with this answer.

Question 10

DISCUSSION: As with other specific detail questions, the passage literally answers this one. If you can't find lines to support your answer, your answer is likely wrong.

A. Chopin avoided romantic, sentimental language. See lines 32-37.
B. Lines 38-40 contradict this: Chopin did not mythologize the past.
C. **CORRECT.** Lines 32-37 describe Chopin's detached narrative. She used the conventions of local color to accomplish this detachment.
D. Lines 48-52 describe how Chopin's stories *avoided* crisp plots.
E. Lines 29-30 do say that Chopin used lonely protagonists. But the passage never says why Chopin does this.

Question 11

DISCUSSION: Lines 13-16 say that women's culture disappeared as women went to university, work and politics.

Before that, women were in the home. Lines 22-28 describe this more explicitly: the garden, the house, the artifacts of domesticity. This was the world of women.

It's hard to conceive of the extent women were in the home, pre-1865. My grandmothers were both homemakers....*after* they married. Before marrying, one grandmother left home to work in the city, and the other got a university degree and worked as a schoolteacher.

Pre-1865, this was not possible. Women....stayed....at....home. They read, they knitted, they played piano, they walked in the garden. If they left the house, they did so in the company of a male relative. They went to balls, and received suitors at home. If there was a match, they went to their new husband's house, and the cycle began again.

That was their life.

A. **CORRECT.** "Domestic" experiences means experiences in the home. Which is where women were before 1865. See lines 13-16 and 22-28.
B. Regional life was what the local colorists explored, *after* women escaped from the home. See lines 16-20.
C. The local colorists were the only artists mentioned (line 20), and their movement arose *after* women's culture ended. I'm not sure what else this answer could refer to, but it certainly doesn't refer to the world of women's culture.
D. Women did not go to university until women's culture dissolved. See lines 13-16.
E. Same as D. Politics was off limits to women until women's culture started dissolving. See lines 13-16.

Question 12

DISCUSSION: The passage places Chopin's work in context. The sentimental novels were the types of books written before women's culture began to dissolve in 1865.

These were the books Chopin read when growing up. They described a period that she had just narrowly avoided living in. Chopin would have had living female relatives who grew up during the period of "Women's Culture".

So these sentimental novels were part of the context of Chopin's life. The passage mentions them to show us what kind of world Chopin was reacting against.

A. Chopin avoided the dramatic style of the sentimental novels. See paragraph three.
B. Lines 38-40 say that Chopin rejected the work of the local colorists because of their nostalgia, not because of sentimentality.
C. **CORRECT.** The best answer. The passage takes us through Chopin's literary influences: The sentimental novelists, the local colorists, the New Women.
D. The local colorists were *not* sentimental (i.e. emotional). They described what they saw "with almost scientific detachment". (line 20)
E. This answer would make sense if the passage was arguing something like "Women *did* write novels before Chopin". The passage is not trying to prove when women wrote novels. The passage isn't even an argument.

Question 13

DISCUSSION: To answer a question like this, you *must* reread the section of the passage that talks about *The Awakening*.

I just did that, and it took me all of five seconds to find the answer. *The Awakening* is discussed in lines 51-57. It used impressionism more fully than the New Women did.

A. The New Women did this too: lines 50-52.
B. The New Women did this too: lines 44-47.
C. **CORRECT.** Lines 52-54 say this directly.
D. Total nonsense. Lines 52-57 don't mention fantasy. Only line 45 mentions fantasy: The *New Women* used it.
E. Line 55 contradicts this: *The Awakening* was *not* unified by style or content.

Question 14

DISCUSSION: The purpose of the passage is to describe Kate Chopin's style and literary influences.

A. We're not told *anything* about Chopin's life. Were her books successful? Did she marry? Where did she live? We have no idea.
B. **CORRECT.** The best answer. We see the evolution of women's literature from sentiment to local color to New Women, and we're told how this influenced Chopin.
C. The passage didn't say whether Chopin was a typical example of women's literature. She doesn't appear to fit neatly into any category.
D. The passage didn't discuss Chopin's external social circumstances. E.g. Was she rich/poor? In good health/sick? Married/single? Urban/rural?
E. The passage never says whether Chopin's books are *better* than other books. The author doesn't specify what's good and bad about Chopin compared to other authors.

Question 15

DISCUSSION: The New Women are discussed only in the fourth paragraph.

Most of the answers discuss things that never happened anywhere in the passage, or only happened in other paragraphs.

Note that you must think broadly. Answer D mentions "aspects of reality that had been neglected". That specific phrase wasn't in paragraph four, but it corresponds exactly with lines 50-52.

I worked first by eliminating those answers that were clearly wrong, then skimmed through paragraph four to find the lines that justify D.

A. The passage never talks about literature changing social customs. We don't know why social customs change.
B. We're not told whether the New Women advocated social change, and regret is never mentioned.
C. The passage didn't say this. "Invariably" is a strong word. We only know about *one* change in social custom: the dissolution of women's culture.
Further, the dissolution of women's culture was in paragraph two. The passage doesn't say whether the New Women cared about the dissolution of women's culture. The New Women were only mentioned in paragraph 4.
D. **CORRECT.** Lines 50-52 support this directly. The New Women experimented with impressionism *in order to* describe female consciousness. This consciousness had been neglected in prior works.
E. The local colorists were dispassionate and uninflected. See line 37, where Chopin was using their techniques. We don't even know if the New Women were uninflected, so this answer has no support.

Passage 3 - Ocean Magnetism
Questions 16-21

Paragraph Summaries

1. The ocean floor has magnetic variations. Newly formed magma on the ocean floor takes its polarity from the Earth's magnetic field, and this magnetic field has changed over time.
2. The mid-ocean ridge has rows of rocks with alternating polarity. Scientists theorize this is because the ocean floor is being pulled apart and new magma continually rises from the ridge.
3. The young rocks near the crest have normal polarity. The rock gets older as it is further from the crest. Scientists are able to judge the age of the ocean rock from samples of land rocks. The stripes of polarity of the rock appear to have reversed whenever the Earth reversed its magnetic field in the past.

Analysis

Many students find this passage very difficult. I suspect there are two major errors:

1. Moving too fast, without trying to understand the passage.
2. Not visualizing what the passage is describing.

This is a complex, technical passage. You should read it slower than other passages. You absolutely have to understand what it's talking about in order to do well.

This isn't like university, where you can skim the course readings and do fine. You need to know what this passage is talking about.

Visualization helps. This passage is describing magma coming out of the ocean floor, and forming a crest over time. The polarity reverses in stripes.

I imagined a crest rising from the ocean floor, and stripes of rock in different colors (I saw purple and black). This image of reversing polarity helped immensely. (I draw it for you later on)

Visualization is a learnable skill. Just....try imagining things, and you'll get better at imagining things in the future. When you review a passage, try to form an image in your head.

This may be slow at first, but soon it becomes instinctive. For me it happens simultaneously with reading.

For instance, the previous passage was partly about "women's culture", the period when women were confined to the home. I had flashes of women reading, strolling in the garden, knitting, talking in the parlor, and other common activities of the era. This imagery helped me retain information and answer questions.

Here, while writing this explanation, I can still imagine the crest with colored stripes. I remember *exactly* what the passage is talking about, thanks to this image in my head.

For some passages (such as this one) you can make a drawing instead. But other passages are easy to visualize but not to draw. I use this process of visualization on all reading comprehension passages and logical reasoning questions, and it speeds me up immensely.

Alright, time to talk about the passage itself. First, if you have any confusion about the passage itself, I suggest you go back and reread it and try to understand it.

Did you reread it? Good. Let's talk about it. The author is discussing magnetic patterns on the ocean floor. Here are the important actors:

Earth's magnetic field: This reverses over time. Compasses will either point north or south, depending on which way the magnetic field goes.

Magma: This is like lava, under the Earth's crust. It is very hot, and liquid. Eventually, it solidifies into rock.

While magma is liquid, it picks up the polarity of the Earth's magnetic field. Once magma becomes rock, it keeps this polarity even if the Earth's polarity changes.

Mid Ocean Ridge: A big ridge under the sea. Sort of like an undersea mountain.

At this point, the earth's crust is weak and being pulled apart by tectonic forces. As the crust is pulled apart, magma comes up from under the Earth's crust.

The ocean cools the magma, and it turns into rock. This process keeps happening. So the rock furthest from the top of the ridge is oldest.

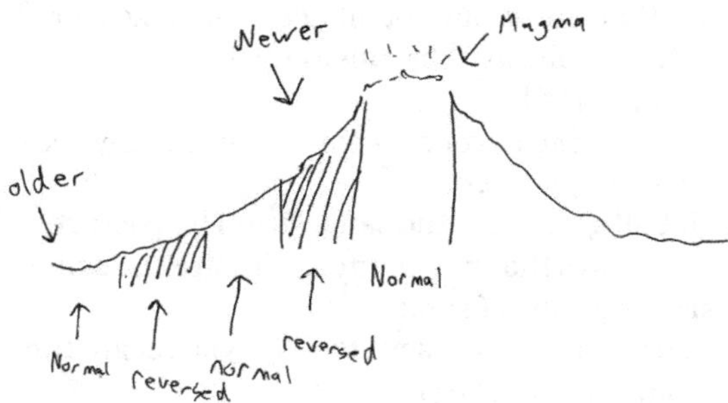

I've drawn a diagram to illustrate this. The newest rock and magma is in the center. This is normal polarity. Moving away from the center, the rock gets older. Some of it is reversed: that means it formed during a time when the Earth's polarity was reversed.

Earth's polarity switched back and forth over time, which is why there are stripes of rock with different polarities. The rock doesn't change its polarity once it has formed.

Polarity, by the way, refers to whether Earth's magnetic field points towards the North or South pole. Currently, our polarity is North.

Question 16

DISCUSSION: Main point answers must first be true. All four wrong answers are either contradicted by the passage, or totally unsupported by the passage.

A. The passage isn't talking about how the entire ocean floor formed. It's about why the ocean floor has polarity, and how this explains the alternating magnetic strips around the mid-ocean ridge.

B. Total nonsense. The passage doesn't say the entire ocean floor doesn't have magnetic striping. The *mid-ocean ridge* is the part of the ocean floor that has alternate striping. See lines 30-31.

C. **CORRECT.** The two discoveries are: magnetic variations and the mid-ocean ridge (lines 5-6 and lines 26-30). This led to the theory in lines 33-40, and the justification in paragraph 3.

D. Lines 9-11 mention local distortions on land. The passage doesn't mention local compass distortions underwater. Totally irrelevant answer.

E. The passage doesn't say why the ocean floor was mapped in the 1950s. This answer combines two unrelated ideas from the passage.

Question 17

DISCUSSION: Look back at the passage analysis section. I described the whole theory: the mid-ocean ridge forms from magma. This ridge spreads out as the crust is pulled apart. The sections of the ridge have differing polarity, as they formed in different magnetic eras.

We know how old land-based rocks are, and we thus figured out when the Earth reverse polarity. Scientists then looked at the mid ocean ridge, and assumed it moved apart at a constant rate. This would let them judge the age of each section of the ridge.

There was a strong correlation between the predicted age/polarity of each section of the ridge, and the measured polarity of that age derived from land based rocks.

So this "remarkable" correlation is consistent with the theory and helps prove the theory correct.

A. The passage says that the spreading may occur at a rate of several cm per year (line 54). But we don't know if that is fast or slow: we have no context for such a statement.
B. We're not just trying to explain the existence of the ridge. We're trying to explain the magnetic striping of the rock extending away from the ridge. The correlation is between the age of this rock and the magnetic history of the Earth, so this correlation supports the full theory.
C. Strength of the magnetic field is never mentioned as being a factor for anything.
D. CORRECT. The theory has multiple parts: why the mid-ocean ridge exists, why there are strips of alternating polarity extending from the ridge, etc. The correlation supports all parts of the theory.
E. The passage never mentions if the reversals happen at set intervals. This isn't part of the theory.

Question 18

DISCUSSION: You can and should prove the right answer by referring to the passage.

Basalt contains magnetite. Magma turns into basalt. You can basically view all three terms as interchangeable for the purpose of answering this question. Magma becomes basalt, which takes on the Earth's current polarity as it hardens.

A. CORRECT. Basalt takes on the polarity the Earth has at the time the basalt forms. The youngest basalt is forming as we speak. So the youngest basalt has the Earth's current polarity. See lines 20-23.
B. Lines 20-23 simply say that basalt takes on the current polarity of the Earth. The passage doesn't say that "most but not all of basalt" takes on current polarity. This answer is totally unsupported.
C. The passage never says this. Maybe many rocks have magnetite.
D. Not all grains are the same size. The passage never says that magnetite grains are the same size as grains of sand.
E. The passage never says this. Maybe magnetite grains are very large.

Question 19

DISCUSSION: Lines 53-55 show that scientists assume the ocean floor is spreading at a constant rate.

Thus, if time periods between reversals fluctuate, some magnetic strips will be wider than others. More spreading will occur if an interval is 500,000 years, compared to an interval of 100,000 years.

A. The peaks of the ridge formed during the *current* polarity. So the basalt matches our polarity and won't distort anything. This answer is just here to confuse you by throwing in a term mentioned in the passage, in an irrelevant context.

B. We don't know why the ridge goes all around the Earth. Scientists speculate it is because the ocean floor is spreading apart....but we don't know *why* the spreading occurs. This is another nonsense answer intended to confuse you.

C. **CORRECT.** Suppose the ocean floor spreads 2cm per year. Then suppose during one period, polarity doesn't reverse for 2,000,000 years. That strip will be 4,000,000 cm wide. If during another period polarity reverses after 20,000 years, then that strip will be just 40,000 cm long. Lines 53-55 say we're assuming the spreading is at a constant rate.

D. Gibberish. I don't even know how to explain this is wrong. This translates as:

"If some magnetic periods are longer than others, then land-based rock is more reliable than ocean-based rock."

Nothing in the passage suggests this is true.

E. If some magnetic ages last a long time, then some magnetic strips will be very wide. The basalt at the start of the strip will be older than the end of the strip.

Question 20

DISCUSSION: All of the wrong answers throw irrelevant terms at you. They say things that have nothing to do with the passage, except that they contain a term used in the passage somewhere.

Merely parroting a term from the passage doesn't make an answer relevant. It's like if a car mechanic said: "The windshield lubricant is jamming the brake in the trunk, so we'll have to replace the driver's seat using the spare found in the gear shaft."

The words are the right words, but they don't make any sense. Honestly, almost all reading comprehension wrong answers read like this if you know what's going on. They're total nonsense.

The right answer supports the argument by verifying data the argument was based on.

A. This could just mean that other rocks have magnetite. The theory never said that only basalt is magnetic.

B. **CORRECT.** More verification is always good. The evidence in the fourth paragraph supports the theory, and this evidence in turn depends on the age measurements being accurate.

C. The passage never said that basalt is only found underwater.

D. The passage never said that the height of the ridge is important.

E. The passage never said if other types of volcanic rock matter.

Question 21

DISCUSSION: The right answer is a bit weak. But it's a "most strongly supported" question, so the answer doesn't need absolute support.

Further, none of the wrong answers have any support from the passage. In fact, some contradict the passage.

A. CORRECT. The mid-ocean ridge is in the middle of the ocean. Rock gets older the farther it is from the ridge. So rock near the continents is likely to be oldest, especially if the whole ocean floor formed from this ridge.

This answer is easiest to support because it only says "some of the oldest rock". There could be older rocks elsewhere in the ocean. Further, the question is just "most strongly supported".

We mainly know that the youngest rock is in the middle of the ridge. It's a *bit* of a stretch to say for sure that the rock by the continents is among the oldest. But given the wishy-washiness of the question type, and the vagueness of this answer, we can say that it is "most strongly supported".

B. Lines 20-23 say that basalt doesn't reverse polarity once it forms.

C. You may have found this tempting, because basalt distorts compasses. But the basalt is all the way at the bottom of the ocean, presumably too far to distort compasses.

Also, use some common sense: for centuries, sailors navigated with compasses. They couldn't have done this if basalt on the ocean floor was constantly interfering with compass readings.

If the passage doesn't support an answer AND the answer defies common sense, it's definitely wrong.

D. Why? The passage never mentions that magnetite grains grow weaker.

E. The passage *contradicts* this answer. The magnetic field of the earth has reversed many times. So many pieces of old basalt have current polarity because they formed in a past age when polarity was the same. Polarity *reverses*. That means it only has two states.

Passage 4 - Historical Objectivity (comparative)
Questions 22-27

Paragraph Summaries

Passage A

1. Historians aim to be objective.
2. Objective historians say that facts exist independently of interpretation.
3. Objective historians must be neutral, like judges. They must not have outside allegiances.

Passage B

1. Objectivity does require self-discipline.
2. Objectivity is not neutrality. An objective argument makes a point, but has carefully considered alternate arguments, and rejected them.
3. The "powerful argument" is the highest form of objectivity. It is not the same thing as "giving equal time to all sides".

Analysis

The passages both talk about historical objectivity. It is not quite clear whether the passages disagree.

The first author describes her ideal of objectivity:

- Facts and interpretation are clearly separate.
- The objective historian will abandon theories and facts if they are mistaken.
- Facts exist independently of opinion.
- The objective historian has no biases.
- The objective historian is not an advocate or propagandist.

The second author has a slightly different view. They believe that the objective historian should make an argument. Of course, the objective historian should still avoid bias and self-delusion. But the goal is to *prove* the truth.

The second author thinks the objective historian should consider all competing theories. But the objective historian should not merely *present* the theories. They must argue which one is correct.

Now, it's possible the two authors don't actually disagree. The first author says that objective historians should be like judges. And judges make *judgements*. Which is what the second author argues that objective historians should do.

We would need more information to determine whether or not these authors actually disagree, or whether the difference is merely a matter of emphasis. The first author places more emphasis on neutrality, the second author places more emphasis on the fact that historians should judge.

Note: several wrong answers mention changes in history over time, or historians from different time periods. But neither passage mentions how history has changed over time!

In fact, almost all the wrong answers simply don't occur in either passage. I don't know how to "explain" that these are wrong: they're hallucinatory answers.

The solution is to read the passages a second time or skim them quickly, and slow down if you don't understand. Rereading is much faster than reading – most students can reread a passage in 30 seconds. You'll remember many more details this way, and dodge hallucinatory answers that describe things that weren't in the passage.

Question 22

DISCUSSION: You're looking for something mentioned in both passages. If even one passage fails to address the topic, the answer is wrong.

However, in practice, most answers are not mentioned in *both* passages. So it is better to eliminate answers with no support, first.

I incorrectly semi-eliminated answer B because I thought it had no support in the first passage. However, I knew it had support in the second passage, so I kept it in the back of my mind.

I then easily eliminated the other answers. At that point, I searched the first passage and found some support for B.

A. Neither passage mentions recent historical scholarship, and neither passage gives examples of flaws.

B. CORRECT. The first author uses paragraphs 1 and 2 to describe how to be objective. Bias is only mentioned by name in paragraph 3, but the ideals described as paragraphs 1 and 2 are synonymous with neutrality and lack of bias.

The second author shows how to avoid bias in the first paragraph of their passage.

C. We're never told the history of objectivity.

D. Passage B doesn't even mention relativist scholarship.

E. This is never addressed. Both passages imply that ideally, interpretations change due to better objective scholarship. But the passages never say if this actually happens.

Question 23

DISCUSSION: The right answer needs to be in both passages. As with question 22, most answers aren't mentioned in *either* passage, so it's best to eliminate those first, then prove one of the remaining answers correct using the passage.

I used this technique to quickly decide between C and E. It was easy to check both of them using the passage, once I had eliminated the other answers.

A. Neither passage mentions other disciplines. Paragraph 1 of passage B mentions "self-discipline". This answer choice was probably trying to confuse you by hoping you would remember the word "discipline", out of context.

B. Outside knowledge makes this answer tempting, as this sounds like a reasonable tactic. But, neither passage mentions methodologies. Common sense can be used to judge whether an answer is reasonable, but answers still need support from the passage to be correct.

C. CORRECT. See paragraph 2 of passage A and lines 30-32 of passage B.

D. This answer is insane, if taken literally. And you have to take LSAT answers literally. This says a historian must answer *all* objections. That means if I say "this theory doesn't cure cancer!" then the historian must address my crazy concern.
Of course, the real reason this answer is wrong is because it's not mentioned in the passage. But our common sense judgement that this answer is insane tells us that neither author would ever say it. This makes it a prime candidate for fast elimination.

E. Tempting, but passage A doesn't mention rival interpretations, or giving "consideration" to interpretations. Paragraph 2 says interpretations are not that important: they are valuable only if they accord with and explain facts.

Question 24

DISCUSSION: I discussed disagreement to some extent in the passage analysis. It's not clear whether the authors actually disagree. But this question is just asking about "likelihood" of disagreement.

The core of the potential disagreement is that the author of passage B says objective historians should make arguments. The author of passage A leans more towards neutrality.

Most people would agree that in disputes, it's possible for one side to be objectively right, and another to be objectively wrong. So the author of passage B might think an objective historian should take sides in some disputes. Whereas the author of passage A seems less likely to think that objective historians should take sides.

A. On line 36, the author of passage B agrees detachment is useful. We have no reason to think that the author of passage A would disagree: detachment is neutrality.

B. CORRECT. The author of passage B says historians should make powerful arguments for the truth. Such a historian might judge that a certain political party is objectively correct, and support that party.
Lines 20-22 in passage A say that objective historians should avoid political commitments.

C. Neither author mentions whether today's historians are more or less objective.

D. Both authors dislike propaganda. See lines 16-18 and paragraph 1 of passage B (line 28).

E. Neither passage mentions historians of different eras.

Question 25

DISCUSSION: The authors have somewhat different opinions on objectivity. The only thing they have in common is that they agree it's important.

A. Neither passage says what is possible for most historians.

B. CORRECT. See lines 1-2 and 27-33. The author of passage B doesn't explicitly say that "objectivity" is what separates history from propaganda. The author of passage B uses their first paragraph to describe the traits that separate history from propaganda. Then they mention objectivity in line 33. The "yet" at the start of that sentence links objectivity with the concepts described in the first paragraph. It should be clear from context and objectivity is what separates history from propaganda.

C. Only passage A says this. Passage B says objective historians should make "a powerful argument". This might include a political alliance if the historian judged that one political group was objectively correct.

D. Neither passage mentions this: it seems a pretty big obstacle to objectivity.
You'd need to use other historians to judge whether you are objective, and neither passage mentions doing this.

E. Neither passage mentions changes in historical scholarship over time, or how common objective historians are.

Question 26

DISCUSSION: Propaganda is mentioned in two places: lines 16-18 and 27-28.

(Note that you should be able to find these lines quickly. When I read these passages, I saw both authors mentioned propaganda, to make an argument. So I remembered where propaganda was mentioned.)

The first author mentions propaganda to describe what a historian must not do. The second author mentions propaganda as something historical scholarship is distinct from.

This means that both authors think historians *could* become propagandists. It's what historians must try to avoid.

A. No rival approaches to history are mentioned.
B. The passages never mention scholarship in other fields.
C. "Discredit" means to destroy the good reputation of something. Propaganda has never had a good reputation. More specifically, the passage never mention anyone discrediting propaganda.
D. **CORRECT.** See the discussion above. Historians can become propagandists if they're not careful.
E. D is a better answer. The authors are not merely contrasting history from propaganda. They are arguing history should *not* be propaganda. Also, this answer says "kinds" of writing, plural. Propaganda is only one kind of writing. The LSAT is maddeningly precise – that plural alone is enough to eliminate this answer.

Question 27

DISCUSSION: The wrong answers are simply never mentioned in the passages. They're intended to distract you and confuse you.

The solution is to have a good idea of what's in the passage, and assume an answer probably isn't right unless it matches your memory of the passage.

Don't give stupid answers consideration. Answers have to *prove* they're right.

A. Neither passage cites any scholarship.
B. The passages never talk about any recent developments.
C. The authors never gave opposing arguments.
D. The passages never mention other fields.
E. **CORRECT.** See lines 22-26 and lines 27-32.

Preptest 64
Section I - Logical Reasoning

Question 1

QUESTION TYPE: Identify the Conclusion

FACTS:

1. There are many reasons why getting a second doctor's opinion can be awkward.
2. It can be a good idea to get a second opinion.

ANALYSIS: The stimulus hasn't told us when second opinions are needed. We only know they're *sometimes* (a very vague word) a good idea. We also don't know whether we should worry that our first doctor will get embarrassed.

The stimulus just tells us a few facts about doctors. Their vanity can be hurt, and they may feel professionally incompetent. And their patient *might* worry about embarrassing them. These are statements of fact. They're not telling us what we *should* do. This distinction between normative statements of opinion ("what should I do?") and positive statements of fact ("This is what will happen) is incredibly important on the LSAT.

Most of the wrong answers aren't even true. The answers need to be true to be the conclusion.

A. Many things in life are worth a little awkwardness; maybe we should get a second opinion even if it's awkward.
B. The argument only said the process of getting a second opinion *can* be awkward. Maybe most doctors are professional about it.
C. **CORRECT.** The second sentence said getting a second opinion can be weird for patients, and the rest of the stimulus describes how doctors can find the process awkward.
D. The final sentence never says that the second doctor *always* feels uncomfortable. The second doctor might often see that the first doctor made an excellent diagnosis and confirm it.
E. This is true ("Often" is a synonym for "many"), but it's not the main point. The stimulus also talked about how doctors feel awkward too.

Question 2

QUESTION TYPE: Must be True

FACTS: Florida panthers need a larger habitat for their population to grow. And their population is too small to sustain itself right now.

ANALYSIS: We need more panthers, or else the panther population can't sustain itself. But their habitat won't support any more panthers.

So the panthers need a larger habitat to have a chance of being self-sustaining. You could draw this as:

S → 250 → LH (sustaining - -> 250 → larger habitat)
~~LH~~ → ~~250~~ → ~~S~~ (contrapositive form)

A. This is never mentioned. Maybe the panthers' entire habitat is high quality, but they need more habitat.
B. False reversal. I need food to live, but I won't live simply because I have food. Likewise, the panthers might need something else to be self-sustaining, apart from higher numbers.
C. **CORRECT.** Without more habitat, the panthers' population will stay stuck at 70-100. That's not enough to sustain them.
D. The panthers might get a larger habitat somehow. Their forest might grow back, for example.
E. We know there are more panthers than in the 1970's. But their habitat might be the same size. Their population could have grown to the limits of their existing habitat.

Question 3

QUESTION TYPE: Method of Reasoning

CONCLUSION: We can create a society that is both diverse and equal.

REASONING: We can support complementary interests. (E.g. we provide support for scientists and artists, in equal measure. Then we get scientific results that look beautiful. People are different, but they have equal support and opportunity.)

ANALYSIS: The political scientist first tells us his opponent's argument: equality means we'd all be the same, and everything would be boring. Then the political scientist contradicts this. If we support complementary interests, we can be equal but different.

It may or may not be a good argument; a lot depends on how you define "equal". But we're concerned with the author's method of argument: he launches a straightforward attack on his opponents' claim.

A. What undesirable consequence? This answer choice is a description of the political scientist's opponents' argument. *They* say that equality would lead to boring sameness.
B. **CORRECT.** The political scientist says that his opponents assume that equality requires everyone to be the same. He contradicts them by saying we can be equal but different instead.
C. The political scientist never says this. Maybe his opponents are very poor, and they would benefit from equality.
D. This might be something that the author's *opponents* say. "If the group is equal, then every person must be the same.", they might say.
E. Which counterexample is being undermined? The author's opponents never gave any examples for the author to weaken.

Question 4

QUESTION TYPE: Weaken

CONCLUSION: Magnetic fields can reduce back pain.

REASONING: An experiment, with two groups: those with magnets on their backs and those without. Those with magnets felt less back pain.

ANALYSIS: There were *two* differences between the groups:

1. The first group had magnets on their back.
2. The first group knew they were being treated.

The second difference could be the cause. This is called the placebo effect. The body can heal itself if it believes it's being healed. It's a useful effect, but it's also very frustrating for doctors who design medical experiments. The LSAT often mentions it.

A. **CORRECT.** The experiment would have been better if the second group had devices that looked like magnets applied to their back. Then the experiment would have isolated the magnetic fields' effect.
B. Who cares what doctors believe? The entire medical profession could be wrong. That's happened before: doctors used to believe that hand washing before surgery was silly.
C. So? The doctor only claimed that magnets helped the back. Other parts of the body don't matter. The doctor only claimed magnets help the back. There could be *thousands* of other studies about how magnets help the back, even if no studies have been done on, say, foot pain.
D. Scientists are allowed to have hypotheses (beliefs). That's why we use experiments: to test beliefs. If the experiment is well designed, scientists' beliefs don't matter. Not having the original scientists involved is a sign that the experiment *was* well designed: their beliefs can't bias the results.
E. I'll explain with an example: headaches happen for many different reasons. That doesn't change the fact that Advil can help with most headaches. The cause of the sore back doesn't necessarily affect whether magnets can help sore backs.

Question 5

QUESTION TYPE: Flawed Reasoning

CONCLUSION: Discipline makes dogs behave badly.

REASONING: Dogs that behave badly get disciplined more often.

ANALYSIS: What a stupid argument. If your dog never misbehaves, why would you discipline it? And if your dog often does terrible things, wouldn't you discipline it?

The argument mixes up causes and effects. Discipline *could* cause misbehavior, but it's also possible that misbehavior causes owners to punish their dogs. Or maybe some third factor both causes dogs to misbehave and owners to treat their dogs poorly. This argument is making a correlation/causation error.

A. CORRECT. If your dog does something bad, you might punish it. It's possible that dogs would behave even worse without discipline.
B. It sounds like the argument *didn't* consider this. Because if this were true, then dogs would quickly learn not to misbehave, unless they like punishment.
C. The argument is only talking about dogs. We all know dogs behave differently from other animals in important ways, so evidence about cats or rabbits (for example) wouldn't tell us much about dogs.
D. The evidence only compared kennel club members with other members, so the skill of non-members is not a factor. It's still true that more punishment was correlated with more misbehavior.
E. This doesn't contradict the argument. The author would reply that this means that kennel club owners' dogs must be more likely to misbehave.

Question 6

QUESTION TYPE: Paradox

FACTS: We spot more tornados, but weather scientists say that no more tornados are forming.

ANALYSIS: The LSAT loves to point out the difference between what we think we know and how things actually are in the real world. We see statistics, and mistake them for absolute truth. Statistics are not reality; they're just our attempt at measuring reality.

We don't see every tornado that ever occurs. Some are very small, and some happen in isolated places like deserts. Some tornados that are seen might not get reported. So official statistics do not accurately count the actual number of tornados.

The right answer should show us the difference between reality and statistics.

A. This doesn't matter, as long as meteorologists knew the factors well from 1953 onwards. The comparison is between 1953 and now.
B. The question talks about the *number* of tornados. Intensity doesn't matter.
C. So? It's still true that we have more than three times the number of tornados we had in 1953. This just means that the increase has slowed recently.
D. Same as B. The question is about the *number* of tornadoes. Property damage is irrelevant.
E. CORRECT. This will increase the number of tornados recorded. If authorities can't detect a tornado then they can't record it. But the number of tornados that actually occur stays the same whether or not we detect them.

Question 7

QUESTION TYPE: Flawed Reasoning

CONCLUSION: The vast majority of foods will eventually be reported to be good for you.

REASONING: Two foods have been reported to be good for you.

ANALYSIS: Another terribly silly argument. *Two* examples can never prove a general claim. It's doubtful, for example that "poison death berries" or "Oreos" will ever be reported to be healthy. The argument makes a claim about *almost all* food, so it needs evidence about all food.

A. It's true that the chocolate makers are a biased source. But the argument only concluded that food will be *reported* as healthful. So biased reports are fine. The author didn't claim that chocolate actually *is* healthy.
B. The argument uses specific examples to prove a general rule. This answer choice gets things backwards.
C. **CORRECT.** It's like saying "I saw two redheads, so most people must have red hair".
D. It isn't necessary that all research results be reported. The author only needs one positive result to be reported for each food.
E. The author didn't say there would be no reports that food was unhealthy. He just argued that there would be reports that most food was healthy, as well. Reports can contradict each other.

Question 8

QUESTION TYPE: Weaken

CONCLUSION: Removing predators won't hurt an ecosystem.

REASONING: No evidence is given for the conclusion.

ANALYSIS: The theory predicts that plants are most important. More plants leads to more herbivores. Predators eat herbivores, so their numbers will increase too.

This is *true*, but it's not the end of the story. Nature is a system, and effects go both ways. Most ecologists know that if you remove predators, herbivores will run wild and reproduce like mad. Then they eat all the plants, and die. The theory ignores this possibility.

The theory already predicts things will go wrong if you remove plants or herbivores. The right answer has to show a problem that happens because we removed *predators*.

A. The theory would have predicted this. It says that plants are the most important thing.
B. **CORRECT.** This sounds like a problem, and it was caused by removing predators. It seems that predators *do* play an important role in the ecosystem: they keep herbivores in check.
C. This is what the theory would predict. Plants are the most important thing, and removing them destroyed the ecosystem.
D. This is consistent with the theory. Plants feed herbivores. So if herbivores can eat the new plant, there's no problem.
E. The theory says that the number of plants determines how many herbivores can survive. This implies that it will be hard to eliminate a herbivore by hunting, as long as there are plenty of plants to eat. If you cut the herbivore population in half by hunting, each herbivore will have more plants to eat and they'll reproduce more frequently.

Question 9

QUESTION TYPE: Flawed Parallel Reasoning

CONCLUSION: If a kid has unhealthy bones, it's because they didn't eat enough calcium. (~~HB~~ → ~~C~~)

REASONING: If a kid doesn't get enough calcium, their bones will be unhealthy. (~~C~~ → ~~HB~~)

ANALYSIS: This argument reverses its terms. Sure, lack of calcium is bad for bones. But there are other things that are bad for bones. Not every case of bad bones is caused by lack of calcium.

A. This is a good argument. Being baked at the right temperature is a necessary condition for a good crust. GC → BR, ~~BR~~ → ~~GC~~

B. **CORRECT.** Here we go. I can make a cake that tastes terrible, even if I put in enough flour. Would you like to try my moldy lettuce cake? You can draw the statements as: TG → F and ~~TG~~ → ~~F~~. Notice the error is slightly different; the argument incorrectly negated instead of incorrectly reversing. But it's the best answer; the two flaws are essentially the same.

C. The past doesn't guarantee the future. Maybe this year, a brilliant young baker will win. This is a completely different flaw; there's no sufficient-necessary reversal.

D. There are many flaws here. First, maybe baking powder doesn't cause exactly the same amount of rising. Second, maybe baking powder affects taste. Third, maybe there's some other difference. So, baking powder and yeast may not be great substitutes. But there's no reversal flaw, as in the stimulus.

E. Maybe? The reverse is also possible; maybe the best chef in the world always enters the cake category, and so people bake pies to avoid competing with him. But this isn't the reversal flaw from the stimulus, it's just unsupported reasoning.

Question 10

QUESTION TYPE: Weaken

CONCLUSION: Inertia is more important than our desire comfort or safety.

REASONING: People with bad working conditions often didn't like technology.

ANALYSIS: This argument is incredibly vague. Which technologies did the working people oppose? Were the technologies going to help them, or make them worse off? This argument doesn't say that the technologies were going to improve working conditions. Also note the argument doesn't say why working people opposed technology. It pulls inertia out of thin air.

In other words, the working people may have been completely correct to resist the new technology. Technology often helps, but not always, and not everyone.

A. **CORRECT.** This shows that people realized the new technologies were going to cost them their jobs. Their behavior showed self-interest, not inertia.

B. The argument doesn't mention any challenges associated with the technology. The argument didn't say what effects the technology had, good or bad.

C. So? This could mean that 1% of technologies were accepted and 99% were opposed. "Some" and "many" are very vague.

D. The stimulus didn't say whether the technological innovations were rapidly or gradually put into place. And if people "tend" to do something, they may still often *not* do it.

E. We don't know if workers like or dislike being more productive. (They produce more, but maybe the work will be duller). And we don't know if these specific technologies were among those that increase productivity. There still could be quite a few technologies that didn't increase productivity.

Question 11

QUESTION TYPE: Sufficient Assumption

CONCLUSION: Flattery didn't cause the promotions.

REASONING: Bosses usually notice flattery.

ANALYSIS: This is a bad argument. Don't we all like being flattered, even if we know we're being flattered? Maybe bosses promote people who flatter them.

But if we assume that flattery doesn't work when it's noticed, then this argument makes sense.

A. This doesn't tell us whether or not bosses promote people who flatter them. It just says bosses expect flattery.
B. So? Bosses might ignore official guidelines when they promote people. This is irrelevant.
C. The psychologist is talking about flattery that *is* noticed. That might still be effective.
D. This seems to weaken the argument. Some bosses might promote flatterers because they mistakenly think the flatterers admire them.
E. **CORRECT.** If flattery doesn't influence bosses when it's noticed, then the bosses must be promoting flatterers for some other reason.

Question 12

QUESTION TYPE: Principle - Strengthen

CONCLUSION: We shouldn't censor groups that argue it's good to eat raw meat.

REASONING: The author claims that it isn't a good idea to censor political groups for having opinions that could harm people.

ANALYSIS: The author tries an argument by analogy. But analogies can't definitively prove a point. Even if it's true that we shouldn't censor political groups, food groups might be a special case. We might want to censor food groups even if we leave political groups alone.

We need a reason that shows that the reasoning from the political analogy applies to raw meat groups.

A. We don't know if many people think eating raw meat is a good idea.
B. This doesn't help. Maybe it's in the best interests of society to avoid the dangers of raw meat.
C. This tells us what *raw food* advocates should do. It doesn't tell us what the government should do.
D. **CORRECT.** If fear of danger is our only reason, then this principle tells us we have no good reason to censor raw foodists.
E. The argument is talking about what the government should do. It's not talking about what we should tell the government to do.

Question 13

QUESTION TYPE: Weaken

CONCLUSION: Stretching doesn't help joggers prevent injuries.

REASONING: A large group of joggers was split into two. One part stretched, the other didn't. Both had the same injury rate.

ANALYSIS: Consider this: "People who inject insulin live about as long as people who don't. Therefore insulin has no effect on health."

I make the same flaw as in the stimulus: some people (diabetics) need insulin, and that explains why they take it. They live as long as non-diabetics *because* they take insulin. It's silly to say insulin has no effect. Some joggers might know they'll get hurt if they don't stretch, and so they stretch often. Whereas joggers who don't get injured don't stretch. The stretching protects the first group, and brings their injury rate to a normal level.

A. "Lower" is incredibly vague. Maybe the rate was .0001% lower, which is just randomness.

B. How much difficulty did those joggers with injuries experience? Did this affect their future injury rate? And how "many" did this affect? 150 out of 50,000 had difficulties (that's still "many"). This information is too vague.

C. If stretching works, then it would prevent the preventable injuries. It makes sense that the remaining injuries couldn't be prevented. That doesn't mean stretching wasn't useful. This is like saying fire extinguishers don't work because most destructive fires couldn't have been stopped by a fire extinguisher.
Also, "most" is as low as 51%. Maybe stretching can reduce the other 49% of injuries, such as pulling a muscle.

D. CORRECT. Here we go. The joggers who stretched normally had a higher risk of injury, but their injury rate ended up the same. Stretching likely helped lower their rate of injury.

E. This answer talks about severity of injury. The conclusion talks about likelihood of injury. Also, "Certain forms of exercise?". Does that include jogging, or does that just refer to weight-lifting, sprinting, swimming etc?.

Question 14

QUESTION TYPE: Role in Argument

CONCLUSION: Superconductors will increase industrial productivity.

REASONING: Superconductors will let us transport energy more efficiently. Oil and natural gas did the same thing (compared to coal) and productivity increased.

ANALYSIS: Learn which words introduce premises. The word "for" (second sentence) usually introduces a premise that supports the claim that the argument just made.

e.g. "Dogs make good pets (Conclusion), *for* they are friendly (premise).

Synonyms for "for" that serve the same role are: since, because, as, etc. They usually mean that the thing said earlier was the conclusion.

A. CORRECT. The word "for" means that what came earlier was the conclusion.

B. Superconductor development allows more efficient transport. This is a *premise* supporting the conclusion that superconductor development will increase productivity. It doesn't illustrate the claim; we're not told how or why energy efficient transport increases productivity.

C. Not so. Superconductor development will definitely make transport more efficient, whether or not it improves productivity. First sentences are sometimes conclusions, but only if a word such as "for", "because", "since" etc. indicates they're not definitely true and we need to support them with reasons.

D. Those fossil fuels are mentioned as an example. The transition already happened, in the past. Oil replaced coal a long time ago.

E. The statement about shipping costs needs no support. It's given in a dependent clause, surrounded by commas. When writers do this, they're giving us a definition or clarification. i.e. "Winter, the coldest season of the year, came earlier in 1972."

Question 15

QUESTION TYPE: Necessary Assumption

CONCLUSION: Colette wasn't indifferent to moral questions.

REASONING: Colette's works must have raised moral questions.

ANALYSIS: I can raise a moral issue ("Is it *right* to rob this bank?") while being indifferent to it ("I don't care about that, I like money"). This argument assumes that people who raise moral issues care about those issues.

A. Even if the critics didn't greatly underestimate Colette, they might still misunderstand Colette's use of emotional and moral issues.

B. CORRECT. If a novelist who condenses emotional crises *does* have to be indifferent to moral issues, then Colette must have been indifferent to moral issues. This wrecks the argument.

C. The negation is: a novel might be greatly praised even if it doesn't raise moral questions. That doesn't do anything. The author wasn't making a general claim about when a novel deserves praise. They only claimed that Colette did care about moral issues.

D. Who cares why Colette's language was vivid? The only issue was: Did Colette care about moral issues? Her use of language has nothing to do with her beliefs about morality.

E. This would support the author, but it's not *necessary*. Colette might have cared about moral issues, even if that wasn't why she condensed her characters' emotional lives. Also, you don't negate "all" to none. You negate it to 99.9% ("not all").
Negation: "In 99.9% of the cases where she condensed moral emotional crises, it was to explore moral questions. In 0.01% of cases, however, she just did it for fun.", OR
"Collete's novels were concerned with moral issues, even though that isn't why she condensed emotional crises."
Tip: Negations are not some technical issue where you find the right word. You're just identifying the concept, and making it "not true".

Question 16

QUESTION TYPE: Flawed Reasoning

CONCLUSION: The social theorists in question think that trying to achieve democracy is useless.

REASONING: Democracy is impossible if people care only about their own interests. Social theorists think people care only about their own interests.

ANALYSIS: There are at least two flaws. First, it might still be worthwhile to *aspire* to democracy, even if we can never achieve it. Aspiring to run 100 yards in ten seconds can make you run faster, even if you never meet your goal.

Second, the social theorists may not realize what their ideas mean. Few people follow their beliefs to their logical conclusions. Most people who are convinced the world will end soon (for whatever reason) nonetheless contribute to their retirement accounts. Abstractly, the author says: "If A is true, then so is B. These guys believe A, so they must believe B." (the problem is that those guys might not realize A leads to B)

A. CORRECT. The social theorists might just be idiots. They may think that self-interested people can have democracy, even if that is impossible.

B. This answer choices describes a whole-to-part flaw e.g. "America has a mighty military, so you personally must have a mighty army, because you're American". This didn't happen here.

C. This is a part to whole flaw. e.g. "Every cell in your body is tiny. So you must be tiny." It's a common logical flaw, but the author didn't make any claim about the *group* of social theorists who believe we are self-interested. He made a claim about the individuals in that group.

D. Did the author say the social theorists smelled bad? Do they have tiny brains? Do they drool when they speak? You need to find a specific insult if you pick an ad hominem flaw answer.

E. Here's an example of this flaw. Suppose I say: "All humans must die someday. So you will die tomorrow". It's a bad argument, but my premise (we all must die) is still valid. This is completely different from what author does. He says: If A is true, then so is B. These guys believe A, so they must believe B.

Question 17

QUESTION TYPE: Strengthen

CONCLUSION: We should have left the mosaics in the archaeological site that was going to be flooded.

REASONING: We didn't need the mosaics for archeological reasons, and there were archaeological reasons to leave the mosaics: future archaeologists can't find them now.

ANALYSIS: The archaeologist is very self-centered. There might have been other, non-archaeological reasons to take the mosaics. Maybe it would be nice to let people look at them in a museum.

The correct answer eliminates all non-archaeological reasons. If we're only considering archaeological reasons, then the archaeologist is right.

A. CORRECT. The archaeologist has shown there was no *archeological* reason to take the mosaics, and there was an *archaeological* reason to leave them. So if archaeology provides the only reasons, then the argument is good.
B. Future archaeologists might be able to tell whether the site was flooded. But they won't be able to look at the mosaics, because we took them. That was the archaeologist's point.
C. The archaeologist wasn't talking about what mosaics are made of. His point was that if we remove the mosaics, future archaeologists might not realize there ever had been a mosaic at the site.
D. This weakens the argument. It implies that future archaeologists might not be misled.
E. The archaeologist was arguing that future archaeologists might be confused. He didn't mention the environment.

Question 18

QUESTION TYPE: Must be True

FACTS: Financial Predicament Resolved → traffic flow increased → computer modeling investment. (F → T → CM)

ANALYSIS: This is a prime example of a question that's worth diagramming. The stimulus is a collection of sufficient-necessary statements. I find it hard to keep track of what's going on without a diagram to show how they all fit together. Sufficient conditions go on the left, and they lead to necessary conditions on the right. Investing in computer modeling software is therefore a necessary condition for fixing the city's finances.

A. The modeling package worked. But another modeling software package might also have worked just as well. The stimulus didn't say which software was necessary.
B. CORRECT. Computer modeling was essential to increasing traffic flow, and increasing traffic flow was essential to fixing the city's finances. (~~CM~~ → ~~T~~ → ~~F~~)
C. Careful. The question was talking about rush hour traffic. This talks about *all* traffic. Maybe there is less traffic over the bridge during the rest of the day, due to better traffic management.
D. We don't know what the mayor's highest priority was. We only know computer modeling software was *one* of the city's priorities.
E. We have no idea why the mayor wanted computer modeling technology. We know if helped traffic, but the mayor might have wanted it for another reason.

Question 19

QUESTION TYPE: Flawed Reasoning

CONCLUSION: Courts *shouldn't* allow DNA evidence.

REASONING: Scientists don't agree exactly how reliable these tests are.

ANALYSIS: The LSAT loves to play with the precise meaning of words. Controversy doesn't mean that scientists think the tests are worthless. It just means they disagree on how useful they are. So some scientists could think that the tests are 99.9% reliable, while others violently disagree and claim the tests are...99.1% reliable. That's a real difference, but either way the test is useful.

Note that the author gives advice on what courts *should* do. She's aware they're *allowed* to admit DNA evidence, she just thinks they shouldn't.

A. This describes what courts are *allowed* to do. The argument was about what courts *should* do.
B. The argument didn't say evidence had to be 100% certain. The author implied that DNA tests are *much* less than 100% unreliable. It's not a flaw to say that unreliable tests are bad.
C. **CORRECT.** Experts can passionately argue over whether a test is 99.1% or 99.9% accurate. Either way, the test is still very reliable.
D. This *strengthens* the argument. The author thinks we shouldn't admit DNA evidence.
E. So? The author is talking about DNA evidence in criminal cases. Controversies about evidence (all types of evidence) in non-criminal cases aren't relevant.

Question 20

QUESTION TYPE: Must be True

FACTS:

1. Member + more than ten → coupon only at your local store.
2. Member + fewer than ten → coupon only at the Main Street store.
3. Pat has rented less than ten movies and can get a coupon at a local store (Walnut Street, which is not Main Street)

ANALYSIS: Pat rented fewer than ten movies. If Pat were a member, she could only get coupons at the main street store.

Since Pat can get coupons elsewhere, she must *not* be a member. This is the contrapositive of fact #2 above: Can get coupons elsewhere → ~~Member~~ or ten or more movies.

Since Pat is *not* a member, we can say "some people" (i.e. Pat, at least) can get a coupon even if they aren't members. One or more = some. Why can Pat get coupons even if she isn't a member? Maybe it's a special promotion to get people to sign up.

A. The stimulus never says anything about non-members. Maybe they can get coupons at all stores (as a special promotion, for example).
B. We know from the stimulus that Pat is *not* a member. So we *don't* know anything about individual members. Maybe they all rent more than ten movies. The second fact tells us what happens *if* someone rents fewer than ten movies. But that doesn't mean anyone actually *does*.
C. We only have Pat's example, and she isn't a member. We don't know about any members.
D. **CORRECT.** If Pat were a member, she would have to get her coupon at Main street, as she's rented fewer than ten movies. Since she gets her coupon at Walnut street, she must not be a member. And since she can get a coupon, that means at least "some" people can. "Some" can be as few as one.
E. Who knows? Pat isn't a member, so maybe she can get a coupon anywhere. Lots of stores will let you get a discount in exchange for signing up to be a member of their program.

Question 21

QUESTION TYPE: Parallel Reasoning

CONCLUSION: Ed will choose the expensive prize

REASONING: If two prizes are just as good, people will choose based on familiarity or price. These two equally good prizes are equally familiar to Ed.

ANALYSIS: This argument only gives us two factors, and it eliminates one of them. So Ed must choose based on the other factor.

It's important to note that the stimulus describes how someone will behave, in the future. Not all answer choices talk about future behavior.

You might have noticed that I described the prizes as "equally familiar" instead of unfamiliar. This was intentional. "Equally unfamiliar" could mean "not at all unfamiliar", as in: "My mother and father are equally unfamiliar to me". The LSAT is agonizingly precise, and you must learn to think in these terms. "Equally familiar" and "equally unfamiliar" mean the same thing, on the LSAT.

A. This doesn't predict future behavior. The stimulus told us how Ed would choose between two things. In this answer, the choice has already been made: The professor will get an advance. It's a good argument, but the structure is different.

B. This is a bad argument. Maybe the Rocket and the Mouse are right beside each other, at the entrance to the park.

C. Another bad argument. Asteroid X might be affected by another planet's gravity. So asteroid X could also have a highly elliptical orbit.

D. This is a bad argument. Maybe Miyoko really wants to be a physicist. So she enters the program, even though she doesn't want to take classes, because she knows it will let her work as a physicist.

E. CORRECT. This makes a prediction about the rabbit's future behavior. This answer also says that rabbits do one of two things. This answer eliminates one of the possibilities, so the rabbit must do the other.

Question 22

QUESTION TYPE: Strengthen

CONCLUSION: Heavy metals in sludge make bacteria resistant to antibiotics.

REASONING: Heavy metals made bacteria resistant to heavy-metal poisoning.

ANALYSIS: This is a causation-correlation error. Humans brains (including yours) are wired to misunderstand correlations. We see that two things happen and assume that one causes the other.
So the LSAC tests us on this quite a bit. But once you learn to recognize the error, the questions aren't hard. They usually don't add additional tricks. So remember: the fact that two things happen together doesn't mean one causes the other.

You can strengthen a correlation/causation relationship by ruling out alternate explanations. You may know in real life that sewage is full of antibiotics. This is a plausible way to cause antibiotic resistance. You can strengthen the argument by ruling out this possibility. You're definitely allowed to use outside knowledge to form hypotheses, as I just did.

A. So? Thankfully, most bacteria aren't antibiotic resistant. And the stimulus said heavy-metal resistance is unusual. So we shouldn't be surprised that most bacteria are vulnerable to both antibiotics and heavy metals.

B. CORRECT. This amounts to a controlled experiment. Everything else is kept equal, except for heavy metals. And bacteria *don't* become antibiotic resistant. So it must be the heavy metals that cause the resistance to antibiotics.

C. This weakens the argument. It shows that the bacteria were likely antibiotic resistant already. They developed heavy-metal resistance as a result.

D. This weakens the argument. It could be the antibiotics that cause antibiotic resistance.

E. So? This is vague. Many could be "150 kinds of bacteria out of 10 trillion total". And why are they resistant to both heavy metals and antibiotics? This does nothing to help prove that heavy-metals lead to antibiotic resistance.

Question 23

QUESTION TYPE: Sufficient Assumption

CONCLUSION: Love doesn't mean "feelings" when used in marital vows.

REASONING: Love is a feeling, and we can't control feelings. It makes no sense to promise to do something we can't control.

ANALYSIS: The ethicist is an idiot. People make wedding vows to express their deep feeling of commitment and love for each other. They are not making a literal promise that is within their power to uphold, and everyone knows it. So what? It's absurd to think that couples aren't referring to the feeling of love in their wedding vows.

To be fair, the ethicist has correctly proved there are two possibilities: Either the promises don't make literal sense, or "love" refers to something that isn't a feeling. But the ethicist gives no evidence for their conclusion that the second option is more likely correct. The correct answer helps the ethicist by eliminating the first option.

A. This doesn't tell us what people refer to in their wedding vows. They might be making a promise about something they can't control: love.

B. This tells us what people *should* do. But the ethicist was talking about something people *are* doing, and what they mean when they do it. "Should" and "is" are different.
Note: When the ethicist says "no one should take" he's describing what a wedding vow *is,* not what it should be.

C. It's necessary for the ethicist to assume that love can refer to something other than a feeling. But it is not sufficient. Married couples still might refer to feelings in their wedding vows, even if love can refer to other things.

D. CORRECT. If this is true, then "love" must refer to something else. Because the ethicist is right that wedding vows don't make sense. It's just that the ethicist hasn't considered that it might make sense to make a vow that makes no sense. This answer eliminates that possibility.

E. This isn't needed. We already know the wedding vow cannot be kept. So it doesn't matter if other vows that cannot be kept make sense or not.

Question 24

QUESTION TYPE: Principle - Flawed Reasoning

CONCLUSION: We don't need to label this food as containing genetically engineered ingredients.

REASONING: Most people wouldn't care that it contains genetically engineered ingredients. If most people do care, then we should label.

ANALYSIS: This is a classic logical flaw – an incorrect negation of the sufficient condition. We know this statement: Most people care → should label

But that doesn't mean we *shouldn't* label in all other situations. There could be other reasons to say that a food contains genetically engineered ingredients. Maybe a small percentage of people are deathly allergic to the genetically engineered ingredients in question. How can evidence that we should label in some situations also be evidence that we *shouldn't* label in other situations? It doesn't make any sense.

I'll give an example to make things clear: If I say that a park is a good place to walk your dog, do I mean that's the only place you should walk your dog? No. It's good to wear a jacket when it's raining. Do I mean you shouldn't wear one when it's snowing? Not at all. It's good to label products if most people would get upset otherwise. Do I mean you should never label products under other circumstances? Of course not.

A. So? Consumers of food in general don't matter; we only care about consumers of specific foods. For those foods, do most consumers care whether certain ingredients were on the label?

B. The argument claims that Crackly Crisps *shouldn't* be labelled. This answer says the ingredients are safe, which *helps* the conclusion.

C. Which value judgment? The application doesn't say whether labeling is good or bad.

D. This answer choice is about whether people would buy something. The question is about whether we should label something.

E. CORRECT. We should label if people would get upset otherwise. That doesn't mean we don't have to label if few people will get upset. There could be other reasons to label.

Question 25

QUESTION TYPE: Role in Argument

CONCLUSION: The voluntary recycling system is better.

REASONING: A forced recycling system would make some people sort trash, but cause many others to refuse out of resentment. The two systems cost the same.

ANALYSIS: This argument would be stronger if we knew how many people would sort trash under each system. "Some" and "many" are vague words.

But that doesn't matter, we're just supposed to figure out the role of the first sentence. It gives context, by telling us why we should care whether people sort their trash. It explains why some people want to force people to sort their trash: the town would save money.

A. The editorial never casts doubt on this statement. Search all you want, it's not there.The first sentence is presented as fact.
B. **CORRECT.** Normally, we wouldn't want to cause resentment by forcing people to sort their trash. But if it saves money, it might be a good idea.
C. Not at all. The editorial implies that a voluntary program might convince just as many people to sort their trash. A forced program would make make people resist out of resentment.
D. The sentence *weakens* the argument; it's not a premise. The argument would be even *stronger* if sorting didn't save the town money. Then it's hard to see why we should force people to sort their trash.
E. No. There are no words like "for", "since" or "as" that show the first line is the conclusion. It's just a fact. The conclusion is that we shouldn't force people to sort their trash.

Section II – Logic Games

Game 1 – Administrator Parking

Questions 1–6

Setup

This is a linear/sequencing game. You have to figure out how to order the six employees. The last rule is the most restrictive and it makes sense to start there (I always read all the rules before drawing).

The last rule says that R can't go in 5 or 6:

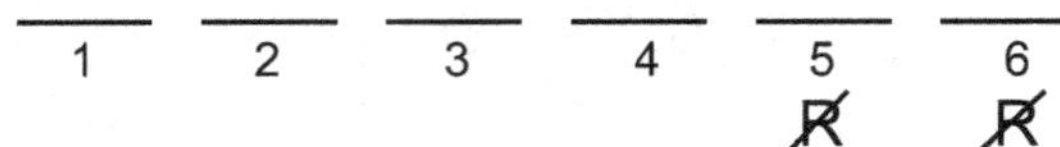

Now you can look at the sequencing rules. Start with one rule, and see what you can add on to it. You can usually combine some or all of them.

T – Y – R

Above, I've combined the first and third rules. It's a good idea to focus first on rules that can be combined. No one said you have to do them in order.

Note that "higher numbered" is to the right in this game. Often "higher" is to the left on sequencing games, so it's easy to get confused. If you're ever uncertain, look to the first question. You'll see they've set it up with the higher numbers to the right.

Here's the second rule. S comes before X. This can't be combined with anything

S – X

The final thing to notice is that V has no rules. You should always check for random variables that have no rules. I draw circles around them.

Before moving on, think about how everything fits together. R has two people in front of it, so it can only go in 3 or 4. Here's what things look like if R is in 3:

S – X, V

T Y R ___ ___ ___
1 2 3 4 5 6
R̸ R̸

Since T and Y come before R, they have to go in 1 and 2.

I've drawn "S – X, V" above the diagram. That shows those three variables come after R. S is before X, and the comma before V shows V is also there, in any order.

There are other ways to draw this, but you should always try to fit rules and variables directly onto the diagram. Otherwise it's easy to forget them. I find placing variables above the lines is a very useful way to remind myself of what the other variables are and where they go.

So in my diagrams, if you see things above the diagram, separated by a comma, it means they go in that area, in any order.

Here's R in four. This diagram is a bit more flexible:

S – X, V

T – Y

R

___ ___ ___ R ___ ___
1 2 3 4 5 6
R̸ R̸

Either S or V could go before R, and S/V could go before, after or between T – Y. You should be aware of these possibilities, but don't try to draw all of them.

I like having this template to help me visualize the possibilities when a question calls for it. Note that the template is a bit unclear. I've drawn S and V after R, but one of them will go before R.

Main Diagram

S – X, V

T Y R
1 2 3 4 5 6
R̸ R̸ (under 5 and 6)

S – X, V

T – Y

R (in 4)
1 2 3 4 5 6
R̸ R̸ (under 5 and 6)

(1) T – Y – R

(2) S – X

(3) (V)

Question 1

The first question is usually easiest to answer by taking the rules one at a time and applying them to the answer choices.

Rule 1 eliminates **A.** Young should be after Togawa.
Rule 2 eliminates **C.** S should be before X.
Rule 3 eliminates **D.** R should be after Y.
Rule 4 eliminates **B.** R cannot be in 5 or 6.

E is **CORRECT.**

Question 2

This question gives us a new rule; these are called local rules because they're specific to the question. They only apply "locally".

You should always draw local rules.

S – T – Y – R
\ X

Now S is in front of T, Y and R. Since R can't go in 5 or 6, this means R must go in 4.

X, V

S T Y R
1 2 3 4 5 6
R̸ R̸ (under 5 and 6)

I've drawn X and V above to show that they come afterwards, in either order. There are no rules about where to put X and V, as long as X is after S.

We can see from the diagram that none of the answer choices can be true except **B**, which is the **CORRECT** answer.

There's only one way to draw STYR with the new rule. Everything becomes clear once you draw the new rule.

Question 3

LSAT games have a lot of moving parts. These questions ask you to pin everything down. That can seem hard, so here's a tip: start with the answer that mentions a random variable. Random variables have no rules, so they're the hardest to force into one place. Watch what happens if we put V in 3:

		V			
1	2	3	4	5	6
				~~R~~	~~R~~

T – Y – R

S – X

I've drawn the ordering rules above. R has to come after T – Y, and R can only go in 3 or 4, so we have to put R in 4, and TY in 1 and 2.

T	Y	V	R		
1	2	3	4	5	6
				~~R~~	~~R~~

Only S and X are left, and we know S comes before X.

T	Y	V	R	S	X
1	2	3	4	5	6
				~~R~~	~~R~~

C is **CORRECT.** Often, it's best to pick the most likely answer and start drawing. It's hard to see how things fit together unless you try.

We saw **A** and **B** and **D** in question 2. S was in 1, Y was in 2 and R was in 4, but we still could choose where to put V and X.

X, V

S	T	Y	R		
1	2	3	4	5	6
				~~R~~	~~R~~

E is wrong because if you put X in 5 you can still choose to put S before or after T – Y.

S, T – Y

			R	X	V
1	2	3	4	5	6
				~~R~~	~~R~~

Question 4

Past diagrams can be useful on this type of question. It also helps to think about variables in groups. Start with the most restricted group: T – Y – R.

R, T and Y can only go in two spots each. R goes in 3 or 4, and that leaves T and Y only two spaces to move in too.

T	Y	R			
1	2	3	4	5	6
				~~R~~	~~R~~

	T	Y	R		
1	2	3	4	5	6
				~~R~~	~~R~~

Most people choose **C.** But X is also restricted to two places. That's because X has to go after S. That leaves only slots 5 or 6 open for X. There's no space for both S and X to go before R.

Here are three different diagrams with X in five or six. I'm also using these diagrams to prove that V and S can go in more than two places:

T	Y	R	S	X	V
1	2	3	4	5	6
				~~R~~	~~R~~

T	Y	R	V	S	X
1	2	3	4	5	6
				~~R~~	~~R~~

S	T	Y	R	X	V
1	2	3	4	5	6
				~~R~~	~~R~~

So T, Y, R and X can only go in two places.
D is **CORRECT.**

Question 5

This question gives us another local rule to draw. If you're not comfortable changing your diagram, or you're not fast at it, then *practice*. It's a supremely important skill for logic games, and you can get better at it.

This should only take about 5–10 seconds to draw. You draw T – Y – R, then draw the new rule showing S in front of Y, then add in your old rule that puts X afterwards:

T — Y — R
  /
S — X

R has to go in 4 because three variables come earlier. Y is in 3 because S and T come earlier. X and V are left to go after R.

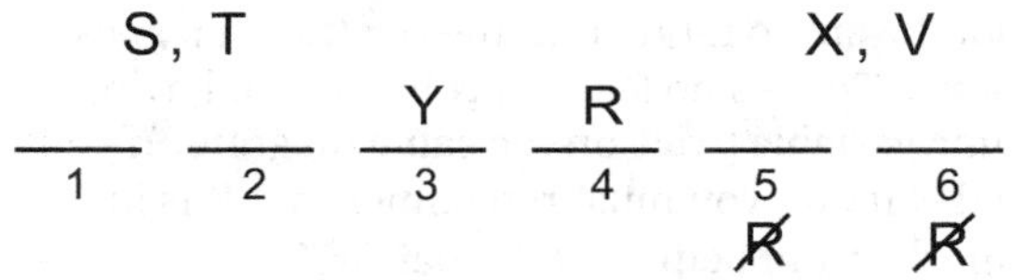

S, T (1, 2) — Y (3) — R (4) — X, V (5, 6)

1	2	3	4	5	6
S, T		Y	R	X, V	
				~~R~~	~~R~~

A is **CORRECT.** T can go in 1 or 2.

You can see from the diagram that **B–E** are wrong. Y and R *have* to be in 3 and 4, and S and V *can't* be in 3 and 4.

Question 6

Another new rule. R is in 3. We saw this at the start. If R is in 3 then T and Y are forced into 1 and 2.

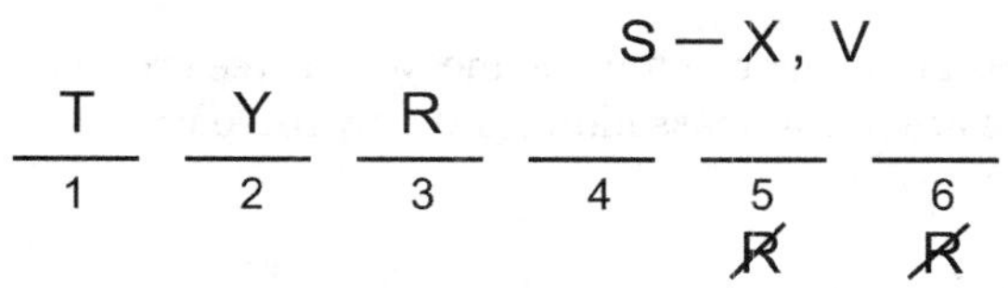

S — X, V

1	2	3	4	5	6
T	Y	R			
				~~R~~	~~R~~

S and X come afterwards, in that order, and V can go anywhere.

A is wrong because S could also go in 5.

B is wrong because T has to be in space 1, not 2.

C is wrong because V could also go in 4 or 6.

D is wrong because X could also go in 5.

E is **CORRECT.** Y is always between T and R. So if R is in 3, Y goes in 2.

Game 2 – Ambassadors
Questions 7–12

Setup

This is an in-out grouping game, with three groups. There are five ambassadors, and only three will be chosen.

The first thing you should always do is read through the rules and think about how to setup the game. Some people start drawing right away, but you should think about the best way to set up the game before you draw anything. Taking the time to do things right usually helps you go faster.

If you're stuck, the first question often shows the best way to do it. On this game, the countries are the groups, and it's easiest to arrange them vertically.

~~L~~ V ___
~~L~~ Y ___
Z ___

I've drawn the final rule on the left of the diagram. L can only go to Zambia. Another way of saying that is: L can't go to Venezuela or Yemen.

There are a couple of ways to draw the first rule. This diagram shows that K and N are never together.

$K \not\leftrightarrow N$

But this is incomplete. It doesn't show that one of K and N has to be in. Also, you can't connect this type of diagram to other rules.

I've come to prefer drawing this type of rule a different way, on games where you can join several rules together (like this one. We'll get to that soon).

K ⟶ ~~N~~ ⟶ K

N ⟶ ~~K~~ ⟶ N

This is confusing at first, but it's very effective. If you have K, you don't have N. And if you don't have N, you do have K.

If you draw the two halves of the rule separately, it's very easy to forget half of the rule. I get to watch a lot of students do logic games, and forgetting easy rules is one of the most common problems.

So I've drawn the two halves together as a reminder. You don't want to forget that the relationship goes both ways. There's no logical problem with having the same variable twice on the same diagram. If you are told N if out, you must remember that K is in, and this diagram helps you do that.

Once you split these diagrams into two and write down the full rule, there's quite a bit you can do. Look at the second rule. We can add it to the first diagram, to get this.

J ⟶ K ⟶ ~~N~~ ⟶ K

O/L

If J is in, you know almost everything. You have J and K, and you're missing N. You need one of O and L too, to get three ambassadors.

N → K → N was the other diagram. Here's the second rule combined with the other diagram:

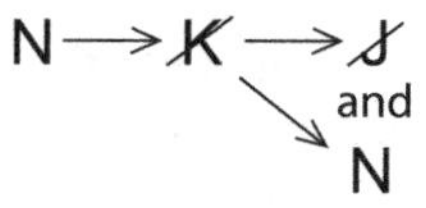

N ⟶ ~~K~~ ⟶ ~~J~~
  ↘ and
  N

If you have N, you don't have K and you don't have J. And if you don't have K, you do have N.
You may still be wondering why it's important to write N twice. Well, some questions may start by saying "K is not assigned to an ambassadorship". If you don't write the second N, you might forget about that rule, and only focus on the rule that says J isn't in.

I can't count how many times I see students forget rules; the games are designed to make you forget.

When you write both rules on the diagram this way, you literally cannot forget. It's right there, staring you in the face. You no longer have to think about it, you can simply apply the rules. Most students' mistakes come from forgetting rules they drew correctly.

Drawing both rules also lets you make a further deduction from this diagram. You need three out of five candidates. If N is in, you lose K and J. So you need O and L to make three.

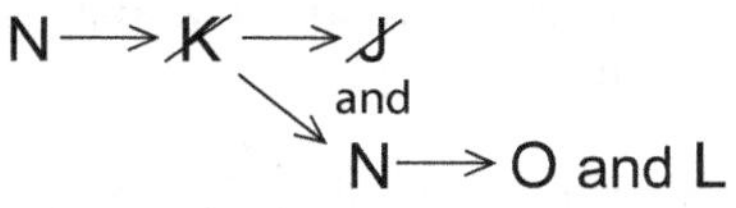

N ⟶ ~~K~~ ⟶ ~~J~~
  ↘ and
  N ⟶ O and L

If N is in, we know almost everything that happens. L is assigned to Z, and N and O go with V or Y.

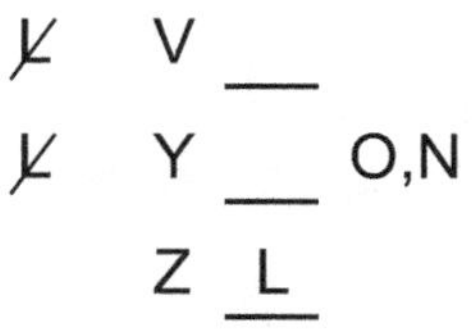

~~L~~ V ___
~~L~~ Y ___ O,N
Z L

The last rule is simple. If you see O with V, then K is not with Y.

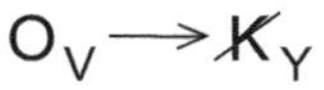

$O_V \longrightarrow$ ~~K~~$_Y$

As it turns out, these diagrams aren't much use on the questions for this game. But I wanted to show you how to make them, for two reasons:

They usually *are* very useful.
If you know how to make this sort of diagram, then you truly understand the game. You'll do well on the questions, whether or not you actually need the diagrams.

You should get in the habit of making deductions and making complete diagrams whenever you can.

There's one other thing you should know for each game. You should know all of the rules, by heart if possible. If you can't remember them, then have them all in a list. On this game, you can solve most questions by mechanically applying the rules to eliminate answer choice. The rules are:

1. Exactly one of K or N is in.
2. If J is in, K is in. If K is out, J is out.
3. If O is in assigned to V, K is not assigned to Y.
4. L can only be assigned to Z.

Know these four rules, and the game is simple. A good setup for this game would be the two diagrams I drew below, and the list of rules.

Main Diagram

Scenario 1

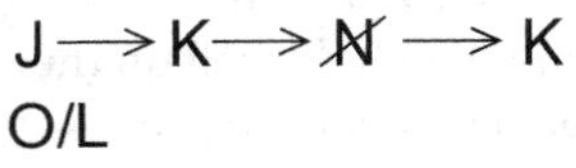

$J \rightarrow K \rightarrow \not{N} \rightarrow K$

O/L

Scenario 2 (Contrapositive)

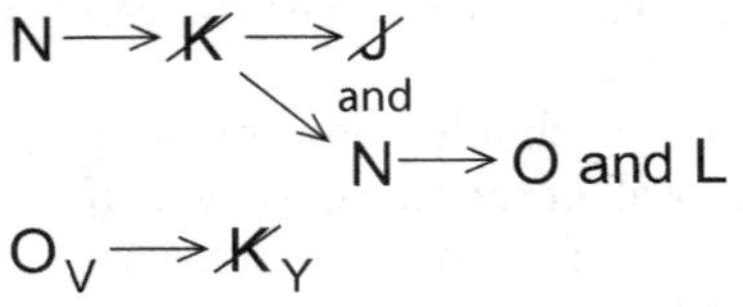

$N \rightarrow \not{K} \rightarrow \not{J}$

and

$N \rightarrow$ O and L

$O_V \rightarrow \not{K}_Y$

This game can be reduced to three simple diagrams that let you solve everything easily. If you're unsure about them, then go back to the rules and try to set them up yourself. Learning to make this sort of diagram makes many games incredibly easy.

Here are the rules again:

1. Exactly one of K or N is in.
2. If J is in, K is in. If K is out, J is out.
3. If O is in assigned to V, K is not assigned to Y.
4. L can only be assigned to Z.

Question 7

As with almost all first questions, you should use the rules to eliminate each answer choice, one by one. Each rule generally eliminates one answer.

A is wrong because J needs K (second rule).

B is **CORRECT.**

C is wrong because L can't be assigned to any country except Z (last rule).

D is wrong because N and K can't go together (first rule).

E is wrong because if O is assigned to V then K can't be assigned to Y (third rule).

Question 8

These questions are hard, because you also have to think about the candidates who *are* assigned to ambassadorships. The easiest way is to write down the three ambassadors beside each answer choice.

A is **CORRECT.**

B assigns K, N and L to ambassadorships. K and N can't go together (first rule).

C is wrong because J is in. If J is in then K has to be in too, not out (second rule).

D is wrong because one of K or N always has to be in (first rule).

E is wrong because it puts J, K and N in ambassadorships. K and N can't both be assigned (first rule).

Question 9

Your first step on local rule questions should always be to draw the new rule, and make deductions. If O is in V, then K can't be assigned to Y (the third rule).

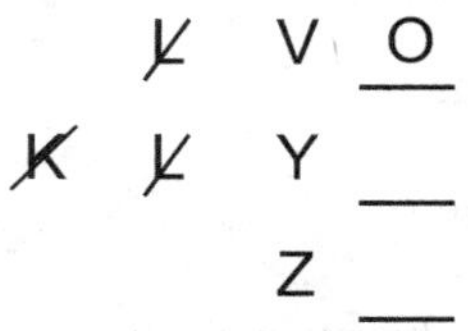

~~L~~ V O

~~K~~ ~~L~~ Y ___

Z ___

A is wrong because one of K or N needs to be in (first rule).

B is wrong because if J is in, K needs to be in too (second rule).

C is wrong because K can't be assigned to Y in this case (third rule) and L can never be assigned to Y (fourth rule). Y needs someone to be assigned to it.

D is wrong because K and N can't go together (first rule).

E is **CORRECT.** L can be assigned to Z and N can be assigned to Y.

Question 10

You should also draw this local rule question. Since K is in Yemen, O can't be assigned to Venezuela (third rule). We know N can't be in, because K is in (first rule). L can never be assigned to Venezuela either.

So the only person left who can be assigned to Venezuela is K. One of L or O will be assigned to Z.

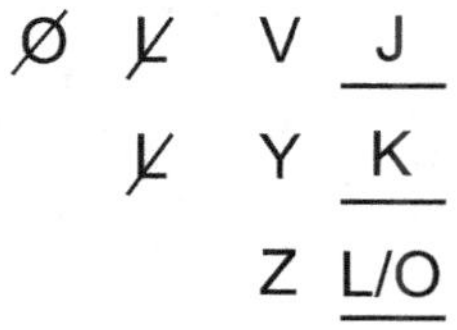

Ø ~~L~~ V J

~~L~~ Y K

Z L/O

A is **CORRECT.** J must be ambassador to Venezuela.

B could be true, but O could be assigned to Z instead.

C could be true, but L could be assigned to Z instead.

D *cannot* be true. J has to be assigned to V, because no one else can go there.

E could be true, but it's possible for O to be assigned to Z.

Question 11

This diagram proves **A** could be true:

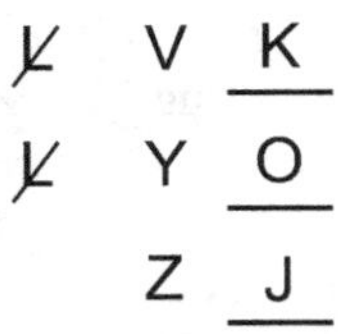

L̸ V K
L̸ Y O
Z J

This diagram proves **B** could be true:

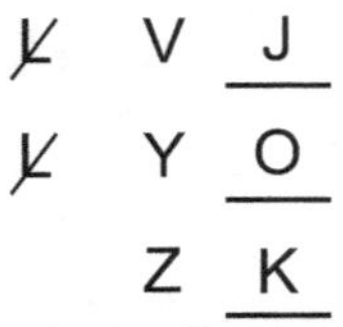

L̸ V J
L̸ Y O
Z K

C is **CORRECT.** We saw in the setup that if N is in, K and J are out, and O and L are in. If L is in, L must be assigned to Zambia, so N cannot go there.

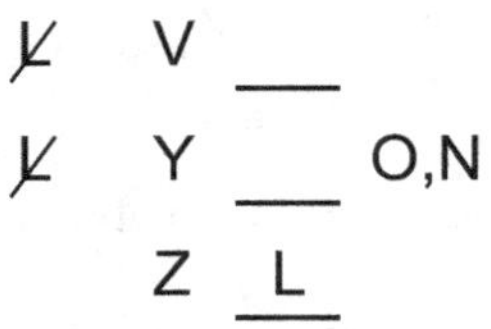

L̸ V ___
L̸ Y ___ O,N
Z L

This diagram from question ten proves that **D** and **E** could both be true. Either L or O can sit out:

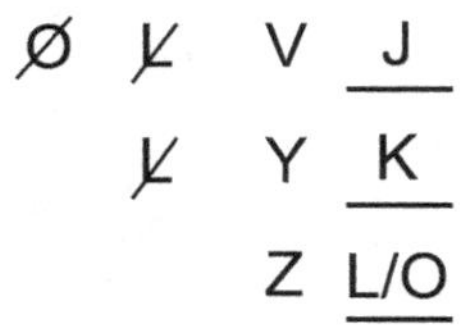

Ø L̸ V J
L̸ Y K
Z L/O

Question 12

The final question of a game sometimes asks you to substitute a rule. Many people find these questions very difficult, but they don't have to be. You should ask yourself what the main effect of the rule is.

If J is in, K is in. That forces N out.

If N is in, K is out. That forces J out.

So J and N can never go together, because of the combination of the first and second rules. And if J is in, and N is out, then K must be in, because we always need one of either N or K (the first rule).

So the right answer has to force N out if J is in, and force J in. Any secondary effect of a rule is almost the only way the LSAT can make a rule substitution answer work.

Answer choice **D** is **CORRECT.** It captures all of this information. If J being in causes N to be out, then K to has to be in, thanks to the first rule. Everyone works out the same.

A gets the second rule backwards, and so it has a different effect.

B has a different effect as well. Previously, it was possible to have K, O and L all in together. Now this can't happen. And this answer also ignores the main effect of the second rule: now J no longer forces K in.

C is way off base. There was no such relation between O and K in the original setup, and this new rule leave J with no effect on K.

E contradicts the old setup. The original rules combine to the effect that if N is in, O and L are in. See the setup for more detail on this point.

Game 3 – Cycling Study
Questions 13–18

Setup

This is a grouping game. There are four bicycles, and four riders. The riders test one bicycle per day, for two days. They don't test the same bicycle both days.

The first thing you should always do is read through the rules and think about how to setup the game. If you're stuck, the first question usually shows the best way to do it. Here, it's best to arrange the bicycles vertically.

F ___ ___
G ___ ___
H ___ ___
J ___ ___

The first three rules are simple to add. R doesn't test F, and Y doesn't test J. You can draw those variables to the left of each bike, with lines through them. That reminds you not to put that rider with that bicycle.

T has to test H, once. You can draw T to the right of H, to remind yourself. Don't think you won't forget. You might get lucky, but in general, people who don't write down rules forget them at some point. At best, you'll go slower because you'll have to look away from your diagram to remember the rules.

~~R~~ F ___ ___
G ___ ___
H ___ ___ T
~~Y~~ J ___ ___

The last rule is the key to the game. YS go together on one of the bicycles. Y tests it first, then S.

Where can they go? Not J, because Y can never test J. They also can't test H.

Why? Because if YS go in H, then there's no room for T to go in H. So YS go in either F or G.

Note that it's only on the *first* day that Y can't test H. Y could test H on the second day; the rule with S only applies to Y's first day.

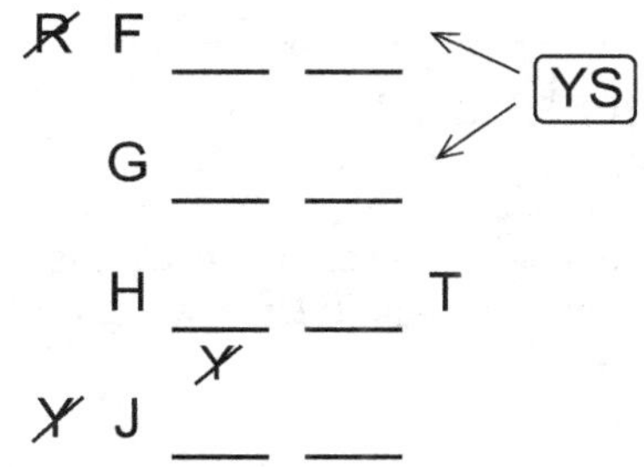

That diagram above tells us every rule. If you're not sure how it works, then reread the rules to see how it's built. If you know this diagram well, the game is easy.

Keep one main diagram that looks like this, then draw a simpler diagram when you have to make one for an individual question. You can usually leave off details like the T, since you'll be often be putting T in H based on information the question gives you.

Main Diagram

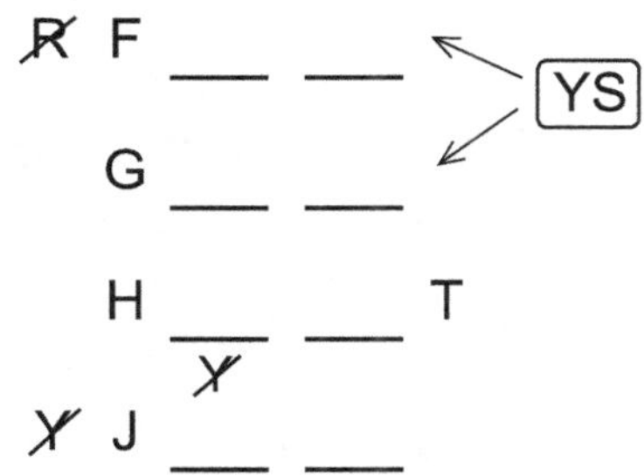

Question 13

It's almost always easiest to solve the first question of each game one rule at a time. Forget your diagram, for this question only.

A is wrong because R can't test F. (rule 1)

B is wrong because T has to test H once. (rule 3)

C is **CORRECT.**

D is wrong because Y can't test J. (rule 2)

E is wrong because S has to test the bicycle Y tests on the first day. (rule 4)

Question 14

As with all local rule questions, you should draw the new rule on a diagram and see what it lets you figure out.

		Day 1	Day 2
~~R~~	F		
	G		T
	H	T ~~Y~~	
~~Y~~	J		

If T tests G on the second day then T must test H on the first day. The third rule says T has to test H at some point.

Next, we see where we can place YS. Y can't test J, so YS must test F.

		Day 1	Day 2
~~R~~	F	Y	S
	G		T
	H	T ~~Y~~	
~~Y~~	J		

This also lets you know which bicycle Y tests on the second day. Only H and J are left. Y can't test J, so Y must test H on the second day.

		Day 1	Day 2
~~R~~	F	Y	S
	G		T
	H	T ~~Y~~	Y
~~Y~~	J		R

R and S both have to test a bike on day 1, so we have to place them in the only two days that are left. R tests G (because R tests J on day 2) and S tests J on day 1.

		Day 1	Day 2
~~R~~	F	Y	S
	G	R	T
	H	T ~~Y~~	Y
~~Y~~	J	S	R

This lets us see that **E** is **CORRECT.** A–D not only don't have to be true, they can't be true.

Question 15

If you followed along in the setup, it's easy to see that **D** is **CORRECT.** If Y tests H on the first day, then S has to test H on the second day. That leaves no room for T to test H.

So Y can't test H on the first day.

		Day 1	Day 2	
~~R~~	F	___	___	
	G	___	___	
	H	Y	S	T?
		~~Y~~		
~~Y~~	J	___	___	

This diagram proves A and C could be true.

		Day 1	Day 2
~~R~~	F	Y	S
	G	R	Y
	H	[S]	T
		~~Y~~	
~~Y~~	J	T	[R]

The diagram from question 14 proves that B and E could be true. R tests J on the second day and Y tests H on the second day.

		Day 1	Day 2
~~R~~	F	Y	S
	G	R	T
	H	T	[Y]
		~~Y~~	
~~Y~~	J	S	[R]

Question 16

The correct answer from question 13 proves **A** can be true. R tests G on the second day.

The following diagram proves **B, D** and **E** could be true:

		Day 1	Day 2
~~R~~	F	[S]	[Y]
	G	Y	S
	H	[R]	T
		~~Y~~	
~~Y~~	J	T	R

C is **CORRECT.** If T tests F on the second day, then T must test H on the first day. YS have to test G, there's no space anywhere else.

		Day 1	Day 2
~~R~~	F	___	T
	G	Y	S
	H	T	Y
~~Y~~	J	___	___

This doesn't work: there's no place to put R for the first day of testing. R can't test F, so R would have to test J on both the first and second days. That doesn't work.

Question 17

By adding the new rule, we get this diagram.

```
R̸ F ___ ___

  G ___ ___

  H ___ _T_
     Y̸
Y̸ J ___ ___
```

This doesn't seem like much of a deduction. But it eliminates answers **C, D** and **E**!

C: H on the second day is now full
D: S's second day has to come after Y, not T. So S can't test J on the second day.
E: T can't test G, because both Ts have been placed.

The following diagram proves **B** is **CORRECT.**

```
R̸ F _Y_ _S_

  G _R_ _Y_

  H [S] _T_
     Y̸
Y̸ J _T_ _R_
```

And this diagram shows why **A** can't be true. There's no place to put Y on the second day. Y can't test J.

```
R̸ F _Y_ _S_

  G _S_ _R_

  H [R] _T_
     Y̸
Y̸ J _T_ ___  Y?
```

The trick to solving these questions is to eliminate answers. Once you realize the local rule eliminates **C, D** and **E,** you can take a bit of time to draw diagrams and decide between **A** and **B.** There's no other shortcut. Diagrams let you understand how everything fits together.

For example, the diagram that proves R can't test H on the first day should draw itself, once you try putting R there and see what other rules are affected. If you're not sure how I got that diagram, recreate it yourself. It's the best way to learn.

Question 18

Past questions can be useful on cannot be true questions. Any past diagram that works can prove an answer could be true. Could be true answers are wrong.

The diagram from question 14 proves that R and S can both test J. **A** is wrong.

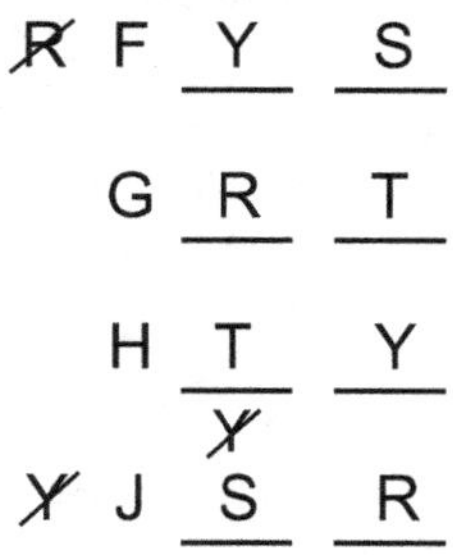

```
R̸ F  Y   S
   G  R   T
   H  T   Y
      Y̸
Y̸ J  S   R
```

The diagram from question 17 shows that R and T can both test J. It also shows that R and Y can test G. So **B** and **C** are wrong.

```
R̸ F  Y   S
   G  R   Y
   H  S   T
      Y̸
Y̸ J  T   R
```

D is **CORRECT.** Seamus' second day always has to come after Y's first day. So Seamus could only test G with T on his first day.

That means T goes in the first day of H. Y and S have to test F, since Y can't test J.

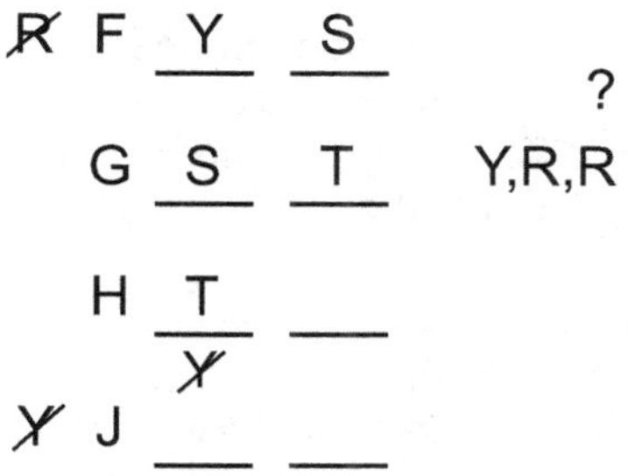

```
R̸ F  Y   S
                 ?
   G  S   T    Y,R,R
   H  T   __
      Y̸
Y̸ J  __  __
```

There's no way to fit Y's other test and both of R's tests in the remaining spots, since Y can't test J. If you have Y test H on the second day, R is forced to test J both days, which isn't allowed.
This diagram shows that T and Y could both test F, so **E** is wrong.

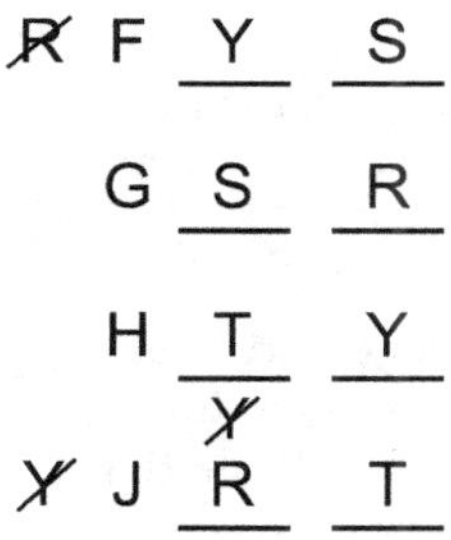

```
R̸ F  Y   S
   G  S   R
   H  T   Y
      Y̸
Y̸ J  R   T
```

Game 4 – Bookshelves
Questions 19-23

Setup

This is a grouping game, with a bit of numerical uncertainty. There are at least two books on each shelf, but there are two different possibilities for the number of books on shelves 1 and 2.

That comes from the first rule. The third shelf (bottom) has more books than the first shelf (top). There are eight books in total. Each shelf has to have at least two books. The only way we can put more on the bottom is to put at least three books there and put only two books on the top shelf. These are the two orders, from top to bottom:

2 - 3 - 3

2 - 2 - 4

Both total to 8. If we put three books on the top shelf and four books on the bottom, we'd only have one book left for the middle shelf.

You can draw the last three rules together. K is higher than F and M (which are on the same shelf). O is higher than L. The vertical lines indicate that one variable comes higher than the other.

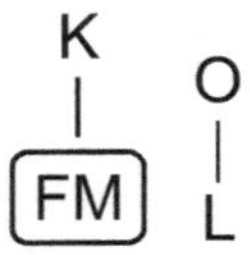

```
  K
  |     O
 [FM]   |
        L
```

It's best to draw rules 3 and 5 rules together: K is higher than both F and M. I often see students draw rules separately, then get lost on their own page. Drawing a smaller number of rules, together, helps you go faster and avoid mistakes.

We can add those rules to a main diagram. I've drawn three horizontal rows to show books on the three bookshelves.

O and K can't go on the bottom shelf (labelled shelf 3) and L, F and M can't go on the top shelf. If K were on the bottom, for example, there'd be no way for FM to be below K.

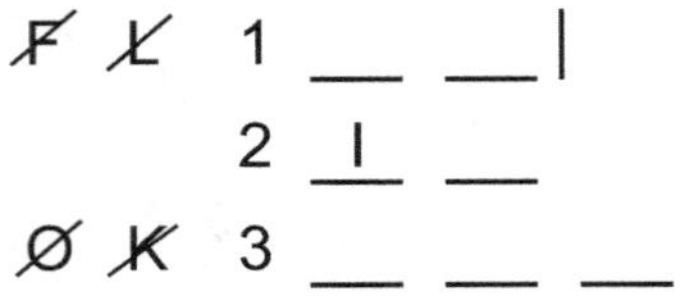

```
F̸ L̸  1 ___ ___|
      2 _I_ ___
Ø K̸  3 ___ ___ ___
```

I is on the middle shelf. It's best to draw that directly on the diagram. Order doesn't matter, so I just put I on the left.

The vertical line by shelf 1 means that there can only be two books on that shelf.

The lack of a vertical line by the other two shelves means an extra book can be added to one of them. Shelf three has at least three books, because the bottom shelf needs more books than the top shelf.

G and H are random variables, with no rules attached to them (I draw circles around random variables).

F,Ⓖ,Ⓗ,I,K,L,M,O

If it helps you visualize things, you could draw two separate shelf setups to show the different numbers of books that could go on the bottom two shelves. One diagram would have four books on the bottom, and one would have three books on the bottom and three on the middle.

I didn't find that useful. Instead, I thought it was helpful to visualize what happens when F and M go on the second shelf.

```
F̸ L̸   1 _K_ ___|
      2 _I_ _F_ _M_|
Ø K̸   3 ___ ___ ___|
```

K has to go on the top shelf, because K must go above F.

O has to go on the top shelf too, because O has to go above L.

```
F̸ L̸   1 _K_ _O_|
      2 _I_ _F_ _M_|
Ø K̸   3 _L_ ___ ___|
```

In this case, the random variables G and H are forced to go on the bottom shelf. There's no space elsewhere.

```
F̸ L̸   1 _K_ _O_|
      2 _I_ _F_ _M_|
Ø K̸   3 _L_ _G_ _H_|
```

So if F and M are on shelf 2, everything falls into place.

The other scenario (F and M are on the bottom) is less interesting, but it's still worth drawing. Drawing it will remind you that FM are on the bottom shelf in all scenarios that *don't* look like the one I drew above.

```
F̸ L̸   1 ___ ___|
      2 _I_ ___
Ø K̸   3 _F_ _M_ ___
```

Main Diagram

First scenario – FM are on bottom:

```
F̸ L̸   1 ___ ___|
      2 _I_ ___
Ø K̸   3 _F_ _M_ ___
```

```
(1)  K
     |
    [FM] =

(2)  O
     |
     L

(3)  F,(G),(H),I,K,L,M,O
```

In the first scenario, there are either two books in the middle and four books on the bottom, or three books on each shelf.

Second scenario – FM are on middle shelf. See setup for how to build this:

```
F̸ L̸   1 _K_ _O_|
      2 _I_ _F_ _M_|
Ø K̸   3 _L_ _G_ _H_|
```

Question 19

Usually, the first question on a game is a list question. When there's no list question, it's a strong sign that you were expected to make many deductions.

A is wrong because there must be at least three books on the bottom shelf. The bottom shelf must have more books than the top shelf.

B is **CORRECT**, as shown by this diagram which obeys all of the rules.

~~F~~ ~~L~~ 1 O K |

2 I L G

Ø ~~K~~ 3 H F M

C and **D** are wrong because K and O can't be on the bottom shelf. K has to be above FM, and O has to be above L.

E is wrong because M needs to go with F.

Question 20

A is **CORRECT.** M always goes with F. If M is with I, that means FM goes on the middle shelf.

In the setup, we saw that placing FM on the middle shelf determined everything:

~~F~~ ~~L~~ 1 K O |

2 I F M |

Ø ~~K~~ 3 L G H |

This is what the diagram looks like if FM are on the bottom shelf instead:

~~F~~ ~~L~~ 1 __ __ |

2 I __

Ø ~~K~~ 3 F M __

If FM are on the bottom shelf, this game is almost impossible to lock down. There's one more book to place: the 8th book can go on shelf three or four.

None of the remaining answers deal with this. Answers **B, C** and **E** place one of the random variables, G and H. That really doesn't do much in this game.

K and G (answer **B**) and H and O (answer **E**) could both go together on either the top or the middle shelf. They're very easy to move around, if F and M are on the bottom shelf.

If F, H and M are all on the bottom (**D**), we still get to decide whether we want to put a fourth book on the bottom, or put a third book on the middle shelf.

The same is true of **C**. If you put L and F together, they go on the bottom. M goes there too, with F. You still get to decide whether to put a fourth book with them, or a third book on the middle shelf instead.

Question 21

Let's start with **A.** It says O must always be higher than M. This is true. O can never go on the bottom shelf: it has to go higher than L. So if FM are on the bottom shelf, O is higher.

When FM are on the middle shelf, O goes on the top shelf. It's the only way to put O above L.
This is the scenario from the setup: placing FM on the middle shelf determines *everything*. It's the only way to put O higher than L.

```
F̸ L̸  1 _K_ _O_ |
      2 _I_ _F_ _M_ |
Ø K̸  3 _L_ _G_ _H_ |
```

So, **A** is **CORRECT.** No matter where you place FM, O is always higher.

The diagram above also proves **C** wrong. I and F can be placed on the same shelf. The diagram likewise proves **D** wrong: G is lower than O.

E is wrong. We've seen plenty of diagrams where FM are on the bottom shelf, lower than L. The diagram below proves it.

Finally, **B** is wrong because G is a random variable. It's really easy to put G above K. Here's one example.

```
F̸ L̸  1 _O_ _G_ |
      2 _I_ _L_ _K_
Ø K̸  3 _H_ _F_ _M_
```

Question 22

The first step with any local rule question is to draw the new rule onto a diagram.

```
F̸ L̸  1 _G_ ___ |
      2 _I_ ___
Ø K̸  3 _F_ _M_ ___
```

In the setup, we saw that placing FM on the middle determines *everything*. When FM are on the middle shelf, G can't go on the top shelf. So FM must go on the bottom shelf for this question.

Both K and O have to be on either the middle or the top shelf. We saw this in the setup. K is above F and O is above L. That leaves at least one of L and H to fill the third space on the bottom shelf.

(The other L/H could go on another shelf.)

```
F̸ L̸  1 _G_ ___ |     K,O
      2 _I_ ___
Ø K̸  3 _F_ _M_ _L\H_
```

There are, at most, three spaces left for K and O: one or two on the middle shelf, and one on the top shelf. I've drawn them up and to the right as a reminder that they must be placed somewhere above the bottom shelf.

The wrong answers fail because of this. They put too many variables on the middle shelf, and thus there's no room for K and O to go above F and L.

A is tricky if you forget that the answer choices show us a *complete* list. H and I could go on the middle shelf if one of K and O went there too, but H and I can't go there alone.

B has the same problem as A. We'd need L, I and one of K and O for it to work.

C is even worse. There's only one spot on the top shelf left for K and O, and no spots left on the middle.

D is **CORRECT.** This diagram shows how it could work.

```
F̸ L̸  1  G  O |
      2  I  K  L
Ø K̸  3  F  M  H
```

E is wrong because if FM are on the middle shelf then both K and O must go on the top shelf, forcing G onto the bottom. It's the scenario from the setup and question 20, where everything falls into place.

It's a major part of the game. If you're not sure how it works, reread the setup and try to create the scenario yourself. Start by placing FM on the middle shelf, and apply each rule in turn. It's a necessary skill to learn.

Question 23

Another local rule, another local diagram. We now know that O is above L and L is above H.

You can draw that rule. Or you can just insert each letter on the diagram; there's only one way to put them in that order.

```
F̸ L̸  1  O  __ |
      2  I  L
Ø K̸  3  H  __  __
```

You're not done yet. When building local diagrams, focus on the most restricted variable. In this game, it's F, which has two rules.

F has to go with M, and the only place you can fit them is on the bottom shelf.

```
F̸ L̸  1  O  __ |
      2  I  L
Ø K̸  3  H  F  M
```

Now we only have G and K left to place. K could go either on the top or middle shelf, and G could go anywhere. Just remember the extra shelf goes either in the middle or on the bottom.

A, B and **D** are wrong because G can still go anywhere. It could go on the top if K went on the middle, or on the middle or bottom if K went on the top.

E is wrong for the same reason. G could go on the top, and K would go on the middle shelf.

C is **CORRECT.** H and M are always on the bottom.

Section III – Logical Reasoning

Question 1

QUESTION TYPE: Complete the Argument

CONCLUSION: We should preserve hot spots.

REASONING: Hot spots have many unique species, and these unique species are the most likely to become extinct. Environmentalists can only fight a certain number of battles.

ANALYSIS: This argument makes sense. Environmentalists should use their limited resources to preserve hot spots, as that gives them the best chance of keeping endemic species alive.

Working to keep hot spots is the only logical way to end the argument. Otherwise, why mention hot spots? The whole argument is devoted to showing how important they are.

A. Which species and which habitats? The argument is talking about a specific type of habitat: "hot spots".
B. **CORRECT.** Hot spots have species that can't be found anywhere else, so it makes sense to protect them first.
C. Why? Some endemic species might be more worthy of preservation than others. If there was an endemic species of plant that cured cancer, wouldn't you rather preserve that than an endemic species that gives people itchy rashes?
D. The conclusion is that we should "give up"? That's encouraging....but seriously, the argument isn't saying everything is hopeless. It's just saying we need to pick our battles. Hot spots seem like a logical place to direct our efforts.
E. How would changing the meaning of a word help preserve species? This is just useless semantics.

Question 2

QUESTION TYPE: Principle – Flawed Reasoning

CONCLUSION: Wilton committed fraud.

REASONING: Wilton didn't know whether the bicycle was good, but he said it was. If you *know something is not good* and say it is good, then you commit fraud.

ANALYSIS: Wilton was just reckless. For all he knew, the bicycle might have been good; he just got unlucky. It would only have been fraud if Wilton was sure the bicycle wasn't good.

A. Why would Wilton have tried to fix the brakes if he got the chance? He didn't know there was anything wrong with them.
B. Fraud is a flexible word. Fraud can be worth $1 or $1,000,000,000.
C. Defective is clear both times. It means: not working.
D. You can commit fraud even if the other person doesn't believe you. The principle doesn't say anything about the buyer's belief.
E. **CORRECT.** Lying means saying something you definitely know is false. Wilton just took a risk. As far as he knew, the bike *could* have been fine.

Question 3

QUESTION TYPE: Complete the Argument

CONCLUSION: Boats affect killer whales' hearing. (my guess at the conclusion)

REASONING: Engine noise is on the same frequency as killer whales' hearing. And it can be loud enough to hurt their hearing.

ANALYSIS: If whales scream at frequencies between 100-3000 hertz, they must be able to hear at those frequencies. And the boats engines make noise on those frequencies that is loud enough to damage whales' hearing.

So it's reasonable to conclude that the engines affect whales ability to communicate, either by hurting their hearing or by drowning out their screams.

A. The argument never says whether younger or older whales are most affected.
B. The argument says whales don't seem to behave differently when boats pass overhead. So maybe they do try to communicate just as often.
C. **CORRECT.** The whole argument is leading to this point. It's less specific than B, which makes it more likely to be correct. We don't know exactly how whales' communication is impaired, but the boat engines probably make things difficult. The engines make noise on the same frequency as whale screams, and the noise is so loud that it hurts hearing.
D. We have no idea where whales will be. Maybe their best feeding grounds also happen to be beneath shipping lanes.
E. Who knows? Maybe the engines confuse fish, and make it easier for whales to eat them.

Question 4

QUESTION TYPE: Flawed Reasoning

CONCLUSION: Bruch Industries isn't a member.

REASONING: Bruch Industries isn't on the list. Every company on the list is a member.

On list → Member

ANALYSIS: Let's say I give you a list of 100,000,000 US citizens. Does that mean anyone not on the list isn't American?

Obviously not, there are over 200,000,000 other Americans. The journalist's list is accurate, but it might not be *complete.*

The flaw here is negating the sufficient condition.

A. Why do we care what Bruch Industries wants? We only need to know whether or not they are in the trade group.
B. **CORRECT.** The list might only include half of the organization's members. No one said the list was complete.
C. Who cares why the journalist has the list? We only need to know whether it is accurate and complete.
D. The argument claims Bruch Industries *isn't* a member. So how could this answer be a flaw in the argument? This answer says Bruch *is* a member.
Also, it might not up to the members to say whether they are members. It could be group policy that no one can reveal their membership, even if they want to.
E. The representative *could* be lying, but it doesn't matter. Whether or not the list is accurate, it can't prove that Bruch isn't a member. Even if the list is accurate, the argument is still bad.

Question 5

QUESTION TYPE: Point at Issue

ARGUMENTS: Peter says that children's stories should have immoral characters so that kids can learn from them.

Yoko argues that children's stories still have immoral characters, but that the characters are less frightening than they used to be.

ANALYSIS: The two of them disagree over whether children's stories still have immoral characters. Peter says no, Yoko says yes.

A. Peter doesn't say anything about whether children's stories are or should be frightening.
B. Same as A. Only Yoko mentions that stories used to be frightening.
C. Neither of them mentions whether children's stories are good.
D. CORRECT. Peter complains that children's stories don't have immoral characters anymore. Yoko says they do, the characters just aren't frightening anymore.
E. Peter thinks stories should improve children's morals. Yoko doesn't say, she just thinks stories shouldn't frighten kids.

Question 6

QUESTION TYPE: Flawed Reasoning

CONCLUSION: An excess of algae is bad for the small fish in the pond.

REASONING: The gardener has seen lots of algae whenever he has seen many small fish wash up dead on the shore.

ANALYSIS: The gardener is confusing correlation and causation. He could have also said that dead fish cause algae to bloom. Just because two things happen together doesn't mean one causes the other.

It's possible there is something in the water which both kills fish *and* helps algae grow.

Note that the gardener says nothing about larger fish. There may not even be any in the pond; the gardener could be comparing the pond's "smaller" fish to the larger fish found in rivers and oceans.

A. The gardener didn't say anything about larger fish. Maybe there aren't any in the pond. The gardener could have said "smaller fish" just to make clear that the fish were small compared to bigger fish that live in lakes and oceans.
In any case, there is justification: small fish from the pond are clearly dead.
B. The gardener was only talking about the pond. He might agree that algae can't harm fish in a river or big lake.
C. The gardener didn't say whether algae hurts larger fish too. He only talked about the pond, and there may be no large fish in the pond.
In any case, the gardener explicitly said that smaller fish are vulnerable, and implied larger fish might not be.
D. CORRECT. There could be something in the water which hurts fish but which nourishes algae.
E. The gardener didn't say what happens when the pond has a shortage of algae. He might agree that it would be bad too. But perhaps the pond has never had an algae shortage so far.

Question 7

QUESTION TYPE: Point at Issue

ARGUMENTS: Tanner says political debates help voters decide which politician would do the best job.

Saldana says that debates just help the candidate who is the better debater. She thinks debates aren't a good indicator of who is the best candidate.

ANALYSIS: The two of them disagree over whether debates are useful at letting us know who is the best candidate. Tanner says yes and Saldana says no.

A. Neither of them said how much of a benefit a debate has for the winner. Maybe the underlying political trends are much more important.
B. **CORRECT.** Tanner thinks this is true, that's why he thinks voters should ask for debates. Saldana argues that debates just help smooth talkers.
C. Nobody says this; it's a pretty extreme statement. Debating (i.e. persuasion) skills can help almost *anyone* do their job.
D. Tanner doesn't even mention debating skills, so he can't agree or disagree. He might not agree debates are always won by the person with the best debating skills. (A skilled Democratic debater would probably lose a debate held at a Republican convention, and vice-versa)
E. Neither of them says how much effect debates have.

Question 8

QUESTION TYPE: Paradox

FACTS: Congested highways have the lowest accident rate.

ANALYSIS: Think of any real, congested highway you've been on. Things tend to move slowly. And it's hard to have a major accident when traffic doesn't move. It helps to think through situations based on your real life experiences, as long as you don't contradict anything from the question.

A note about the correct answer: it talks about serious accidents. The stimulus talks about the number of *all* accidents. Serious accidents are a small portion of all car accidents. So this is a weak answer choice. But it's still stronger than the others, and the question stem just asked for the answer choice that did the "most" to explain.

A. People seem more likely to be bored and distracted on a congested road, so this adds to the confusion.
B. This is consistent with the stimulus, but it doesn't explain anything. We already knew that non-congested roads have more accidents than congested roads.
C. Does commuting make you more or less likely to have an accident? I have no idea, and this doesn't say.
D. **CORRECT.** Congested roads move slowly. So this tells us that they'll have a lower rate of serious accidents, at least, since serious accidents require speed.
E. "Do not always carry" more trucks? That's impossibly vague. I don't know if that means 2% of the time or 99% of the time.

Question 9

QUESTION TYPE: Strengthen

CONCLUSION: Lawmakers think that bribery and theft are equally harmful.

REASONING: The law's penalties for bribery and theft are the same.

ANALYSIS: This sounds like a good argument. But harm is only one reason we send people to jail. Another reason is deterrence. If we think a high penalty will stop people from committing one type of crime, we may set a higher penalty for that crime. Punishment is another reason. Some people just want the criminal to suffer.

Not everyone believes in all of these reasons, and not to the same degree. But they show that there are a mix of reasons why laws punish criminals; harm is just one. So this is a weak argument. It would be stronger if we said that the punishment for a crime was directly related to the harm the crime caused.

A. CORRECT. This does it. "Proportional" means "directly related to". So more harm = a longer sentence. Any two crimes with similar sentences must be thought to cause similar harm.
B. Deciding to make something a crime is not the same as deciding on the length of the punishment.
C. This shows that sentencing lengths are somewhat random. The sentences are the same today, but a bribery scandal tomorrow could make bribery seem worse. The sentences don't tell us much about what politicians actually think about crimes; it sounds like politicians are reacting to media hype.
D. We're talking about how much harm politicians *think* people suffer. How much harm people actually suffer is not relevant.
E. The stimulus doesn't talk about deterring crimes. This is way out of left field.

Question 10

QUESTION TYPE: Role in Argument

CONCLUSION: People are wrong to tell us we should learn the lessons of history.

REASONING: It's very hard to figure out the lessons of history, and hard to apply them, because the future will never present an identical situation.

ANALYSIS: The word "but" in the first sentence should be a big tip off. The author disagrees with the claim in the first sentence. It's very hard to learn from history, and harder still to apply its lessons.

Really, how useful is it to know, for example: "Don't let Hitler annex the Sudetenland"? That precise situation will never happen again. The right move back then might be the wrong move now.

A. There's no problem (question) to be solved. The sentence just presents a claim: we should learn from history. The argument argues against the claim.
B. Not at all. The argument's conclusion is that this claim is wrong. We shouldn't try to learn the lessons of history.
C. This goes too far. The argument gives reasons why the claim is false: it's very hard to learn the lessons of history, and harder still to apply them.
D. CORRECT. The author strongly disagrees with the idea that we should learn the lessons of history. It's nearly impossible to do, and the lessons don't seem very useful.
E. Huh? The argument's conclusion is that it's really, really hard to learn or use history's lessons. The argument disagrees with the claim in the first sentence.

Question 11

QUESTION TYPE: Flawed Reasoning

CONCLUSION: Sigerson's proposal isn't honest.

REASONING: Sigerson wants to ban contributions from firms that do business with the city. But Sigerson has taken such contributions!

ANALYSIS: The argument is no good. Sure, Sigerson took campaign contributions. It wasn't illegal! Sigerson will hopefully stop taking contributions once his law passes. Then there wouldn't be any dishonesty. This argument focusses on Sigerson's past behavior, while his law affects the future.

The conclusion is specific: Sigerson was dishonest. Three of the wrong answers talk about whether the proposal will or should pass. But the conclusion was that the proposal wasn't *honest*. Whether or not the proposal passes doesn't affect its honesty.

A. This answer describes mixing up sufficient and necessary. The argument didn't do that.
B. The argument *didn't* reject Sigerson's proposal. The author just said the proposal was dishonest. If you bring me a gift and are dishonest about why you're doing it, I might still accept the gift.
C. Who cares what other politicians think? The conclusion was that the proposal is *dishonest*. Whether or not it passes doesn't change whether it is dishonest.
D. Sigerson is very familiar with campaign contributions. He took many of them himself.
E. **CORRECT.** Sigerson might agree not to take contributions if his law passes. Then there would be no dishonesty. It currently isn't illegal to take contributions.

Question 12

QUESTION TYPE: Necessary Assumption

CONCLUSION: Some of Garden Path's books are bad.

REASONING: A good gardening book must explain the basics of composting. Some of Garden Path's books don't explain hot and cold composting.

ANALYSIS: Are hot and cold composting part of the basics of composting? If not, then this argument is worthless. It hasn't given any other evidence to show that Garden Path's books don't explain the basics.

A. This doesn't tell us anything about Garden Path's books. Also, the conclusion was that the books *were* flawed. This says some books are *not* flawed. This wouldn't help even if it were talking about Garden Path's books.
B. This tells us what gardeners should do, but it doesn't tell us whether Garden Path writes good books.
C. **CORRECT.** If you can explain basic composting without mentioning hot and cold composting, then maybe Garden Path's books are good.
D. So? I could say that everyone who understands the theory of relativity understands basic math. But that doesn't mean relativity is part of basic math!
You need the basics to understand advanced material, but that doesn't mean advanced material (like hot and cold composting) is part of the basics.
E. Imagine a gardening book that explained the basics of composting, but also gave horrible paper cuts to anyone that held it. That's not a very good book! My examples negates answer E, but the negation doesn't weaken the argument. The argument didn't say that all books that explained basic composting were good.

Question 13

QUESTION TYPE: Paradox

FACTS: Astronomers haven't changed their estimates of the universe's weight, even though we've discovered 40 billion more galaxies.

ANALYSIS: Shouldn't more galaxies mean the universe is heavier? There are more stars, planets, etc.

Well, the right answer tells us that galaxies are only a small part of the universe. Sure makes you feel tiny.

A. CORRECT. This would do it. If Galaxies were only 0.0001% of the universe, then even 40 billion more galaxies wouldn't add much weight.
B. We found *four times* the number of galaxies that we thought existed. That should let us make at least a rough estimate of their weight: they're probably heavy, compared to the galaxies we knew about.
C. This explains why we found more galaxies, but it tells us nothing about their weight.
D. This goes the wrong way. We're trying to figure out why theories about the universe's weight weren't affected by the discovery about the universe's mass.
E. One astronomer's estimate might say the universe is twice as heavy as another astronomer's estimate. But if both astronomers didn't change their estimates, then we can say they agree that the new galaxies didn't affect the weight of the universe, even if their estimates are different.

Question 14

QUESTION TYPE: Flawed Reasoning

CONCLUSION: We can't get rid of our social ills by fixing government.

REASONING: Arnot thought we could solve our social problems by fixing government, and Arnot's plan includes a silly assumption.

ANALYSIS: The subscriber argues that Arnot's *conclusion* is false, because his reasoning is bad. This itself is terrible reasoning. Let me give an example. "Gravity is less strong on the moon. This is true because the moon is made of blue cheese, which produces less gravity."

My reasoning is silly, but my conclusion is true. You've probably heard the phrase "right for the wrong reasons". The newspaper subscriber ignores this possibility.

A. CORRECT. Arnot's claim might still be true, even if his argument for the claim isn't good.
B. This describes the error of mistaking a necessary condition for a sufficient condition. I.e. "All cats have tails. This thing has a tail, so it's a cat." It's a bad argument, but it's not what happens in the stimulus.
C. This gets it backwards. The argument fails to consider that a conclusion might be true even if some premises that support it are false.
D. What is the distortion? The subscriber just argues that Arnot's argument makes poor assumptions. As far as we know, the author accurately describes Arnot's argument.
E. Government isn't defined here, but presumably the subscriber means "group that leads society" both times, or something like that. There's no indication of a switched definition.

Question 15

QUESTION TYPE: Weaken

CONCLUSION: The city council made the right choice by hiring an investment advisor.

REASONING: Other cities have hired advisors. The decision paid off for them.

ANALYSIS: The first half of the stimulus is just fluff. The analogy about doesn't serve any real purpose in the argument.

Just because other cities did well with advisors doesn't mean that it's a good move for this city. As a start, we'd want to know the other cities' situations were similar to this city's situation.

A. Does this mean the city will break down and need a repair? The analogy to cars only goes so far.... Also, maintenance can still be a good idea, even if it's not 100% effective.
B. CORRECT. This is a major difference. An economic advisor might only be useful when a city reaches a certain size. It might be *harmful* to hire one too early, if the advisor gives you strategies that are only appropriate for a large city.
C. Who cares about motorists? They were just used as an example to make you think about the wisdom of long term planning.
Also, this answer choice doesn't tell us whether drivers had good or bad non-financial reasons to avoid maintenance.
D. This sounds good, but it doesn't mean those advisors are a bad deal. People often hesitate to buy things that will clearly benefit them.
E. The columnist admits this; they say the payoff will likely come in several years.

Question 16

QUESTION TYPE: Role in Argument

CONCLUSION: We shouldn't allow cell phones on airplanes.

REASONING: Cell phones are annoying on buses and trains, and they would be even more annoying on planes. This is because airplanes are crowded and you can't change seats.

ANALYSIS: This question can be difficult if you depend on trigger words to decide whether something is a premise or a conclusion. The sentence in question is an intermediate conclusion, but there are no keywords to let you know that.

Instead, you need to ask: why are they telling me this? Don't be a robot, as one of my students says. Think about the plain English meaning of the argument.

Cell phones are annoying on planes, so this sentence is evidence for the main conclusion: don't allow cellphones on the planes. The last two sentences are evidence for the sentence itself. Cell phones are annoying on planes *because* planes are crowded and you can't change seats. So the statement is an intermediate conclusion. It's supported by some statements, and it supports the main conclusion.

A. Not quite. The main conclusion is that we shouldn't allow cell phones on planes, *because* they'd be even more annoying than on buses.
B. The *entire* argument talks about how cell phones are annoying, and especially annoying on planes.
C. This description is true of the last two sentences, if you consider an intermediate conclusion a premise. But the sentence we're talking about *directly* supports the conclusion.
D. CORRECT. The sentence is supported by the argument, and it supports the conclusion. Cellphones are more annoying on planes. Why? Because planes are crowded. What does this let us conclude? Don't allow cellphones on planes.
E. The entire argument is about cell phones on planes and whether they are annoying. So it seems relevant that phones are more annoying on planes than on buses.

Question 17

QUESTION TYPE: Strengthen

CONCLUSION: Microglia (immune cells in the brain) cause Alzheimer's.

REASONING: Microglia attack the proteins that build up during Alzheimer's, poisoning the brain in the process. Also, acetylsalicylic acid (aspirin) can slow Alzheimer's, but we're not told how.

ANALYSIS: Part of the argument is okay. If microglia release poison when removing proteins from the brain, then *maybe* this could cause Alzheimer's. This doesn't prove the conclusion, but at least it shows how the brain could get hurt. We could strengthen this part of the argument by showing that microglia's removal of PA proteins is the actual cause of Alzheimer's.

But what does Aspirin have to do with it? The argument didn't say how anti-inflammatories prove that microglia cause Alzheimer's. We can strengthen the argument by showing how Aspirin proves that microglia cause Alzheimer's. The right answer tells us that Aspirin reduces the amount of immune cells in the brain.

This is a hard question, with unfamiliar words. Note that *I* had to read this 2.5 times before I looked at the answer choices. If you read this, felt confused, but looked at the answer choices anyway, you made the mistake the LSAC wanted you to make.

The answers choices are no good to you if you don't understand what you've read. You should always reread any stimulus you don't understand. Even a quick look-over can do wonders for your understanding of the question.

A. This explains why proteins buildup in the brain, but it doesn't prove that microglia cause Alzheimer's. It's true that microglia are part of the brain's immune system, but maybe another part of the system causes the protein buildup. This also doesn't help prove that PA proteins are part of the real cause of Alzheimer's.

B. CORRECT. Microglia are immune cells in the brain. If Acetylsalicylic acid gets rid of them *and* improves Alzheimer's then maybe microglia are a cause of Alzheimer's. It's still weak evidence, but this at least explains why the argument mentioned Acetylsalicylic acid.

C. This might slightly weaken the argument. The argument said Alzheimer's patients suffer from a buildup of BA protein. This answer means that microglia help effectively combat one symptom of Alzheimer's. We already know that microglia poison the brain, but this answer suggests there's at least one benefit to the poisoning.

D. This suggests that BA might be the cause of Alzheimer's. So maybe microglia do the brain a favor by getting rid of BA, even if they have to use a bit of poison. This weakens the argument, slightly.

E. So? This doesn't tell us if microglia cause those diseases or whether the microglia are helping fight the diseases.

Question 18

QUESTION TYPE: Principle

FACTS: A sufficient condition and necessary condition for accessing computers are given.

Justified in accessing files without permission → the computer must be a business computer.

If the computer is a business computer AND you reasonably think it has data that can be used against the owner in a legal case → you can access the computer.

ANALYSIS: Four of the situations are wrong, and designed to confuse you. On this type of question, make sure you understand *exactly* what the necessary and sufficient conditions say.

We can conclude "justified" only with the sufficient condition. We can conclude "not justified" only if we're missing the necessary condition (i.e. the computer isn't for business). There might be other ways to prove a search was or wasn't justified, but we don't know about them.

A. Who knows? The passage doesn't talk about authorized access.
B. **CORRECT.** All you need is a reasonable belief that a business computer has relevant evidence. It doesn't matter if you're wrong, as long as the belief was reasonable.
C. The police officer's search could have been justified. Maybe her belief was reasonable. Maybe a judge ordered the search. Who knows? We can only conclude "not justified" if the computer isn't a business computer.
D. This answer doesn't mention any legal proceeding. We can only say for sure that a search was justified if the evidence will be used in a legal case.
E. We can only conclude "not justified" if the necessary condition is missing. But here the computer was used for business, so the necessary condition was met. The search still might not have been justified, but we can't say for sure.

Question 19

QUESTION TYPE: Necessary Assumption

CONCLUSION: It costs less to tan leather using biological catalysts.

REASONING: Tanning leather with biological or chemical catalyst costs the same, if we leave out waste disposal costs. But the biological catalysts make less waste, and getting rid of waste is expensive.

ANALYSIS: The reasoning and conclusion are about the costs of using each type of catalyst. They cost the same to use, if we don't include getting rid of the waste.

So waste disposal costs are the only weak area. We know biological catalysts produce less waste. But what if that waste is much more expensive to get rid of? The argument assumes that isn't true.

A. If this were negated and leather tanned conventionally *was* lower quality, then biological catalysts would be an even better idea. Though technically this has nothing to do with cost.
B. Who cares about the cost by weight of the materials? We already know that the total costs for using each type of catalyst work out to the same amount.
C. It doesn't matter if biological catalysts have always been affordable, or whether they just recently became affordable. Either way, they're cost effective now.
D. **CORRECT.** If you get 20% less waste with biological catalysts, but that waste costs seven times more to get rid of, then maybe biological catalysts aren't such a good idea.
E. The second sentence clearly says that the two tanning processes cost the same amount if you leave out waste. That means all other costs are included: labor, machines, materials, etc. If biological catalysts' labor costs are higher, that just means some other cost is lower.

Question 20

QUESTION TYPE: Principle

FACTS: You shouldn't play a practical joke under two conditions: if it will show contempt for the person you're playing the joke on, or if you think the joke will hurt the person.

Harm OR Contempt for subject of joke → Don't do it

ANALYSIS: We have information to conclude when not to play a practical joke: if one of the two conditions is true then you shouldn't play the joke.

We have no information to tell us when a joke is a good idea. Even if there's no contempt and no one will be hurt, a joke might still be a bad idea.

A. This says the person should have known the joke would cause harm. The stimulus only talked about *actually* knowing. "Should have known" isn't good enough for us to say a joke was wrong. Also, the stimulus didn't talk about harm to "someone". It only warned against causing harm to the person the joke was being played on.

B. It's true that the two conditions for proving a joke wrong are missing. But there might be other reasons not to do a practical joke. Maybe the joke is rude, or not funny, etc. We can never prove it's right to play a joke.

C. **CORRECT.** The person believes the joke might cause harm, so they're correct that it would be wrong to play the joke.

D. It's not necessarily wrong to play a joke that shows contempt for "someone". It's only wrong to play a joke that shows contempt for the person the joke is being played on.

E. We don't know whether the joker believed the joke would cause harm. It's the belief in harm that's important.

Question 21

QUESTION TYPE: Sufficient Assumption

CONCLUSION: Checkers wanted to hurt Marty's pizza when it refused the coupons.

REASONING: Accepting the coupons would have cost Checkers nothing and pleased Checkers' customers.

ANALYSIS: We know two things about Checkers.

1. They would not have been hurt by accepting the coupons.
2. They would have pleased their customers.

We're trying to prove that Checkers refused because it wanted to hurt Marty's. We can prove the argument correct by showing that refusing + 1 or 2 above = wanting to hurt a competitor. Either one of these would work:

No harm to accepting, but company refuses → motive to hurt competitor, OR
Customers would have been pleased, but company refuses → motive to hurt competitor

---

A. **CORRECT.** This is the second sufficient-necessary statement above. We know Checkers could have pleased some customers, but they refused the coupons. This proves that their only motive must have been to hurt Marty's.

B. This tells us what happens when a company wants to hurt a competitor. But we don't know that's true of Checkers....that's what we're trying to prove!

C. So, one company wants to hurt a competitor. But is it Checkers pizza, or some unrelated company?

D. This tells us why Checkers might have thought refusing the coupons would hurt Marty's. But it doesn't tell us that Checker's did refuse the coupon's in order to hurt Marty's. They might have had some other reason. Maybe Checkers' owner is philosophically opposed to coupons?

E. This is completely off target. Checkers *would* have satisfied customers by accepting coupons. Further, this answer choice only lets us conclude that someone was motivated to help customers. We want to conclude Checkers was motivated to hurt a competitor.

Question 22

QUESTION TYPE: Most Strongly Supported

FACTS:

1. Scientists usually choose which problems to work on.
2. When others choose problems for scientists, the scientists help write the question in a way that makes the question easier for science to solve.
3. Scientists rarely have to answer questions not designed to be answered by scientists.

ANALYSIS: The whole passage suggests that scientists might not do so well with problems they haven't helped to design. Scientists have stuck to questions that science is good at answering.

This probably isn't the only reason science is successful, but it helps to have a good question to work on.

A. There's no support for this. There are many problems that are scientifically solvable, but that no one asks scientists to look at. Think of small things from your daily life that you wonder about. Sure, scientists could solve them, but you haven't asked, have you?

B. The stimulus says scientists can answer most questions they formulate. This answer mistakenly negates that.
It's possible scientists can solve problems while being unsure how to ask the question. Choosing the right question can be hard sometimes. In more concrete terms, this would be doing something right without knowing why.

C. **CORRECT.** If scientists were asked to solve every type of question, then they would probably do less well on questions that weren't designed to be answered by scientists. They get an advantage by asking their own questions.

D. Who knows? Maybe most problems scientists are called upon to solve are chosen by scientists and not business leaders.

E. This goes too far. Science has *some* power. If science were terrible, then scientists probably couldn't solve even those problems they chose themselves.

Question 23

QUESTION TYPE: Flawed Parallel Reasoning

CONCLUSION: Most car mechanics know how electronic circuits work.

REASONING: Most experienced mechanics know how electronic circuits work. And most car mechanics are experienced.

ANALYSIS: There are other types of mechanics, besides car mechanics. Maybe the mechanics who understand electronic circuits are those who work on tanks, submarines, airplanes, etc....machines that have electronic circuits.

Abstractly, the flaw is that even if something is true for most people in a group, it doesn't have to be true for most people in a subset of that group. For example, suppose most pets are dogs. That doesn't mean that most pets that live in fish tanks are dogs. So look for an answer that talks about most people within a larger group.

A. This is a good argument. Traffic → high gas price → complaints.

B. This is a bad argument. The most common species could account for, say, 10% of the total birds in the area. So even when that species leaves, 90% of the birds stay. But this is not the same flaw as in the stimulus.

C. This is not quite a good argument. It hasn't told us that drivers who want to drive fast *do* buy sports cars. Maybe drivers who want to go fast only buy trucks. But this is not the "most" flaw from the stimulus.

D. Why would nature photographers find it especially boring to take pictures of famous people? They might prefer that to taking pictures of random people in a studio. But this is not the same flaw.

E. **CORRECT.** This repeats the flaw. Why would a *snow-removal business* hire more people in the summer? Just because most people that run lawn care businesses do, doesn't mean that most companies within a sub-group (snow-care) also hire in summer. Use common sense; snow-removal companies lose business when the snow goes away. Whereas companies that only do lawn care will hire in the summer.

Question 24

QUESTION TYPE: Strengthen

CONCLUSION: You should pretend to be confident if you want to succeed.

REASONING: It's easier to be successful if you truly believe you can be successful.

ANALYSIS: This is the "fake it till you make it" argument, and it tends to be good advice. But it's missing a step. The reason it works is that pretending to be confident can make you confident. This works in other areas too: it's hard to be sad if you're smiling, etc. Faking a feeling can produce that feeling.

But this is outside knowledge. An argument is stronger if you make this kind of information explicit, and the right answer does that.

A. The passage didn't talk about convincing others you could succeed. It's giving advice on how to *actually succeed*. You can convince others you'll succeed, but then fail.
B. **CORRECT.** Genuine confidence helps you succeed, and this tells us that fake confidence helps you get genuine confidence.
C. Is fake confidence the same thing as determination? This answer doesn't match up with anything from the stimulus.
D. This tells us many people aren't faking confidence. But it doesn't tell us whether we should fake confidence if we *don't* feel confident.
E. The argument already told us we should feel confident and try to get rid of self-doubt. But this doesn't help us prove that faking confidence will actually get rid of self-doubt.

Question 25

QUESTION TYPE: Parallel Reasoning

CONCLUSION: A strike is likely.

REASONING: A strike will definitely happen unless everyone agrees to obey the arbitrator. But the union probably won't agree to that.

ANALYSIS: This is a good argument. Past experience can't guarantee the future, but it can help predict the future. The conclusion is appropriately hedged. A strike isn't certain, but it's probable.

Note: There's a potential flaw in this question. I wrote the LSAC about it. If you're interested in seeing their response, go to this link:

http://lsathacks.com/lsac-responses/

I had no difficulty choosing the right answer under timed conditions. I only noticed the potential flaw when a student asked about it. Under timed conditions I wouldn't worry about an ambiguity as small as this.

A. This is a good argument, but it's too certain. The stimulus was uncertain. (The structure is "no stock → downsize → shareholders want change")
B. This is a bad argument. Rodriguez will donate *only if* the wing is named after her. That's a necessary condition, so she might still not donate.
C. This is a good argument. The two business partners fail to meet a necessary condition for being good partners. But this doesn't have the uncertainty of the stimulus.
D. **CORRECT.** The conclusion is appropriately uncertain. It's unlikely that Lopez will win, because a necessary condition for his winning (hydration) is unlikely to be met.
E. This is a bad argument. The department might get a qualified instructor before spring.

Question 26

QUESTION TYPE: Sufficient Assumption

CONCLUSION: Consumers are rational when they are too lazy to research the products they buy.

REASONING: It's rational not to research products unless you think the benefits of the research will justify the effort.

ANALYSIS: Sometimes it is worth it to research products you buy. It takes time, but you get a much better product as a payoff. Other times, research isn't worth it.

The argument assumes that if someone didn't do research then the research must not have been worth it. But that's not a good assumption, because sometimes people don't act in their own best interest.

We can prove the conclusion true if we assume that consumers are always correct that it would not be a good idea to research products. If it's not worth it to research, then it's rational not to research. It's almost a circular argument, but not quite.

A. We're trying to prove certain consumers are rational. This only tells us something about consumers we already know are rational.
B. This would help us prove someone was irrational if they did research. But the argument wasn't trying to prove anyone was irrational.
C. We don't care about what is "usually" true. The argument said that *every* consumer is rational when they refuse to research a product.
D. Same as A. This tells us something about rational consumers. But we're trying to prove that certain consumers *are* rational, and this doesn't help do that.
E. **CORRECT.** Here we go. Consumers don't think that research will benefit them. And the second sentence says it's rational not to research if you don't think the research will benefit you.

Section IV – Reading Comprehension

Passage 1 – Crime and Economics

Questions 1–6

Paragraph Summaries

1. Debate: should we help give potential criminals access to economic opportunity, or should we deter them with punishment?
2. Utility maximization theory says both views are correct. The theory says *deliberate* crime is a rational decision. Do the costs of crime outweigh the benefits?
3. According to this theory, deterrence reduces the reward for crime, and increasing economic opportunity increases the reward for *not* committing a crime.

Analysis

The first paragraph is confusing. It's hard to figure out what the first group of scholars wants. Access to economic institutions? What is that?

Academics often find it hard to communicate with human beings. What the professors mean to say is: we should help poor people find jobs, start businesses, feed their families, etc. That way they'll be less likely to commit crimes. "Work", "jobs", "community", etc. are all "economic institutions".

The other scholars have a clearer opinion. They want to punish criminals, and try to convince potential criminals that they'll suffer if they commit crimes.

Utility maximization theory says these are two sides of the same coin. The first group (institutions) raises the rewards of not committing crimes. The second group (deterrence) raises the costs of committing crimes. Remember that we're only talking about intentional crimes (line 2).

So, according to the theory, if you earn $20,000 per year and you could steal $1,000,000 with little risk, you might be tempted to steal. But if you earn $60,000 per year, and you'll almost certainly go to jail for ten years if you steal any amount of money, you probably won't be tempted.

Question 1

DISCUSSION: For main point questions, ask yourself: *why* did they tell me that? LSAT passages always have a point. Here, the point is that the two plans to deal with crime are really just opposite sides of the same coin.

A. This is true, according to the passage, but it isn't the main point. This answer ignores the fact that utility maximization theory will let us settle the debate.

B. The passage's point was broader. Utility maximization theory can be used to settle the debate between the two camps.

C. The point was that utility maximization theory could settle the debate between the two sides. Quantification of effects wasn't mentioned.

D. **CORRECT.** Utility maximization theory lets us see that both sides are right. Deterrence and better opportunities are both important for stopping crime.

E. Utility maximization theory demonstrates this is wrong. Norms and institutions affect whether someone will commit a crime. If no one gives you a job, your business idea fails and the government won't give you money, you may be tempted to steal rather than starve.

Question 2

DISCUSSION: The author is telling us to ignore crimes of passion. He only wants to talk about crimes people consciously intend to do.

Crimes of passion are those crimes that people commit in the heat of the moment. They are not rational.

A. Crimes of passion *aren't* deliberate crimes. They're crimes people commit without thinking.
B. **CORRECT.** Now that we know crimes of passion aren't deliberate, we have a better idea of what deliberate crimes are.
C. The author never said it's impossible to deter crimes of passion. People might sometimes restrain their passions if they fear the consequences.
D. The debate comes later in the paragraph. At the start of the paragraph, the author is just defining crimes for us.
E. The passage says *deliberate* crimes might be due to social factors (line 6). Crimes of passion are impulsive, and we don't know what causes them.

Question 3

DISCUSSION: The rational model says that we'll go after things that help us and avoid things that hurt us. So if the benefits outweigh the drawbacks, a decision is rational.

A. This helps the waiter, and he doesn't face much risk. Sounds like a smart move.
B. It sounds like a good idea not to speed. There's little benefit to speeding, and a high risk.
C. The industrialist isn't being a very good citizen, but he is acting rationally. He's financially better off paying the fine than cleaning up the pollution.
D. The official's situation isn't as clear as the situations in A-C. We're not told whether the benefit of the bribes outweighs the risk of prosecution. But at least there is a benefit, unlike answer choice E.
E. **CORRECT.** The worker doesn't get any long term benefit from assaulting his supervisor and he risks going to jail. It's a dumb move.

Question 4

DISCUSSION: The legal scholars used research from another discipline (economics) to correct a mistake in legal scholarship.

You need to find a situation where experts:

1. Use information from another field.
2. To solve a problem within their own field.

A. There's no debate being settled. And the astronomer's information comes from within cosmology.
B. **CORRECT.** The drawing instructor uses knowledge from another discipline (physics) to correct a mistake within her own discipline.
C. The biologist isn't settling any debate or correcting a mistake. The biologist likely could have made their point without help from the Olympic athlete.
D. Here we aren't told if the judge's decision was *correct*. The judge's evidence from anthropology might be completely inappropriate.
E. The mediator understands the importance of tact. But they're hardly using knowledge from another discipline to correct a mistake.

Question 5

DISCUSSION: The passage starts with a debate between legal scholars. Then utility maximization theory is used to settle the debate: it turns out both sides actually agree.

A. CORRECT. The general principle (utility maximization theory) shows that the two sides actually agree.
B. Close, but utility maximization theory proves that *both* sides have a point. Punishment does help deter crime, and opportunity does help persuade people that crime isn't worth it.
C. Discredit? Utility maximization theory shows that both sides have a point (55-60).
D. The LSAC is hoping that "instantiated" will confuse you and slow you down. You don't need to know what it is (I had to look it up). All you have to know is that this answer choice says the general principle comes first. In the passage it only comes in the second paragraph.
E. Same as D. The general principle (utility maximization) comes in the second paragraph of the passage, not at the start. And while the two sides are different, the general principle is used to bring them together.

Question 6

DISCUSSION: The author thinks utility maximization theory is accurate. That means the author believes that deterrence prevents crime by raising the risk of crime, and increased opportunity reduces crime by convincing people they're better off being honest. It's covered in the third paragraph.

A. The author agrees that stronger penalties deter crime.
B. The author would agree. Rehabilitation includes making a prisoner better able to fit in with society. This increases the likelihood that they'll benefit from society (e.g. they might get a job) and they'll be less tempted by crime.
C. CORRECT. This is backwards, but disguised by fancy language. It says that people will commit fewer crimes if society offers them fewer opportunities. The author says people will commit *more* crimes if society gives them fewer opportunities.
D. Access to economic institutions is jargon for things like the ability to get a job or get loans to start a business. If this gets harder, the author agrees that people will be more tempted by crime.
E. Vary inversely means: go in opposite directions. So stronger punishment leads to less crime. This means that deterrence works. The author agrees with that.

Passage 2 – Mexican-American Proverbs

Questions 7–12

Paragraph Summaries

1. Definition of proverb, and origins of Mexican-American proverbs.
2. The role of proverbs in the Mexican-American community: they're often educational.
3. Proverbs also link Mexican-Americans with their heritage.

Analysis

The passage is a description of the role of proverbs within the Mexican-American community. The material is easy to understand compared to other passages. I encourage you to reread if it you've got any points of uncertainty. I don't have anything to add beyond the paragraph summaries above.

On easier passages it's vital to have a good map of the passage. Since the concepts aren't difficult, the questions test you on knowledge of specific details. Questions 8-12 are all about specific details. It's easiest to answer by finding a specific line in the passage that supports the right answer.

The best way to make a mental map of the passage is to skim over it again after reading it. 15-20 seconds should be enough. This lets you see the order of the passage more clearly, and seeing the details a second time helps confirm them in your memory.

Question 7

DISCUSSION: The passage introduces the idea of a proverb, and discusses the origins of the proverbs used by Mexican-Americans. Then it gives examples of how they are used: for education and as a connection to tradition.

A. Lines 10-12 say that Mexican-American proverbs have much in common with the European tradition. We have no evidence proverbs are used differently in Europe.

B. **CORRECT.** This covers every paragraph. Paragraph 1 introduces proverbs, paragraph 2 mentions education, and paragraph 3 discusses heritage.

C. This only covers the first paragraph. The passage was mainly about how the proverbs are used in the Mexican American community.

D. Lines 19-21 say that teaching is just *one* purpose of proverbs. They're used for other things. Proverbs are likely also used by everyone in the community, and not just "many" people, which is a vague term.

E. This answer doesn't even mention Mexican Americans. They were the focus of the passage.

Question 8

DISCUSSION: The translation gives us an example of how Mexican Americans think about community: "Tell me who you run with and I'll tell you who you are." The passage says this means that an individual is formed by their community.

The sample proverb shows us how proverbs are used, and what effect they have. By repeating this proverb, Mexican Americans reinforce their ideas about community.

A. CORRECT. Lines 25-30 show that this is true. The proverb in question is given as an example of how Mexicans view the relationship between individual and community.

B. We're not told anything about the tone of the proverb. It could be used humorously, or seriously. We know it's used frequently, but we're not told much about the context in which it's used.

C. An appeal to traditional wisdom is mentioned in lines 38-39, but this example hardly shows how the proverb acts as an appeal to traditional wisdom. We'd need a description that shows how the proverb linked present to past.

D. There's no evidence that translating proverbs is hard. While some may lose their meaning, lines 10-12 show that some Mexican-American proverbs can be translated to an English equivalent.

E. We're not told whether this proverb is effective at getting its message across. Maybe Mexican American kids are instead listening to the individualist message of American culture.

Question 9

DISCUSSION: One of these answers has support from the passage, and the other four are designed to trick you. You should always check your answer against the passage. That way you can be 100% certain you're correct.

A. Lines 7-12 mention the origins of proverbs, but they tell us nothing about proverbs that comes from outside Europe.

B. Lines 7-12 tell us that some English proverbs have equivalents in Spanish, but we don't know if any English proverbs came from Mexican Americans.

C. English proverbs are only mentioned in lines 10-12 and line 24. We don't know much about them. We only know that English shares some proverbs with Spanish, and that English speakers are less likely to use proverbs for education.

D. No other ethnic groups are mentioned.

E. CORRECT. Lines 21-24 say this is true.

Question 10

DISCUSSION: Like question 9, one of these answers has support from the passage and four of them are designed to confuse you. You can side-step the trap by learning to quickly find information in the passage. Then you can check your answer against the passage to be sure you're correct.

If you need to get better at finding information: practice. Have a friend identify a fact, then see how fast you can find it. Then do it again, and try to find the next fact faster.

A. Lines 33-35 suggest that proverbs *are* intended to strengthen community norms.

B. CORRECT. Lines 10-12 say that Mexican Americans and English speakers have proverbs in common. Yet lines 22-24 say that proverbs are used differently between the two communities. So it's likely that the two communities sometimes use the same proverb differently.

C. Lines 27-30 show that this is a common use of proverbs. But we're not told if it's the most common use of proverbs. There might be another use that's even more common. If I say "rain is common frequent", I don't necessarily mean it rains most days.

D. Lines 45-48 say that proverbs help pass on the Spanish language. But we're not told if proverbs are used *in order to* help kids learn Spanish. Language learning might just be a beneficial effect of proverb use.

E. We are never told how many purposes people have when they use proverbs.

Question 11

DISCUSSION: Yet another specific detail question. There's no way to answer these well without having a good grasp of the passage.

A. Lines 10-12 say that *some* proverbs come from Europe, but we don't know if *most* do.

B. Only lines 38-39 mention traditional wisdom. It's lines 20-24 that compare Mexican American to English-speaking Americans. Mexican (note: not Mexican American) tradition is more likely to use proverbs for education, but this is not the same thing as valuing traditional wisdom.

C. We have no idea. These traditions are mentioned in lines 7-12, but the passage never says which tradition has more proverbs.

D. CORRECT. Lines 33-39 support this; they say that Mexican Americans may use proverbs because community norms are threatened ("Perhaps....authority").

E. There's absolutely no evidence for this. Lines 10-12 even point out that there are a lot of proverbs common to many European countries. That means there is a version in each language.

Question 12

DISCUSSION: The final question, and the final specific detail question of five. The fact that there were so many detail questions shows that you were expected to know this passage like the back of your hand. It's easier to find details if you skim over the passage once more after reading it. While looking over the passage, make sure you know the function of each paragraph; they all have one.

A. This strings together an idea from the second paragraph with an idea from the third paragraph to form a nonsense sentence that has no support in the passage.

B. The third paragraph says this is true of the Mexican American community. We don't know if it's true of all communities.

C. Lines 7-10 tell us that Mexico got many proverbs from Spain, but we're not told whether Spaniards use proverbs the same way as Mexican Americans do.

D. **CORRECT.** This is devilishly abstract. It refers to the proverb on lines 32-33. We can understand it, even though it has been translated (therefore, it is outside of its Spanish verbal context). But we understand it differently from Mexican Americans, because we don't share their social context, which emphasizes group-individual relations.

E. Lines 22-24 say that Mexican Americans are different from English-Speaking Americans in that Mexican Americans use proverbs for *education*. But maybe English speaking communities do frequently use proverbs to teach about peer-group relations in particular. That's narrower than education in general.

Passage 3 – Evolutionary Psychology (Comparative)
Questions 13–19

Paragraph Summaries

Passage A

1. What is evolutionary psychology? Can it explain altruism?
2. Altruistic behavior can help spread your genes, if you help a relative.
3. Altruism would have helped groups pass on their genes. When these groups became large and successful, individuals' genes would still cause them to help others. We now help others even though they we are not genetically related to everyone in our large societies.

Passage B

1. Evolutionary psychology theorizes our genes have secret motives.
2. Evolutionary psychology's arguments *seem* to make sense.
3. But there are many different reasons that could explain our behavior. Just because evolutionary psychology proposes a *plausible* explanation doesn't mean that explanation is correct.

Analysis

To succeed on the second passage (Mexican American proverbs), you had to know specific details. The difficulty on the third passage is understanding what this says (for non-science students).

I generally look over all passages after reading them the first time. I find it solidifies my understanding of the content. Something that was confusing on the first read often makes sense when you look at it again.

If you don't understand something, you should always reread the relevant section. It's much better than moving on to the questions without having understood what you read. The key concepts to understand here are:

1. What evolutionary psychology is. (It's the theory that our genes influence our actions. We do things that help spread our genes).
2. What the main critique of evolutionary psychology is. (Just because its explanations are plausible doesn't mean they are correct).

The second passage is more complex. The author is saying that wanting to pass on our genes *could* explain why we protect our children. But maybe we protect our children because we *like* doing it, and we'd do it even if it didn't help our genes. Or maybe some other explanation is true.

The second author says we can only know an evolutionary explanation works if the behavior would *never* happen if the explanation weren't true. And very few cases are like that.

The first author seems to be in error. They examine behavior based on whether or not it helps reproduction. If a plausible story can be made that an action helps reproduction, then the first author accepts it as true. The second author directly critiques this line of reasoning.

Question 13

DISCUSSION: The first passage uses evolutionary psychology to explain altruism. We evolved in small groups, and when we helped our relatives we helped our genes (because we share genes with relatives). Groups that did this were successful, and grew larger. Their genes for altruism spread. We kept the genes for altruism, even though we are no longer helping relatives when we help strangers in large groups.

A. Lines 9-10 said we have to use energy to help others, but the passage never said we have less chance of reproducing if we help people.
B. There's no new evidence. The passage describes evolutionary psychology by showing how it explains a puzzling situation. The explanation is not new; it's just unfamiliar to many people.
C. This is true, but it's not the main point. This answer doesn't even mention evolutionary psychology.
D. The author doesn't mention critics, and the author also never claims that *most* behavior is due to selfish genes.
E. **CORRECT.** Lines 15-16 mention cues that made early humans altruistic. Lines 18-21 mention psychological states and how helping others allowed early humans' genes to be more successful. So our genes cause us to feel altruistic (a psychological state) when see people that look like us (cues).

Question 14

DISCUSSION: The author of passage A thinks that evolutionary psychology is correct (lines 1-2 even say that it has "taught us"). The author of passage B think evolutionary psychology hasn't proven its case. Lines 35-36 call it a "conspiracy theory", which is not usually language you use for a theory you like.

A. Neither author mentions the "logical implications" of evolutionary psychology. The first author uses evolutionary psychology to explain a situation, and the second author criticizes evolutionary psychology.
B. **CORRECT.** The author of passage A accepts evolutionary psychology as a correct theory, and he uses it to explain altruism. The author of passage B calls evolutionary psychology a "conspiracy theory" (lines 1-2). He doesn't sound very committed to evolutionary psychology's principles.
C. The opposite is true. The author of passage A gives us an evolutionary explanation for altruism, while the author of passage B ridicules evolutionary psychology as a conspiracy theory.
D. Careful. The author of passage B is skeptical of evolutionary *psychology.* That's different from evolutionary *theory,* which refers to Darwin's theory of natural selection.
E. The author of passage B thinks that evolutionary psychology is dumb, but he doesn't attack the motives of evolutionary psychologists. He ridicules the theory by calling it a conspiracy theory, but he's referring to the fact that we can never prove that genes did or did not cause our actions.

Question 15

DISCUSSION: Lines 60-65 show that the author is skeptical that desire to spread our genes is what causes us to help our children.

The author is also indirectly skeptical of evolutionary psychologists' explanation for monogamy. His second paragraph explains their arguments, but lines 53-54 and the rest of the third paragraph show he doesn't think much of this explanation. The author first says that evolutionary psychologists might be wrong (i.e. their explanation is questionable), and he goes on to say that they're generally never right.

A. The author of Passage B never mentions this. It's only mentioned on lines 27-28, in passage A.

B. Lines 46-47 show that human kids mature slowly. But neither author explains why. The fact that kids grow slowly is used by evolutionary psychologists to explain why humans are monogamous.

C. **CORRECT.** The second paragraph mentions that evolutionary psychologists say we form monogamous families because we want to spread our genes. Lines 53-54 show the author's skepticism, and the third paragraph expands on this: evolutionary psychologists rarely show that their theory is the only explanation. So the author likely thinks the evolutionary psychologists' explanation of monogamy is bunk.

D. The author of passage B criticizes evolutionary psychologists for misinterpreting motives. But the question asks us which *explanation* the author of passage B criticizes.

E. The evolutionary psychologists *ignore* this possibility. This isn't one of their explanations. The author of passage B criticizes them for not realizing this, see lines 64-66.

Question 16

DISCUSSION: Passage A argues that evolutionary psychology can explain human behavior. If your genes make you do something that helps you reproduce, then you'll likely pass on those genes.

The genes for altruism increased the survival of our relatives, who also had the gene for altruism. So the genes for altruism were passed on. The spread of altruism led to better group survival, and the further spread of the genes.

In general, genetic behaviors which helped survival were passed on. So evolutionary psychologists claim that most of our behavior can be explained by this genetic process.

A very simple way to get the right answer is to notice that only answer choice A mentions genes. For a passage about *evolution,* that makes things fairly obvious.

A. **CORRECT.** This was the whole point of passage A. Lines 27-30 mention it specifically.

B. This describes altruism. That was just an example used in passage A. The passage's overall point was about all behaviors. This answer choice also leaves out genes.

C. This is never mentioned. You might think a behavior would have to improve health to get passed on. But a behavior that hurts you might get passed on if it increased your chances of reproducing or if it kept your children alive.

D. Who knows? The author of passage A was mainly concerned about genes being passed on. You might pass on genes even if you're bad at finding food.

E. Altruism helped make groups mutually dependent, but that was just an example. Some other behaviors may have helped survival even if they didn't make us live in groups.

Question 17

DISCUSSION: Passage B criticizes evolutionary psychology. Passage A is an explanation of altruism, using evolutionary psychology. So Passage B is attacking the sort of explanations made in Passage A.

Passage B's main criticism is that there are many possible explanations for any behavior. Just because evolutionary psychology seems to make sense doesn't mean it's right.

- **A.** Not at all. The author of passage B *criticizes* evolutionary psychology.
- **B.** The first part of this is right, but the author of passage B never uses an analogy.
- **C.** The author of passage B never said evolutionary psychologists observe the world wrong. An example of that criticism would be to say that humans aren't monogamous or altruistic. Instead, the author of passage B criticizes evolutionary psychologists' *explanations* for these observations.
- **D.** Lines 56-59 say it's rare that you could definitively prove one of evolutionary psychology's explanations correct. But the author never says its *impossible*.
- **E. CORRECT.** Just because an explanation is plausible (line 43) doesn't mean that it is correct (line 53, lines 59-61).

Question 18

DISCUSSION: Be careful on this question. The author of passage B doesn't think evolutionary psychologists are conspiring against us.

Instead, the author of passage B argues that evolutionary psychologists believe *our genes* are secretly conspiring to control our behavior. We aren't aware they are making us altruistic, but they do make us altruistic.

The answers are all taken directly from passage A. You should read the answer you choose in context, and make sure it makes sense according to passage B's description of a conspiracy theory.

Common sense can do much to answer this, even if you didn't understand what the author meant by conspiracy in this case. None of the wrong answers describe a secret situation, while conspiracies involve hidden motives.

- **A.** This sounds nice and open. A conspiracy theory involves secrecy.
- **B.** There's not even a whiff of secrecy in that statement. Evolutionary psychologists are being open and honest by saying that they find altruism difficult to explain.
- **C.** This is a description of altruism. There's nothing that seems secret.
- **D. CORRECT.** Here's the secrecy we need. Genes appear altruistic, but really they're just plotting in secret to spread themselves.
- **E.** There's not necessarily anything secret about a small group of humans.

Question 19

DISCUSSION: This is a specific detail question. You'll want to support the answer using the passage. Remember that both authors are talking only about the influence of genes on psychology and behavior.

A. Neither author talks about how genes affect our appearance. They were talking about psychology.
B. The author of passage A wasn't an extremist. Lines 31-34 say that altruism "may" be explained by genes. The author never says *everything* we do is directly controlled by our genes.
C. **CORRECT.** See lines 60-61. An explanation can make sense without being correct. So just because evolutionary motives *could* explain behavior doesn't mean they *do*.
D. No one mentions animal behavior. This is just here to slow you down and confuse you if you don't know what to look for.
E. The author of passage A never makes this extreme claim. We still do stupid things. The author of passage A only talks about one example, altruism.

Passage 4 – Dostoyevsky
Questions 20–27

Paragraph Summaries

1. The two camps of Russian literary criticism (idealists vs. realists), and Dostoyevsky's mixed view.
2. Dostoyevsky says that there is no fixed reality.
3. Dostoyevsky's view that artistic merit is the most important thing.
4. It's very hard to measure how great art will eventually be useful.

Analysis

Each paragraph has a clear purpose. When reading a passage, you should have two goals.

1. Understanding everything.
2. Understanding how it fits together and knowing where information is located.

So if, for example, you didn't understand the third paragraph, it's vital that you reread it. You need to know that Dostoyevsky didn't believe art should necessarily serve political goals. Instead, art should be judged on whether the reader understood the author's thoughts.

None of the ideas in this passage are particularly difficult, but they're hard to keep track of. If you're still unclear what any part of the passage means, practice looking over the passage a second time to make sure you understand it and get a sense of its organization.

A few key points. Dostoyevsky was a realist, but he mixed realism with fantasy, because he knew that there is no single, objective reality.

Art could serve a goal, but Dostoyevsky thought it could only fulfill its goal if it had merit. He said a novel had merit if it was well written and the reader could understand the author's thoughts. Dostoyevsky thought it was silly to focus on usefulness. It's hard to say whether something will be useful, or when. We value some art (such as the *Iliad*) even if we're not sure how it was useful.

Question 20

DISCUSSION: The passage presents Dostoyevsky's view; three separate points are covered in paragraphs 2, 3 and 4. The author of the passage seems to agree with Dostoyevsky. The right answer covers all of Dostoyevsky's criticisms of his critics.

A. We're never told if other Russian novelists followed Dostoyevsky's lead.
B. Lines 10-11 show that Dostoyevsky was a realist.
C. This ignores the second and third paragraphs. Dostoyevsky had several criticisms.
D. This only covers the second paragraph.
E. **CORRECT.** The first paragraph set up the dispute. The three themes mentioned cover the second, third and fourth paragraphs.

Question 21

DISCUSSION: Lines 35-41 say what Dostoyevsky thought "artistic" meant. He said it means the author writes well, and is understood by his readers.

A. Will the readers understand the author's opinions? This doesn't say.
B. **CORRECT.** It sounds like readers will have no trouble understanding this author's opinions, whatever they are. That was Dostoyevsky's main criteria, see lines 35-41.
C. "Attempted"? It doesn't sound like this author was very good at making himself understood.
D. We have no idea whether this author wrote well. He may have bored his readers to tears.
E. Again, we have no evidence that the author was clear. Lines 35-41 show that Dostoyevsky thought clarity was the most important thing.

Question 22

DISCUSSION: Lines 16-20 explain Dostoyevsky's views on reality. There is no single reality, everything depends on how each person perceives things.

A. **CORRECT.** This is directly supported by lines 16-20.
B. The second paragraph never mentions politics. Politics is only mentioned on lines 26-27, where Dostoyevsky scorns them as unimportant.
C. Lines 10-12 make clear that Dostoyevsky was a realist. This answer gives the view of the critics from lines 3-4; they're mostly irrelevant to the passage.
D. *Realists* cared about creating a new society (lines 5-9). Dostoyevsky took a different view. He was more concerned about artistic merit (paragraph 3) than politics (lines 26-27).
E. Lines 10 and lines 23-25 show that Dostoyevsky did use reality as a source. He just mixed it with the fantastic.

Question 23

DISCUSSION: Lines 7-9 explain what the radicals meant by useful. They wanted literature to help create a new society.

A. It was Dostoyevsky who used fantasy in his work, and he didn't care whether art was demonstrably useful (paragraph 4).
B. Lines 35-41 mention a novel should communicate an author's ideas. That was part of *Dostoyevsky's* definition of "artistic merit"; he wasn't talking about usefulness.
C. **CORRECT.** This matches lines 7-9, which describe the radicals' idea of the purpose of literature. They thought literature should help reform society.
D. This is Dostoyevsky's view from lines 20-21, but he was describing whether or not artists should be realistic. Dostoyevsky didn't mention anything about usefulness until paragraph 4.
E. Nobody mentioned the importance of promoting their theory of literature. The radicals wanted literature to promote social change, and Dostoyevsky seemed mostly concerned with artistic merit (paragraph 3).

Question 24

DISCUSSION: The three positions are the idealists (lines 3-4), the radicals (lines 5-9) and Dostoyevsky. The idealists are never mentioned again (In fact, I had to make up the name "idealists" to refer to them). The rest of the passage describes Dostoyevsky's criticisms of the radicals.

A. This isn't true. The critics from lines 3-4 are never mentioned again; I'd hardly say we know them in much detail.
B. This has the same problem as A. The idealists from lines 3-4 are never mentioned again, so we can hardly say the passage compared them to Dostoyevsky.
C. **CORRECT.** Dostoyevsky's view is the third position. Paragraphs 2-4 describe Dostoyevsky's disagreements with the realists (the second position).
D. There are two problems. First, the author never compares Dostoyevsky's views with those of the idealists from lines 3-4. Second, the author never explicitly says whether he agrees Dostoyevsky was right and the realists were wrong.
E. The author spends the entire passage telling us about Dostoyevsky's criticisms of the realists (the second position). We can suspect the author agrees with Dostoyevsky and not the realists. There's certainly no evidence for the opposite conclusion.

Question 25

DISCUSSION: The critics from lines 3-4 are never mentioned again, so we have to base our answers on Dostoyevsky's opinions. While Dostoyevsky did use fantasy, lines 10-12 show that he was a realist. He wouldn't have liked the idea of standing above the present and mundane reality.

Note that the critics from lines 3-4 never mention fantasy. Standing above the present doesn't necessarily refer to fantasy. It could refer, for example, to only writing heroic descriptions of important, real events from Russia's history.

A. The critics from lines 3-4 never said anything about the fantastic. They said art should stand above the present. Those aren't necessarily the same thing.
B. Dostoyevsky does think that reality is more than just the everyday. But line 10 makes clear that Dostoyevsky *was* a realist. He didn't think art should stand above reality.
C. **CORRECT.** Lines 10-12 support this. Even though Dostoyevsky used fantasy, he thought literature must be grounded in reality.
D. Lines 3-4 never mention fantasy. So we have no idea whether or not the idealist critics made such a distinction.
E. This describes the view of the critics from lines 5-9. We're talking about the critics from lines 3-4.

Question 26

DISCUSSION: Lines 33-34 help give us the answer. Dostoyevsky thought only true art could serve other goals. And lines 40-41 show that Dostoyevsky thought true literature was simply well-written literature.

A. CORRECT. Read the lines mentioned above. Art can't fulfill its purpose (political or otherwise) unless it is good art. For a book, that means the book must be well written.

B. Lines 35-41 contradict this. Dostoyevsky thought a book was well written if it made the author's thoughts clear.

C. This is just dumb. There are plenty of terrible books that also have no political goal.

D. If you picked this, you probably remembered lines 26-27, where Dostoyevsky disagreed that art must serve political goal.
But that doesn't mean Dostoyevsky thinks are *should never* have political goals. It's just that Dostoyevsky doesn't think political goals are the main thing: he's mainly concerned that books are good art. But if a book is well written, Dostoyevsky wouldn't reject it merely because it also had a political goal.
Lines 35-41 imply that Dostoyevsky would agree political literature was well written if it expressed the author's thoughts.

E. There's no reason that political literature must be bad literature. Lines 35-41 imply that Dostoyevsky would agree political literature was well written if it expressed the author's thoughts.

Question 27

DISCUSSION: Dostoyevsky had three major criticisms of the radicals. In paragraph 2, he thought they misunderstood reality. In paragraph 3, he thought they didn't understand the importance of good writing. In paragraph 4, he said it was impossible to know when and how art would be useful.

The critics could have made Dostoyevsky happy by improving their opinions on any of those points.

A. This would have annoyed Dostoyevsky. Lines 23-25 show he wanted to mix fantasy and reality.

B. Lines 30-33 show that Dostoyevsky thought a work's formal aspects were important.

C. Lines 10-12 show that Dostoyevsky was a realist. This would have horrified him.

D. CORRECT. The third paragraph shows that Dostoyevsky thought artistic merit was very important. See lines 35-41. The critics would have pleased Dostoyevsky by agreeing on this point.

E. This refers to lines 16-19. Dostoyevsky wasn't saying he didn't understand when he called their position "meaningless". He understood what the critics meant, but he thought there was no such thing as "reality as it is."

Preptest 65
Section I - Logical Reasoning

Question 1

QUESTION TYPE: Strengthen

CONCLUSION: A diet may not have to be extremely low in fat in order to protect the heart.

REASONING: Two diets were compared. A moderate fat mediterranean diet, and a low fat western diet. The mediterranean diet produced a significantly lower risk of heart attack.

ANALYSIS: The risk of heart attack from the Mediterranean diet could still be *high,* even if the Mediterranean diet gives you a *lower* risk.
This question makes an error between a comparison (e.g. higher) and an absolute quality (e.g. high).
For instance, it's significantly *safer* to jump out of a two story window, compared to shooting yourself in the head. But neither activity is *safe.*

That's why the conclusion doesn't follow. Even though the Mediterranean diet is *safer,* maybe it's still quite unsafe and does a terrible job protecting the heart. The right answer addresses this, by showing that the fat in the Mediterranean diet is healthful. This strengthens the idea that the fatty Mediterranean diet is actually safe, rather than merely being less unsafe.

A. The argument's conclusion was that eliminating fat was not necessary. This answer weakens the argument by saying that limiting fat can be good.
B. **CORRECT.** This strengthens the argument by showing that the fat in the Mediterranean diet was, in fact, helpful. So a moderate fat diet could be an advantage, rather than a drawback.
C. Great, the Mediterranean diet is delicious. So what? The conclusion is about the effects of the diet, not whether it is easy to follow.
D. It's not clear how this affects the argument. We don't know if the study participants exercised.
E. This shows that drugs might make the Mediterranean Diet more effective.
So what? We have no reason to believe that participants in the study were given these drugs.

Question 2

QUESTION TYPE: Identify The Conclusion

CONCLUSION: Florists should buy white carnations for St. Patrick's day.

REASONING: People like green carnations on St. Patrick's Day. Green flowers are rare in nature. It's easy to dye white carnations green.

ANALYSIS: This argument gives advice to florists. Anytime an argument says someone 'should' do something, that recommendation is almost certainly the conclusion.

A. **CORRECT.** The rest of the argument supports this. It's easy to dye white carnations green. People like green flowers, and naturally green flowers are rare.
B. This is evidence to support the conclusion that florists should buy white flowers instead.
C. This is evidence for the conclusion. This is the reason that florists should buy white flowers and dye them green.
D. This is a reason that florists should buy white carnations, rather than rare green carnations.
E. This explains why florists must use white carnations instead.

Question 3

QUESTION TYPE: Evaluate The Argument

CONCLUSION: Everyone should use low-wattage bulbs.

REASONING: Low-wattage bulbs offer great advantages to homeowners, even though low-watt bulbs are more expensive than regular bulbs.

ANALYSIS: To evaluate an argument, you should follow the same process as with any argument: ask yourself why it might be flawed.

The argument doesn't list any actual advantages to low-wattage bulbs, so the conclusion raises questions. For instance:

- Should renters buy these bulbs, even if renters don't pay for electricity?
- Is the light quality from low-wattage bulbs worse somehow?
- Are the bulbs so much more expensive that it takes decades to pay them off?
- Are there any safety risks?
- How long do low-wattage bulbs last?

The key to answering these exception questions is to open your mind to all possible flaws in the argument.

You don't need to prephrase all possible answers, just put yourself in the shoes of someone buying a low-wattage bulb and ask if the answer is relevant.

A. This seems relevant. If the actual operating cost of low-wattage bulbs is unusually high, then people shouldn't use them.
B. **CORRECT.** Who cares about profits? If the bulbs produce a benefit, I don't mind if a company makes profits.
C. If a low-wattage bulb costs $10,000, few people will want one.
D. This is relevant. Current users of low-wattage bulbs are better placed to spot hidden flaws.
E. If you have to replace low-wattage bulbs every two weeks, it gets expensive and inconvenient to use them.

Question 4

QUESTION TYPE: Complete the Argument

CONCLUSION: It is even more important to teach children to want healthy food.

REASONING: It's more important to teach children to swim than to close off pools with fences. Similarly, restricting access to junk food is not the most important thing.

ANALYSIS: Complete the argument questions often involve analogies. You have to think about the logic of the analogy.

If a kid can swim, it doesn't matter if he falls into a pool that isn't fenced off.

Likewise, if a kid doesn't want junk food, then it doesn't matter whether she's allowed to have it.

A. This doesn't make sense. If we teach kids to trust TV then they might believe that junk food ads are accurate and that kids should eat nothing but chocolate bars.
B. This is over-broad. We don't know if all ads are misleading.
C. **CORRECT.** If children know how to make good nutritional choices, then they won't be as tempted by junk food ads on TV.
D. Physical activity won't save you if your diet is nothing but ice cream. This is beside the point of the argument, which is about nutrition.
E. This completely ignores food. The argument was about how kids should eat.

Question 5

QUESTION TYPE: Weaken

CONCLUSION: The TV program is biased against the freeway.

REASONING: Most of the people that the TV station interviewed were against the freeway.

ANALYSIS: This question plays on an American notion that news coverage must be 'balanced', with equal coverage given to both sides.

This idea of 'balance' didn't exist at all prior to the second world war, and it only became strong in the 1990's. It generally doesn't exist in other countries. If you're a university age American, the idea of 'balanced' coverage is one of the mental biases you're prone to, and the LSAT tests for this error.

Maybe the dam is a terrible idea and almost everyone hates it. In that case, it would make sense to show more interviews with residents who were against the dam. To give equal coverage would give a misleading view of citizens' opinions about the dam.

A. It doesn't matter what viewers think. The question is about whether the program itself was biased.
B. Same as A. Whether or not a program is biased is an objective fact. Who cares what people *believe*.
C. This might slightly strengthen the argument, by showing that the station selected more emotional, persuasive interviewees to speak against the dam.
D. CORRECT. This shows that the proportion of interviewees against the freeway accurately represented the general population's views.
E. This gives a reason that the TV station might be biased. It slightly strengthens the argument.

Question 6

QUESTION TYPE: Principle

CONCLUSION: We shouldn't eat seafood.

REASONING: We don't know if sea animals can feel pain. We should err on the side of caution, assume sea animals do feel pain, and not eat them.

ANALYSIS: Evan says vegetarians should err on the side of caution. Vegetarians shouldn't eat seafood until they know *for sure* that sea animals can't feel pain.

This means that vegetarians risk being wrong. It's possible sea animals feel no pain, and it would be alright to eat them. But since there's some chance that sea animals feel pain, vegetarians should risk being wrong.

The correct answer must say what someone should do, and it should advise that person to err on the side of caution.

Many of the wrong answers don't even offer advice.

A. CORRECT. This answer errs on the side of caution. We should make sure we pay Farah, even if we risk paying her twice. That's like making sure we avoid causing sea animals pain, even if we risk needlessly avoiding eating them.
B. This is just common sense, and a statement of fact about the world. It doesn't tell us what anyone *should* do.
C. This answer has nothing to do with erring on the side of caution.
D. Same as C.
E. This is a bad argument. It's possible Allende writes joyful characters because that joy is missing from her own life. In any case, this has nothing to do with erring on the side of caution.

Question 7

QUESTION TYPE: Complete the Argument

CONCLUSION: Governments should only intervene when not intervening would cause much more harm than intervening.

REASONING: Medicines have harmful side effects. We should only use them when the benefit to using them greatly exceeds the harm.

Government intervention in the economy is similar.

ANALYSIS: The author dislikes medical and government intervention.

They'll accept intervention in only one situation: Not intervening will cause even more harm.

Suppose you will die without an antibiotic. Then it makes sense to give you the drug, even if the drug causes horrible damage to your intestines.

Likewise, suppose the economy will collapse unless you bail out the banks. Then it might be justifiable to bail them out, even though the bailout causes harm.

You *can't* intervene unless non-intervention will cause even more harm. Harm from non-intervention is a necessary condition. Here's a diagram:

Intervening OK → Not intervening causes more harm

A. Whether people *approve* isn't the question. A patient might approve of a terrible treatment because it seemed easy. What matters is whether government policies are helpful or harmful.
B. This isn't enough. The policy needs to do less damage than not intervening.
C. This isn't quite it. It might be ok to exacerbate (make worse) existing problems if not intervening would cause even more problems.
D. CORRECT. Here we go. The author clearly dislikes intervention. They'll accept it only when the harm from not intervening is even worse.
E. The solution might not be worth it if intervention caused a lot of harm as well.

Question 8

QUESTION TYPE: Flawed Reasoning

CONCLUSION: Reading labels promotes healthy behavior.

REASONING: People who read labels tend to eat less fat.

ANALYSIS: This argument makes two errors. One is a causation-correlation error. It could be that people read labels *because* they want to avoid fat. So it's the healthful behavior that causes label reading, and not the reverse.

The argument also assumes that eating fat is unhealthy. There is, in fact, little to no evidence that saturated fat is harmful. So we can't conclude that people are healthier because they avoid fat.

The LSAT sometimes recognizes that fat isn't harmful, and it sometimes doesn't. In this case, the correlation is the surer error.

A. CORRECT. This reverses the arrow of causation. It could be that people try to eat less fat and therefore they look at labels to avoid it.
B. Actually, the sample here is the entire population. The stimulus looks at the behavior of those who read labels and those who don't: that's 100% of people.
C. This answer refers to mixing up sufficient and necessary conditions. But the stimulus doesn't contain any sufficient or necessary conditions. For instance, looking at labels is not a *sufficient* condition for avoiding fat. There's just a correlation between the two. Some people might look at labels and eat lots of fat.
D. This is a different error, a false dichotomy. It's like saying: 'either is will rain or it will be a nice day'. That's wrong: it's possible it might not rain, but be really humid and unpleasant. This wasn't the error in the stimulus.
E. This is a different error. It's like saying "John dropped the dishes and broke them. So John must have *intended* to destroy our dishes". It ignores the possibility that the consequences didn't match the intentions.

Question 9

QUESTION TYPE: Identify The Conclusion

CONCLUSION: It's unlikely that *Apatosaurus* could gallop.

REASONING: We calculated that galloping would have broken *Apatosaurus'* legs.

ANALYSIS: This is a reasonable argument. It shows that since galloping would have disastrous consequences, *Apatosaurus* probably couldn't gallop.

Some words help you find conclusions. Notice that the stimulus says 'however'. That usually shows that the author disagrees with a previous statement. What follows 'however' tends to be the conclusion.

A. This is evidence that supports the conclusion that *Apatosaurus* couldn't gallop.
B. This tells us how we know that galloping would have broken *Apatosaurus'* legs.
C. **CORRECT.** See the second sentence. The author said 'however', which almost always indicates a conclusion.
D. The author didn't actually say this. It's an implicit premise that allows them to draw their conclusion. The conclusion is that *Apatosaurus* is unlikely to have been able to gallop.
E. This is a necessary assumption, not the conclusion. If *Apatosaurus'* bones were much stronger than modern bones, then maybe *Apatosaurus* could have galloped without breaking its legs.

Question 10

QUESTION TYPE: Role in Argument

CONCLUSION: The new advance could reduce anemia worldwide.

REASONING: We can now put iron in salt. Lots of people eat salt. Anemia is caused by lack of iron.

ANALYSIS: The sentence in question shows that people will get a decent amount of iron from salt. If people just ate a tiny bit of salt, then salt couldn't help fix iron deficiency.

Thus, the sentence in question helps show that adding iron to salt really could help solve the problem.

A. The conclusion is that the new advance could help reduce anemia.
B. **CORRECT.** The sentence supports the conclusion by showing that people will get a meaningful amount of iron from salt.
C. The argument doesn't try to disprove *any* claims. And the fact that people eat a lot of salt *supports* the argument.
D. 'Qualifying' a conclusion means putting limits on it. An example would be 'not everyone eats salt, so this won't work for everyone'. The sentence in question supported the conclusion, it didn't restrict the conclusion.
E. Not at all. Illustrating a principle means giving an example of something abstract. I could say:

'Technological advances can improve health. For instance, improved monitoring can catch diseases early.'

That's a principle, and an example illustrating the principle. The sentence in question wasn't an example of anything.

Question 11

QUESTION TYPE: Flawed Parallel Reasoning

CONCLUSION: The thief must have worn gloves.

REASONING: The only fingerprints in the building belong to the owner, Mr. Tannisch.

ANALYSIS: The first rule of detective stories is that anyone is a suspect. Yes, there *could* have been a thief with gloves. Or maybe there are no other prints because....Mr Tannisch is the thief!

The detective improperly excludes the owner from suspicion, without giving a reason why.

To parallel this argument, you need to find a situation where the author incorrectly excludes a possible suspect.

A. CORRECT. This ignores the obvious possibility that the camp cafeteria made everyone sick.
B. This doesn't ignore an obvious, named suspect. Instead, it ignores a possible (unnamed) alternate cause. For instance, maybe the inclement weather was worse when the second prototype was tested.
C. This is a different error. It's true that an individual swimmer has low odds of winning. But there will always be *one* winner out of a group. There's a 100% chance of *someone* winning the meet.
D. This is possible, but incomplete. We'd need more information about what can cause cavities. This argument isn't like the stimulus, it doesn't exclude any obvious suspect.
E. This is a bad argument. Maybe peas are different from tomatoes. But it doesn't exclude any obvious suspect.

Question 12

QUESTION TYPE: Paradox

PARADOX: Different reefs contain shrimp with big genetic differences. Yet, ocean currents should allow the shrimp to interbreed.

ANALYSIS: For paradox questions, you must think carefully about what you're trying to explain. The question doesn't always spell it out for you. Figure out the paradox *before* you look at the answers.

Here, the shrimp can travel between reefs. So they *could* interbreed. But there are large genetic differences between reefs. This suggests the shrimp *don't* interbreed.

Answer B is very tricky. There will always be some genetic differences within a population. But, the differences might be very small, and not matter.

The paradox in the stimulus is that there are *large* genetic differences between reefs.

A. This just tells us that shrimp are similar to each other. That makes sense. It's like how you have more genetic heritage in common with a Norwegian than with an Elephant.
This information doesn't explain why you do have some genetic differences from Norwegians despite easy air travel.
B. This is very tempting. But the stimulus said there are *substantial* genetic differences from one reef to another. Whereas this answer choice just says there are 'differences'. It could be that within a reef there are only tiny differences. We need to explain large differences between reefs.
C. CORRECT. This shows that even though shrimp *could* breed at other reefs, they don't. Shrimp come home to breed.
D. This answer adds to the confusion. If shrimp leave reefs when they're old enough to breed, then presumably they breed with shrimp at other reefs. Why are there still big genetic differences?
E. This doesn't affect anything. We don't care about shrimp that left coral reefs to live in the open ocean. The stimulus refers to genetic differences among the shrimp that stayed at reefs.

Question 13

QUESTION TYPE: Strengthen

CONCLUSION: Seawater agriculture might work in desert regions near sea level.

REASONING: Halophyte plants can survive on sea water. Halophytes need more water than normal crops, but it's cheap to pump seawater, compared to pumping from wells.

ANALYSIS: Halophyte irrigation can be cost-effective. Great.

But, irrigation is not the only factor in agriculture. You've also got to consider the cost of fertilizer, labor, machines, seeds, transport to market, etc.

The right answer shows that irrigation is a major cost in agriculture. Since halophyte irrigation is cost-effective, this helps show that raising halophytes in desert regions could make sense.

A. The 'volume' of food isn't necessarily relevant. A small volume of meat gives you more calories than an equivalent volume of vegetables. That doesn't necessarily make meat 'better'.
The key factor is how much it costs to feed an animal using halophytes, and whether animals can survive on halophytes. This answer doesn't address those issues.

B. This is tempting. But the stimulus wasn't about whether you should irrigate halophytes with salt water. The question was whether to grow halophytes at all.

Halophytes are less productive, but also the only plants that can use seawater.

C. This weakens the argument. If research spending were required, then that would be an obstacle to making halophyte agriculture work.

D. This tells us that costs are different.
But it doesn't tell us whether halophytes cost more, or less.

E. CORRECT. We know that irrigation costs are cheaper for halophytes in desert areas. So if irrigation costs are a major part of agricultural costs, then that is a big advantage.

Question 14

QUESTION TYPE: Principle

PRINCIPLE: No reasonable person would read the policy → Uphold a reasonable person's understanding of the policy

APPLICATION: The insurance company should cover hail damage, even though the policy barred hail damage.

ANALYSIS: We must show that the sufficient condition of the principle applied. So it has to be true that a reasonable person wouldn't have read the policy.

We also should show that it was reasonable to expect the policy to cover hail.

Since this is a 'most justifies' question, the answer doesn't need to cover both factors. The correct answer does get them both, however.

A. This doesn't show whether the policy was written in a way that would prevent an ordinary person from reading it.

B. CORRECT. This shows the sufficient condition applies: a reasonable person would have read the policy. And Celia reasonably expected it to cover hail. This meets both conditions in the principle.

C. It's not clear if it matters that Celia read the policy. The sufficient condition was that 'a reasonable person wouldn't have read thoroughly'. This answer doesn't address that point.

D. It's possible to make an unreasonable decision, and then make a reasonable decision.

For instance, perhaps it was unreasonable not to read the policy thoroughly. Then, to get into Celia's position, you would have to take an unreasonable decision. You could reasonably assume the policy covered hail, but only because you took the unreasonable decision not to read the policy.

E. This doesn't say whether Celia was reasonable to expect the policy would cover hail.

Question 15

QUESTION TYPE: Flawed Reasoning

CONCLUSION: If we could stop all iatrogenic disease, the number of deaths would fall by half.

REASONING: Half of deaths are due to iatrogenic error.

ANALYSIS: This argument ignores that people are going to die of something.

If I save you from cancer, you might die of a heart attack within a month.

If you die from a doctor's error, you're already in the hospital. So you were probably sick. Your odds of dying from something are higher than normal.

So if the doctor doesn't kill you, you might die from whatever sent you to the hospital in the first place.

Answers B, D and E refer to reality. But the researcher isn't making a realistic argument. They're asking us to imagine a *hypothetical* situation. What would happen *if* we could end all iatrogenic disease.

It's like asking what would happen if humans could grow wings and fly. An interesting question, but nothing to do with reality.

A. The stimulus wasn't talking about preventing non-iatrogenic diseases. (i.e. regular diseases)
B. Actually, the argument assumes we can use safer treatments. Less invasive treatments might be a major way to prevent iatrogenic error.
C. **CORRECT.** Exactly. If you survive doctor error, you might still die from a heart attack or pneumonia.
D. The argument wasn't saying whether it's actually possible to end all iatrogenic error. The researcher is describing a hypothetical situation: what would happen *if* it were possible to end all iatrogenic deaths.
E. It's reasonable to assume that there's always a risk of iatrogenic error. The author is asking us to imagine a hypothetical situation where we can get rid of this risk and end all iatrogenic error.

Question 16

QUESTION TYPE: Sufficient Assumption

CONCLUSION: At least one member should vote against the proposal.

REASONING: Members should either vote against or abstain. If they all abstain, voters will decide the issue.

ANALYSIS: The argument doesn't say why it's a bad idea to let voters decide the issue.

It's clear that council members shouldn't vote for the proposal. It's not clear why they shouldn't let it get decided by voters.

To prove the argument correct, we must say that it's a bad idea to let the issue go to the voters.

A. This is very tempting. But the argument didn't say the proposal shouldn't pass. The argument just said that council members shouldn't be the ones to vote for it.
B. **CORRECT.** If this is true, then at least one council member should vote against the proposal so that it doesn't reach voters.
C. This still doesn't tell us whether council members should abstain or vote against the proposal.
D. This tells us that voting against the proposal will prevent it from going to voters. It doesn't tell us whether we should care if the proposal goes to voters.
E. The stimulus didn't say whether all members ought to vote against the proposal - this is irrelevant. The conclusion is just that ONE member should vote against the proposal. The rest are presumably free to abstain.

Question 17

QUESTION TYPE: Flawed Reasoning

CONCLUSION: The media critics are wrong to say that negative economic news will harm the economy.

REASONING: People spend based on their confidence in their own economic situation.

ANALYSIS: The argument ignores the possibility that negative news about the economy makes people less confident in their own economic situation. That would cause them to spend less.

A. This is backwards. We don't care what causes people to think the economy is doing well. As far as we know, spending is only related to people's confidence in *their own* situation.
B. It would be astounding if news reports about the economy were 100% accurate. This answer just points out the obvious. It has no impact on the stimulus, which was about whether negative news affects confidence.
C. This doesn't tell us anything about people who *do* pay attention to media reports about the economy.
D. CORRECT. Suppose negative news makes people less confident about the economic situation. This answer says that people's lack of confidence in the wider economy will reduce their confidence in their own situation, which will make them spend less.
E. This tells us what will happen *if* an economic slowdown occurs. The stimulus was about whether negative news could cause a slowdown in the first place.

Question 18

QUESTION TYPE: Necessary Assumption

CONCLUSION: It would be hard or worthless to domesticate the remaining large wild mammals.

REASONING: Past generations would have tried to domesticate every large mammal which *seemed* worth domesticating.

ANALYSIS: The premise of this argument is that people would have tried to domesticate any seemingly useful large mammal. Since some mammals aren't domesticated, those animals must not have seemed useful, or have been hard to tame.

So far so good. But then the conclusion is that *now,* none of those species *are* worth domesticating, or easy to domesticate. But things change. There are at least three possible flaws here:

* With our modern techniques, maybe it's much easier to domesticate animals now.
* Ancient peoples only tried to domesticate animals that *seemed* useful. The conclusion is about whether mammals *are* worth domesticating.
* Maybe some animals were not useful in the past, but would be useful in our modern economy.

A. The argument was only about species that *seemed worth domesticating*. It doesn't matter whether people tried to domesticate animals that weren't worth domesticating.
B. CORRECT. If it's much easier to domesticate animals today, then maybe we could domesticate a few more mammals.
Negation: It is much easier to domesticate large mammal species than it was in the past.
C. It doesn't matter if some species went extinct. The conclusion is about existing species.
D. Use the negation test on necessary assumption questions. The negation here is: "There isn't always a correlation between how easy it is to domesticate an animal and how worthwhile it is." That has no impact on the conclusion. Why the devil would such a correlation matter? We only care about: **i.** can you do it? **ii.** Is it worth it?
E. Why would this matter? We don't care how easy it was to domesticate goats or cows.

Question 19

QUESTION TYPE: Strengthen

CONCLUSION: Last year's mild winter is responsible for the growth in bird population.

REASONING: Last year's winter let birds stay up north, in their summer range. This stopped them from dying during migration. The birds were able to forage naturally rather than eat at feeders.

ANALYSIS: Bird migrations are a wonderful thing. Birds fly north in summer, and fly south in winter. So they stay in similar temperatures year round.

But it's a hard trip. This stimulus tells us that birds avoided dying from migration because they stayed up north during the winter. That *might* explain the population growth. But maybe another factor caused the increase in population. Population growth = number of births - number of deaths.

Anything that increases births or reduces death increases population. We can support the conclusion that the winter was the cause by providing further reasons that the mild weather let the birds survive, or by ruling out other causes of population growth.

A. This is really vague, and can't provide much support. We don't even know if a mild winter is an unusual weather pattern.
B. Differ how? This doesn't tell us whether these mating behaviors can increase population.
C. **CORRECT.** We already know the mild winter led to fewer deaths during migration. This says the mild winter led to fewer deaths at home, too. Foraging helped keep birds safe from predators.
D. This shows that the birds would have run out of food by staying the winter. So why did their population *grow?* This answer suggests a factor other than the mild winter helped them.
E. This doesn't tell us whether visiting feeders helps birds survive. So we have no idea if visiting feeders impacts population growth.
Also note that the answer says 'sometimes'. That could mean birds visit feeders 0.0000023% of the time. Answers with 'some' have little impact.

Question 20

QUESTION TYPE: Flawed Reasoning

CONCLUSION: Small observational studies are more likely than large controlled studies to have dramatic findings.

REASONING: Newspapers report more frequently on small observational studies. Newspapers tend to report only dramatic findings.

ANALYSIS: This question confuses odds for a group and odds for an individual. This is also called confusing number and rate.

There are more rich people in China than in Switzerland. So does that mean that the average person in China is more likely to be rich than the average Swiss citizen?

No. China is much bigger than Switzerland, and so it has more rich people. But it's poorer on average.

Maybe there are many more small observational studies than large randomized studies. So small studies could be less dramatic on average, yet produce a greater *number* of dramatic results.

You're allowed to use intuition. It might have occurred to you that small studies are easier to do, and so there are more of them. The LSAT expects you to use this kind of insight to form hypotheses.

A. The author never said that newspapers were wrong to report dramatic findings.
B. The author didn't say that drama always meant a study was unscientific. They just said that large studies have stronger evidence on average.
C. This answer is pure nonsense, so I don't know how to explain why it is wrong. There simply were no two 'similar claims' about both groups. If something doesn't happen, it can't be a flaw.
D. **CORRECT.** If small studies are more common, then they could produce more cases of dramatic results even if they are less dramatic on average.
E. Actually, the first sentence rules out this possibility. Newspapers only report on stories that sound dramatic. So the drama comes first.

Question 21

QUESTION TYPE: Necessary Assumption

CONCLUSION: Government incentives to plant trees increase global warming.

REASONING: Trees don't store CO2 as well as native grasses do. Governments give farmers incentives to plant trees.

ANALYSIS: You can conclude that the incentives aren't encouraging the best possible policies. Farmers could trap more CO2 if they planted grasses instead of trees.

Further, if farmers remove native grasses to plant trees, then the incentives are clearly bad.

But you don't know what farmers would do without the incentives. Maybe farmers would plant crops, rather than grasses. Crops might not store CO2. There'd still be no native grasses. So the argument assumes farmers would plant grasses if there were no incentives.

A. It doesn't matter. The stimulus said that trees reduce CO2 on average. The point is that grasses are even better at reducing CO2, so we're not encouraging the best use of the land.

B. The only necessary assumption with respect to trees is that at least some farmers plant trees in response to incentives. "Most" statements are poor answers on necessary assumption questions, as the negation of most is just 'not most', which could be as high as 50%.

C. This might strengthen the argument, but it's not necessary. It just adds an additional reason trees are bad. We don't *need* two reasons.

D. CORRECT. Negate this answer. If *no* trees are replacing native grasses, then there's no problem. **NEGATION:** No trees planted due to the incentives are planted where native grasses grow.

E. This isn't necessary. In fact, the argument is stronger if this isn't true and many governments promote native grasses.

Question 22

QUESTION TYPE: Role in Argument

CONCLUSION: The position of the driver's seat probably affects driving safety.

REASONING: The driving seat affects comfort and vision. These affect safety.

ANALYSIS: The sentence in question introduces two reasons why the position of the driving seat may affect safety.

The argument goes on to justify those two reasons. So the sentence is question is evidence that supports the conclusion. It is also supported by other evidence.

You might think that the sentence is therefore an intermediate conclusion. Don't get hung up on this type of distinction. Just know which way the evidence flows and you'll be able to find the best answer, whether it says 'premise' or 'intermediate conclusion'.

You should be able to see that the second sentence is the conclusion. Any sentence that gives the author's opinion or a probability is usually the conclusion. The second sentence does both.

A. The second sentence is the conclusion. The author gives his *opinion* on whether car seat position affects safety (it probably does).

B. The author doesn't disprove any claims in the argument. This is nonsense.

C. The author didn't explain any phenomena. He's speculating about whether seat position affects safety. He thinks it doesn't, but he hasn't looked at evidence to see if he is correct.

D. Same as B. The author doesn't argue against any claims.

E. CORRECT. The sentence in question gives us two reasons why seat position probably does affect safety.

Question 23

QUESTION TYPE: Point At Issue

ARGUMENTS: The doctor says trampolines are dangerous because they cause many injuries. He thinks we should require professional supervision for trampolines.

The trampoliner points out that injuries have increased less quickly than trampoline sales (so the injury rate is falling). Every activity has risks, even with supervision.

ANALYSIS: It sounds like they disagree on whether the level of trampoline related injuries is acceptable, and whether trampolines require professional supervision.

The right answer has to be something that both people have an opinion on. Many wrong answers talk about things that one or both of the two people say nothing about.

A. The trampoline enthusiast doesn't deny that trampolines cause injuries.
B. Neither person talks specifically about home trampolines.
C. The physician doesn't say anything about the injury rate.
D. It sounds like the enthusiast agrees that supervision can reduce (but not eliminate) injuries. However, they don't think it's justified to require supervision.
E. **CORRECT.** The trampoline enthusiast says no. All activities carry risks, even with supervision. But the doctor thinks we should supervise.

Question 24

QUESTION TYPE: Principle

CONCLUSION: The story was good journalism.

REASONING: The public was interested and the story was true.

ANALYSIS: For principle-justify questions, pretend you don't know what's right and wrong.

The editorial describes some things the station did. You must prove that those things lead to good journalism.

So, the right answer will be along the lines of 'if something is true and interests the public then it is good journalism'.

Identify the things the station did, then say they're good things. That's it.

A. This tells us when we should criticize journalists. We want to *not* criticize journalists.
B. Same as A.
C. **CORRECT.** The station did provide accurate information, and the public was interested. Therefore, according to this answer the station produced good journalism.
D. This is a necessary condition for good journalism. We want a sufficient condition.
E. This helps us prove that something *isn't* good journalism. We want to prove that the story was good journalism.

Question 25

QUESTION TYPE: Must Be True

FACTS:

1. Coffee or Restaurant → Public Place
2. ~~Comfortable~~ → ~~Well Designed~~ (For public places)
3. Well Designed → Comfortable (contrapositive)
4. Comfortable → Spacious Interior

ANALYSIS: You can combine the 3rd and 4th claims to get this statement about public places:

Well Designed → Comfortable → Spacious Interior

This chain applies to coffeehouses or restaurants, since they are public places. So any well designed coffee house is spacious.

I didn't draw the most statement. It doesn't connect with anything. I prefer to leave most statements alone until I've drawn the rest of the diagram, as you generally can't use them to form logical chains.

This most statement turned out to be useless fluff.

A. We know comfortable places have large interiors. But this answer mixes up necessary and sufficient. A large public place doesn't have to be comfortable.

B. This answer just gets the 'most' statement backwards. You can't reverse a 'most' statement.

C. There are lots of public places: museums, libraries, malls, subway stations. We know *most* well designed public places have artwork, but maybe the art is in the public places I listed and not in coffee houses.

D. CORRECT. Coffee houses are public places. We know that well designed public places are comfortable, and that comfortable places are spacious. So any well designed coffeehouse is spacious. See the diagrams above.

E. This answer confuses sufficient and necessary. We only know:
'Well designed → comfortable → spacious'

The reverse doesn't have to be true. I've been in large, ugly coffee houses.

Section II - Logic Games

Game 1 - Piano Recitals

Questions 1-5

Setup

The setup of this game is quite simple. However, the questions make up for it. A few of the later questions are harder than normal, for a pure sequencing game.

Ok, time to make a diagram. You should always read the rules before drawing, it lets you make additional deductions.

For instance we can combine rules 1 and 3. G is before HF, which are in either order. The box with a line over it indicates HF can be reversed:

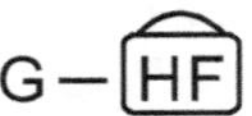

Secondly, K is before both HF and J. You can combine all three rules in one diagram:

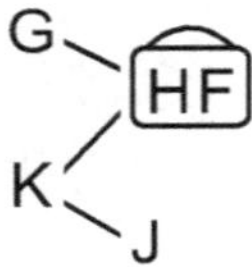

That's it. Of course, it's important to know how to read this diagram.

J could go before G, for example. Even though J is to the right of G on the diagram, there's no line connecting them.

The only rule for J is that it goes after K.

Draw a few sample orders and refer to the original rules if you're still unfamiliar with how to read sequencing diagrams. It should become second nature to make correct scenarios.

Hint: there are LOTS of different ways to make a correct scenario. Any scenario that doesn't violate a rule is 100% fine.

Main Diagram

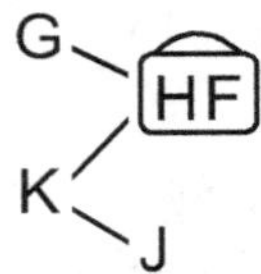

Remember that K or G could be first, and that G could go before or after J.

J or HF could be last.

Question 1

For list questions, go through the rules and use them to eliminate answers one by one.

Rule 1 eliminates **E.** G must be earlier than F.

Rule 2 eliminates **A** and **B.** K has to be earlier than H and J.

Rule 3 eliminates **C.** H must be beside F.

D is **CORRECT.** It violates no rules.

Question 2

It's helpful to make a new diagram when a question gives you a new rule. Just put G after J, and copy the other rules from the main diagram:

K–J–G–[HF]

A is **CORRECT.** F can go fourth or fifth. All the other answers are impossible.

Question 3

You're looking for something that can't be true.

This question tests whether you combined the third rule with the other rules. If you did that, then you know H has to come after G and K.

C is **CORRECT.**

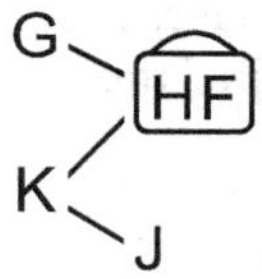

G \ [HF]
K / [HF]
K \ J

I'm not drawing scenarios to prove all the other answers correct, as you'll benefit more from trying them yourself. But here's proof that **A** is possible, for example:

G	K	H	F	J
1	2	3	4	5

The general rule is that if something isn't explicitly forbidden by the rules, it's allowed. So this diagram would also work to disprove **A:**

K	G	H	F	J
1	2	3	4	5

F is fourth in both diagrams. Neither is better than the other, they're both perfectly good proofs that **A** is possible and therefore wrong.

For all the wrong answers on this question there are many scenarios that disprove them.

Any drawing you make that doesn't violate one of the rules from the setup is a valid drawing. It's good practice to make them for all answers, quickly, when reviewing.

Question 4

Main Diagram

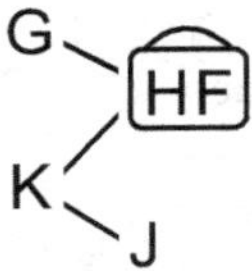

Here's where the questions start to get trickier. This question asks us what would 'fully determine' the order of the students.

The big wildcard in this game is HF. Those two variables can go in either order. So the right answer has to lock down their order.

Unfortunately, that insight doesn't help here. All the answers include H or F.

But there are other variables, and there are no rules that tell us the order of G and K, or G and J. So you need to settle that.

This is important, so I'll repeat it. The correct answer must lock down the relative order of G, K and J. If an answer leaves some uncertainty about where they go, it's wrong.

A doesn't work, because it doesn't affect G, K or J.

B is a poor candidate, because we already knew G was before HF.

C is a bit better. It tells us the order of FHJ. But it doesn't tell us the order of G and K. Either could be first.

D is also partly successful. It tells us the order ends with JHF. But it doesn't affect the order of G and K. Either could go first.

E is **CORRECT.** The answer tells us that KFH go in a row. We still have to place G and J.

G must go before F, so we get GKFH. And J must go after K. So we get this order:

G	K	F	H	J
1	2	3	4	5

Question 5

Main Diagram

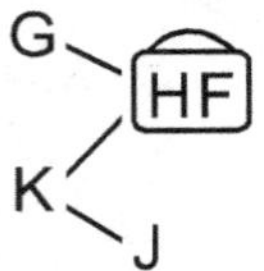

This question is a bit tricky. I almost got it wrong, because I mistakenly thought J could go fourth.

First, it's obvious H and F can each go fourth. We've seen many scenarios that put them there.

Here's one, just for proof. Remember that HF are reversible, so either could go fourth in this scenario:

G	K	J	H	F
1	2	3	4	5

So at least two students can go fourth: H and F.

G and K *can't* go fourth, because they're stuck earlier than HF. G and K can go third at the latest.

That leaves only J as a candidate.

The problem with putting J fourth is that it leaves no open spaces for HF to go beside each other. Have a look. Both G and K need to go before HF:

G	K		J	
1	2	3	4	5

HF ?

J leaves no space for HF. And if you put HF earlier than third, then there would be no way to put G and K in front of HF.

So **B** is **CORRECT.** Only H and F can go fourth.

Game 2 - Craft Open House
Questions 6-11

Setup

This is a linear game. It's *less* complicated than it looks.

My central theory for logic games is that success depends on figuring out how to make a complicated situation less complex.

Our brains can't handle more than about 7 facts at the same time, and the more facts we have to keep track of, the worse we do. So every rule you simplify improves your effectiveness.

For instance, the game lists three teachers, so you might think they're an important part of the game.

They aren't. Instead, the six presentations are all you have to worry about.

So you *could* draw this list of teachers, but I don't find it helpful.

j : N,O

k : P,S,T

l : W

Exactly *one* question asked about a teacher (question 9), and you can just look back to the rules to see what classes that teacher teaches.

The first rule does involve a teacher, but we can turn this into a rule about the presentation.

The rule says K can't give two presentations in a row. What this *really* means is that P, S and T can't be beside each other. Here's how I drew it:

If you studied Powerscore, you'll have seen this diagram, and you'll recognize that I'm using it the wrong way. Technically, in the Powerscore system, this diagram means that PST can't form a group of three.

Who cares? I'm giving the diagram a new meaning for this game. I know the context of the game. Only the first rule keeps people apart. So I read my diagram as meaning you can't have PS, SP, PT, TS, etc.

The traditional way to draw this rule would be like this:

I personally find this diagram hard to read quickly. On logic games I care most of all about being right AND fast.

You should be copying this diagram on the page as you follow along with these explanations. Use whichever method makes more sense to you.

Rule 2:

S–O

Rule 3:

T–W

This game only has six spaces. That's pretty restrictive. Here's the setup:

1	2	3	4	5	6
Ø					S̸
W̸					T̸

I've added in the deductions from the first and second rule.

We've drawn all the rules. But before starting a game, you should always see if a logic game has a particularly restricted point. Here, P, S and T are very restricted. Especially S and T.

You always have to space PST apart from each other. You'll get diagrams that look like this. The X's represent PST in any order:

X _ X _ X _
1 2 3 4 5 6
Ø (not O in 1), S̶ (not S in 6)
W̶ (not W in 1), T̶ (not T in 6)

X _ _ X _ X
1 2 3 4 5 6
Ø (not O in 1), S̶ (not S in 6)
W̶ (not W in 1), T̶ (not T in 6)

There are too many possibilities to bother drawing each one, but you should be aware that whenever you place one of PST, the others may be forced into specific spots.

Especially if there is no PST in spot 1 or 6. PST take up 5 spaces at minimum. The first diagram with the X's is an example of this.

I said S and T are particularly restricted. This is because they are affected by other rules. Their order is S - O and T - W.

So out of PST, P tends to have to go last. If P goes before S and T, there often isn't enough space to put S - O and T - W. A couple of questions test this deduction.

Main Diagram

_ _ _ _ _ _
1 2 3 4 5 6
Ø (not O in 1), S̶ (not S in 6)
W̶ (not W in 1), T̶ (not T in 6)

(1) P̶S̶T̶ (PST not adjacent)

(2) S–O

(3) T–W

Question 6

For list questions, go through the rules and use them to eliminate answers one by one.

Rule 1 eliminates **A** and **E.** PST can't be together.

Rule 2 eliminates **D.** S must be earlier than O.

Rule 3 eliminates **B.** T must be earlier than W.

C is **CORRECT.** It violates no rules.

Question 7

When a question gives you a new rule, draw a new diagram and ask how the new rule affects existing rules.

The question places T fifth. We know that T is before W (rule 3):

```
                T   W
__  __  __  __  __  __
1   2   3   4   5   6
not O               not S
not W               not T
```

Next, T can't be beside P or S (rule 1).

PST need five spaces to spread out. Since T is fifth, then P/S must go first and third.

Whenever there's only two possibilities, it's helpful to draw both. It should only take you a few seconds to draw these two diagrams:

```
P       S       T   W
__  __  __  __  __  __
1   2   3   4   5   6
not O               not S
not W               not T
```

```
S       P       T   W
__  __  __  __  __  __
1   2   3   4   5   6
not O               not S
not W               not T
```

Now you can make separate deductions on each diagram. For instance, you know O is after S:

```
P   N   S   O   T   W
__  __  __  __  __  __
1   2   3   4   5   6
not O               not S
not W               not T
```

```
        N,O
S       P       T   W
__  __  __  __  __  __
1   2   3   4   5   6
not O               not S
not W               not T
```

In the second diagram, N and O go in either order.

D is **CORRECT.** S can go third or first.

It turns out we solved a bit more than we needed, but it's always helpful to practice the process of making deductions.

Alternate Method - Elimination

You could also solve this question by elimination.

A is wrong because W has to go sixth, so N can't go there.

B is wrong because P can't go beside T, and T is fifth.

E is wrong because W has to go after T, so W is sixth.

Elimination is a very effective method. Now we're down to two answers, **B** and **C.**

To solve the question at this point, you would just try a couple of diagrams to see whether S can go second, or third.

Question 8

This question places N first. Remember that PST need five spaces. If N is first, then PST must go in spaces 2, 4 and 6, represented by X's:

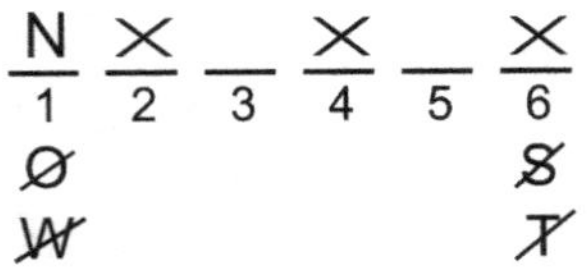

```
N  X  _  X  _  X
1  2  3  4  5  6
Ø              S̸
W̸              T̸
```

S and T can't go last, due to rules 2 and 3. So P goes last, and ST go in 2 and 4, in either order. We can draw two diagrams to capture both possibilities:

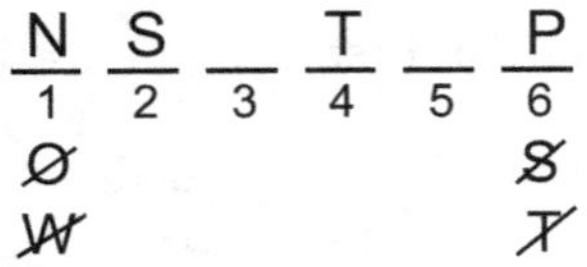

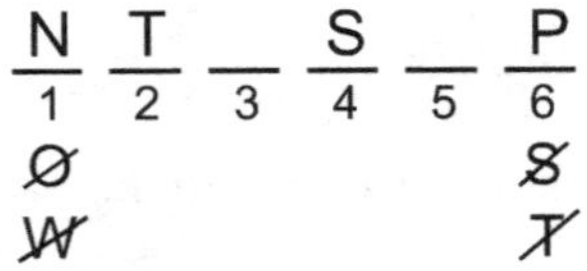

```
N  S  _  T  _  P
1  2  3  4  5  6
Ø              S̸
W̸              T̸
```

```
N  T  _  S  _  P
1  2  3  4  5  6
Ø              S̸
W̸              T̸
```

Next, apply rules 2 and 3 (T-W and S-O) In the first diagram, W must go in spot 5, after T.

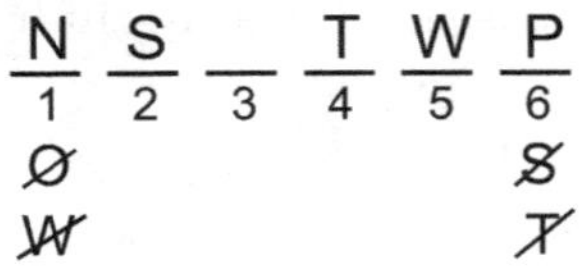

```
N  S  _  T  W  P
1  2  3  4  5  6
Ø              S̸
W̸              T̸
```

In the second diagram, O must go in spot 5, after S.

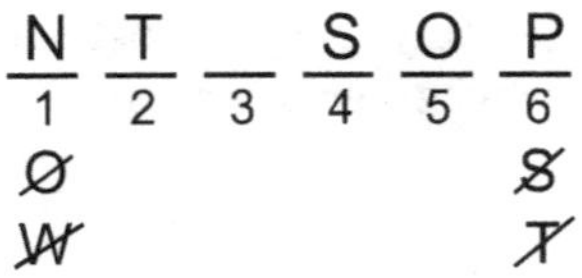

```
N  T  _  S  O  P
1  2  3  4  5  6
Ø              S̸
W̸              T̸
```

That leaves space 5 open for the remaining variable. In the first diagram, O goes in space 3, and in the second diagram, W goes in space 3.

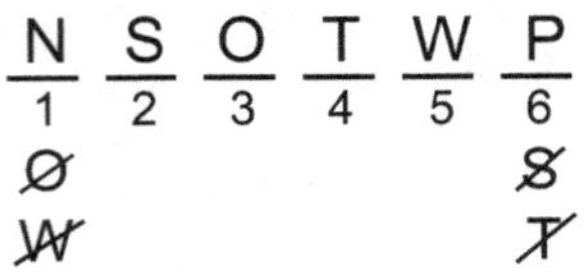

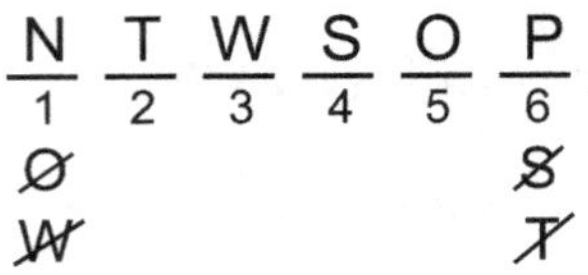

```
N  S  O  T  W  P
1  2  3  4  5  6
Ø              S̸
W̸              T̸
```

```
N  T  W  S  O  P
1  2  3  4  5  6
Ø              S̸
W̸              T̸
```

If that was confusing, draw the diagrams yourself and you should see how it works. Another way of looking at it is that TW and SO are interchangeable, in spaces 2-3 and 4-5.

E is **CORRECT**. Woodworking can be third.

Question 9

This is the only question that references one of the teachers: Jiang. We know they present N and O. So you can read this question as asking which two spaces can't be filled by N and O.

I solved this question by drawing each answer. Sometimes there's no other method, so you should practice getting fast at making correct diagrams.

You should try making diagrams to disprove the answers yourself, now, before looking at mine.

Any diagram that follows the rules will disprove an answer, if the diagram has NO in the right places.

O is important, remember that O comes after N. That means O can't go first. So for answers A-C, you'd have to put N first and O in the other spot.

The other rules are that PST are spread out, and T goes before W.

This diagram disproves **A:**

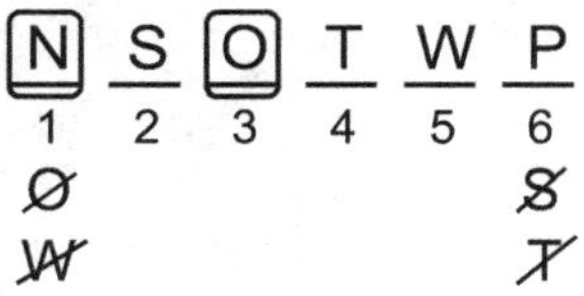

```
[N] S [O] T W P
 1  2  3  4 5 6
 Ø            S̸
 W̸            T̸
```

This diagram disproves **C:**

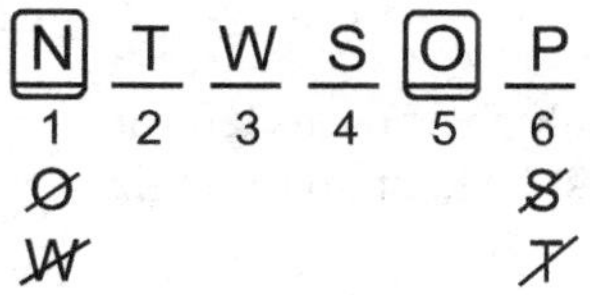

```
[N] T W S [O] P
 1  2 3 4  5  6
 Ø            S̸
 W̸            T̸
```

This diagram disproves **D:**

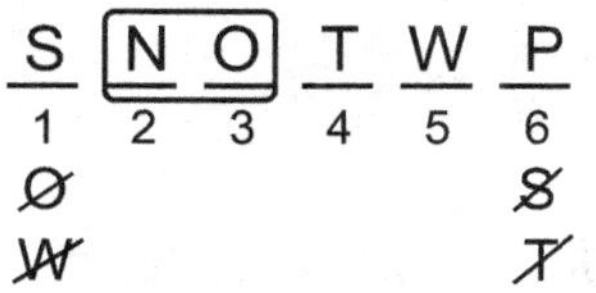

```
S [N O] T W P
1  2 3  4 5 6
Ø           S̸
W̸           T̸
```

This diagram disproves **E:**

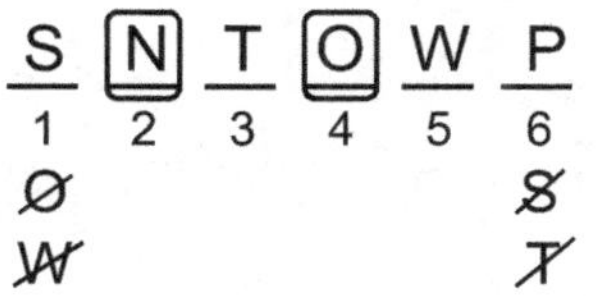

```
S [N] T [O] W P
1  2  3  4  5 6
Ø             S̸
W̸             T̸
```

B is **CORRECT.** If you put NO in one and four, there's no place to put PST without putting them together:

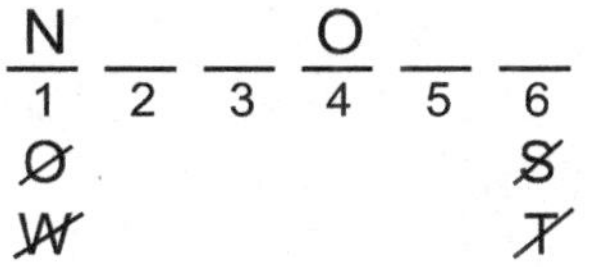

```
N _ _ O _ _
1 2 3 4 5 6
Ø         S̸
W̸         T̸
```

You'd be forced to put two of PST together in 2-3 or 4-5.

Question 10

If N is 6th, then there are only five spaces left for PST. Since these letters must be kept apart, their positions looks like this:

X _ X _ X N
1 2 3 4 5 6
Ø S̸
W̸ T̸

We can deduce a bit more. Rules 2 and 3 say that both S and T need a variable after them (S-O and T-W). So neither S nor T can go fifth.

Therefore P must go fifth.

Once again there are two possibilities. Either S is first and T is third, or the opposite:

S _ T _ P N
1 2 3 4 5 6
Ø S̸
W̸ T̸

T _ S _ P N
1 2 3 4 5 6
Ø S̸
W̸ T̸

Next, apply rules 2 and 3. The 4th spot is the limiting spot in both cases.

In the first diagram, W must go 4th to be after T.

S _ T W P N
1 2 3 4 5 6
Ø S̸
W̸ T̸

In the second diagram, O must go 4th to be after S.

T _ S O P N
1 2 3 4 5 6
Ø S̸
W̸ T̸

There's only one spot left in each diagram, so put the other variables there. In the first diagram, O goes second:

S O T W P N
1 2 3 4 5 6
Ø S̸
W̸ T̸

In the second diagram, W goes second:

T W S O P N
1 2 3 4 5 6
Ø S̸
W̸ T̸

Once again, I've shown more deductions than we needed. We could have stopped with the very first deduction: P is 5th. **B** is **CORRECT**.

However, you never know which deduction will be tested. So it's valuable to practice making all of them. Usually it doesn't take long to add the extra deductions.

Question 11

It's helpful to use scenarios from past diagrams to disprove answers.

This scenario from question 9 disproves **A:**

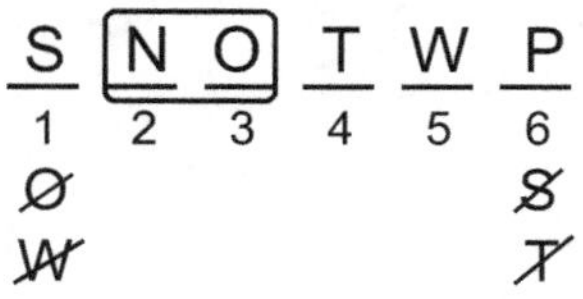

```
S [N  O] T  W  P
1  2  3  4  5  6
Ø              S̸
W̸              T̸
```

The correct answer to question 6 disproves **B.**

This scenario from question 8 disproves **D:**

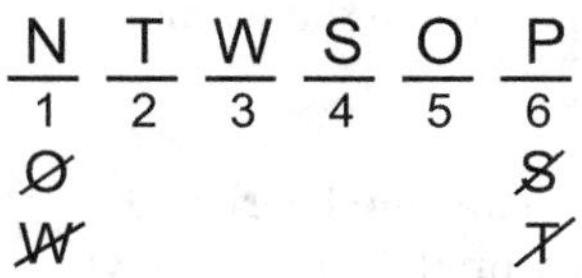

```
N  T  W  S  O  P
1  2  3  4  5  6
Ø              S̸
W̸              T̸
```

This scenario from question 10 disproves **E:**

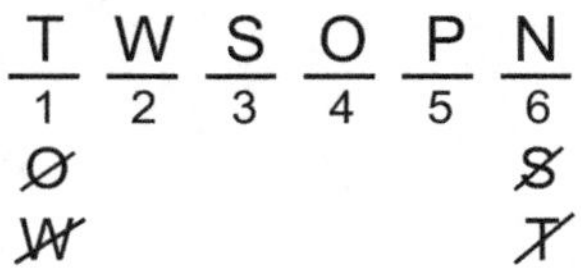

```
T  W  S  O  P  N
1  2  3  4  5  6
Ø              S̸
W̸              T̸
```

C is **CORRECT**. PST are pretty restricted. Placing one of them fifth creates this order:

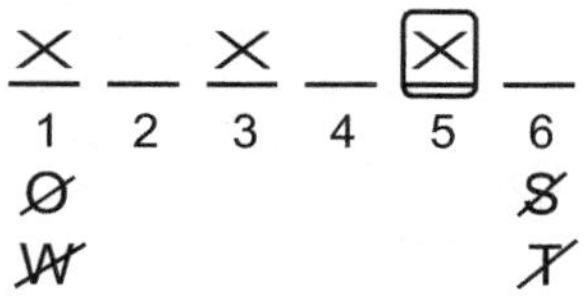

```
X  _  X  _ [X] _
1  2  3  4  5  6
Ø              S̸
W̸              T̸
```

Placing one of PST second creates this order:

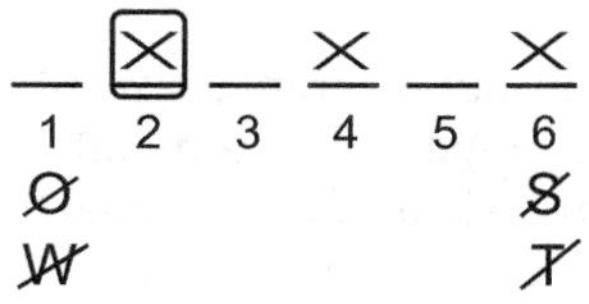

```
_ [X] _  X  _  X
1  2  3  4  5  6
Ø              S̸
W̸              T̸
```

This is the central point of the game. PST need at least five spaces. If you're still unsure about how this works, you should redo this game in a day or two, and keep redoing it until this makes sense.

So, **C** doesn't work because if you place P 2nd, then S and T must go 4th and 6th.

Except, S and T can't go 6th. They both need another workshop after them. Therefore P can't go 2nd.

Game 3 - Luncheon
Questions 12-16

Setup

This is a grouping game. You need a firm grasp of the rules to solve this game. Make sure you've reread them before reading this explanation.

I set this game up using an in-out diagram (drawn later). I usually don't use this type of diagram, but for this game I found it extremely useful to be able to show which variables are out.

This is because the game often places three variables out, which means that *all* the other variables are in.

There are two things I want to point out. First, it's fine to modify your diagramming style based on circumstances.

Second, you don't have to do games perfectly. I didn't use an in-out diagram when I first did this game. I got everything right, but I struggled.

When I sat down to explain it, I realized an in-out diagram would be much simpler.

So my original diagram wasn't the same as my final diagram. You might ask: why bother studying these final diagrams then?

Well, even though I didn't draw an in-out diagram, I was very aware of which variables are out. That comes with practice, and from having drawn 'out' diagrams on previous games.

So by practicing with the best diagrams, you'll stand a better shot of coming up with great diagrams when you see new games. And even if you don't get the ideal diagram, your intuition will be better for having studied ideal diagrams.

Ok, on to the rules. There are eight foods, and five of them are included. Take note whenever a game includes only some of the variables. We know, for instance, that if three variables are left out, then the other five must be in. This comes up a lot in this game.

The dishes are desserts, main courses, and sides. Some are hot. Here's the list. I indicated the hot foods by putting a box around them.

d : [F],G

m : [N],O,P

s : [T],V,W

You could draw a separate list of hot foods, but it's best to stick to the smallest possible number of diagrams. That makes it easier to see the whole setup.

Here's the in/out diagram I mentioned earlier. I included the first rule directly on it. That rule says that at least one dessert, main course and side dish are in:

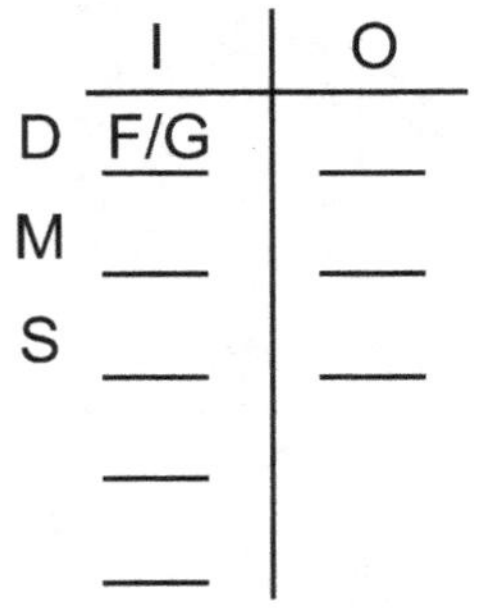

	I	O
D	F/G	___
M	___	___
S	___	___
	___	
	___	

I included one slot for dessert, main course, and side dishes. **Note that these only refer to the in group. The out group can be any type of dish.**

There are only two desserts: F and G. So at least one of F and G is in. I drew that on the diagram.

Rule two I just memorized: it says you always need at least one hot food. You could draw '1+ Hot' in your list of rules if you prefer.

Rule three says either PW are both in, or both out:

[PW] or ~~[PW]~~

Rule four says that if G is in, O is in:

G → O

Rule five says that if N is in, V is out:

N → ~~V~~

If you're still making mistakes or forgetting contrapositives, you should draw the contrapositives for rules four and five. Otherwise it's not necessary. Here are the contrapositives:

~~O~~ → ~~G~~
V → ~~N~~

Rule five is important. One of N or V is always out. This type of rule comes up again and again on logic games.

N and V could both be out together, mind you. The rule doesn't say 'if N is out, V is in'.

But at least one always has to be out. You can put this deduction on the main diagram:

	I	O
D	F/G	N/V
M	___	___
S	___	___
	___	
	___	

We could stop here. But there's one more deduction which is somewhat useful.

It has to do with the third rule. PW are either in or out. When the game gives you only two possibilities, you should try both of them. This usually leads to deductions.

Not much happens if we put PW in. Still, this lets us view the scenario more clearly.:

	I	O	
D	F/G	N/V	N/V
M	P	___	T
S	W	___	F/G
	___		O
	___		

I drew the remaining variables to the right of the diagram. It's much easier to visualize combinations when the open slots and remaining variables are written down in front of you.

Note that I put P and W in the M and S slots. This makes it clear that rule one is fulfilled in this scenario.

Now, if we put PW out, then three variables are out: P, W, and one of N/V.

That means everyone else is in!

	I	O
D	F	N/V
M	O	P
S	T	W
	G	
	N/V	

So if PW are out, then the only uncertainty is which of N or V is in.

I actually don't use these scenarios very much in the explanations. But I'm definitely aware of them, and you should be too.

Studying these deductions upfront is worthwhile. Sometimes you'll get them, and even if you don't your intuition will be better.

Main Diagram

	I	O	
D	F/G	N/V	N/V
M	P	___	T
S	W	___	F/G
	___		O
	___		

	I	O
D	F	N/V
M	O	P
S	T	W
	G	
	N/V	

1. PW or ~~PW~~
2. G → O
3. N → ~~V~~

I didn't draw one rule. The second rule says that there's always at least one hot food: F, N or T.

Some rules are hard to draw, and I find it easier to memorize them.

Question 12

For list questions, go through the rules and use them to eliminate answers one by one.

Rule 2 eliminates **E.** We need at least one hot food.

Rule 3 eliminates **D.** P can't be in the in group without W.

Rule 4 eliminates **C.** G needs O.

Rule 5 eliminates **A.** N and V can't be together.

B is **CORRECT.** It violates no rules.

Question 13

I skipped this question the first time I did the game. I hoped later questions would give me scenarios that I could use to eliminate answers.

That didn't end up helping much. So I came back and make scenarios to disprove wrong answer. Fortunately, with practice, you can learn to make correct scenarios quite quickly.

Try to disprove the wrong answers on your own first before you check my scenarios. Aim to do it correctly, and fast. If it feels slow, redo it until it's quick and second nature.

This scenario eliminates **A:**

	I	O
D	G	V
M	N	F
S	W	T
	O	
	P	

This scenario eliminates **B:**

	I	O
D	F	V
M	N	G
S	T	O
	P	
	W	

This scenarios eliminates **C:**

	I	O
D	F	N
M	O	T
S	V	G
	P	
	W	

The second scenario from the setup eliminates **E.** V can be out with W, since either N or V could be out:

	I	O
D	F	N/V
M	O	P
S	T	W
	G	
	N/V	

D is **CORRECT.** It says P and O are out. You also have to put one of N/V out. That's three variables.

But then you have to put W out, because PW are always in or out together. So P, O, W and one of N/V are out.

That's four variables out, which is too many.

Question 14

Whenever a question gives you a new rule, you should draw a new diagram that uses that rule.

O is the only main course. That means the other main courses are out (N and P):

	I	O
D	F/G	N
M	O	P
S	___	___
	___	
	___	

Since P is out, W must be out too (rule 3):

	I	O
D	F/G	N
M	O	P
S	___	W
	___	
	___	

All three out spaces are full. That means every other variable is in:

	I	O
D	F	N
M	O	P
S	T	W
	G	
	V	

Once again, we've done too much work. But I wanted to walk you through all the deductions that are possible.

Since P is out, W can't be selected. **E** is **CORRECT.**

A small note on how to fill in the final diagram. It's helpful to have a default way to fill in variables, so you don't get stuck wondering who goes where.

If I'm filling in the listed D, M and S spots, I just go with the hot foods, F, N and T. There's no reason not to put them there.

So if I'm trying to build a scenario, I will fill it with F, N and T unless there is some reason to use other variables.

In this case, I did F, O and T because the question told us to put in O for the main course.

This meant that when filling in all five variables, I automatically filled in F and T. Then I stopped to consider which variables remained, and filled in G and V.

With a default order to fill things in, you can create diagrams much faster. Obviously, your default order must obey all the rules.

Question 15

If we don't have F, then we have G, since at least one dessert must be in. That means we have O as well:

	I	O
D	G	N/V
M	O	F
S	___	___
	___	
	___	

The next step may not be obvious. PW must be in or out. That requires two spaces. There's only one space in the out column.

So PW have to be in:

	I	O
D	G	N/V
M	O	F
S	W	___
	P	
	___	

Finally, we need a hot food (rule 2). The hot foods are F, N and T.

F is already out, so one of N or T is selected. That means V has to be out, because there's no space left:

	I	O
D	G	V
M	O	F
S	W	N/T
	P	
	N/T	

So we can figure almost everything out, based on the local rule!

A is wrong because both P and O must be selected.

B is wrong because W must be selected.

C is wrong because there's only room for one hot food. It's one of N/T.

D is **CORRECT.** We could place N in, and T out:

	I	O
D	G	V
M	O	F
S	W	T
	P	
	N	

E is wrong because V is always out for this question.

Question 16

If T and V are in, then W is out. So P is out.

Sound familiar? This is the second scenario from the setup. N, P and W are out, so everything else is in:

	I	O
D	F	N
M	O	P
S	T	W
	G	
	V	

A is **CORRECT.**

Game 4 - Television Programming
Questions 17-23

Setup

This is a linear game, with a slight twist. The six slots include hours and half hours. You must keep track of which variables can start on the hour, and which ones start on the half hour.

One of the variables, G, is an hour long. I kept track of this by drawing it GG. But, you have to remember that GG = 1 variable. Some questions require you to count the number of variables.

Here's my variable list:

GGRSTW

Here's the main diagram:

__ __ __ __ __ __
1 1.5 2 2.5 3 3.5

The first rule says that GG can only start on the hour. There's no great way to draw this rule. Better just to memorize it. I'll add it to the main diagram later, which is another way not to forget. But if you do want to draw a way to list the rule, just make something up, like this:

GG = 1.0 h

You can do the same for rule 2. I do prefer to memorize it and/or put these rules on the main diagram. But here's a plausible way to draw the second rule:

T = 0.5 h

Rule 3 says R is before S:

R—S

Rule 4 says that either W is directly before T, or T is somewhere before W:

[WT] or T—W

A couple questions require you to remember this rule. Hint: if W is first, then it's definitely before T.

I like to put rules 1 and 2 directly on the main diagram:

__ __ __ __ __ __
1 1.5 2 2.5 3 3.5
T̸ $G̸_1$ T̸ $G̸_1$ T̸ $G̸_1$

The G's are labelled G1, as a reminder that it's just the first G that can't go on the half hour.

Honestly, it's probably better just to memorize those two rules. It's not hard. Just read them a few times each, and remember that there are two rules that deal with hours and half-hours.

I'm keeping the 'not' rules under the main diagram for the rest of these explanations. Not everyone reading these will memorize the rules, so that will make the diagrams clearer for them.

But if you're serious about doing well, I recommend practicing simply memorizing these rules. It's not hard to memorize 1-2 key rules on each game, and you go *so* much faster when you do. Your diagrams will also be simpler and quicker to draw.

Main Diagram

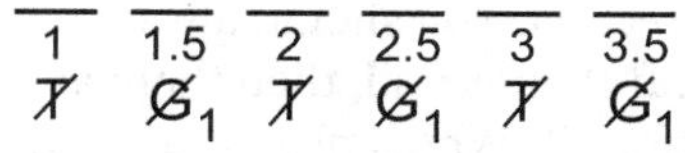

1	1.5	2	2.5	3	3.5
~~T~~	~~G~~$_1$	~~T~~	~~G~~$_1$	~~T~~	~~G~~$_1$

(1) R—S

(2) [WT] or T—W

I've drawn rules 1-2 directly on the diagram. G must start on the hour, and T goes on the half hour.

It's also a very good idea just to memorize them, as you can make new diagrams much faster, with fewer mistakes.

Question 17

For list questions, go through the rules and use them to eliminate answers one by one.

Rule 1 eliminates **C.** GG can't start on the half hour.

I did find it hard to eliminate this answer. I solved it by counting R, T, W as 1.0, 1.5, and 2.0. I then realized that GG starts on 2.5, which doesn't work.

Rule 2 eliminates **A.** T has to start on the half-hour. I had the same difficulty eliminating this answer as I did with C. I got around it by counting.

Rule 3 eliminates **E.** R has to go before S.

Rule 4 eliminates **D.** If W is before T, then W has to be *immediately* before T.

B is **CORRECT.** It violates no rules.

Question 18

When a question gives you a new rule, you should draw it.

We know that if W is before T, then W has to go *immediately* before T.

If W is first, then it's definitely before T. So the diagram starts like this:

W	T				
1	1.5	2	2.5	3	3.5
$\not T$	$\not G_1$	$\not T$	$\not G_1$	$\not T$	$\not G_1$

Now, we need to know how many orders are possible. It's probably a small number.

Best to start by placing a restricted variable. GG can only go on the hour. So there are only two possibilities:

W	T	G	G		
1	1.5	2	2.5	3	3.5
$\not T$	$\not G_1$	$\not T$	$\not G_1$	$\not T$	$\not G_1$

W	T			G	G
1	1.5	2	2.5	3	3.5
$\not T$	$\not G_1$	$\not T$	$\not G_1$	$\not T$	$\not G_1$

Only R and S are left. We know R goes before S (rule 3). So there are only two possibilities:

W	T	G	G	R	S
1	1.5	2	2.5	3	3.5
$\not T$	$\not G_1$	$\not T$	$\not G_1$	$\not T$	$\not G_1$

W	T	R	S	G	G
1	1.5	2	2.5	3	3.5
$\not T$	$\not G_1$	$\not T$	$\not G_1$	$\not T$	$\not G_1$

B is **CORRECT.**

Question 19

This question places R second. You should always look at restricted spots. If R is second, then there is exactly one program before R. Which program could it be?

Not T. T can't start on the hour.

Not W. If W goes before R, then W is also before T. But the fourth rules says that T has to come right after W is W is before T.

Not S. S has to go after R.

So only GG can go before R. This means R is in the third slot (but they are still the second variable). Remember that GG only counts as one variable:

G	G	R			
1	1.5	2	2.5	3	3.5
$\not T$	$\not G_1$	$\not T$	$\not G_1$	$\not T$	$\not G_1$

T, W and S are left to place. S can go anywhere, since it's automatically after R. So let's focus on T and W.

T can only go on the half hour. So T can go fourth or sixth. If T is fourth, W and S can go in either order:

G	G	R	T	W,S	
1	1.5	2	2.5	3	3.5
$\not T$	$\not G_1$	$\not T$	$\not G_1$	$\not T$	$\not G_1$

If T is sixth, then W must go immediately before T (rule 4). S is left to go fourth:

G	G	R	S	W	T
1	1.5	2	2.5	3	3.5
$\not T$	$\not G_1$	$\not T$	$\not G_1$	$\not T$	$\not G_1$

D is **CORRECT.** There is no way to put W third.

All of other answers are possible, on one of the two diagrams.

Question 20

There are two possibilities, if S is third. Either S is in the 3rd slot:

		S			
1	1.5	2	2.5	3	3.5
$\not T$	$\not G_1$	$\not T$	$\not G_1$	$\not T$	$\not G_1$

Or S is in the 4th slot, but is the third program, because GG comes earlier. GG would have to go first:

G	G		S		
1	1.5	2	2.5	3	3.5
$\not T$	$\not G_1$	$\not T$	$\not G_1$	$\not T$	$\not G_1$

Let's try to complete the first diagram.

We know R has to go before S. And in this diagram, GG has to go at 3 o'clock, because it's the only open spot left that is on the hour:

R

		S		G	G
1	1.5	2	2.5	3	3.5
$\not T$	$\not G_1$	$\not T$	$\not G_1$	$\not T$	$\not G_1$

T and W are left. There aren't two open spaces to place WT, so T must go somewhere before W instead (rule 4):

R	T	S	W	G	G
1	1.5	2	2.5	3	3.5
$\not T$	$\not G_1$	$\not T$	$\not G_1$	$\not T$	$\not G_1$

R goes first and T goes second because T must go on the half hour.

Let's try to fill out the second diagram, where GG goes first and S goes in the fourth slot.

We know R goes before S:

G	G	R	S		
1	1.5	2	2.5	3	3.5
$\not T$	$\not G_1$	$\not T$	$\not G_1$	$\not T$	$\not G_1$

Only T and W are left. T has to go on the half hour, so we get this order:

G	G	R	S	W	T
1	1.5	2	2.5	3	3.5
$\not T$	$\not G_1$	$\not T$	$\not G_1$	$\not T$	$\not G_1$

In both diagrams, W is fourth. **E** is **CORRECT.**

The other answers don't have to be true. At least one diagram shows that each of the other answers could be false.

Question 21

If GG is the third program, then it must be in the third spot, at 2 o'clock:

		G	G		
1	1.5	2	2.5	3	3.5
~~T~~	~~G~~$_1$	~~T~~	~~G~~$_1$	~~T~~	~~G~~$_1$

T is the next most restricted variable. T can only go on the half hour. So T can go second or last:

	T	G	G		
1	1.5	2	2.5	3	3.5
~~T~~	~~G~~$_1$	~~T~~	~~G~~$_1$	~~T~~	~~G~~$_1$

		G	G		T
1	1.5	2	2.5	3	3.5
~~T~~	~~G~~$_1$	~~T~~	~~G~~$_1$	~~T~~	~~G~~$_1$

If T is second, there are two main possibilities. Either W is first, and RS are last. Or R is first, and WS are last in either order:

W	T	G	G	R	S
1	1.5	2	2.5	3	3.5
~~T~~	~~G~~$_1$	~~T~~	~~G~~$_1$	~~T~~	~~G~~$_1$

W,S

R	T	G	G		
1	1.5	2	2.5	3	3.5
~~T~~	~~G~~$_1$	~~T~~	~~G~~$_1$	~~T~~	~~G~~$_1$

Both scenarios obey the fourth rule: W is either directly in front of T, or W is somewhere after T. Both diagrams also put R before S.

Let's look at the second diagram from above, where T is last. There is only one possibility. W must go fifth, directly before T, and RS must go first and second. (rules 3 and 4):

R	S	G	G	W	T
1	1.5	2	2.5	3	3.5
~~T~~	~~G~~$_1$	~~T~~	~~G~~$_1$	~~T~~	~~G~~$_1$

C is **CORRECT.** S could be the fourth program in this diagram, since W and S are reversible. Remember that GG is just *one* program:

W,S

R	T	G	G		
1	1.5	2	2.5	3	3.5
~~T~~	~~G~~$_1$	~~T~~	~~G~~$_1$	~~T~~	~~G~~$_1$

None of the other answers are possible.

Question 22

You can use past questions to eliminate answers on many must be true or must be false questions.

Any scenario that worked on a previous question is something that could be true.

This scenario from question 21 eliminates **A:**

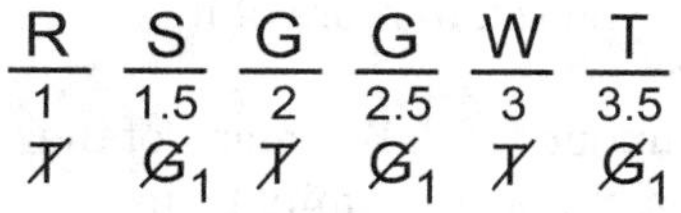

R	S	G	G	W	T
1	1.5	2	2.5	3	3.5
$\not{T}$	$\not{G}_1$	$\not{T}$	$\not{G}_1$	$\not{T}$	$\not{G}_1$

This scenario from question 20 eliminates **D:**

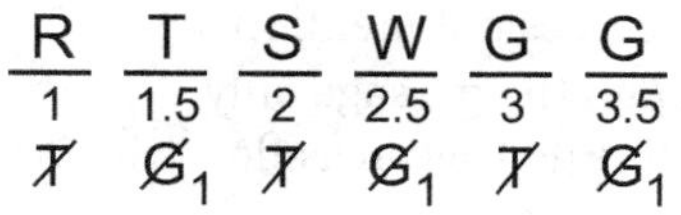

R	T	S	W	G	G
1	1.5	2	2.5	3	3.5
$\not{T}$	$\not{G}_1$	$\not{T}$	$\not{G}_1$	$\not{T}$	$\not{G}_1$

This diagram from question 19 shows that **E** is possible. W could be at 3 o'clock:

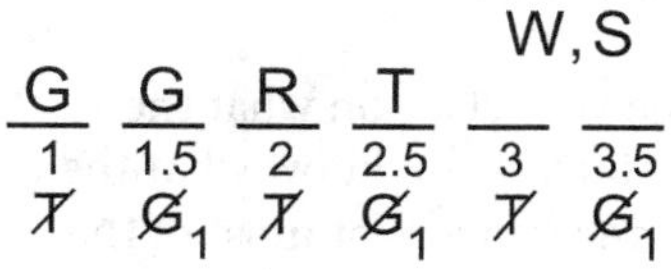

				W, S	
G	G	R	T		
1	1.5	2	2.5	3	3.5
$\not{T}$	$\not{G}_1$	$\not{T}$	$\not{G}_1$	$\not{T}$	$\not{G}_1$

That leaves **B** and **C.** This scenario eliminates **C:**

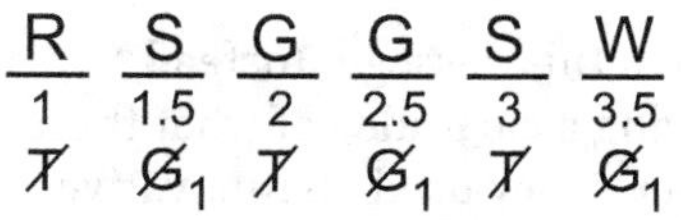

R	S	G	G	S	W
1	1.5	2	2.5	3	3.5
$\not{T}$	$\not{G}_1$	$\not{T}$	$\not{G}_1$	$\not{T}$	$\not{G}_1$

B is **CORRECT.** There's no way to put W right before R without placing T on an hourly slot, or breaking the rule about W coming immediately before T.

Try drawing it, and you'll see it can't be done. There's no good drawing I can make to show you, because you'd only think this answer works if you're forgetting a rule. I don't know which rule you're forgetting.

If you draw it yourself and refer carefully to the rules, you'll learn it better anyway.

Question 23

For rule substitution questions, you should consider the full effect of the rule in question. Usually the right answer is just a rephrasing of the rule's effects.

If GG can only go on the hours, then that means GG *can't* go on the half hours.

So GG can't start 2nd or 4th. **C** is **CORRECT.**

You might have noticed there's another half hour slot: 6th. This rule doesn't say GG can't go there. So how is this a complete answer?

Well, we don't need the first rule to tell us that GG can't start 6th. Since there are two G's, they couldn't start on the last spot. There's be no place to put both G's.

A is wrong because it would allow GG to start on the half hour as long as T was elsewhere.

B is wrong because it is too restrictive. GG should also be able to start 3rd.

D is just weird. It has nothing to do with the original rule. Normally putting G third doesn't affect R.

E also makes little sense. Avoid answers that introduce conditionals that weren't obviously part of the original rules.

Section III - Reading Comprehension

Passage 1 - Innovative Latina Autobiography

Questions 1-7

Paragraph Summaries

1. Literature by American Latinas was prominent in the 1980's. Latina autobiography also became popular in the late 1980's.
2. The Latinas' stories are innovative, confronting linguistic and cultural boundaries. Their autobiographies use innovative styles.
3. A lengthy description of the mixed styles used in three autobiographies.
4. These Latina authors have revolutionized autobiographies and shattered the silence that the world assumed Latinas were confined to.

Analysis

This is a classic theme for an LSAT passage. It's all here:

- Autobiographies no one has read, outside of a specialized community
- A minority group
- Innovative styles
- Breaking of multiple traditional boundaries
- Mixing of styles and genres

There's been some debate as to why these themes occur on the LSAT. My guess is that it's because almost no one knows anything about them. If this passage were about Shakespeare, then English majors would have an advantage. With this topic, almost no LSAT students have an edge.

A familiarity with LSAT themes will help you interpret these passages. An LSAT author will almost always be supportive of everything that nontraditional authors do. This supportive perspective can help you assess answer choices.

This support for nontraditional artists will generally exist on all passages of this type, though of course you must make sure the passage you are reading fits the model.

In this case, the Latina authors successfully cross boundaries and mix styles. The third paragraph is very important. You don't need to know all the details there, but it has a lot of useful information. A second reading will help you retain more of it.

This passage is hard to understand. But many of the answer choices are actually easy to eliminate, if you're clear about what the passage says.

For instance, the passage does not mention academics, or scholars, and the passage only mentions a critic once (line 30), as an aside.

Yet on question 5, all the wrong answers talk about scholars, critics, and academics. Those answers assume you were hallucinating when you read the passage. Stick to what the passage says!

This is why you should be very clear on what the passage says before you start. If you know what the passage says, then you'll recognize that most of the wrong answers are fancy nonsense. If you're interested in *why* the LSAC uses nonsense answers, I've written a note below.

There's little to analyze in this passage. Instead, success depends on having a clear idea of what these Latina authors have done. They used an innovative structure that mixes genres.

Note on Hallucinatory Answers

I mentioned that the answers to question 5 assume you were hallucinating. It's an odd situation: why do the wrong answers talk about academics, scholars, and critics? Those groups aren't mentioned in the passage.

This goes to the heart of what reading comprehension is testing. Many people are lazy readers. I am sometimes, too, but not when reading the LSAT. You shouldn't be either.

The Latina biographies sound vaguely scholarly. You can imagine a stereotypical left-wing professor talking about them over coffee. A literary critic might review these books for a newspaper. Booo-ring.

I'm not suggesting that these elites are the actual readers of the biographies. What I'm suggesting is that your entire cultural experience has given you stereotypes and biases. And most people in your culture will share the stereotype that only scholars and critics will read boring, fancy books like these Latina autobiographies.

Note that I am not saying that the autobiographies actually *are* boring. The books may in fact be very interesting. But the LSAC knows that most readers of this passage would assume the books are boring. Further, readers will assume that the books are boring in a specific, liberal, scholarly, lit-crit fashion.

And that's where LSAC hits you. They know most readers *associate* these books with dull academics and literary critics. So a lazy reader will *assume* the passage mentions those groups at some point.

Hence, several wrong answers refer to scholars, academics and critics, even though those groups are *not* in the passage. The LSAC knows *exactly* what biases you're prone to.

There's a method to this madness.

This is just one example, but it's part of a trend. On many passages wrong answers will refer to think that weren't in the passage. These answers are calculated to play to your unconscious biases. Know the passage well, and you can easily avoid them.

Question 1

DISCUSSION: For main point questions, the right answer must be true, and cover the main points of the passage.

You can first eliminate answers that aren't true.

A. This isn't even true, necessarily. The first paragraph mentioned poetry and fiction, then autobiographies. But the author didn't say that the *same* authors wrote poetry/fiction and autobiographies.

B. CORRECT. This is a weak answer, but it's the best one. I say it's weak because the author claimed that the Latina authors revolutionized autobiography (line 52), while this answer doesn't compliment the Latinas' achievements.

Nonetheless, this answer does adequately summarize how the Latina authors experimented to find an innovative way to tell their stories.

C. This answer isn't even true. The passage doesn't mention *traditional* Latina autobiography.

D. The passage's point wasn't that nonfictional narrative can be combined with other genres. We don't even know if Latinas were the first to mix genres. The author's idea is specific: these Latina authors revolutionized *autobiography*. Other authors may have already mixed styles in other non-fiction genres.

E. A critic is only mentioned on line 30. They talk about gender differences, but not ethnic/cultural differences. This is hardly the main point.

Question 2

DISCUSSION: The last paragraph covers this. Lines 53-55 say that the Latina authors used new structures to better tell their own stories.

The second paragraph expands on the multiple identities these women have: Mexican, American, Hispanic, English speaking, women, etc.

The passage says that the Latina authors needed a varied, non-traditional style to express their fragmented identities.

The wrong answers are all nonsense that rely on you being confused about the meaning of the passage. The main point was this: the authors were non-traditional, and they mixed genres.

A. Lines 28-30 say that these autobiographies were *not* chronological.
B. Non-narrative means poetry, essays, etc. The authors *did* use these genres. See lines 18-21. And no line says that the Latina authors excluded any non-narrative genres.
C. Line 30 says that at least one author wrote her autobiography in terms of her political development.
D. **CORRECT.** See the explanation above. The Latina authors had complex identities, so they needed a complex style to express their stories.
E. Stuff and nonsense. The authors *did* use poetry in their narratives.

Question 3

DISCUSSION: After I first read the passage, I couldn't remember a thing about *Getting Home Alive*.

I correctly assumed that the details of each book were not particularly relevant to the overall point of the passage. And I knew that if a question asked about *Getting Home Alive,* I could just reread that short section and refresh myself on the details.

So for this question, I reread the relevant section. It only took 5-10 seconds. That's how you should approach detail on RC passages: Don't worry about remembering it, but know where it is.

The relevant section starts at line 35. The previous discussions said that the other two books departed from convention. Line 35 says that *Getting Home Alive* departed even further. The rest of the paragraph describes the mixed voices used by the book, and how this was a good thing.

This question asks about the author's purpose in mentioning *Getting Home Alive,* so the right answer should focus on how the book's structure was different from traditional autobiography and even from the other two Latina autobiographies.

A. Line 35 implies that *Getting Home Alive* is similar to the other books in that all three use innovative structure.
B. Only line 39 mentions poems, and it doesn't explain how they are integrated into the book.
C. We know that this book used multiple voices. We don't know if this was common.
D. Not even true. Lines 42-43 say that the book's structure may *seem* confusing. The passage didn't say whether readers actually *do* find the book confusing.
E. **CORRECT.** Lines 35-49 are all about the book's innovative, multi-author structure.

Question 4

DISCUSSION: This question gives us no hints, so we can't go back to the passage before looking at the answers. We'll have to evaluate the answers one by one.

Remember the main point of the passage: the autobiographies have innovative structures.

A. CORRECT. See lines 17-21. These autobiographies use poetry, sketches and other forms commonly found in literature or other books. Line 36 mentions that the books are departing from the conventions of autobiography.
B. Line 20 mentions journal entries, but we don't know if they were unpublished, and we don't know if each autobiography used journal entries.
C. Careful. We know each author's cultural background was influential. But the authors may not have *analyzed* how their cultural background influenced their books' content.
D. We only know this is true of *Getting Home Alive*. The other authors may have written their own poetry.
E. Same as C. The authors used innovative structures. They surely had their reasons and methodologies for doing so. But the passage doesn't say that the authors explained their methods to their readers.

Question 5

DISCUSSION: See line 44. The author thinks that the book's structure is 'well-designed'. The author compliments *Getting Home Alive* and says nothing negative about the book.

(It's true that the book may *seem* confusing, but as the author says, it's *actually* well designed.)

So the author likes the book's innovative structure.

A. Total nonsense. The passage doesn't mention any other books by these authors. And the passage doesn't express any disappointment with the authors.
B. CORRECT. See lines 42-45. The author is aware readers may find the structure confusing.
C. Academics aren't even mentioned in the passage. This is just confusing fluff.
D. Same as C. Scholars aren't mentioned in the passage. This answer is ridiculous.
E. Except for line 30, the author never mentions critics. The author does say that the books have revolutionized autobiography (line 52), but they don't say whether critics have noticed.

Question 6

DISCUSSION: This is a passage about autobiographies. You've probably read one or two. An autobiography is usually a book where someone tells the story of their own life, chronologically. Traditional autobiographies tend to just be prose; they don't use poetry, sketches, song, etc.

'Existing generic parameters' refers to this traditional structure of autobiographies.

You can also answer this question by choosing something that the Latina authors *don't* do. Since they violate traditional structures, anything Latina authors don't do will probably fall into traditional 'existing generic parameters'.

A. CORRECT. Traditional autobiographies are chronological. And these untraditional Latina autobiographies are not chronological (line 29).
B. A traditional autobiography would not even use other modes of presentation, such as poetry.
C. This isn't clear. Many autobiographies are political, such as biographies written by politicians.
D. Same as B. Traditional biographies wouldn't even use poems. If they did, they'd be separate from the main text.
E. Traditional biographies only tell personal experiences in chronological narrative. They don't use poems, journal entries, sketches, etc.

Question 7

DISCUSSION: The question references lines 50-55. In those lines, the author claims that the Latina authors revolutionized autobiography.

Revolutionizing autobiography would require two things:

1. The Latinas were the first to use these new techniques.
2. The Latinas' autobiographies influenced how other authors wrote autobiographies.

If the Latinas weren't first, or if nobody paid attention to them, then they couldn't have revolutionized the field of autobiography.

A. This answer is complex and may sound like nonsense. If you don't understand an answer, focus on it one part at a time. Use the sections you understand to isolate the sections you don't.

'Chronological linear prose' is traditional autobiography, the opposite of what Latina authors use. This answer says that since the Latina autobiographies came out (around 1985) *few* authors have been recognized for using that traditional style. This suggests that the Latina authors had an impact and it strengthens the argument. We want to *weaken* the argument.

B. The author claimed that all autobiography was revolutionized, not just Latina autobiography.

So the number of critically acclaimed Latina autobiographies doesn't matter. Maybe there simply aren't that many Latina autobiographies.

What matters is whether there were other, non-Latina autobiographies that adopted the innovative techniques used by these Latinas. That would mean that the Latina autobiographies had influenced autobiography as a whole. This answer doesn't disprove that possibility.

C. 'Some' is a vague word. This answer could mean that 3 out of 1,000 autobiographies use a traditional structure. Who cares?

D. **CORRECT.** This shows that earlier autobiographies used the same structure that these new Latina autobiographies used. So the Latina autobiographies were not necessarily that innovative in their style.

E. Who cares about books that *aren't* autobiographies? The author's claim was only about autobiographies.

Passage 2 - Digital Archives
Questions 8-13

Paragraph Summaries

1. We have more information than ever, and it's harder to preserve.
2. Computers might help, but file types keep changing.
3. There's a lot of information, and it's deteriorating quickly. We won't have time to decide what information is worth saving before it starts to disappear.

Analysis

This passage describes a serious issue. We have a lot of information, and it's disappearing.

The passage has a clear structure.

1. Information is disappearing faster than ever.
2. Computers are tricky, because file types change.
3. Lastly, information is vanishing so rapidly that we won't be able to save all of it or even decide what is important to save.

Most of the questions involve details. To solve this passage effectively, you should have a clear grasp of the information in the passage, and be able to locate line references quickly.

I'm not going to repeat all the passage's information here, but the answers have line references to all the relevant information.

I will discuss the main themes. It's important to know what archivists do. They sort through all the information that we have, and decide what to keep.

Much of what we know about the past is thanks to past archivists. For instance, some people decided to save the works of Plato, and not other authors. So we know more about Plato. But as the passage mentions, we almost *lost* the works of Plato, too.

Today we have more information than ever, and it's getting harder to store. In the past, there wasn't that much information, and it lasted a long time. We have some paper that's thousands of years old.

Contrast this with technology. I'll bet there are some floppy disks in your parents' basement that you can no longer run. I personally have some Wordperfect files on my computer that I can't open. Remember wordperfect? It was still popular in 2001. Now there's nothing I can do with those files.

So all of our new storage methods can have short shelf lives. But at the same time, we're producing more information than ever. Think about everything you've seen on the internet today. Will future historians be able to access it? Will they be able to access this book that I'm writing?

Archivists thus face a difficult task.

1. There is more information than ever.
2. Much of it is unimportant.
3. Information is being destroyed rapidly.

These difficulties are the theme of the passage. Each paragraph gives specific details. As I mentioned, the best way to answer the questions is to know *where* to look to find specific details.

Note that computers are both part of the problem and the solution. Computers are what have allowed us to produce so much information. But lines 36-40 offer hope that computers might finally allow us to store things for the long term.

Question 8

DISCUSSION: The main point is that we have more information than ever, and it's decaying rapidly.

A. CORRECT. This is a good summary. We have more information, and it's decaying rapidly. So archivists have a tough job.
B. This completely contradicts the third paragraph. See lines 58-59.
C. Lines 34-36 show that archivists are reluctant to use computers. But this is hardly the main point of the entire passage.
D. Actually, the *capacity* of modern storage media is enormous. Hard drives are cheaper than ever. See line 23. It takes very little space to store information electronically.
E. This may be true, but it's not the main point. This is just a factor that makes things harder for archivists. With so much useless information, it's hard to sift through and find the stuff worth storing.

Question 9

DISCUSSION: This question asks which answer choice we're able to answer using the passage. This question type gives no guidance for which information will be relevant. You have to consider each answer choice with the whole passage in mind.

However, the question says the passage has information that allows you to answer the question in the right answer. So when you choose an answer, you should be able to check the passage to answer the question.

A. Lines 45-46 mention Vergil and Homer. Those lines don't say if any copies on parchment survived. Parchment was mentioned separately, on line 12.
B. We have no idea why acidic paper degrades. It was only mentioned in passing on lines 14-15.
C. CORRECT. Lines 27-29 say that optical storage disks were cutting edge in the 1980s.
D. Lines 9-11 say the tablets still exist, but we don't know how many survive.
E. Lines 49-53 mention Plato. They don't say how he originally wrote his works.

Question 10

DISCUSSION: As with question 9, you should justify the answer you choose by using a line from the passage.

If you can't justify the answer using the passage, there's a good chance you've made an error.

A. CORRECT. Lines 33-35 strongly suggest this. Those lines say that if archivists don't start using computers, they will run out of time.

We have more information than ever. Only computer storage (line 23) lets us store all of our information using very little space.

B. Lines 33-35 contradict this. We are running out of time and can't afford to wait.

C. It's true that digital storage has durability problems (second paragraph). But the first paragraph describes how even non-computerized information is decaying rapidly.

D. The author doesn't mention paintings. There's no reason to think that it's hard to store photographs. The author doesn't mention any reasons, and you surely know that computers already store photographs very effectively.

E. This is total nonsense. The author never mentions that storing a large amount of information *causes* the data to be unstable.

It is true that we have more information than ever, and that it degrades faster than ever. But that's just a correlation.

Question 11

DISCUSSION: The author mentions computers to show a possible solution to our storage problems.

They are a flawed solution, but in lines 19-23 the author is showing that they are a possibility.

A. Actually, computers offer us the chance of preserving some information. So this goes against the first sentence, which says we'll lose information.

B. CORRECT. Ostensible means 'so-called'. As in, something that seems like it might work, but has a hidden problem. Computers have issues of their own in terms of losing data.

C. The last sentence has nothing to do with lines 19-23. The last sentence of the passage simply emphasizes the urgency of saving information.

D. It's true that computers are another example of how data is quickly lost. But lines 19-23 don't tell us that. Instead, those lines serve to mention a *possible* (but misleading) solution to the problem.

E. Computers might solve the problem. But there definitely is a problem. The final paragraph makes clear that even if computers work we will still lose much information.

Question 12

DISCUSSION: As with questions 9 and 10, you should justify the answer using the passage. There's almost always a line that lets you prove the right answer correct.

A. The passage never talks about stealing information.
B. Unfortunately, we have no idea how much information was transferred from disks. It's possible we lost most of the information stored on disks.
C. Actually, line 23 implies that computer storage doesn't cost much. Documents take up little space.
D. CORRECT. The second paragraph says that some digital information lasts only ten years. This is less durable than the information mentioned in the first paragraph. Even videotapes last 20 years (line 18).
E. Lines 56-59 suggest that we have so much information ('sheer volume') that much of it is useless. It is hard to sift through and find the valuable information. So unfortunately most new information isn't essential.

Question 13

DISCUSSION: As with questions 9, 10 and 12, you should justify your answer using the passage. There will almost always be a line that proves the right answer 100% correct for this type of question.

A. Lines 37-40 suggest that new computer storage systems may be more durable.
B. Lines 58-59 suggest that it would be a good idea to sort through information and get rid of some dispensable material. So presumably we can predict what *won't* be a great work.
C. The general public doesn't care about keeping stuff for that long, at least not compared to archivists. In any case, we have no idea whether the public are misled by manufacturers. This simply isn't mentioned.
D. The author implies that archivists have always wanted to keep only valuable information. The problem is greater in recent years simply because we have much more information and it degrades faster.
E. CORRECT. Lines 46-54 imply this. Our view of the past is shaped by what survived. We would have a different view of history if Plato's works had perished.

So future generations will have a different impression of our time depending on what we preserve today.

Passage 3 - Blackmail (comparative)
Questions 14-19

Paragraph Summaries

Passage A

1. It's not clear why blackmail is illegal. It is a combination of two legal acts.
2. Blackmail laws are unclear as a result.
3. We can make a theory of blackmail. Blackmail is illegal because it misuses a third party.

Passage B

1. Roman law had no category for blackmail. Actions were considered illegal based on whether they caused harm.
2. Blackmail was considered harmful. A blackmailer had to show why they should be allowed to reveal information.
3. Truth wasn't enough. There had to be a public purpose to revealing the information.

Analysis

The two passages discuss theories of blackmail.

First, there is our own theory of blackmail. It's not clear why blackmail is illegal, since free speech is allowed. But threats aren't legal. Passage A claims that blackmail is illegal because we use third parties to make threats.

Roman law had a different view of blackmail. Truth and free speech weren't important values. There had to be a public purpose to reveal information. Blackmail wasn't illegal as such, but it would be illegal if it caused harm.

It's worth rereading both passages to see how they relate and how they differ. You need to have a clear idea of our blackmail and roman blackmail before you look at the questions.

I want to be very clear about Roman law. It was much more restrictive than North American law. In the US, you can say something harmful about a public figure, as long as its true, and you're not blackmailing them.

In ancient Rome, you could *not* harm people by telling the truth about them, *unless* there was a clear purpose to doing so.

So if you embarrassed a public figure with the truth, he could sue you because you harmed him. Truth was *not* a defense. Only public interest was a defense.

Blackmail was therefore illegal by consequence of this law. If you couldn't harm someone by telling the truth, then you certainly couldn't harm someone by telling the truth AND blackmailing them.

Question 14

DISCUSSION: The passages discuss blackmail. The first passage discusses blackmail in our current North American legal system. The second passage discusses blackmail in the Roman system. The passages don't have much in common beyond that.

A. Only the first passage mentions triangular transactions (line 22). It doesn't say that all triangular transactions are illegal. It only says blackmail is illegal because it is triangular.
B. Rome didn't have a right to free speech.
C. **CORRECT.** Passage A discusses blackmail in modern North America. Passage B discusses blackmail in Ancient Rome.
D. Passage A doesn't discuss the history of blackmail. Passage B discusses blackmail in one historical period (ancient Rome), but that doesn't make passage B a complete history of blackmail in every time period.
E. This only covers passage A. Ancient Rome (passage B) didn't even have blackmail, as such.

Question 15

DISCUSSION: Lines 27-29 talk about threatening to turn in a criminal. That's 'bargaining with the state's chip'.

It means using the government as a threat. Bargaining with a chip seems like a gambling reference. But what I really want you to know is that it doesn't *matter* if you don't understand what "bargaining with the state's chip" means, exactly. You just need the gist of it. You surely know what "bargaining" and "state" mean. So a blackmailer uses the state in negotiations with their victim.

If you blackmail someone by threatening to report their crime, you're not threatening the criminal with your own resources. You're letting the government's threat do your dirty work.

A. You're not determining that the criminal's actions are a crime. The criminal knows that he committed a crime, and you know. But the government doesn't know. That's why you can threaten to turn him in.
B. **CORRECT.** 'The state's chip' is that it wants to hear about crimes and will punish them.

This question is a little confusing. It's easiest to answer if you think about what the blackmailer is threatening to do: they will tell the government that you committed a crime.
C. The crime already occurred. The blackmailer is considering telling the government about the crime.
D. Err....a government definitely doesn't rely only on citizens for information. They also have police and bureaucrats to gather information.
E. The government can't compel the blackmailer to testify. The government doesn't know that the blackmailer knows anything. That's the entire point of the threat: the crime is unknown to the government.

Question 16

DISCUSSION: You should justify the answer you choose by finding a specific line in the passage.

A. CORRECT. The blackmail paradox exists because free speech is normally legal and protected (lines 9-10). Likewise, it's legal to ask someone for money. The paradox is that you can't ask someone for money to prevent you from speaking - that's blackmail.

The final paragraph of Passage B shows there was no paradox in Roman law. This is because there were no free speech protections in ancient Rome. You had no right to harm someone by speaking against them, even if what you said was true, and even if you weren't threatening them. So if merely speaking the truth was illegal, then blackmail was definitely illegal - no paradox required.

B. There was no specific Roman law against blackmail. But blackmail was definitely still illegal if it harmed the victim (lines 41-43).

C. We have no idea how many freedoms are granted by Roman or North American law in general. We're only told about blackmail.

D. This is true of Roman law, not North American law. Normally free speech protects you in North America (lines 9-10), even if you harm someone. The third paragraph of Passage A gives the best justification for why blackmail is illegal in North America: you're using someone else as a threat.

E. We're not told if US and Canadian law recognizes the public's interest in certain information being disclosed. It's implied though, since our law protects free speech (lines 9-10).

Question 17

DISCUSSION: North American blackmail is the combination of two legal acts: free speech, and seeking money.

Roman was different. In Rome, *any* disclosure was illegal if it caused harm, and did not have a legitimate public purpose. That's a very strict law. Roman law had the effect of prohibiting blackmail as well.

So Roman law had no paradox. In North America the paradox is that blackmail is the combination of two legal acts. But in Rome, almost any harmful speech was illegal, so blackmail would often have been illegal even without a threat.

A. CORRECT. See the description above.

B. Roman blackmail was still triangular. For example, suppose someone threatens to expose a man for cheating on his wife. His wife is the one that would harm him.

C. Actually, the second paragraph says the laws are unclear and not meant to be precisely enforced.

D. This is true of both North American and Roman law.

E. Blackmail is a crime in North America. See the very first lines. It's *Roman* law that has no category for blackmail.

Question 18

DISCUSSION: Revealing information was sometimes legal in Rome, if it had a public purpose.

Public authorities presumably cared about losing money. It's doubtful they cared about politicians who had affairs. Public authorities (i.e. politicians) would probably prefer to keep that secret.

A. Bribery was presumably illegal in both Rome and North America.
B. There is a public purpose to revealing embezzlement. This might have been allowed in Rome.
C. Lying in court is presumably illegal in both Rome and North America.
D. There's a public purpose to revealing tax fraud, so this was presumably legal in Rome.
E. **CORRECT.** It's not clear the public ought to know about the affair. This revelation might be illegal in Rome, even if it were true.

It's definitely legal to say this in North America, as long as you're not blackmailing the politician.

Question 19

DISCUSSION: North America specifically bans blackmail, even though it's a combination of two things that are normally legal.

Rome didn't officially ban blackmail, but their laws on harmful disclosures had the indirect effect of banning actions we would consider blackmail.

Further, Rome didn't allow harmful disclosures even if there was no blackmail. There were no rights to free speech. Disclosures were allowed only if they had a public purpose.

A. Both systems need to have similar effects. It seems like one country has no effect on carpenters.
B. This answer talks about making the same thing illegal in different places. But Roman law actually made *different* things illegal.
C. The effects of North American and Roman laws were fairly similar. In this answer, they're different.
D. **CORRECT.** Here, the law has the same effects. Felons can't own guns. In fact, in one country, guns are only allowed for an official purpose.
E. This is a totally different situation. Here something dangerous is allowed in one country, but you're on the hook if you misuse it.

Passage 4 - Recovering Farmland
Questions 20-27

Paragraph Summaries

1. It is difficult to restore farmland to its natural state. Nutrients are depleted and weeds have spread. A dutch experiment may speed things up.
2. The experiment produced varying results.
3. Microorganisms can speed up recovery. Farmed land is depleted of microorganisms.

Analysis

This is a complex passage. It's very hard to keep track of everything that's going on, or draw an overall conclusion. Sometimes you'll get a reading comprehension passage you just don't understand. When you do, try to get the key points as best you can. Then when you review, aim for complete understanding. This will help you on future passages.

Here are the key points underlying this passage:

* Farmed soil is depleted, we want to restore it.
* Biodiversity is good and helps us restore land.
* Thistles are bad.
* More diversity above ground helps restore land.
* More diversity underground helps restore land.

If a question asks about specific details, you can refer back to the passage. It's very difficult to keep everything straight on a first read; I didn't try.

I noticed that the experiments were well controlled. Every experiment showed that diversity helped.

The first paragraph describes the main goal: restoring the biodiversity of old farmland.

The rest of the passage describes how to restore farmland *faster*. It's a way to help achieve the goal. The passage never modifies or criticizes the goal.

Lines 30-33 are potentially confusing. You should know there were four different types of plots:

1. Corn: Lots of thistles
2. Nothing: Lots of thistles
3. Fewer varieties: some thistles, but thistles are eliminated from certain mats of grass.
4. Most varieties: all thistles gone

The final paragraph is even more confusing. I'll try to break down what's going on. Imagine some land that's been out of production for 20 years. It's been left to grow wild.

Then we've got new land, near the old farm. This new land was farmed until recently. Now let's name three plots, A, B and C:

Plot A: A field from the old farm. Has been out of production 20 years.

Plot B: A field from the new farm. Recently out of production. Covered with soil from plot A.

Plot C: A field from the new farm. Recently out of production. Not given any new soil.

The passage says that plot A does best, plot B does second best, and plot C does worst. We can conclude that the soil from plot A helps plot B, but there's still some factor missing.

Disease micro-organisms are the problem. Both plots B and C have horrible creatures living underground that harm plants. Soil from plot A helps defend against these diseases, but more time is needed to eliminate them.

One helpful analogy is the human body. You probably know that microorganisms help you to digest food. For example, certain bacteria help you digest the lactose in milk. Without them, milk will cause problems. Likewise, certain bacteria harm you.

You can eat a perfect diet, but if your stomach is full of bad bacteria, you will not do well.

Good food is like clover and native grasses. Bad food is like corn and farming. Disease micro-organisms are like the bad bacteria that give you stomachaches. The soil from plot A is like probiotics: they help you digest food, but you need to solve the bad bacteria problem before you can say your digestion is good.

One small note. It's easy to be confused about the word 'overproduction'. This refers to total agricultural production in Europe. Overproduction means it's too high.

If people only want 100 million tons of food, and Europe produces 110 million tons, then there is overproduction. Overproduction has absolutely nothing to do with how intensely a given piece of land is cultivated.

Question 20

DISCUSSION: The passages describes how a dutch experiment may help restore farmland. The researchers grew diverse plants, and spread diverse microorganisms in the soil.

A. **CORRECT.** This covers all paragraphs. Paragraph 1 talks about rehab. Paragraph 2 talks about how surface diversity helps recovery. Paragraph 3 talks about how microorganisms under the soil can help recovery.

B. This is probably true, but the main point of the passage is to describe a dutch study that can speed up the restoration process.

C. The passage never said if we should change how we use farmland. Paragraphs 2 and 3 are mainly about a dutch study that will help speed up farmland recovery.

D. This is only mentioned in lines 15-17. It's not even necessarily true. This is just something generally believed.

E. This mixes together two unrelated concepts. Agricultural overproduction refers to the total amount of food we produce. It does not refer to how intensely we farm individual plots of land.

Farming would still produce weeds and disease organisms even if Europe produced exactly as much food as we required (no overproduction).

Question 21

DISCUSSION: Each answer has three parts. These match the three paragraphs in the passage.

You can eliminate answers by looking at each part individually. For instance, A and C say that the study is described/evaluated in the first paragraph.

Nope. The first paragraph describes the problem. The study is described in paragraphs 2-3. So A and C are out.

You can eliminate B and D similarly, by identifying parts that simply aren't true.

A. The study is described in paragraphs 2-3, not the first paragraph.
B. The hypothesis is in lines 17-21: the Dutch study can help speed recovery. The rest of the passage *supports* this hypothesis. There's no evidence against it.
C. The study is evaluated in the 2nd and 3rd paragraphs, not the first.
D. The goal in the first paragraph is that we should restore farmland. The passage never modified this goal, it just told us how to achieve it faster.
E. **CORRECT.** Close enough. The first paragraph describes a problem, and the second paragraph describes the study.

The third part isn't quite right. The final paragraph continues to describe the study. The passage doesn't give us much of a plan of action: it just says to spread diversity above and below ground. But, that's at least practical advice.

This is still the best answer, which is what we're looking for. The other answers are all clearly wrong.

Question 22

DISCUSSION: This is covered on lines 35-44. It's a bit confusing.

The land in the experiment was recently cultivated. Some nearby land had been out of production for 20 years.

Researchers took soil from the land that had been out of production, and they spread the soil on the recently cultivated land.

Plants grew better on the recently cultivated land when researchers scattered the soil. This was because the soil had helpful microorganisms. (lines 38-41).

However, plants still grew better on the land that had been out of production (lines 43-44). That is, the land that had been out of production for 20 years.

The reason? The recently cultivated, farmed land was overrun with harmful microorganisms, and lacking helpful microorganisms (lines 44-50).

A. This fact is out of context, it comes from lines 5-8. Lines 44-50 make clear that the problem with these particular plots of land was that they were overrun with harmful microorganisms.
B. **CORRECT.** See lines 44-50.
C. This is a fact from lines 8-12, it's out of context here.
D. It's worse than this. Not only does farmed land lack helpful microorganisms: farmed land is full of *harmful* microorganisms (lines 44-50).
E. This is backwards. The *farmed land* had harmful microorganisms (lines 44-50).
The land that was out of production had *helpful* microorganisms (lines 38-41).

Question 23

DISCUSSION: This is lines 12-15. The farmland is heavily fertilized. The quickest way to fix this would be to replace the topsoil.

Logically, we must be replacing the over-fertilized topsoil with soil that has less fertilizer. Otherwise, why bother?

A. We know that thistles grow in fertilized land (lines 10-11). Fertilized land is a *sufficient* condition. But it's possible thistles can grow even in soil that isn't fertilized.
B. We have no idea if replacement topsoil has fungi. Presumably all soil has some fungi. The third paragraph shows that both farmed and unfarmed soil has fungi (lines 38-50).
C. Why would this be true? We're not told anything about the replacement soil. Maybe it has tons of good plants.
D. **CORRECT.** This would make sense. We're replacing over-fertilized topsoil. So it would make sense to use soil that has *less* fertilizer.
E. Who knows? The soil just has to be good soil. It's possible it was used to grow corn, then rehabilitated.

Question 24

DISCUSSION: There is a lot of land across Europe that has to be restored. It would be nice if it could be done quickly.

Lines 16-17 emphasize that natural restoration will be quite slow. That's why the dutch experiment is so exciting: it will speed up land restoration.

A. The dutch study doesn't say that natural recovery is fast. The study is about whether humans can speed up the natural rate of recovery by intervening.
B. This makes no sense. Nowhere does the passage justify intense agricultural production. The passage is only about restoring former agricultural land.
C. Not quite. First, overproduction refers to how much food is produced, not how much soil is depleted. Second, the passage never argues that agriculture isn't harmful. The passage is about how to restore damage, not how much damage exists.
D. Agricultural overproduction refers to producing more food than we need, in all of Europe. The passage never says why that is harmful.
E. **CORRECT.** The dutch study showed us how to speed up recovery of agricultural land. This study was necessary *because* natural recovery is slow.

Question 25

DISCUSSION: See lines 13-21. The fastest way to restore land is to replace the topsoil, but that's difficult (lines 13-15).

Natural recovery is slow (lines 15-17).

The dutch study lets us speed up natural recovery (lines 18-21).

So the dutch methods are useful if we have to rely on natural recovery. But replacing topsoil would be faster.

The wrong answers all talk about problems caused by agriculture. The dutch methods are useful for accelerating recovery in all such cases.

A. This is just a normal result of using land for agriculture (lines 7-8). The dutch study can help.

B. **CORRECT.** Lines 13-15 say that replacing topsoil is the fastest way to restore land. So it may make sense to replace topsoil in cases where it's easiest to do so.

The dutch method is only for when we're relying on natural processes to restore land.

C. Fertilization is a common agricultural practice that can help milk thistle grow (lines 8-11). Lines 30-34 show that the dutch study can help with this.

D. Commercial grass plants and rye are never mentioned in the passage. This answer is just meant to confuse and mislead you.

E. The passage never talks specifically about restoring land that is adjacent to current cornfields. This is misleading.

Question 26

DISCUSSION: Lines 45-46 don't make sense on their own. Line 45 says "that this is because".

What is "this"? You have to look to earlier lines to see what lines 45-46 refer to. This is a common reading comprehension trick.

You should read lines 35-45. They say that plots enriched with microorganisms grow better than unenriched plots. However, plots that were left out of production grow even better.

Now lines 45-46 make sense. Agriculture lets disease organisms spread in land. They slow down recovery, even if we introduce beneficial microorganisms.

Without disease microorganisms, the land would do better and recover faster.

A. Mycorrhiza are only mentioned on line 47. The passage only introduced them as an example of a useful microorganism not present in agricultural land. The author didn't say Mycorrhiza would decline without disease microorganisms.

B. The passage only mentions thistles on lines 10, and 30-34. The author doesn't say whether thistles depend on disease microorganisms.

C. **CORRECT.** See lines 40-46. Seeds sown on depleted land didn't grow as well, because the land had disease microorganisms.

D. Tempting, but we don't know. It's possible that disease microorganisms don't hurt beneficial microorganisms. It might have been agriculture that killed the beneficial microorganisms.
Also, notice that this answer is very broad. It says 'all types' of beneficial microorganisms. We don't have evidence about every single type of beneficial microorganism.

E. We have no idea. The passage never says whether disease organisms are in competition. Maybe eliminating these disease organisms would make it harder for other disease organisms to enter the soil.

Question 27

DISCUSSION: There are four elements in This question:

- **Thistles:** competing with native grasses for space.
- **Native grasses:** Competing with thistles.
- **Bad microorganisms:** Attacking native grasses, letting thistles win.
- **Good microorganisms:** Defends native grasses against bad microorganisms, indirectly stopping thistles.

Good microorganisms *indirectly* help. In the right answer, Party A is thistles. We need to find an answer that *indirectly* attacks party A by helping defend a supporter.

If you still find this question confusing, concentrate on the relationships between the four parties above. Thistles and native grasses are competing. The microorganisms directly hurt or help native grasses, and thus indirectly hurt or help thistles.

A. This would be like directly attacking organisms that support thistles. But the stimulus doesn't mention any organisms that help thistles. We're looking for an answer where the newspaper defends a rival party.

B. **CORRECT.** Party A is thistles. The rival candidates are other plants. The editorials are beneficial microorganisms, and the broadcast journalists are disease microorganisms.
The researchers indirectly stopped thistles by introducing beneficial microorganisms. The beneficial microorganisms defended native grasses against disease microorganisms, which let the grasses outcompete thistles.
Here, the newspaper indirectly attacks party A by defending a rival party from attacks by other journalists. So in both cases, there is only indirect offense.

C. Same as A.

D. This is like attacking microorganisms that support thistles. The passage doesn't mention any microorganisms that support thistles.

A. This would be like attacking thistles directly.

Section IV - Logical Reasoning

Question 1

QUESTION TYPE: Paradox

PARADOX: Acid rain lowers calcium levels in the soil. Sugar, fir and sugar maples all need calcium. But, sugar maples seem more affected by acid rain.

ANALYSIS: You need to find an answer that shows a difference between sugar maples and the other trees.

A. This is a vague answer. We don't know what these other changes are, or if they affect sugar maples differently.
B. This makes things more confusing. In the stimulus, sugar maples decline even more rapidly when acid rain depletes calcium. Yet this answer shows that they should be more resistant.
C. **CORRECT.** This shows that spruces and firs have a second source of calcium. Sugar maples don't have this source, so they suffer when acid rain lowers calcium.
D. This doesn't tell us anything about spruces and firs. Maybe the increased calcium requirement also applies to them. The stimulus also implied the decline would occur in any season.
E. This doesn't matter. The stimulus was only talking about areas that did receive acid rain. Some spruces and firs do receive acid rain.

Question 2

QUESTION TYPE: Necessary Assumption

CONCLUSION: Columnists rarely persuade voters.

REASONING: By the time columns appear, almost all voters who will vote have decided who to vote for.

ANALYSIS: This sounds like a good argument. But it treats coming to a decision as being set in stone. You know that people often change their minds. Maybe someone has *decided* to vote Republican, but then a persuasive column convinces them to switch their vote.

The argument has to assume that once someone decides who to vote for, they don't change.

A. This would weaken the argument. The argument argues that columns don't have influence.
B. This shows that columns backfire. Tell someone to vote Republican and they'll vote Democrat. The argument doesn't have to assume this.
C. The argument doesn't have to assume you only read people you agree with. They just have to assume that you won't change your mind if someone tries to persuade you to switch candidates.
D. This "regular readers" idea is misleading. The stimulus never mentioned it. They were talking about all people who read columns.
E. **CORRECT.** Exactly. I often change my mind, even after I've decided to do something. The argument has to assume that voters won't change their ideas once they come to a decision.

Question 3

QUESTION TYPE: Weaken

CONCLUSION: Airlines should focus on making economy class seats more comfortable.

REASONING: 80% of ticket sales are made by leisure travelers.

ANALYSIS: Ever booked a flight, and seen that economy class is $259, and business class is $2765?

Economy class is the majority of seats. But airlines make most of their money from business class.

So maybe it makes sense to ignore economy class. In fact, the worse you make economy class, the more business people will want to pay to get better seats.

I'm using outside knowledge to form a hypothesis. This is a perfectly valid way of forming hypotheses and pre-phrasing answers. You're not supposed to shut off your brain on the LSAT.

A. This doesn't explain why we should care about business travelers.
B. So? 'Some' could mean one airline. And this doesn't tell us what other airlines should do.
C. The argument wasn't just talking about sleeping in comfort. It was talking about comfort in general.
D. CORRECT. This shows that business travelers are more important than leisure travelers, even though they don't buy many tickets.
E. This shows that leisure travelers are cheap. But it's still true that leisure travelers buy 80% of tickets. This answer doesn't show that business travelers are more important than leisure travelers. D is a better answer.

Question 4

QUESTION TYPE: Point At Issue

ARGUMENTS: Gaby says children should follow their own interests, supported minimally by experienced teachers.

Logan says children should learn fundamentals in a disciplined, systemic way.

ANALYSIS: Gaby and Logan disagree on what kind of structure children should have.

Gaby thinks there should be little structure, and Logan thinks there should be much structure. They also disagree on who should set the curriculum: children or teachers.

A. Gaby doesn't mention fundamentals.
B. CORRECT. Gaby thinks teachers should offer almost no direction. Logan thinks education should be highly structured.
C. They both agree children should have access to good teachers.
D. Neither of them mentions the school environment, as such. School environment is not the same thing as teaching style.
E. Neither Gaby nor Logan mentions whether children have any interest in fundamentals.

Question 5

QUESTION TYPE: Principle

CONCLUSION: The judge will not order that defendants can be questioned without their codefendants or their codefendants' legal counsel.

REASONING: Two of the defendants have the same lawyer.

ANALYSIS: This is a sort of a necessary assumption question. The judge is assuming that if you question a defendant, their lawyer will be present.

Since the defendants share lawyers, that means the lawyer will be both the defendant's lawyer and the codefendant's lawyer.

But what if defendants aren't allowed to have their lawyer present? Then it doesn't matter that they share a lawyer.

A. This is totally beside the point. The court order wasn't going to force a lawyer to disclose information.
Negation: A court can issue an order that forces legal counsel to disclose information revealed by a client.

B. **CORRECT.** If this is true, then there's no way to question a defendant without their codefendant's lawyer being there. Negating this wrecks the argument.
Negation: Defendants do not have the right to have a lawyer present during questioning.

C. This has nothing to do with lawyers.
Negation: People may not refuse to answer self-incriminating questions during legal proceedings.

D. The plaintiff wants permission to question the defendant. That doesn't sound like a right, and in any case the defendant might be able to get the same permission.
Negation: There are occasions when it is correct to grant a plaintiff a right not given to a defendant.

E. No one mentioned questioning the plaintiff.
Negation: A defendant's legal counsel does not have the right to question the plaintiff.

Question 6

QUESTION TYPE: Must Be True

FACTS:

1. Sewage can fill estuaries with nutrients.
2. This causes algae.
3. This causes microorganisms.
4. This kills most of the fish.

ANALYSIS: It sounds like sewage can indirectly kill fish.

Sewage → Algae → Microorganisms → Most fish die

A. The passage mentioned that fish die from microorganisms. It didn't mention fish dying directly from sewage.

B. We know that the microorganisms reproduce more quickly when algae is present. We don't know whether they reproduce more quickly than other organisms. This is the wrong comparison.

C. It's quite possible that sewage poisons fish directly. The fact that sewage has an indirect effect doesn't prevent it from having a direct effect.

D. Sewage is a sufficient condition for algae, but it's not a necessary condition. There may be other things that cause algae to spread.

E. **CORRECT.** This is a straightforward combination of the facts from the stimulus. You should read all the answers before thinking too hard about any of them: this answer is fairly obviously correct, but the LSAC placed it at the end to make you waste time.

Question 7

QUESTION TYPE: Evaluate the Argument

CONCLUSION: Archaeologists think the stones were transported on reed boats.

REASONING: Archaeologists transported a 9 ton stone on a reed boat built from local materials. The ancient stones weighed up to 40 tons.

ANALYSIS: There are several things that would be helpful to know:

- Was it difficult to transport the stones with the boats?
- Could the boats have transported a 40 ton stone?
- Were there other available methods of transport?

The right answer uses information I didn't think of. It's definitely relevant to know whether the traditional techniques were available at the time the stones were transported. "Traditional" doesn't mean the techniques were around forever. A traditional technique could be only 500 years old. Tiwanaku was prehistoric – that's *very* old.

A. CORRECT. If the techniques weren't available when the stones were transported, then maybe the Tiwanakuans couldn't have transported the stones in reed boats.
B. It doesn't matter whether the stones were used locally. We only care how people managed to get the stones far away to Tiwanaku.
C. It doesn't matter what people do today. We only care what people did at the time the stones were transported.
D. It doesn't matter if there are bigger stones at the site. Those weren't transported. We only care how the Tiwanakuans transported the 40 ton stones to their building site.
E. It only matters that the boats were useable long enough to transport the stones.

Question 8

QUESTION TYPE: Flawed Reasoning

CONCLUSION: We shouldn't strike now.

REASONING: A strike would be financially difficult.

ANALYSIS: This union organizer only mentioned the downsides of striking now. They ignored whether there are benefits.

Strikes *always* pose financially difficulties to unions. The reason unions strike is that they hope to get benefits from the strike that outweigh the downsides.

A. Actually, the organizer did consider this: a strike would reduce the strike fund, even if there is no fine.
B. This doesn't matter. Union members probably have enough context to understand what a major financial cost would look like.
C. CORRECT. The union member only mentions downsides to striking. They ignore any possible benefits.
D. The union member wasn't comparing all factors that affect the union's bargaining position. They were just claiming that the financial loss would be unacceptable.
E. It's possible there will never be a good time to strike. That doesn't mean the union should strike now.

If there's never a good time to strike in the future, and now isn't a good time, then the union simply shouldn't strike, ever.

Question 9

QUESTION TYPE: Most Strongly Supported

FACTS:

1. Birds and mammals can only catch West Nile from mosquito bites.
2. Mosquitos can catch West Nile only from biting animals.
3. Humans can catch West Nile, but they can't spread it to mosquitos.
4. West Nile started in north Africa, and spread to North America.

ANALYSIS: It's fairly strongly supported that there are animals in North America capable of spreading the West Nile virus.

West Nile virus is in North America, and humans can't spread it. Mosquitos can't spread it on their own, so something else is spreading it. We know that animals can help mosquitos spread the virus.

A. West Nile could definitely be common. Humans can't spread the virus directly, but if enough animals spread West Nile it could become common among humans too.

B. Hard to say. West Nile only spread to North America recently. So perhaps the virus is only present in New England, but the densest concentration of mosquitos is in Louisiana, where the virus hasn't reached yet.

C. The stimulus doesn't mention symptoms. We have no idea if people can catch the virus and not show symptoms.

D. The virus started in North Africa. But it might affect more people in North America. Perhaps it spreads easier here. We have no idea, really.

E. **CORRECT.** This is probably true. Humans can't spread the virus to mosquitos, and mosquitos are the ones that spread the virus.

It's likely that an infected animal arrived, and spread the virus to mosquitos.

Question 10

QUESTION TYPE: Paradox

PARADOX: Those who reduced red meat the most eat more fat than those who didn't reduce.

ANALYSIS: It could be that people replaced red meat with other fatty foods.

Or maybe they ate more fat in the first place, and that's why they decided to reduce red meat consumption. So they still eat more fat, but less so than they used to.

A. It doesn't matter how many people reduced their red meat consumption. The stimulus talked about the two groups on average. Total numbers are irrelevant for averages: it doesn't matter if two million reduced, or twenty million.

B. The stimulus said that people reduced by one half in order to reduce fat. If they reduced even further because of high prices, that just adds to confusion. Further reduction is a second reason we would expect their fat consumption to be lower.

C. This just shows that the two groups are equal in terms of fat in other foods. So if one group reduced red meat, we would expect that group's fat consumption to be lower.

D. **CORRECT.** This shows that people replaced red meat with fattier foods. So no wonder they eat more fat.

E. This doesn't explain why people that stopped eating red meat are eating more fat. D is a better answer because it specifies that people replaced red meat with fattier food.

Question 11

QUESTION TYPE: Flawed Reasoning

CONCLUSION: The house on Oak Avenue isn't the best one to rent.

REASONING: The yard isn't as big as it looks. Part of the yard is city property.

ANALYSIS: Tom correctly points out that the yard is smaller than it seems.

But Yolanda says that *every* yard it smaller than it seems – every yard has 20 ft of city property. So Tom is mistaken. The house on Oak Avenue does have the biggest yard of the houses they saw.

A. If anything, this is an error Yolanda makes. She say the house on Oak Avenue is the best simply because it has the biggest yard. Tom attacks her by trying to prove that the yard isn't big.

But Tom could also have argued that a big yard doesn't mean the house will be good.

B. Actually, Tom says that city property is not part of the yard. Presumably city property is not available for private use.

C. The house on Oak Avenue is in Prairieview, so Tom's generalization is relevant in this case.
Example of flaw: Property lines in Mongolia start 20 feet from the street. So this house in California doesn't have a large yard.

D. CORRECT. Tom only applied the city property rule to the house on Oak Avenue. He should have also applied it to the other houses that he and Yolanda looked at, since they're all in Prairieview.

E. This is a different error.
Example of flaw: "Because part of the yard is city property, the whole yard is city property."

Question 12

QUESTION TYPE: Role in Argument

CONCLUSION: Jazz is mostly hornlike voices and voicelike horns.

REASONING: Jazz singers use their voices like horns. Jazz hornists use their horns like voices.

ANALYSIS: The word 'so' usually indicates a conclusion. So, the last sentence is the conclusion.

The facts about singers and horn players are premises that support the conclusion.

The first sentence is an intermediate conclusion. It's supported by the second sentence, which tells us that Billie Halliday used her voice like a horn.

A. The final sentence is the main conclusion.

B. Same as A.

C. CORRECT. The second sentence provides evidence that some jazz singers use their voices like horns. The sentence in turn provides support for the main conclusion.

D. The second sentence provides evidence for this claim.

E. This is true of the second sentence.
But the line in question is the first sentence. The first sentence supports the conclusion directly, and it receives support from the second sentence.

Question 13

QUESTION TYPE: Necessary Assumption

CONCLUSION: Smaller classes probably wouldn't improve education.

REASONING: To reduce class sizes, we need to hire teachers. There aren't enough qualified teachers in the region. Bad teachers don't improve education.

ANALYSIS: This sounds like a good argument. But, the educator only says there's a shortage of qualified teachers *in the region.* There might be qualified teachers in other areas. The school district could hire those teachers. Then the district could increase class sizes and maintain quality. This argument has to assume that it's not possible to hire qualified teachers from other regions.

A. The educator didn't say whether we *should* reduce class sizes. He just said that reducing class sizes probably wouldn't improve education.
Negation: "It might be a good idea to reduce class sizes even if achievement didn't increase."

B. This would be needed if we were arguing that we *could* use smaller classes to improve outcomes.
Negation: "No qualified teachers could improve education if class sizes were reduced"

C. The argument is about a fact: whether or not smaller classes could improve education. This answer addresses public opinion. Fact and public opinion are unrelated. What students think has no effect on whether smaller classes will work.
Negation: "Students place at least as much value on class size as on qualified teachers."

D. This says that unqualified teachers will help NO ONE. To test an answer, negate it only slightly. If it's the right answer, even the slightest negation will destroy the argument. The negation here is not significant to overall education quality.
Negation: "Unqualified teachers might help one or two students".

E. CORRECT. If we could relocate large numbers of qualified teachers, then the local shortage isn't a problem.
Negation: "We could relocate significant numbers of qualified teachers from other regions."

Question 14

QUESTION TYPE: Identify The Conclusion

CONCLUSION: The prediction is wrong. Global warming probably won't cause more storms.

REASONING: Unstable wind and other factors will work against global warming's impact on storms.

ANALYSIS: This argument has several structural words: 'because', 'for this reason', and 'but'.

In the first sentence ,'because' introduces evidence. This evidence supports the second sentence.

The second sentence introduces a viewpoint. 'For this reason' shows that the first sentence is the evidence for this viewpoint.

The third sentence says 'but'. The word 'but' is *very* important on the LSAT. It usually introduces the author's opinion, which tends to be the conclusion.

In this case, the word 'but' shows that the author disagrees with the researchers. The final sentence supports the author's claim.

You can figure out which of two statements is the conclusion by asking which one supports the other. The claim about the prediction doesn't support the final sentence. But the final sentence gives a reason why the claim about the prediction is probably true.

A. This is just a fact that explains why global warming might cause more tropical storms.

B. This definitely isn't the conclusion. It wasn't even in the argument. No 'earlier discussions' said that *only* global warming affects tropical storms.

C. Same as B. This wasn't even in the argument. True, some scientists said that global warming would increase storms. But reversal of a cause doesn't always lead to the opposite effect.

D. This is evidence for the conclusion: because of these other factors, the prediction is likely false.

E. CORRECT. The word 'but' shows that this is the conclusion. The final sentence supports it by giving a reason that global warming probably won't lead to more storms.

Question 15

QUESTION TYPE: Strengthen

CONCLUSION: Copyright sometimes goes beyond its original purpose.

REASONING: Copyright's sole purpose is to spread ideas by giving authors a reward from their works.

ANALYSIS: This is an unusual question type. It looks like a 'complete the argument' question, but really it's asking us to strengthen a statement.

We have no idea why copyright might go beyond its original purpose. So you should approach the answers with a clear sense of the original purpose.

The idea behind copyright is to encourage the spread of ideas. Letting authors earn money was the mechanism that allowed ideas to spread. So letting authors earn money is only important if it spreads ideas.

A. So? It's possible there are alternatives to copyright. This doesn't show that copyright is exceeding its purpose.

B. Tempting. But the purpose of copyright is to *increase* the circulation of ideas. Maybe authors will circulate *even more* works if they can make money.

C. The stimulus ends with 'sometimes'. It doesn't matter if authors *sometimes* can't find a publisher, as long as they can generally profit from releasing good works.

D. Tempting. This would prove that copyright doesn't work. But we're trying to prove that copyright *goes beyond its purpose.* Copyright can't go beyond its purpose if it doesn't work.

E. CORRECT. If an author is dead, then what good does continued copyright on his works do for him?

Note: This isn't a great objection to copyright. If your work has value after death, then you can sell it for more money, or leave it to your children. So copyright isn't necessarily going beyond its purpose if it provides money beyond death. But it *might,* so this is still the best answer.

Question 16

QUESTION TYPE: Method of Reasoning

CONCLUSION: The economist says his advice was correct.

REASONING: The economist's advice prevented the recession.

ANALYSIS: The critic has a silly interpretation of the economist's prediction. The economist made a conditional prediction. *If* we don't do anything, there will be a recession.

Well, the government did something, thanks to the economist's warning. Since the government did something, the economist prediction no longer applied. But the economist could have been right that there *would* have been a recession *if* the government didn't do anything.

The economist's method was to point out his prediction's context and full meaning.

A. CORRECT. This is a complex way to phrase a simple idea. Familiarize yourself with the phrase 'did not obtain' - many questions have used it. It means that something did not happen.
In this case, the economist said that the economy would do badly *if* the government did nothing. Since the government did do something, the sufficient condition "did not obtain" and the economist's prediction no longer applied.

B. The economist wasn't arguing that the economy might still do poorly in the future.

C. Which inconsistency? An inconsistency is when your own statements contradict themselves. The critic only said the economist made a bad prediction, and the economy grew.

D. A general claim would be "all cars are red". A counterexample would be "no they aren't. That car is green". The critic made no general claim, and the economist made no counterexample.

E. The critic only had two factual premises:
i. The economist made a prediction.
ii. The economy grew.
The economist didn't contradict either fact. Instead, he added context to the first fact. This context proves the critic was incorrect.

Question 17

QUESTION TYPE: Parallel Reasoning

CONCLUSION: 1970's music videos weren't representative of the music at the time.

REASONING: 1970's music videos mostly attracted cutting edge artists.

ANALYSIS: This is a good argument, assuming that most music in the 1970's wasn't cutting edge.

On parallel reasoning questions, you should always find an abstract way to describe the structure. An argument might not use formal logic, but it still has structure.

Here, the argument is that a thing (music videos) is not representative of a bigger thing (music) because the thing has a biased sample (cutting edge music).

I put the correct answer in the same form.

A. This doesn't show that the surviving literature was unrepresentative. It might be, but we don't know for sure.
B. This is backwards. The argument said that music videos offer an inaccurate view. This answer says we can trust our view of 1960's TV.
C. CORRECT. This shows that a thing (CD publishing) is unrepresentative of a larger thing (publishing) because the thing has a biased sample (game publishers).
D. There's no bias in the sample here. This just tells us that we lost most silent films, because they disintegrated.
E. This shows that our knowledge is accurate, despite bias. The argument said our knowledge was inaccurate, because of bias.

Question 18

QUESTION TYPE: Principle

FACTS: Organizations can be good even if their individual members are selfish.

ANALYSIS: This situation illustrates that the whole is not the same as the sum of the parts.

The institutions (the whole) work for the public good, even though the members (the parts) are selfish.

By the way, whole-to-part and part-to-whole flaws are very common on the LSAT. You should make sure you understand them intuitively.

The damned thing is, sometimes part-to-whole and whole-to-part arguments work. If a table is made entirely of wood, then every part is made of wood, and vice versa.

So you must use common sense to judge when you can go from whole to part and when you can't.

A. The stimulus never said that some organizations do not have public purposes or fail to achieve them.
B. CORRECT. This is a tricky answer. It requires you to know that 'not all' can include 'none'. The stimulus says that each staff member pursues their own interests. Technically, this means that "not all" of them pursue public purposes.

So organizations pursue public purposes even if 'not all of their members pursue public purposes'.
C. We don't even know if this is true. The stimulus never said that individual members claim altruistic motives for their selfish actions.
D. We don't know what the founders of these institutions intended. This answer is completely unsupported.
E. This is something different. It's like realizing that your house keys can also be used to cut through plastic.

Question 19

QUESTION TYPE: Weaken – Exception

CONCLUSION: There are reasons to avoid irradiated foods.

REASONING:

1. Irradiated food is exposed to radioactive substances.
2. irradiation reduces vitamin content and leaves behind residues.
3. Irradiation produces radiolytic products which can cause cancer.

ANALYSIS: You can weaken the argument by showing that the listed reasons aren't really problems.

You can also weaken the argument by showing that irradiation produces benefits that outweigh the harm it causes.

A. This shows that the third problem is unlikely to apply in the case of irradiated food.

B. CORRECT. This just shows that irradiation isn't the *only* cause of cancer. But irradiation could still dangerous.

Likewise, falling off a cliff isn't the only possible cause of death. But you still shouldn't walk off cliffs.

C. The second reason said that irradiation *can* reduce the vitamin content of foods. This shows that that rarely happens.

D. This shows that irradiation may actually *reduce* the amount of harmful chemicals in food.

E. This shows a lack of correlation between irradiated food and cancer. That reduces the odds that irradiated food causes cancer.

Question 20

QUESTION TYPE: Necessary Assumption

CONCLUSION: Art teachers should use colored paper rather than paint to teach color.

REASONING: Colored paper is more consistent in its color than paint. This lets teachers show color in varying contexts.

ANALYSIS: This is a tricky question. This argument sounds good, but the author didn't actually give a reason consistent color is useful. The LSAC wants you to assume that consistency is a good thing. But who knows? I certainly don't know much about teaching color.

The wrong answers are mostly irrelevant. The stimulus says it's *possible* for two pieces of paper to have the same color. Obviously, in most cases two pieces of paper will be different colors. So what? The stimulus is only talking about those situations where the paper is the same color.

A. The argument didn't mention different textures. Obviously, paper can be different. The important point is that it is *possible* for two separate pieces of paper to be the same.

B. The stimulus said paper was useful because two pieces of paper could have the *same* color. Obviously, you can have two pieces of paper with color differences. But we don't care about those.

C. 'Apparent color' is not the same thing as actual color. It's possible for two pieces of paper to have the same color. The stimulus said this lets us see how the color would look in different contexts. Changing light conditions are an example of a different context. This answer has no effect on anything.

D. CORRECT. Negate this, and you get "observing the impact of color in varying contexts does not help students learn about color". That eliminates the only advantage paper had over paint.

E. The only purpose of using paper was to show students how the same color differed in different contexts. Beyond that, to doesn't matter if students understand anything about paper.

Question 21

QUESTION TYPE: Role in Argument

CONCLUSION: Social scientists need data from several societies to explain cultural phenomena.

REASONING: Suppose you think that a certain political structure is due only to certain ecological or cultural factors. You can only prove this if you know two things:

1. There are no countries with similar political structures that don't face those factors.
2. There are no countries that face those factors, and aren't structured the same way.

ANALYSIS: This question uses unusually complex wording. It's simplest to look for structural words to figure it out. The phrase 'for example' introduces reasoning to support a previous statement.

In this question, the colon after the first sentence further supports the idea that the first sentence is the conclusion and what follows is evidence.

A. The philosopher didn't say that social scientists need certainty. He said that *if* they want to be certain they need data from several societies.

B. Pure bunk. *What* general theoretical claim about cause and effect relationships? An example of such a claim would be "no matter how many times two events occur together, you can not prove they will always occur together".
The philosopher mentioned specific, non-general causal claims relating to particular societies.

C. The philosopher never said that there is a causal relationship between environmental factors and political structure.
Instead, the philosopher described what evidence you would need to prove such a claim.

D. The philosopher never said whether it is difficult to figure out the causes of political structures.

E. **CORRECT.** This answer means the sentence is a conclusion. Which it is. The phrase "for example" shows that the preceding sentence is the conclusion. The example in the stimulus shows the requirements for proving that a certain political structure was caused by political or environmental conditions.

Question 22

QUESTION TYPE: Strengthen

CONCLUSION: Physicists should copy biologists and increase anti-fraud protections.

REASONING: Physicists say that physics is protected from fraud by peer review. Biologists once said they were protected from fraud, but they weren't. But now biology increased its protections against fraud.

ANALYSIS: Don't get fooled by the question stem. This is a strengthen question, not a most strongly supported question. You're supposed to support the conclusion. There are a couple of problems with this argument:

1. We don't know why biology faced fraud. Maybe their peer review system wasn't very effective. Physics might have a better peer review system.
2. We don't know that fraud is bad for physics. The argument concludes that reducing fraud will help physics, but it doesn't give any evidence that fraud will set physics back.

Be careful in how you use outside knowledge. You can use it to generate hypotheses. *Maybe* fraud is bad. It seems like it should be. But you can't use outside knowledge to *prove* anything. You can *suspect* fraud is bad, but you can't *assume* it unless the argument says so.

A. **CORRECT.** This says fraud is bad. Making this explicit strengthens the argument. If fraud isn't bad, then how will reducing it help physics?

B. This shows that biology adopted an effective system. It doesn't show that physics will benefit from increased fraud protection.

C. This very slightly *weakens* the argument, by showing that fraud can't be eliminated. But this doesn't really impact anything. The stimulus didn't say we have to eliminate fraud entirely.

D. This weakens the argument. Physics today is better protected than biology used to be. Maybe more protections are unnecessary.

E. This weakens the argument, slightly. Based on past evidence, physics is already protected against fraud.

Question 23

QUESTION TYPE: Necessary Assumption (principle)

CONCLUSION: Some dogs come from more recently domesticated wolves.

REASONING: Some dogs are more closely related to wolves than other dogs are.

ANALYSIS: On necessary assumption questions, look for a shift in concept in the conclusion.

The conclusion says that some dogs were more recently *domesticated*. The evidence is that these dogs are more *closely related to wolves, genetically*.

The argument assumes that if a dog is more closely related genetically, then the domestication must be more recent. This is a hard argument, and frankly, most of the answers are nonsense. Focus on understanding the relationships in the stimulus.

A. This refers to the wrong thing. We're trying to conclude that some dogs descend from more recently domesticated wolves. This answer tells us what would happen *if* that were true.

B. CORRECT. The negation of this answer breaks the implied link between being genetically related to wolves and being descended more recently from wolves.

Negation: A breed of dog could have more recent undomesticated wolf ancestors even if that breed of dog is less closely related to wolves than another breed.

C. Negation: There's *one* domesticated species of dog that's more closely related to wolves than to dogs.

Who the hell cares? The argument was about when wolves were domesticated. This tells us nothing about date of domestication.

D. Negation: How closely a dog is related to a wolf doesn't affect how closely that dog is related to other dogs.
The argument was about domestication date, not how related two breeds of dog are.

E. This doesn't tell us if some wolves were domesticated more recently than others.

Question 24

QUESTION TYPE: Flawed Parallel Reasoning

CONCLUSION: Professor Mansour must be a paleomycologist. M → PM

REASONING: Paleomycologists know about the writings of other paleomycologists. Professor Mansour knows the writings of one paleomycologist.

ANALYSIS: This argument confuses necessary for sufficient. Yes, all paleomycologists know about paleomycology. That *doesn't* mean that anyone who knows about paleomycology is a paleomycologist. The argument incorrectly reversed this: PM → M

The argument makes a second error. The necessary condition is that paleomycologists know about the writings of *all* other paleomycologists. Professor Mansour only knows about the work of *one* paleomycologist: Professor DeAngelis. The right answer should match both of these flaws.

A. CORRECT. This repeats both flaws. The premise: Flight delayed → all connecting delayed
The argument reverses this to: one connecting delayed → original flight delayed
They also shift from 'all connecting flights' to 'one connecting flight'.
(By the way, the first flight is *not* a connecting flight. Connecting flights happen *after* an initial flight. I'm mentioning this in case you thought a delay on a later flight would guarantee delays on earlier flights.)

B. This is a bad argument, but it makes a different error. Here, the conclusion negates the sufficient condition of the premise, and assumes that the necessary condition is negated.
M → WH, ~~M~~ → ~~WH~~

C. This is a good argument. If expenses decrease and income stays the same, profit goes up.

D. This is a bad argument, but it makes a different flaw. We only know Gavin *can* participate in the plan. That doesn't mean he will do it.

E. This is a bad argument, but it makes a different error. *If* a competitor dropped prices, then it's true that Global must have done the same. But, we don't know whether a competitor did drop prices.

Question 25

QUESTION TYPE: Point At Issue

ARGUMENTS: Lutsina says that Sci-Fi can be a richer source of social criticism than conventional fiction, because authors are free to invent new social arrangements.

Priscilla says Sci-Fi writers are not good at inventing new social arrangements – they are limited by current reality. So, the best social criticism comes from clear presentation of current reality.

ANALYSIS: Lutsina thinks Sci-Fi has the most potential for social criticism. Priscilla thinks conventional fiction has more potential. That's all there is to it.

A. Priscilla doesn't say whether all Sci-Fi writers utterly failed to invent new realities. And Lutsina doesn't say that any Sci-Fi writers succeeded – she just said they have potential. The two authors can't disagree on this point.
B. Neither author said who is more skillful. Lutsina says the *genre* of sci-fi makes it easier to critique social arrangements. Priscilla doesn't say why Sci-Fi writers have found it hard to invent new social structures.
C. **CORRECT.** Lutsina agrees, Priscilla disagrees.
D. Lutsina doesn't even mention technology, this can't possibly be a source of disagreement. Priscilla has no clear opinion on this point.
E. Priscilla doesn't say whether descriptions of radically different arrangements would be useful. She just says Sci-Fi writers have had a hard time creating any.

Question 26

QUESTION TYPE: Flawed Reasoning

CONCLUSION: Our team will almost certainly win the city championship.

REASONING: Our team is the most likely to win the championship. It's the best team, because we recruited the best players.

ANALYSIS: You might think the flaw is the first sentence. Do the best players necessarily work well enough together to make the best team?

Yes, they do. The sentence says '*Because* we recruited....'. This implies that the team actually is the best, and the best players are the reason. You must assume that premises are true in LSAT arguments.

The flaw instead lies in the difference between 'most likely' and 'almost certainly'. Maybe the best team only has a 7 percent chance of winning. This is higher than any other team's chance, and therefore 'most likely'. Not very impressive, right? Certainly not 'almost certain' victory.

A. Rubbish. Read carefully. Why did the argument say the team is the best? Because they have the have the best players. This answer can't be the flaw if it didn't happen.
B. What features? The argument said that the best team has the best chance of winning. And 'our club' is the best team, so that seems entirely relevant.
C. Why would this be a flaw? If you want to predict the outcome of a competition, it's a *good* idea to compare the two parties! In any case, like answer choice A, the argument didn't *do* this. There's no comparison.
D. Again, the argument didn't do this. Here's an example of this answer: "Because the team is the best, each player must be the best". It's a whole to part flaw, which simply isn't in the argument.
E. **CORRECT.** 'Most likely' could mean an 8% chance, which is not very likely at all. The argument went from 'most likely' to 'almost certainly'. Almost certainly refers to overall likelihood, +80% or so.

Preptest 66
Section I - Reading Comprehension
Passage 1 - Digital Publishing
Questions 1-7

Paragraph Summaries

1. Printed books will continue, with instant printing of electronic book files, even in small quantities.
2. Digital printing reduces various costs.
3. Authors will demand higher royalties. Unless publishers adapt and get rid of their redundant functions, authors will go to new digital firms.

Analysis

This passage is an argument. The author is making predictions about the future.

Books won't disappear. Instead, when you go to a 'bookstore' you will look through a digital catalogue for the books you want. When you tell the clerk, he'll give your order to a machine, which will instantly print your books. The quality will be the same as traditional books.

Right now, publishers get most of the money from book sales. They use this to pay for printing books, warehousing books, shipping books, etc.

If books can be printed in a bookstore, then these costs are unnecessary. So authors will demand higher royalties. Since publishers won't be willing to get rid of their traditional functions, authors will choose new digital publishers who have lower costs.

You may have wondered whether LSAT RC passages are true. This passage is actually spot on.

If you bought the paper copy of this book, then you bought a digitally published book. I sent a pdf file to a printing company. They waited for your order with amazon.com or barnesandnoble.com. When the order came in, they printed an instant copy of the book and shipped it to you directly. It never went to a warehouse. My royalty is higher than with a traditional publisher, because of lower costs.

Question 1

DISCUSSION: Main Point answers must be true, and describe the entire passage.You can first eliminate any answers that are false, and then focus on finding an answer that best describes the passage as a whole.

Here the main point is that the internet won't destroy printed books. Instead, digital publishing will keep printed books alive and disrupt the traditional publishing industry by lowering costs.

A. This makes it sound like economic shifts are the main point. They're not. They were only mentioned (lines 51-53) to support the case that the digital publishing transition will happen.

B. The emphasis is wrong here. It's true that further change in economic factors (lines 26-29) and social factors (publisher resistance) could speed the transition to digital books. But the author doesn't present either of these as major obstacles to digital printed books. Indeed, he thinks it's inevitable that things will change.

C. Actually, the third paragraph shows that digital publishing will *not* be profitable for publishers, unless they get rid of many redundant functions (lines 47-50). Authors *will* move to new digital publishing houses, but there won't necessarily be a great deal of movement back and forth once they've switched over.

D. This ignores the economics of publishing and the effect of digital publishing on the traditional publishing industry. Also, the author was only arguing that printed books wouldn't disappear. He didn't say whether or not they would be more popular than e-books.

E. **CORRECT.** This covers all three paragraphs. The only part is leaves out is the argument that traditional publishers will be forced to pay higher royalties or go out of business, as authors move to traditional publishing houses.

Question 2

DISCUSSION: 'Elimination of whole categories of expense' refers back to the second paragraph.

Whenever an LSAT line reference refers to an earlier point in the passage, you should find that section and reread it.

The second paragraph said that many costs would be eliminated such as shipping and warehousing. These are retail costs, so D is correct.

A. Literary agents will always collect fees. Being an agent is not charity work.
B. Digital publishing will still have printing costs. Printing will take place on the spot, but it won't be free.
C. Actually, the third paragraph says publishers will have to pay *higher* royalties.
D. CORRECT. See lines 16-21. Digital publishing will eliminate many costs.
E. This answer is throwing in a reference to something vaguely related in an attempt to confuse you. The passage mentioned returning unsold books (line 20), but it never mentioned the calculation described in this answer choice.

Question 3

DISCUSSION: For an inference question, you should try to justify your answer using lines from the passage. Many trap answers sound plausible but have no support from the text.

If you have trouble finding line references, then you should practice forming a mental map of the passage, and finding lines references on review. You can get much faster at it. Most of my students learn to find lines in 2-3 seconds, at most.

A. CORRECT. See lines 47-51.
B. The author never said that digital publishing will be threatened. He presents its success as inevitable.
C. The author never mentioned how retail would be affected by digital publishing.
D. The author never made claims about *all* books. Maybe a very small number will require traditional publishing methods for best quality. And the author didn't say digital publishing will increase sales compared to the old method. Rather, it will *replace* traditional publishing. Book sales might drop regardless, for other reasons.
E. The author only says publishers can reduce shipping and warehousing costs. But authors presumably still have to market digitally published books.

Question 4

DISCUSSION: Much like question 3, you should be able to identify wrong answers in the passage.

If you find this takes a while, then this type of question is excellent practice on review. See how quickly you can eliminate the wrong answers. Then wait a few days, try again and try to go faster. Use it as a drill to get faster at finding line references.

This question makes it easy to find line references. Costs are mentioned only in lines 16-20.

A. Line 18.
B. **CORRECT.** Book covers are never mentioned.
C. Lines 18-19.
D. Line 20.
E. Lines 19-20.

Question 5

DISCUSSION: The scenario in the first two paragraphs is that digital publishing succeeds. Printed books remain popular, and many traditional publishing costs are eliminated.

A. **CORRECT.** This makes sense. Digitally published books will still need the same amount of paper, so it will need to be warehoused before being sent to bookstores.
B. We're not given any reason why consumers would prefer used books.
C. We're not told whether publishers will continue to use stores. They may be the most convenient place to print books. Printing in store would avoid shipping costs.
D. Lines 16-20 describe cost reductions. The costs are related to physically moving books. Books will still need nice design and editing to sell.
E. This is unlikely, because the author believes that printed books will continue to be popular. Books will be printed on demand, but they'll still need book-grade paper.

Question 6

DISCUSSION: For this type of question it's important to understand the why's of the passage:

- Why is the author telling us this?
- Why does he think digital publishing will succeed?
- Why are costs lower with digital publishing?
- Why will publishers be forced to change?

These are things you should already know before starting the questions. If you don't know the answers to these questions, use this question as a review exercise to improve your understanding of the passage.

A. Nonsense. The transition will happen because books are available digitally and because the technology exists to print them.
B. The author never said exactly why the new digital model will be accepted. It's true that low costs will make it affordable (lines 16-20), but the author never explained why people wouldn't prefer entirely e-books, rather than digitally printed books.
C. **CORRECT.** Literary agents are mentioned on lines 38-41. Agents will recognize that the publishing landscape has changed, and ask for higher royalties for their authors. If publishers don't comply, then they will send their authors to new publishing houses (lines 44-46).
D. The passage doesn't mention how books are marketed.
E. The passage never says how many people will be familiar with new publishing methods.

Question 7

DISCUSSION: It should go without saying that before answering this question you should read the final sentence, *and* the text before it, to get context.

The last sentence shows that other industries have also faced difficult adjustments. The difficulty and uncertainty help explain why publishers are slow to change.

They can't easily get rid of their old model. And they're afraid that getting rid of their old model might be the wrong move. So they hesitate.

A. Just the opposite. The author suggests that publishers have a reason for their caution.
B. **CORRECT.** Lines 53 says that the adjustments typical of an economic transition may explain publishers' reluctance. It shows that other industries have faced similar dilemmas.
C. Not at all. This sentence adds some doubt and shows that the future is not 100% certain. This explains some of publishers' reluctance.
D. Actually, the primary obstacle is that traditional publishers are invested in the old publishing infrastructure (lines 45-51).
E. Actually, the author suggests that publishing houses stand to gain if they move quickly and embrace digital publishing. Otherwise authors will go to upstart companies (lines 45-51).

Passage 2 - Fingerprint Analysis (Comparative)
Questions 8-14

Paragraph Summaries

Passage A

1. The defendant says fingerprint analysis is flawed.
2. The defendant says there are no fixed standards for fingerprint analysis.
3. The judge says experts agree that fingerprint analysis is reliable.
4. The judge says that while fingerprint analysis standards differ, the error rate is low.

Passage B

1. There are no objective standards in fingerprint analysis.
2. We don't know the true error rate of fingerprint analysis, because we can't say how likely it is that certain people will share fingerprint characteristics.
3. There haven't been many studies of fingerprint analysis error rates. One study showed rates could be as high as 34 percent.

Analysis

The first passage is a judge's argument (see line 21, where the author refers to himself as 'this court'). The judge considers the defendant's arguments, and decides that the arguments are not convincing. Fingerprint analysis may not be 100% certain, but the error rate is low enough that we can be confident in using it.

The second passage is also an argument. It says fingerprint analysis is uncertain. This argument supports the defendant. It sounds like a scholarly article he might have used in building his case.

Many wrong answer choices speak of a defendant's right to challenge evidence. The judge doesn't deny this right. The judge accepted the defendant's right to challenge evidence, but concluded the defendant's argument was wrong.

The author of the second passage doesn't mention how courts should use fingerprint evidence. Many wrong answers suggest that he did.

Question 8

DISCUSSION: The main point of passage B is that we don't know how accurate fingerprint analysis is. There are also no objective standards for fingerprint analysis.

The author does not say how we ought to use fingerprints in court, if at all.

A. Passage B never mentions how we use fingerprint evidence in trials.

B. Same as A. The author of passage B never says that fingerprint evidence has no use in criminal trials. It's just not 100% effective. Perhaps it can be useful, even if it is not definitive on it's own.

C. Look at the first two sentences of the final paragraph of passage B. The author doesn't say what the error rate is. He said we *don't know* the error rate because we haven't done many studies.

D. **CORRECT.** This sums things up. We lack objective standards for fingerprint analysis, and we don't know what the error rate is.

E. The author didn't say whether legal scholars are aware of the problems with fingerprint analysis.

Question 9

DISCUSSION: Remember that the judge likes fingerprint analysis, while the second author is skeptical. But, the judge admits fingerprint analysis has some weaknesses.

- **A.** See lines 19-21. Though the judge likes fingerprint evidence, they admit that more consistent standards would be desirable.
- **B. CORRECT.** The judge thinks errors are rare (line 35). The author of passage B thinks that we don't know the error rate (lines 59-62).
- **C.** The judge doesn't think fingerprint identification is scientific law (lines 16-18). The author of passage B definitely doesn't think fingerprint analysis is a science.
- **D.** Neither author says which method is better.
- **E.** Neither author is specific about how agencies regulate fingerprint matching.

Question 10

DISCUSSION: To figure out an author's perspective, it helps to read the start and end of a passage.

The first line says the text is written for an appeal of a criminal conviction. The final line says that the trial court was right. Those sound like the words of an appeals court judge.

It's also clear throughout the passage that the author is judging the defendant's argument, and deciding what should happen to him.

See line 21, where the author refers to himself as 'this court'. Really, this line reference alone is enough to eliminate answers B, C, D and E.

- **A. CORRECT.** See the explanation above.
- **B.** A defense attorney would attack the fingerprint evidence. This passage argues for using the fingerprint evidence.
- **C.** A prosecutor would be more forceful in arguing for the defendant's conviction. This passage seems to weigh evidence evenhandedly before coming to a conclusion. Also, in line 21 the authors refers to himself as 'this court'.
- **D.** The author of the passage appears to be coming to a decision as they write. The judgement uses present tense, while a law professor would use past tense.
- **E.** When an academic presents a paper, they usually talk about the paper. This passage is a judgement of a man's future, not an introduction to a scholarly paper.

Question 11

DISCUSSION: There's no shortcut on these questions. You need to find references in both passages. Otherwise you can't be sure an answer is correct.

You can get faster at this by practicing. On review, go through each answer to see if you can find references in both passages, one passage, or neither passage.

A. Neither passage talks about the ability of a defendant to attack the prosecution.
B. Personal integrity refers to things like honesty. Neither passage talks about whether fingerprint examiners deliberately lie.
C. **CORRECT.** See lines 12-15 and lines 44-46.
D. Only passage B mentions this (lines 52-53).
E. Only passage B mentions this (line 44).

Question 12

DISCUSSION: The authors of both passages agree that fingerprint analysis could be useful, and that it has some flaws.

They come to different conclusions. The judge in the first passage thinks that fingerprint analysis is accurate. The author of the second passage implies that fingerprint analysis has not been proven to be accurate.

A. Only passage A says this. Passage B doesn't mention how courts ought to use fingerprint evidence.
B. Neither passage mentions what rights defendants have to challenge evidence.
C. Passage A never mentions partial fingerprints.
D. Passage A never mentions rigorous tests, and they never say what standards fingerprint analysis must meet to be considered accurate. The judge's only evidence is that courts have used fingerprints for a while, and experts agree that fingerprints are reliable (lines 16-19).
E. **CORRECT.** In the final paragraph of passage A, the judge argues that fingerprint analysis is held to consistent standards, which means the same thing as objective standards. The first sentence of passage B complains that fingerprint standards are not objective.

Question 13

DISCUSSION: I personally find this question infuriating. It depends on your ability to check both passage for very specific details.

There's no way to be sure about this type of question without searching the passages for the answer choice that is referenced in both.

Several wrong answers mention things that simply did not appear in the passage. Best to first check answers that you're pretty sure you remember appearing at least somewhere.

A. Only passage B mentions 'holistic' (line 44).
B. A misleading answer. Neither passage mentions databases. This is just a word you might associate with fingerprints.
C. **CORRECT.** See lines 14-15 and lines 39-41.
D. Neither passage mentions statistics about rare fingerprint characteristics.
E. The passage doesn't even contain the word 'computer'. This answer is completely off-base. It's designed to play on your mental association of fingerprints with CSI-like techniques.

Question 14

DISCUSSION: Passage B talks abstractly about fingerprint analysis. Passage A only talks about fingerprint analysis in order to prove a conclusion in a specific case. The judge's argument is focussed on one defendant's claims.

You may have found C tempting. Passage B may seem tentative because they claim we don't know if fingerprint analysis works.

But, they are 100% certain that we don't know. They're making a strong claim. Tentative would mean admitting they're not sure if their argument is correct.

Tentative: I'm 75% certain that we are correct.
Certain: I'm 100% certain that we don't know what we're doing.

A. Passage B is somewhat pessimistic about fingerprint analysis, since we have no idea whether it works.
B. **CORRECT.** Passage B talks about fingerprint analysis in general. Passage A focussed on one defendant's case, even if the judge used evidence about fingerprint analysis to support their argument.
C. Passage B is very clear in its claim: we don't know whether fingerprint analysis works. If the author had been tentative in their claim, they would have said they weren't confident about their evidence.
D. Passage B doesn't show respect or disrespect to opposing claims. The author just makes an argument without reference to opponents. And passage A isn't disrespectful to opposing claims. The judge is fair to the defendant even though they disagree with him.
E. Passage B cites research. Their assumptions are substantiated.

Passage 3 - Jazz Novel
Questions 15-22

Paragraph Summaries

1. Writing has often aspired to be musical, especially in the African-American community. Toni Morrison's *Jazz* was the first novel to use a musical genre as a structuring principle.
2. In *Jazz,* the story is structured as a piece of music. The omniscient narrator controls the first person voices of individual characters.
3. Duke Ellington kept his soloists under his guidance, even if their solos were innovative. Morrison did the same with her book's characters.
4. *Jazz* redefines the possibilities of narrative by combining Morrison's style with a musical structure.

Analysis

The passage is about Toni Morrison's book *Jazz.* The bit about music and writing at the start is just context to introduce Morrison's book; it isn't the main point. The passage focusses on the book.

You need to understand what 'narrative' means. It's how you tell a story. Some books are first person: the narrative is told through the eyes of the main character. Other books are third person, told through the eyes of a narrator.

Morrison's book mixes persons. The narration is done by an omniscient third person narrator. Individual characters speak as well in first person.

But....the narrator has total control. The individual characters are clearly contrasted from the main text, by quotation marks.

Jazz is organized similarly to Duke Ellington's jazz performances. He allowed his performers to do very innovative solos.

But if you listened carefully, Ellington had total control. Every solo had to fit within his overall plan.

The same goes for Morrison's characters. They all fall within the control of the narrator.

Morrison book was very innovative. She wrote the first novel that used a musical style for its structure.

It's important to note that we hardly know anything about the plot or theme of the book. All we know is that the book is set in Harlem in the 1920s. The passage is about the innovative structure of the novel, not its plot.

Question 15

DISCUSSION: It's clear that this passage expects you to be confused about how *Jazz* the book mimics the musical structure of jazz music.

We don't know much about the book or how it uses jazz music, if at all. The book doesn't used jazz music as a metaphor. Morrison's book doesn't describe a jazz performance. In fact, we know nothing about the plot of *Jazz.*

The point was that *Jazz* has a unique narrative structure. Narrative is *how* Morrison tells the story. She has a central narrator controlling when and how the individual characters can speak. This is similar to Duke Ellington's performances.

A. The passage isn't about the plot, theme and setting of *Jazz.* It's about the *structure* of *Jazz;* the book was written like a piece of jazz music.
B. Morrison didn't *describe* a musical ensemble performance. She structured the *narration* of her book as though it was a piece of jazz music.
C. Morrison doesn't use jazz as a metaphor. She uses the structure of a jazz piece to guide how she narrates her story.
D. The passage doesn't say if Morrison uses her jazzlike style of narration in any other books.
E. **CORRECT.** See especially paragraphs 3 and 4. The main point of this passage is that Morrison was the first to write a book that used a style of narration drawn entirely from a musical genre.

Question 16

DISCUSSION: For this type of question, it's important to reread the first paragraph.

The author starts by talking about writing and music in general. Then she moves to how the African American community has merged the two.

Finally, she talks about how Morrison was an innovator in this tradition.

You can eliminate wrong answers that get even one element wrong. It can be helpful to go through the answers one by one.

A. The author never denied that art and music are in competition.
B. **CORRECT.** The general remark is about the tension between art and music. The particular artistic tradition is African-American music and writing. The particular work is *Jazz* by Toni Morrison.
C. The author never really supports the claim that art and music are in tension.
D. The passage starts with a description of *two* art forms: writing and music.
E. The example of the African Americans is not a counterexample to the claim. It *supports* the claim. This answer also says that Toni Morrison was used to disprove something about African Americans, but Morrison fits within the African American tradition.

Question 17

DISCUSSION: The assertion is that Morrison was the first to attempt to use a musical genre to structure a novel.

To weaken this, we ought to show that Morrison was not the first, or that she hadn't attempted to use a musical genre to structure her novel.

A. This supports the point, by clearly showing that *Jazz* was structured on a musical style.
B. **CORRECT.** This shows that these authors tried to structure their work on a musical genre *before* Morrison did. She wasn't the first.
C. Just because a novel *appears* to have been following the narrative style of an art form, doesn't mean the author intended to do this or that the appearance is correct.
D. This doesn't tell us whether authors attempted to structure their novels using a musical genre.
E. Plots and characters are irrelevant. The *narration* of Morrison's book was styled after a musical genre.

Question 18

DISCUSSION: It's worth reading the third paragraph to refresh your memory of what we know about Ellington.

This seems like it will take a while, but it actually makes you go through the answers *much* faster. And if you practice rereading relevant sections, you'll get faster at doing it.

A. The passage never said whether Morrison acknowledged Ellington's influence.
B. Line 39 says that Ellington's musicians *did* perform lengthy solos.
C. Same as A. The passage doesn't say whether Morrison ever acknowledged Ellington or included him in her book.
D. **CORRECT.** See lines 36-39. Ellington composed his music with the styles of particular musicians in mind.
E. The passage never says whether Ellington composed in other genres.

Question 19

DISCUSSION: The main purpose of the passage is to talk about the jazzlike narrative style used in *Jazz.*

A. We're told of at most *one* contribution made by Morrison: the jazzlike narrative structure she used in *Jazz.*
B. The only other artist mentioned was Ellington, and the passage said Morrison's book was similar to his music.
C. **CORRECT.** The work is *Jazz.* The aspect is the jazzlike narrative structure.
D. Music and writing (the two different arts) weren't the main focus of the passage. The passage never said whether they are similar.
E. The author did not discuss the themes of *Jazz.* The focus was on the novel's narrative style.

Question 20

DISCUSSION: The author seemed to like *Jazz*. They thought it was innovative and they approved of the novel's jazzlike narrative style.

A. CORRECT. This answer talks about African-American music.
However, the author seems to think that Morrison's book was an even more interesting contribution to North American art than African-American music was. So this quote is off base.

B. This has to do with the novel's narrative structure, the main focus of the passage.

C. This describes the interaction between the narrator and the individual characters, much like the interaction between Ellington's ensemble and the soloists.

D. This shows how the narrative style of Morrison's book is like a jazz ensemble.

E. This shows that Morrison used a jazzlike style in her narration and combined it with her skillful writing abilities, making a great book.

Question 21

DISCUSSION: For inference questions, you should try to justify your answer by finding a reference in the passage. Otherwise you risk choosing a trap answer.

A. Line 12 says that no one else had attempted a book with the narrative structure of a genre of music.

B. The *structure* of Morrison's book was based on jazz. We don't know what the book's theme was. Morrison may not have focussed on the milieu that jazz musicians lived and worked in.

C. See lines 27-31. It's easy to distinguish individual characters. But, they must follow the narrator's lead.

D. CORRECT. See the third paragraph. Ellington's soloists are always under his control, and Morrison's characters always follow the lead of the narrator. There's more than a simple shift between individual and ensemble.

E. It seems that Ellington made his transitions appear easy as well. This is actually a similarity between Ellington's jazz performances and Morrison's novel's shifts between narrator and individual characters.

Question 22

DISCUSSION: You should try to justify your answer by finding a reference in the passage. Otherwise you risk choosing a trap answer.

Since the prompt says the passage helps answer the question posed by the right answer, you will always be able to find a line reference for this type of question.

A. The passage never mentions visual artists.
B. The passage never mentions Morrison's other books.
C. The passage never says what critics thought of Morrison's book.
D. The passage never mentions other books.
E. **CORRECT.** See lines 10-12. Other writers also used music and musicians as a theme.

Passage 4 - Scientific Uncertainty
Questions 23-27

Paragraph Summaries

1. Scientific discoveries often look easy in retrospect. Nuclear fission is one example. Uranium bombardment experiments produced evidence that we could do fission, but scientists took a while to realize what they had done.
2. There was a theoretical basis for fission, but the uranium bombardment experiments weren't undertaken to produce fission. The researchers weren't expecting fission to occur.
3. Researchers were puzzled by the results of bombardment, and assumed the results were close to uranium.
4. Hahn discovered that the experiments had produced barium.
5. Scientists realize that they've been doing fission.

Note: 3 and 4 refer to the first and second halves of paragraph 3.

Analysis

The first sentence is the most important part of the passage. It shows the author's theme: science sometimes seems obvious when we look back at it. But science is actually very complicated and uncertain.

Scientists will often assemble much evidence, but then take a while to piece everything together. This makes sense. Science is a complicated business, and we have the benefit of hindsight when we look back.

The author introduces the example of nuclear fission in order to illustrate his claim about the messy nature of science. Fission is *not* the main point. It's just an example. See line 5, 'a case in point'.

That said, fission is an extended example, so it's important to understand what's going on. There were two groups of scientists.

First, there was a theoretical group that claimed atoms could be broken apart. But they couldn't prove anything.

Second, there was a group of experimental physicists. They were bombarding uranium with neutrons. We don't know why they were doing this, but we do know they weren't expecting to break apart uranium atoms.

So they were puzzled by their results. They didn't bother analyzing the chemicals produced by bombardment, because it was hard to do. But they also didn't bother because they assumed they would find only uranium.

Eventually, Hahn did an analysis and figured out the the results included barium. Meitner then realized that the scientists had been splitting atoms.

Once Meitner figured this out, then research teams were easily able to replicate the results and produce fission. The big problem had been that nobody realized fission could be done.

There's a large variety of research teams mentioned. The point is that even multiple teams of very smart scientists had no idea what was going on.

Once you figure something out, the solution seems obvious. But it's not. *Before* you solve the problem it can seem very hard. You have all the information necessary, but it takes insight to piece things together in the right way.

Question 23

DISCUSSION: The main point of the passage is that science often seems more obvious than it is. You can see this in the first sentence. The first sentence often introduces the main point of a passage.

The start of the second sentence 'A case in point....' shows that nuclear fission is just an extended example supporting this claim.

A. The author hasn't criticized anyone.
B. **CORRECT.** The first sentence is the main point: science often looks simpler in hindsight. The example of nuclear fission is used to illustrate this sentence.
C. The author never says whether theory or experimentation is more important. The only general claim is made in the first sentence.
D. The author didn't say that there is a better way to do science.
E. The author never mentioned intellectual arrogance. The scientists were faced with a situation they didn't understand and did the best they could to sort it out. They had preconceived ideas, but they were hardly stubborn.

Question 24

DISCUSSION: The theoretical physicists predicted that the atom could be split. But they didn't prove it with experiments.

Meitner realized that experimental neutron bombardment had been splitting the atom. So she proved the that the theoretical physicists were correct.

A. Lines 20-22 say that the researchers doing the bombardment hadn't believed they could produce fission.
B. Theoretical physics was already acceptable. The specific theoretical physicists who predicted fission would be pleased to have confirmation of their theory, but theoretical physics itself didn't need legitimacy.
C. Actually, nuclei are pretty stable. Uranium held together until it was *bombarded by neutrons!*
D. **CORRECT.** The theoretical physicists predicted atoms could be split. Meitner realized that her group *had* split atoms. So she confirmed that the theoretical physicists' prediction was correct.
E. Actually, Meitner and the other scientists *didn't* analyze their data (lines 30-35). They didn't expect any extraordinary results.

Question 25

DISCUSSION: This goes back to the very first sentence of the passage.

Often, in science, there is enough data to make a discovery. The problem is seeing the pattern in the data or making the right connections.

In this case, the relevant evidence was the results of neutron bombardment experiments carried out in Europe. Scientists hadn't realized they had split atoms.

Several wrong answers mention work done in 1938. That's when Hahn did his analysis and Meitner made the discovery. But line 63 says the evidence had been present *for some time*. So it's referring to evidence from years before 1938.

A. **CORRECT.** These experiments split the atom. But it took scientists a while to realize what they had done. They weren't expecting the result. So the relevant evidence was present but scientists didn't know what to do with it.

B. Actually, it was Otto Hahn who produced the results that Meitner used. See the second half of the third paragraph.

C. Hahn's results led Meitner to her insight. But the same experiments had already been conducted, it's just that no one bothered to do the analysis Hahn finally did in 1938.

D. This is what Hahn finally figured out in 1938. But he could have figured it out years earlier if he had analyzed the bombardment experiments.

E. The question asked about relevant evidence. The scientists had a *lack* of evidence because they didn't examine the by products of bombardments. Only when they started examining these by-products did they get relevant evidence.

Question 26

DISCUSSION: A big part of the problem was that scientists never analyzed the results of uranium bombardment experiments.

It was dangerous, and scientists assumed they would just find elements close to uranium. (lines 30-36)

A. This wouldn't have helped. The physicists' techniques didn't assume that bombardment would split the atom.

B. **CORRECT.** If the physicists hadn't expected that the by-products would be similar to uranium, then they might have analyzed them earlier and realized they had split atoms.

C. The problem was that physicists hadn't realized they were splitting atoms. If anything, knowing about the theoretical possibility of splitting atoms would have helped them make this connection.

This answer choice said they would have been better off *not* knowing fission was possible, which makes no sense.

D. The problem was that every research team made the same errors. Only dumb luck let them discover they had split the atom. More research teams couldn't have helped much.

E. We have no idea if neutrons could have split substances other than uranium.

Question 27

DISCUSSION: You'll want to support the answer using a reference from the passage. But make sure to read all the answers before trying to support or eliminate some.

If you remembered lines 33-34 then this was an easy question, otherwise it was hard. That's why it's important to have a clear idea of the passage before starting, even if it means rereading some sections.

A. The experimental physicists didn't disagree with the theoretical findings. They just didn't expect fission to happen from bombardment. (lines 20-22)

B. The passage never mentions anyone revising the earlier theoretical work. Presumably it was correct.

C. Actually, Hahn did identify these by-products. Read the second part of the third paragraph, especially lines 42-44.

D. We're never told about experiments splitting other types of atoms.

E. **CORRECT.** See lines 33-34. Physicists recognized the dangers, that's one reason they hadn't analyzed the by-products of bombarded uranium.

Section II - Logical Reasoning

Question 1

QUESTION TYPE: Flawed Reasoning

CONCLUSION: We should adopt my plan.

REASONING: Council has debated a variety of alternatives. We can either adopt my plan or do nothing. Doing nothing would be bad.

ANALYSIS: The mayor hasn't said why the only alternatives are his plan or nothing. He said council had debated *many* options. The mayor didn't explain why those other options weren't also possibilities. So, the mayor presented a false choice.

A. Conservative estimates are appropriate here. They show that even a best case scenario is bad.
B. Actually, the mayor's plan and 'doing nothing' *are* mutually exclusive. Doing *anything* is the opposite of doing nothing.
C. A decrease in the *rate of increase* is not that helpful. It means we will still have growth in traffic, just smaller growth. Gridlock will continue since road capacity isn't growing. Failing to consider this isn't a flaw.
D. Everyone knows gridlock is pretty terrible. It would be useful to know the cost of gridlock, but everyone agrees it's something that must be avoided on a road system. It's not a flaw to avoid calculating an exact cost of gridlock.
E. **CORRECT.** Exactly. The mayor never said why other options are unthinkable. He even said council had considered other options.

Question 2

QUESTION TYPE: Necessary Assumption

CONCLUSION: The earthenware hippopotamus was a religious object.

REASONING: The ancient Egyptians thought that breaking the legs off a representation of an animal would help the dead win their battles in the afterlife. The hippopotamus had its legs broken off.

ANALYSIS: This sounds like a good argument. But the author is assuming that the legs were broken when the hippopotamus was placed in the tomb.

It's possible the hippopotamus broke by accident after it was placed in the tomb. Perhaps an earthquake or grave robbers broke it.

A. This would help the argument, but just because the tomb was a child's tomb, that doesn't mean that the hippo was a toy. Children need religious objects to help them in the afterlife, too.
B. This would strengthen the argument by showing that the object wasn't a toy. But it's not necessary that all earthenware hippopotami were religious objects.
This hippopotamus could be a religious object even if other earthenware hippopotami were toys.
C. It's fine for the tomb to have been reopened, as long as no one broke the hippopotamus for non-religious reasons.

Indeed, maybe the tomb was re-opened because the priest forgot to break the hippo's legs. Perhaps they went back in to make sure the hippo was a proper religious object.
D. **CORRECT.** If the legs were broken by a natural occurrence such as an earthquake, then we have no reason to think that the hippo was a religious object. The broken legs were the only evidence.
E. The author never said that being upside down was significant. The broken legs were the main point.

Question 3

QUESTION TYPE: Strengthen - Exception

CONCLUSION: Jury instructions should be simple and easy to understand.

REASONING: It's more important for juries to understand their role, than it is for their role to be precisely specified.

ANALYSIS: Many of the wrong answers seem too obvious. That's ok. They still strengthen the argument by making some assumptions explicit.

A. This shows that the current way of writing jury instructions makes them harder to understand. This seems like something we could have assumed, but making it explicit strengthens the argument.
B. This shows that current instructions don't work.
C. This shows that it's *possible* for jury instructions to work when they're simplified. That's helpful.
D. **CORRECT.** This shows a downside to simplified language. It definitely doesn't strengthen the argument.
E. This shows that the argument's reasoning isn't wrong. Precision is not necessary for a basic understanding of a jury's role.

Question 4

QUESTION TYPE: Necessary Assumption

CONCLUSION: Drugs will eventually work just as well as talk therapy.

REASONING: Talk therapy produces chemical changes in the brain. These changes seem to happen alongside improvements in patients' behavior. Drugs can be used to produce chemical changes in the brain.

ANALYSIS: This passage doesn't tell us much about talk therapy. Talk therapy might have other effects, apart from producing chemical changes.

A. Far too broad. We only care about chemical changes that result from talk therapy or drug use designed to treat psychological disorder.
B. **CORRECT.** If talk therapy has other effects apart from chemical change, then drugs probably couldn't match those effects.
C. This would strengthen the argument by setting a low hurdle for drugs to be considered effective. But this assumption isn't necessary. Maybe drugs can match talk therapy even if talk therapy is very effective at treating psychological disorder.
D. What a weird answer. Who cares if psychology and neuroscience become the same? The stimulus was pretty specific, dealing only with whether drugs could be as effective as talk therapy.
E. The stimulus didn't make any claims about the relative costs of the two methods, so this is irrelevant.

Question 5

QUESTION TYPE: Weaken

CONCLUSION: We shouldn't consider *H. pylori* a commensal.

REASONING: *H. Pylori* harms 10% of the people who have it (though it also helps their immune systems). *Mycobacter tuberculosis* only harms 10% of the people who have it and no one would consider it a commensal.

ANALYSIS: This isn't a good argument. *H. pylori* has some good and bad effects. We're not told whether *Mycobacter tuberculosis* has any good effects.

H. pylori was considered a commensal precisely because it had good effects.

A. This actually slightly strengthens the idea that *H. pylori* is a commensal. Its negative effects can be treated. That makes it more likely to have a beneficial effect overall.
B. You know, I'd rather have a cold that lasted a long while than gangrene that only lasted a few days. Length of illness isn't everything.
C. **CORRECT.** This shows there is a major difference between the two bacteria. There's absolutely no reason to consider *Mycobacter tuberculosis* a commensal, because it doesn't help us and only hurts us. *H. pylori does* help us.
D. Whether we consider *H. pylori* a commensal depends on its effects, not how common it is.
E. Same as D.

Question 6

QUESTION TYPE: Sufficient Assumption

CONCLUSION: At least one studio apartment in the building has scenic views.

REASONING: Most apartments on the upper floors of the building have scenic views.

ANALYSIS: We'd need to know that most apartments on the upper floors of the building are studio apartments.

You can make a logical deduction with two 'most' statements. It's the least well known deduction on the LSAT, and it's not very intuitive. If two 'most' statements refer to the same thing, you can combine them to get a 'some' statement. Here's an example:

'I work most days of the workweek'
'You work most days of the workweek'

There are five days in the workweek, and we each work three. That means we overlap for at least one day. So:

'We work together on some days of the workweek'

So if:

'Most upper floor apartments have a great view.'
'Most upper floor apartments are studios.'

Then some studio apartments have great views. Memorize this most + most → some deduction, as it's usually tested once every 1-2 LSATs.

A. This doesn't tell us anything about studio apartments.
B. This doesn't tell us whether there are any studio apartments in the building.
C. This could mean the studios are all on the lower floors and none have scenic views.
D. This doesn't tell us if there are studio apartments in the building.
E. **CORRECT.** See the explanation above.

Question 7

QUESTION TYPE: Principle - Strengthen

CONCLUSION: It would not be wrong for me to use Tom's computer.

REASONING: Tom didn't say I could. But last week he used Mary's bicycle without asking.

ANALYSIS: We don't know if it was 'not wrong' for Tom to use Mary's bicycle.

We need a principle that shows you can treat people the same way they treat others.

A. Mike didn't say anything about theft. He wants to prove that it would 'not be wrong' to use Tom's computer. That's different from stealing Tom's computer. (Heck, for the purposes of this argument, we don't know if theft is wrong)
B. Mike isn't talking about *lying* to Tom. He's just talking about doing something without checking for permission first.
C. Tom *didn't* use Mike's property. He used Mary's property.
D. **CORRECT.** Mike is treating Tom the way Tom treated Mary, so therefore Mike's actions are permissible and not wrong.
E. This provides a sufficient condition for showing something is wrong. We're trying to show that Mike's use is *not* wrong.

Question 8

QUESTION TYPE: Flawed Reasoning

CONCLUSION: The museum didn't waste money.

REASONING: Displaying the items is the only way to show them to the public.

ANALYSIS: The argument completely ignored Wexell's criticism that the objects have no value outside of a performance.

Wexell would say there's no point showing these objects to the public, since they can't be used in a performance.

A. This is a completely different error. It's like saying: 'Everyone I saw today is young. So the entire city must be young.'
B. **CORRECT.** Wexell doesn't care about displaying the objects. He thinks they're useless if they're not used in a performance.
C. Robinson didn't attack Wexell personally. In fact, he ignored Wexell completely.
D. This is a different error. It's like saying 'we won't send humans to Mars because we haven't proven we can'.
E. This is a different argument. It's like saying you *need* a 180 and a 4.3 GPA to get to law school, just because those are (usually) *sufficient* to get to law school.

Question 9

QUESTION TYPE: Principle

FACTS:

1. Someone is told they must guess what a dream was about by asking a group yes or no questions.
2. There is no dream, but the group uses a rule to decide how to answer.
3. The questioner often constructs a coherent dream narrative.

ANALYSIS: It sounds like the questioner is seeing things that aren't there. Because they've been told the group is describing a dream, the questioner imagines the answer mean something. The questioner invents a dream from the group's responses.

It's like how if a trusted friend describes a stranger as intelligent, you will assume they are intelligent unless strong evidence convinces you they aren't. Your brain will interpret the stranger's actions in a way that makes them seem smart.

A. CORRECT. This makes sense. The questioner *assumes* that there is a dream with order. So this causes them to see order in the answers and invent their own story.

B. Actually, the questioner did reach a false understanding of the group's answers.

C. There was no dream in the stimulus. That was a lie to deceive the questioner.

D. Same as C.

E. The questioner isn't explaining *his own* behavior. He's interpreting the group's answers.

Question 10

QUESTION TYPE: Necessary Assumption

CONCLUSION: Computers can't currently be made significantly faster.

REASONING: Making a chip smaller without lowering sophistication will increase speed. We can't do this at the moment.

ANALYSIS: The argument assumes that we can only increase chip speed by making them smaller. They also assume that we can only make computers faster by increasing chip speed.

Maybe we could make chips faster without making them smaller. Or maybe we could make a computer faster by improving other parts of the computer.

This question negates a sufficient condition for increased computer speed, and incorrectly assumes that negates the necessary condition. We have to assume the sufficient condition was also necessary.

A. CORRECT. If there are other ways to make computers faster than maybe we can do it, even if we can't shrink chips.

B. This isn't necessary. We already know that shrinking chips isn't an option.

C. The argument isn't saying we should decrease sophistication. The author just says that we can't shrink chips without losing sophistication.

D. Who cares what manufacturers believe? They could all be wrong.

E. The passage never mentioned increasing sophistication. In fact, if we can increase speed by increasing sophistication, then maybe they argument is *wrong*. This assumption might harm the argument.

Question 11

QUESTION TYPE: Flawed Reasoning

CONCLUSION: It is wrong to say that pollution is killing amphibians.

REASONING: We just discovered many more amphibians.

ANALYSIS: When we 'discover' a new amphibian species, we don't create them out of thin air. The frogs were already there, we just noticed them for the first time.

So it's quite possible that species are dying. It doesn't matter if we find species we had previously missed. Discovering more frog species has no effect on whether species are dying.

This is the difference between reality and our knowledge of reality.

A. This is a different distinction. It's like the difference between 'presidents of the USA' and 'George Washington, Abraham Lincoln...etc'
B. This is a totally different thing. There's no conditional logic in this question.
C. This is a totally different thing. The question didn't talk about cause and effect.
D. This is a totally different thing. The argument didn't mention a correlation. That's where two things change in the same direction.
E. **CORRECT.** We have better knowledge of amphibians. That doesn't have any effect on their survival.

Question 12

QUESTION TYPE: Principle - Strengthen

CONCLUSION: Using peat moss as a soil conditioner is not environmentally sound.

REASONING: Peat moss contributes a lot of oxygen to the atmosphere, and gardeners are using peat moss faster than it can be replaced.

ANALYSIS: The answers to principle questions often seem blindingly obvious.

Approach these as if you were a space alien. What is 'environmentally sound'? The stimulus doesn't say.

We need a principle that says whatever the gardeners are doing (depleting oxygen, etc.) is environmentally unsound.

A. This just shows that it's *possible* that using peat moss is environmentally unsound. It doesn't show that it is unsound.
B. **CORRECT.** The gardeners will eventually significantly reduce the amount of oxygen entering the atmosphere if they deplete peat moss. This shows that doing so is environmentally unsound.
C. This tells us how to show something *is* environmentally sound. We want to show that using peat moss is *not* environmentally sound.
D. Same as C.
E. This tells us when to ban something. But it doesn't tell us when something is 'environmentally unsound'.

Question 13

QUESTION TYPE: Flawed Reasoning

CONCLUSION: Morgenstern says Brooks should quit.

REASONING: The main risk to quitting is not finding another job, in which case Brooks would be unhappy. But Brooks is already unhappy.

ANALYSIS: Morgenstern forgets that there are degrees of unhappiness.

You might dislike a job. But you might dislike not finding another job and being a hobo *even more*.

(I actually recommend leaving jobs you don't like. You're not likely to become a hobo. But that's another story.)

A. CORRECT. Sure, you dislike your job. But, you might be much more unhappy if you couldn't find another job.
B. This is code for circular reasoning. Morgenstern did have (flawed) evidence: Brook's greatest fear has already happened.
(according to Morgenstern)
So the argument isn't circular.
C. Morgenstern was pretty accurate about what Brooks said. Brooks did say he's unhappy, and Morgenstern correctly identified Brooks' main worry: not finding another job.
D. There's only one type of risk here: not finding another job. Being unhappy in Brooks' job isn't a risk, it's a certainty. He's already unhappy.
E. Morgenstern didn't say that everyone who is unhappy should quit their job. He just said that Brooks should. That's not a generalization.

Question 14

QUESTION TYPE: Must Be True

FACTS: Only Canadian films are shown at the festival. Most of the films at the festival won prizes at international festivals.

ANALYSIS: We can say that some Canadian films won prizes abroad, because they were shown at the festival.

You might have gotten confused because the argument goes from 'most' films at the festival to 'some' Canadian films won prizes abroad.

That's because 'most' just refers to films at the festival. E.g. 51 out of 100. But when you consider those 51 films out of all the films that won prizes internationally, they are just 'some' films. The total changed.

Diagrams:

F → C
F most → P

Conclusion:

Some canadian films won prizes abroad
Most films at the festival won prizes abroad

A. This gets things backwards. Maybe 1,000 Canadian films won prizes internationally, while only 100 films were shown at the festival.
B. Similar to B. There could be 1,000 Canadian films, and only 100 were shown at the festival.
C. CORRECT. This must be true, because some films from the festival won prizes and all the films at the festival were Canadian.
D. This could be true, but we have no idea. It's possible that every film that won a prize at that festival was also shown internationally. 'Most' can include 'all'.
E. Who knows? Maybe Canadian films swept the international film festivals this year, and Canadian films won all the prizes.

Question 15

QUESTION TYPE: Flawed Reasoning

CONCLUSION: The critics are wrong to say that journalists undermine society with cynicism.

REASONING: Journalists have always been cynical.

ANALYSIS: The author is mixed up. The critics claim that journalists hurt society by being cynical.

The author responds by saying that journalists have always been cynical. That's irrelevant.

If I say "you're being mean *right now*", I don't care if you've *always* been mean or if you just started.

That is to say, maybe journalists are currently hurting society with their cynicism. And maybe they hurt society in the past with the cynicism, as well.

A. The commentator needn't say that cynicism is good to disprove the social critics. He can disagree with them any way he wants. It seems like a bad argument technique to say that cynicism is good, few would argue that widespread cynicism is a good thing.
B. This would explain why the journalists are cynical, but it doesn't prove that their cynicism is harmful.
C. It doesn't matter if the cynicism is genuine or not. The commentator was only trying to prove it wasn't harmful.
D. This might show that the journalists are just being honest. But it doesn't prove whether or not their cynical portrayals harm the public.
E. **CORRECT.** The social critics were arguing that the cynicism is harmful *right now*. They might agree that it was harmful in the past as well. You can't prove something is good merely by saying it's been happening for a while.

Question 16

QUESTION TYPE: Parallel Reasoning

CONCLUSION: The owners should make the improvements even though they are not directly profitable.

REASONING: The improvements would also increase rents in nearby buildings also owned by the owners.

ANALYSIS: This may be a good argument. We're not told if the total increase in profits is enough to cover the cost of the improvements.

In terms of structure, the argument introduces an outside factor (more rents at nearby properties) that boosts the argument for doing the improvements.

A. **CORRECT.** This gives John *two* reasons to have the painful surgery: he will have a slight long term reduction in pain, and he can exercise again. It's similar to the stimulus in that we don't know how much John cares about exercising.
B. This hardly makes sense. The company is using the boats for fishing during the fishing season. Why would they want to use them for other purposes?
If it had said they could use the boats for other purposes during the 'non-fishing season' then this would have been the right answer.
C. This sounds like a reasonable argument. Better to spend $175 than risk having your car ruined. But this is nothing like the stimulus, which introduced a second factor in favor of a course of action.
D. This is a good argument, but it's not recommending that anyone should get dental problems. The original argument made a recommendation.
E. We have no idea what's in the long term interest of the fruit company. Maybe people will like the fruit, but they won't buy it often and it will be unprofitable.

Question 17

QUESTION TYPE: Strengthen

CONCLUSION: The president thinks sales will increase quite a bit once the games have copy protection.

REASONING: The company's games are copied illegally. The company will introduce copy protection on its games.

ANALYSIS: There are several ways to strengthen the argument. You could show that the copy protection will work or that at least some pirates will buy the game.

The right answer shows that the copy protection will allow pirates to get a taste of the game, and make them want to buy it.

A. This just tells us something about the company's profits. It doesn't prove the sales will increase.
B. This is just a problem faced by the company. It doesn't tell us that copy protection will fix the problem.
C. **CORRECT.** This is clever. You can still use a copied version of the game, but it will show you just enough to get you hooked, and then you have to buy it. This could increase sales.
D. This has always been true. Only a *new* factor will cause a substantial increase in sales.
E. This doesn't tell us whether copy protection will cause pirates to buy the games.

Question 18

QUESTION TYPE: Identify The Conclusion

CONCLUSION: Society wouldn't accept having the government electronically record all transactions.

REASONING: People don't trust governments with too much power. Eliminating paper money would give governments too much power.

ANALYSIS: 'However' often introduces an argument's conclusion. Look for this word on RC passages as well, as it indicates the author's opinion.

By the way, the IRS has announced it can access to all of your emails, Facebook messages, and other electronic activities. So, this world already exists, and then some. They don't need a warrant to look at any of this data.

A. **CORRECT.** Society wouldn't accept this because it would give the government too much power, and society doesn't trust too much government power.
B. The columnist never said whether society's fears are reasonable.
C. This is just a fact. It explains why the columnist is talking about the possibility of government recording of all transactions.
D. Same as B. The columnist never gives his opinion on whether the government can be trusted.
E. This isn't even true. The columnist said that people wouldn't *willingly* accept government transaction recording. But the government might force it on society anyway.

Question 19

QUESTION TYPE: Sufficient Assumption

CONCLUSION: Some observers have misunderstood Marxism.

REASONING: Marxism should be taken as a scientific theory. So it isn't a political program aimed at radically transforming society.

ANALYSIS: The author hasn't shown that being a scientific theory causes Marxism to also *not* be a political program. It could be both.

We need to show that Marxism can't be political because it is a science.

Here's the diagram from the correct answer:

Science → Not Political

We know Marxism is science, so therefore it is not political.

A. The author said Marxism should be regarded as a scientific theory because it *claims* to describe history rigorously. If the claims were not rigorous, then Marxism would simply be a bad scientific theory. It would still be science.
B. This could just mean that Marxism has contradictory aims by being both science and a political program. Lots of ideas contain contradictions.
C. This shows a necessary condition for science. It doesn't help prove that Marxism isn't political.
D. **CORRECT.** This shows that because Marxism is science, it can't be considered political.
E. We're trying to prove that Marxism is not a political program. This doesn't help. It's just a prediction about the future and the means of production.

Question 20

QUESTION TYPE: Point At Issue

ARGUMENTS: Daniel says we must perform some actions due to moral obligations. But to be good, an action must have the right motivations.

Carrie says we can't control our motivations. So the only necessary condition for an action to be good is that it fulfills a moral obligation.

ANALYSIS: They disagree on whether right motivations are required for an action to be good.

A. Neither of them mentions impossible actions.
B. Neither says why an act might not be good even if it meets the necessary conditions, such as fulfilling an obligation or having the right motivations.
C. Neither talks about why we do actions. Maybe some moral obligations are fulfilled by accident.
D. **CORRECT.** Daniel agrees with this. Carrie says that good actions only need to fulfill moral obligations.
E. Nonsense. Neither of them mentioned sufficient conditions for something being good. And this condition doesn't make sense - it's possible for someone to have a mistaken sense of moral duty.

Question 21

QUESTION TYPE: Flawed Reasoning

CONCLUSION: The bridge renovation was wasteful.

REASONING: The Southern Tier project was wasteful. The bridge renovation was part of that project.

ANALYSIS: This argument makes a whole to part error. We know the Souther Tier Project was wasteful.

That doesn't mean that every *part* of the Southern Tier project was wasteful. Maybe the bridge renovation was very efficient.

I originally got this wrong, because I misread the question and thought the tier project was part of the bridge project. Make sure you keep whole and part straight for this type of question!

A. CORRECT. This answer describes a whole to part error.

The author concluded that the bridge project was wasteful because the larger Southern Tier project was wasteful. But individual parts of the Southern Tier project could have been efficient.

B. This is a part to whole error. It's like saying, these students are intelligent, so the entire school must be intelligent.

C. The author never attacked the mayor personally. He did say the mayor lied, but that was his conclusion, not a personal attack supporting a conclusion.

D. This is code for circular reasoning. This argument is not circular, the conclusion is based on evidence from the government commission that found waste in the Southern Tier Project.

E. This is similar to C. It's code for an ad hominem attack. But the author didn't attack the mayor personally or discuss his motives.

Question 22

QUESTION TYPE: Most Strongly Supported

FACTS:

1. When weather is poor, planes can't use adjacent runways.
2. In good weather, 60 planes an hour can land. In bad weather, 30 planes an hour can land.
3. Plane schedules assume good weather. Bad weather creates serious delays.

ANALYSIS: This question tests your ability to identify two different concepts as having the same meaning.

Airlines based their schedules on good weather. That means they assume that up to 60 planes can land at once.

That's the most strongly supported statement!

It almost seems too obvious, like it didn't have to be said. But there's nothing wrong with obvious answers!

A. Half as many planes land at the airport in general, during poor weather. But that's because only half the runways can be used - planes can't use adjacent runways. Bad weather doesn't mean any particular runway is dangerous.
Some runways might get just as much traffic, it's just that the runways right beside wouldn't get any traffic at all.

B. We know that good weather allows up to 60 planes to land. But we don't know if the airport is always working at max capacity.

C. Actually, in good weather, adjacent runways are used simultaneously, without delay.

D. CORRECT. Airlines base their schedules on good weather. In good weather, more than 30 planes can land per hour. Up to 60 planes in fact.

E. There are many reasons a flight can be delayed even if weather is good. Mechanical problems, for example.

Question 23

QUESTION TYPE: Paradox

PARADOX: Bigger primate groups usually spend more time grooming each other. This helps group cohesion.

Based on evidence from neocortex size, early human groups were quite large. But people didn't groom each other apart from parents grooming children.

ANALYSIS: The main dilemma is explaining how early humans groups stayed cohesive. Grooming helps groups bond.

I had no idea how to prephrase this. So I just moved to the answers, keeping in mind that I had to explain how humans bonded.

The right answer shows that humans developed language, an even more effective way of bonding. So grooming became unnecessary for group cohesion.

A. This doesn't explain how human groups stayed cohesive.
B. **CORRECT.** This shows that language let humans bond. So grooming was unnecessary, and presumably used only to keep people clean.
C. This would show that it's easier to keep humans clean. But, the main purpose of social grooming was to keep the group together. This doesn't explain why humans didn't need the bonding effect of grooming.
D. This has nothing to do with grooming or bonding. We need an explanation for how human groups bonded.
E. That's nice. This doesn't explain how human groups maintained cohesion.

Question 24

QUESTION TYPE: Flawed Parallel Reasoning

CONCLUSION: The economic theories were wrong.

REASONING: If the theory was right AND the program was implemented, inflation would have decreased. Inflation increased.

ANALYSIS: We can only conclude that the theory was wrong OR the program was not implemented.

The argument hasn't shown that inflation increased due to bad ideas and not poor implementation.

T AND P → ~~I~~

I → ~~T~~ OR ~~P~~

A. This is a good argument. Since the architecture didn't change, both sufficient conditions for architectural change must be false.
I OR CC → AC   ~~AC~~ → ~~I~~ AND ~~CC~~
B. This is close. It's possible the workers thought that the party simply wouldn't win. But, and here's the difference, it's also possible that the workers are lying when they promise they won't strike. This would only have been correct if we had been told the election was over and the workers didn't strike.
C. **CORRECT.** This ignores the possibility that the company didn't buy the patent.
S AND P → Stock increase
~~Stock Increase~~ → ~~S~~ OR ~~P~~
D. This makes a sufficient-necessary error, which is different. The argument gives us two sufficient conditions for the people to support the rebels. But it's possible that the citizens supported the rebels for another reason. There can be multiple sufficient conditions for any necessary condition.
E. This is a good argument. It uses the contrapositive to show that the sufficient condition wasn't present.
WI → A AND R
~~A~~ → ~~WI~~ (We don't know if ratings changed)

Question 25

QUESTION TYPE: Method of Reasoning

CONCLUSION: If you want an accusation to work, call someone 'unyielding'.

REASONING: To prove someone is unyielding, you can point to the fact that they haven't yielded. They can't deny that.

ANALYSIS: This argument says to choose a word that can be proven using a person's actions as evidence.

It's hard to prove that someone is stubborn, because it's a negative attribute and people will dispute it. But unyielding can be positive, and it's based in objective fact: whether or not someone has yielded.

A. The argument didn't say to avoid character attacks. It just said pick one that is easiest to prove. This doesn't mean that there can never be evidence that someone is pig headed; it's just easier to prove that someone is unyielding.

B. Actually, the author didn't say to avoid insults. They said, *if* you decide to insult someone, call them unyielding, because it's easier to prove.

C. Unyielding isn't necessarily less offensive, it's just easier to prove.

D. Actually, the author says that epithets such as unyielding rarely help a group reach consensus. They're only recommending unyielding because it is at least easier to prove.

E. **CORRECT.** 'Conditionally advocating' just means '*IF* you want to insult someone, *THEN....*'.It's advice for what to do if you feel like calling someone a name. In that case, you should call them unyielding, because it's hard to argue you're not unyielding if you have not yielded.

Section III - Logic Games

Game 1 - Lab Sessions

Questions 1-5

Setup

This game is a mix of linear and grouping. It tests your ability to remember the rules. If you have them in your head and can combine them, then this game is easy. If you have to constantly check the rules, then this game is hard.

I set up the game horizontally. If you set it up vertically, that's fine too. It's a matter of preference.

M ___ ___ ___

A ___ ___ ___

W T F

Next, KR have to be on the same day, in either order:

The line indicates that K and R can be reversed. Think of it like a suitcase handle.

L and O can't be on the same day:

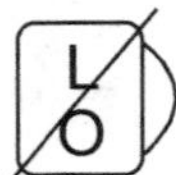

N can only go in the afternoon. I drew this on the diagram itself. I used a 'not' rule to show that it can't be in morning.

That's what we know for certain, it's best to stick to what is definite.

M ___ ___ ___ ~~N~~

A ___ ___ ___

W T F

Finally, J comes on an earlier day than O.

J—O

This diagram is slightly ambiguous. It just shows that J comes earlier. Morning is earlier than afternoon, so you have to remember that it means J comes on a *day* earlier than O does.

There aren't any obvious deductions, but you can make some by thinking about how the rules fit together. If you suspect a game is restricted, it helps to make a sample scenario to see how things fit together.

KR take up an entire day. This is very restrictive. L/O are split between the other two days, and J-O are also split between the other two days.

In fact, JL always have to go together, and ON always go together. I'll show this with an example.

By the way, I didn't figure this out explicitly the first time I did the game, though I knew it intuitively well enough and could draw fast diagrams. You don't need to make a perfect diagram to do well on a game.

Ok, time to prove the deduction. Let's see what happens if you put KR on Wednesday. Remember that they're reversible:

M K ___ ___ ~~N~~

A R ___ ___

W T F

J goes before O (rule 4), so J is on Thursday and O is on Friday. Since L and O can't go together, then L must also go on Thursday with J.

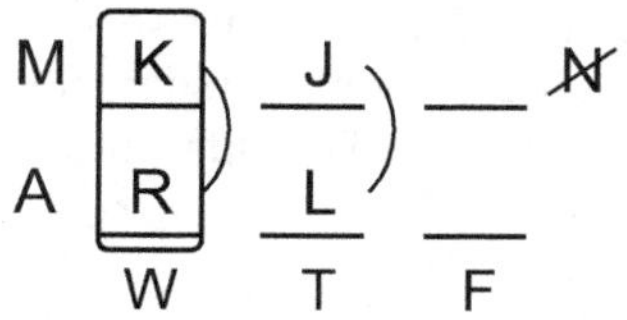

I haven't placed O yet. I'll get to that. First, I'll explain what I've drawn.

KR have a box around them as a reminder that this is based on a rule.

JL have a line between them to indicate that they're reversible, but there's no box because no rule says they must be together. It just so happens that the other rules force them together.

This is an arbitrary style I made up for this game, because it's unique. You could easily draw a box around J/L and do fine.

Ok, now let's place O. We only have O and N left to place. And N can't go in the morning. So this is the only possible diagram when KR go Wednesday:

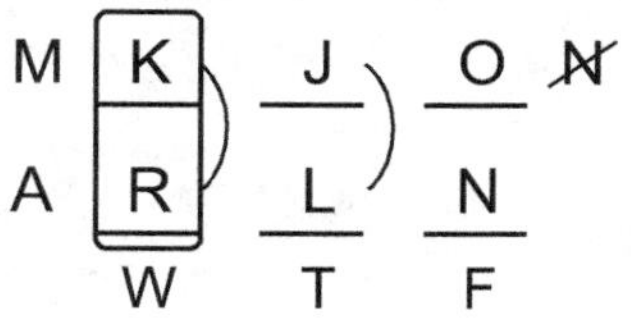

If KR go Thursday or Friday then we get slightly different diagrams, but the principle is the same:

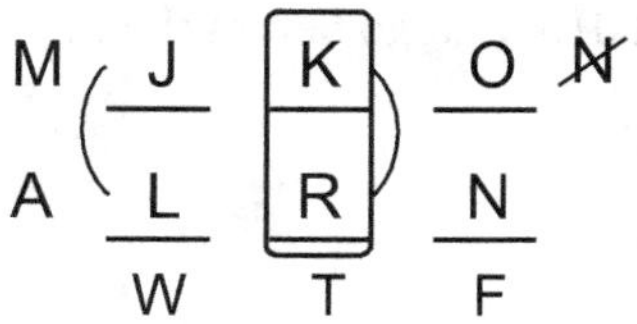

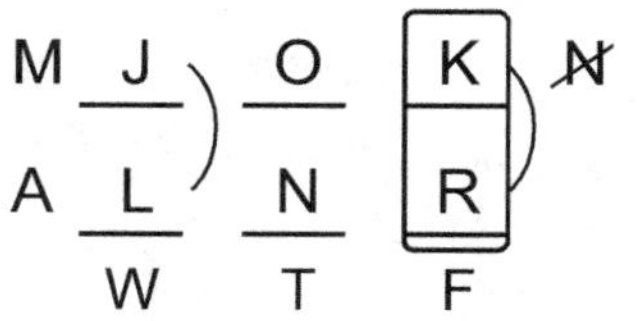

So there are only three possibilities for this game, and they're based on the same idea. JL (in either order) are before ON (in that order). KR (in either order) fill one of three days.

Important. For the rest of the game, I'm going to say things like JL must come before ON. You *must* reread the above explanations if you don't see why JL comes before ON. Otherwise this game won't make sense.

The deduction is based on a combination of rules, which force JL to always go together. J goes before O, and L can't go with O. KR splits JL and ON into two groups.

Main Diagram

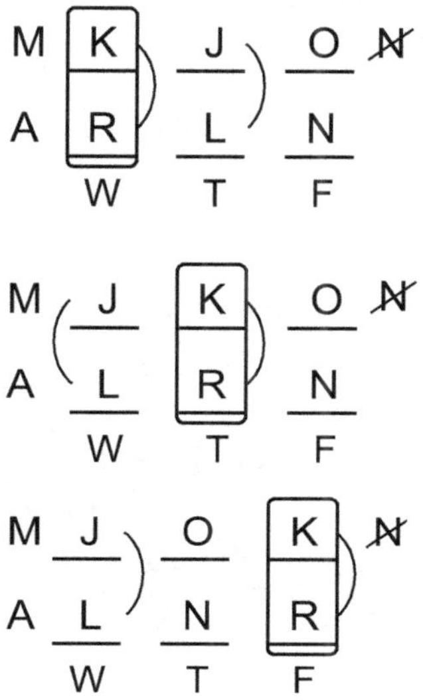

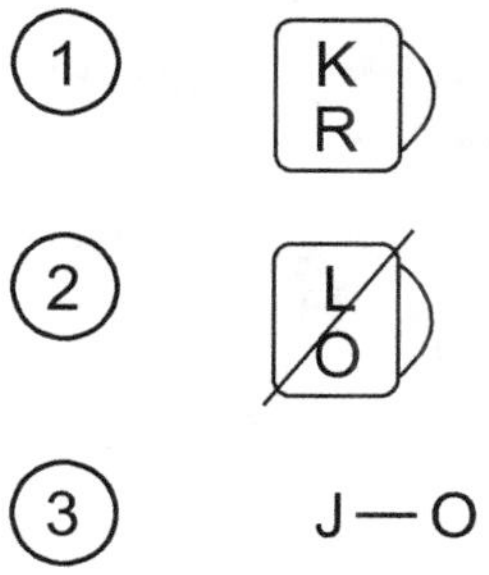

Note that we've already placed all the rules on the diagram in the three scenarios. It's still a good idea to make a list of the rules, and try to commit them to memory.

The questions are easier if you remember *why* the scenarios must be as they are.

Question 1

As with all the list questions, you should go through the rules to eliminate answers one-by-one.

Rule 1 eliminates **C.** KR must be together.

Rule 2 eliminates **D.** O and L can't go together.

Rule 3 eliminates **A.** N must go in the afternoon.

Rule 4 eliminates **B.** J must come before O.

E is **CORRECT.** It violates no rules.

Question 2

Remember from the setup that J and L must go together. L can only go Wednesday or Thursday. So if L is not Wednesday, they must go Thursday and we get this diagram:

	W	T	F
M	K	J	O ~~N~~
A	R	L	N

If you're unsure why this diagram must be true, review the rules and the setup. The idea that JL are before ON is the key to the entire game.

E is **CORRECT.**

Question 3

KR can only go directly before ON only if the two groups go on Thursday and Friday:

	W	T	F
M	J	K	O ~~N~~
A	L	R	N

B is **CORRECT.**

If we tried to put KR on Wednesday, then ON would have to go Friday so that JL could go before them.

Question 4

In the setup, I made three diagrams. Review the setup and draw them yourself if you're unsure why they have to be true.

In all three scenarios from the setup, J and K could be morning or afternoon. That's why they had reversible lines.

Have a look at the diagram in question 3 as a reminder of what the setup diagrams look like. JL and KR are reversible.

If J and K *must* be in the morning, then JL and KR are no longer reversible. L and R must be in the afternoon.

And that's all we can say.

A is **CORRECT.** If J is in the morning, then L must be in the afternoon, not the morning.

Question 5

On this question it makes sense to depart from the setup scenarios and build a new diagram based on the rules.

If J is on Thursday afternoon, then we know O is on Friday. J comes before O (rule 3).

In fact, ON are on Friday, because KR go together (rule 1) and only Wednesday has space to take both of them:

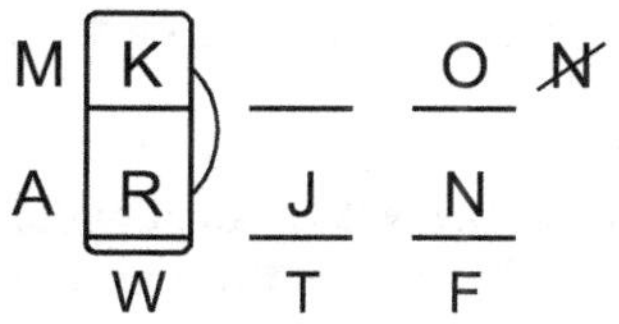

```
M  K   __   O  N̸
A  R   J    N
   W   T    F
```

O is in the morning, because N can only go in the afternoon.

Finally, L must fill Thursday morning.

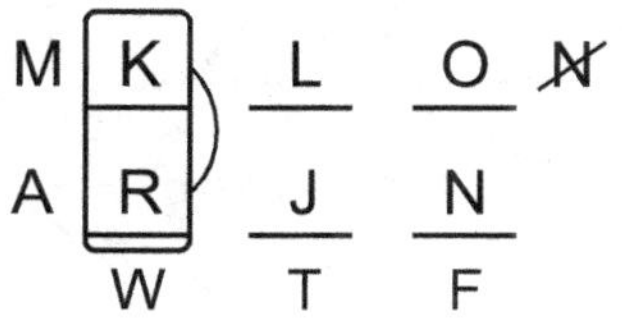

```
M  K   L    O  N̸
A  R   J    N
   W   T    F
```

We can tell where L, O and N are placed, in addition to J. So **C** is **CORRECT.**

KR can go in either order.

Game 2 - Seven Shops
Questions 6-11

Setup

This is a linear game, but it's complicated by the first rule. P and one of the R's must be on either end of the diagram.

When a rule lets you draw something only two ways, it's a very good idea to make two separate scenarios for your main diagram. This helps you visualize the game, and lets you draw separate deductions for each diagram.

Here are the first three rules. Draw it yourself while referencing the rules, then I'll walk you through this diagram:

R					O/V	P
1	2	3	4	5	6	7
	~~R~~	~~R~~				

P	O/V					R
1	2	3	4	5	6	7
				~~R~~	~~R~~	

Here are the first three rules:

- P/R are at either end of the diagram.
- O/V must be beside P.
- And R can't go in the two spots beside the first R.

Makes a simple diagram, right?

The final rule is that T/V can't be together. Remember this rule well, it's the *only* rule that can't be shown on the diagram.

There are no rules for S, so S can go anywhere. I represent random variables with a circle:

Main Diagram

R					O/V	P
1	2	3	4	5	6	7
	~~R~~	~~R~~				

P	O/V					R
1	2	3	4	5	6	7
				~~R~~	~~R~~	

Question 6

As with all list questions, you should go through the rules and use them to eliminate answers 1-by-1.

Rule 1 eliminates **C.** P must be on one end of the diagram.

Rule 2 eliminates **B.** The two R's can't be beside each other.

Rules 3 eliminates **D.** P must be beside O or V, not S.

Rule 4 eliminates **A.** V can't be beside T.

E is **CORRECT.** It violates no rules.

Question 7

If S is 2nd, then we must place R first and P seventh. This is because P must be beside O or V.

R	S				O/V	P
1	2	3	4	5	6	7
	~~R~~	~~R~~				

This eliminates **B, C, and D.**

What about **E**? T and V can't go beside each other (rule 4). If V is in space 4, then only spaces 3 and 5 are left for T.

A is **CORRECT.** There's only one way it would work, but it does:

R	S	T	R	O	V	P
1	2	3	4	5	6	7
	~~R~~	~~R~~				

Question 8

For this question, V is in the 5th space. You should make both scenarios, to see what happens in both of them.

One of O/V must be beside P. Since V is in spot 5, that means O must be beside P.

R				V	O	P
1	2	3	4	5	6	7
	~~R~~	~~R~~	~~T~~			

P	O	T		V		R
1	2	3	4	5	6	7
			~~T~~	~~R~~	~~T~~ ~~R~~	

In both diagrams I've drawn the rule that T can't go beside V. In the second diagram that means T must go third.

Next, you can place the second R, since R must be more than two spaces away from the first R.

R			R	V	O	P
1	2	3	4	5	6	7
	~~R~~	~~R~~	~~T~~			

P	O	T	R	V		R
1	2	3	4	5	6	7
			~~T~~	~~R~~	~~T~~ ~~R~~	

Finally, in the first diagram T/S go in either order in spots 2 and 3. In the second diagram, S must go sixth.

R	T, S (either order)		R	V	O	P
1	2	3	4	5	6	7
	~~R~~	~~R~~	~~T~~			

P	O	T	R	V	S	R
1	2	3	4	5	6	7
			~~T~~	~~R~~	~~T~~ ~~R~~	

The only point both diagrams have in common is that R must go fourth. **C** is **CORRECT.**

Question 9

The question tells you to put OS together. It also tells you that whoever is beside OS are the stores that always *must* be beside OS.

So to find the right answer, you just have to make a single correct diagram. You don't have to make every possible diagram.

The question has told you that if you put OS together, then whoever is beside OS must always be beside OS. They told you it's something that must be true.

O or V has to be beside P. I first tried making a diagram with O beside P, because it seemed simpler to place S. But this didn't work. T and V end up beside each other. That violates the fourth rule:

P	O	S	R	T, V		R
1	2	3	4	5	6	7
				~~R~~	~~R~~	

(R is fourth because of rule 2, it can't be fewer than two spaces away from the other restaurant.)

So let's try again, with V beside P. Remember, we just need to find one diagram that works:

P	V					R
1	2	3	4	5	6	7
		~~T~~		~~R~~	~~R~~	

Let's think about R. R can't go fifth or sixth.

Turns out R also can't be fourth. If you try to place R fourth, then OS will be fifth and sixth. T would have to go third, beside V.

Draw this and you'll see. You should be drawing these diagrams yourself as you follow along, they'll make more sense.

So R is third:

P	V	R				R
1	2	3	4	5	6	7
		~~T~~		~~R~~	~~R~~	

Since OS must be a block, then they either go fourth and fifth or fifth and sixth:

P	V	R	[O	S]	T	R
1	2	3	4	5	6	7
		~~T~~		~~R~~	~~R~~	

P	V	R	T	[O	S]	R
1	2	3	4	5	6	7
		~~T~~		~~R~~	~~R~~	

They are in a block with a line across to show that their order is reversible.

Either way, they are surrounded by T and R.

D is **CORRECT.**

Question 10

For this question, the shoe store is in fourth.

To figure out what must be true, you'll need to make each scenario and check what has to be true in both.

Here's S fourth. I've added a deduction about R which I'll explain below.

R			S	R	O/V	P
1	2	3	4	5	6	7
	~~R~~	~~R~~				

P	V/O	R	S			R
1	2	3	4	5	6	7
				~~R~~	~~R~~	

R has to go between P and S in both cases. Remember, it has to go at least two spaces away from the other R.

Only T and V/O are left to fill the spaces between R and S.

Since T and V can't go beside each other, it must be T and O. So V will be beside P.

	T, O					
R			S	R	V	P
1	2	3	4	5	6	7
	~~R~~	~~R~~				

				T, O		
P	V	R	S			R
1	2	3	4	5	6	7
				~~R~~	~~R~~	

B is **CORRECT.** P is beside V in both cases.

Question 11

The rule says that R must be a placed away from the first R. That's another way of saying that it has to be placed *close* to P.

If you count, you'll see that in any diagram the second R must always be within two businesses of P.

D is **CORRECT.**

Rule substitution questions are tough. You should always think about the full effect of a rule and see if there's another way of describing it.

The other answers are unlikely, because they are complicated. Usually a substituted rule will be simple, and merely describe the effect another way.

This diagram proves that **A, B** and **C** are wrong. It meets the conditions listed in those answers, but violates the rule we're trying to replace. The two R's are too close together.

R	V	R	T	S	O	P
1	2	3	4	5	6	7
	~~R~~	~~R~~				

E is strange. It doesn't even mention restaurants. We've seen many past diagrams that obeyed all the rules and put O and S together, such as the diagrams from question 9.

Game 3 - Sales Representatives
Questions 12-18

Setup

This is a grouping game. There are no ordering elements.

The game has five rules, which is more than most games. It will be important to simplify these and keep a clear list of rules.

I've drawn the three groups vertical, as the game itself did in question 12. You can also draw this game horizontally. These differences are just a matter of personal preference.

1 ___

2 ___

3 ___ ___

I've drawn two spots in group 3, as a reminder of the final rule. You should always read all the rules before drawing, it lets you take shortcuts like this.

The final rule says Group 3 always has more representatives than group 2 does. You can draw something like this as a further reminder on your list of rules:

$$3 > 2$$

But this diagram isn't that helpful. 3 > 2 is sort of ambiguous. It looks like a mathematical equation, referring to the numbers 3 and 2.

In the heat of the moment, it's easy to forget that this actually refers to the numbers of reps in groups 3 and 2.

It's far better just to memorize rules that have no clear diagram. When a game gives you a unique situation, make up a plausible diagram and try to memorize it.

The first and second rules I also prefer to memorize, or partially memorize. They say we need one of two variables in a group, but not both.

This means that, for example, *exactly* one of P or T will be in group 1. But both of them *can't* be there.

I like drawing this directly on the main diagram:

~~P/T~~ 1 P/T

~~T/U~~ 2 T/U

3 ___ ___

There's no great way to draw a 'either-or but not both' rule. I usually draw them like this:

$\not{P}_1 \rightarrow T_1$

$\not{T}_2 \rightarrow U_2$

These are actually 'at least one' diagrams. I memorize the added context that you can't have both at once.

It's true that the diagram leaves out some information, but you can still solve a game very effectively with an imperfect diagram. Memorizing the missing elements is easier than it sounds, and a very powerful tool.

If you want to capture the full effect of the rules, you can draw these diagrams. These are just for the first rule:

$\not{P}_1 \longleftrightarrow T_1$

$P_1 \longleftrightarrow \not{T}_1$

This means that T1 is always NOT with P1, and the reverse. If T is not in 1, P is there.

That diagram is accurate, and if you memorize what it means, it works. But it's big and clunky. For rare situations, I prefer a smaller diagram, and keeping part of the rule in my head.

Ok, the last two rules are simple. PQ and SU go together.

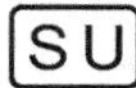

You should also note the random variables. There are two, M and K:

That's all the rules. There aren't any deductions, but you can turn the rules into scenarios.

Scenarios are not essential to solve this game, but the though process involved in making scenarios is very useful.

I didn't make scenarios when I first did this game, but I could construct them on the fly when doing questions because I'm used to doing it. I've built scenarios a bit further on as an example. You should follow along and draw them yourself if you're not clear how to do it on your own.

Before you try this game, make sure you've memorized the full impact of rules 1 and 2. There's no diagram that will be as effective as having them in your head.

There are no shortcuts on logic games. This section tests your working memory. To get better, you have to be comfortable with memorizing at least a couple of the rules.

Main Diagram

~~P/T~~ 1 P/T

~~T/U~~ 2 T/U

3 ___ ___

(1) $\not{P}_1 \rightarrow T_1$

(2) $\not{T}_2 \rightarrow U_2$

(3) PQ

(4) SU

(5) 3 > 2

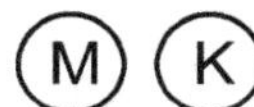

Scenarios

T is involved in both of the first two rules. Wherever you place T, it has an effect. Always look for variable mentioned in more than one rule.

It makes sense to construct scenarios using T. Just place T in a group, and apply the rules to see what you can deduce. Then do the same for the other two groups.

You need to be familiar with the rules to build scenarios. I'm going to say things like 'U has to go with S'. I'll expect you to know that I'm referring to rule 4. Review the rules if you're unsure why I say something has to happen.

Here's T in group 1. That forces U to go in group 2:

~~P~~ 1 T

2 U

3 ___ ___

U has to go with S. This means we need at least 3 in group 3, so that it has more than group 2:

1 T

2 U S |

3 ___ ___ ___

Group 2 can't take any more people. I drew the vertical to show that it's closed.

PQ, M and K are the only variables left to place.

PQ and one of M/K must go in group 3:

1 T M/K

2 U S |

3 P Q M/K

The other M/K can go in either group 1 or 2.

That scenario is complete. Let's try T in group 2. This forces P to go in group 1, and U can't go in group 2:

1 P

~~U~~ 2 T

3 ___ ___

We can't deduce much in this scenario. PQ go together, so Q is in group 1.

SU, M and K are left to place. They can go anywhere as long as you keep more variables in group 3 than group 2:

1 P Q

~~U~~ 2 T [SU],M,K

3 ___ ___

Lastly, try T in group 3. This forces P in group 1 and U in group 2.

1 P

2 U

3 T ___

You know Q goes with P and S goes with U:

1 P Q

2 S U

3 T ___ ___

Since there are two variables in group 2, you need to place three variables in group 3. Only M and K are left.

1 P Q

2 S U

3 T M K

So if T goes in group 3, then everything is determined.

Scenarios

Here are the three scenarios I built above. They're T in group 1, 2 and 3 respectively.

Scenario 1

1 T

2 U S | M/K

3 P Q M/K

Scenario 2

1 P Q

~~U~~ 2 T [S U],M,K

3

Scenario 3

1 P Q

2 S U

3 T M K

Question 12

For list questions, go through the rules and use them to eliminate answers one by one.

Rule 1 eliminates **D.** P or T must go in group 1.

Rule 2 eliminates **E.** T or U must go in group 2.

Rule 3 eliminates **A.** P must go with Q.

Rule 4 eliminates **C.** S must go with U.

B is **CORRECT.** It violates no rules.

Question 13

Look to the three scenarios and you'll see that only scenario two allows the possibility that group 1 has more variables than group 3.

Here's scenario two with two extra slots added to group 1.

```
1  P   Q   __  __
2  T |       [SU],M,K
3  __  __
```

It's the only way to have more people in group 1 without violating the rule that group 3 has more than group 2.

The line beside T in group 2 is a reminder that the group is full. It's the only way to have more people in group 3 than group 2.

The diagram directly disproves **C** and **D.**

Group 2 is full, so K and M can't go there. **A** and **B** are wrong.

E is **CORRECT.** M and K would go in group 1, while SU would go in group 3:

```
1  P   Q   M   K
2  T
3  S  [U]
```

I boxed U because that's what the answer says.

Question 14

To answer this kind of question, you have to become fast at drawing scenarios to disprove wrong answers.

There's no secret to doing this. You need to know the rules, and you need to practice making scenarios. The more you practice drawing correct scenarios, the faster you'll get.

A is **CORRECT.** Let's try it and see what happens.

```
1  S   U   K
2  __
3  __  __
```

SU go together. Now, the second rule says one of T or U goes in group 2. So T must go in group 2. Likewise, the first rule says one of P or T must go in group 1. So P goes in group 1.

```
1  S   U   K   P
2  T
3  __  __
```

Q has to go with P (rule 3), so M is the only one left to go in group 3. This doesn't work, since group 3 needs more sales representatives than group 2.

```
1  S   U   K   P   Q
2  T
3  M   ?
```

B-D are unlikely candidates to be correct. They all involve random variables, and they place variables in group 3. It's easy to place people in group 3, as you need more people in group 3 than group 2.

They're also all the same answer. SU are interchangeable, since they're always together. Likewise, M and K are interchangeable, since they have no rules.

This scenario disproves **B, C** and **D:**

1 P S
2 T
3 M S U K

This diagram disproves **E.**

1 P Q S U
2 T
3 M K

This answer is similar to A, but it only forces four people to go in group 1, whereas A forced five people to go there.

Question 15

A is **CORRECT.** We saw this scenario in answer E of question 14:

1 P Q S U
2 T
3 M K

It's an easy diagram to make because M and K are both random.

B and **C** don't work because they don't have more people in group 3 than in group 2.

For B, if T is in group 3, then SU must be in group 2. So each group has two.

For C, if P is in group 3 then T must be in group 1 and SU are automatically in group 2. So groups 2 and 3 each have two people.

(These deductions are based on rules 1 and 2)

D and **E** violate either the first or second rule. Two our of three of P, T and U must be in groups 1 and 2. Both of these answers place too many of those variables in group 3.

Question 16

Q is always with P (rule 3). P can't be with T (rule 1). That means Q can't be with T.

D is **CORRECT.**

Question 17

This question was removed from scoring. That means it had a flaw.

It's very rare that LSAC does remove a question, but it happens.

Question 18

To answer this question, it's best to create a working diagram, then see what you can change. It turns out you can only place M and S in group 3.

M and S can't go together in group 1, for the same reason that K and S can't go in group 1 (the correct answer to question 14). There's not enough people to go in group 3:

1 S U M P Q

2 T

3 K ?

Briefly, U has to go with S. Since U is in group 1, T must go in group 2.

Since T is in group 2, P goes in group 1. That means Q also goes in group 1.

So only K is left to go in group 3.

Likewise, M and SU can't go in group 2. Then you would have to place four people in group 3, and there would be no one to go in group 1.

So M and SU must go in group 3:

1 ___

2 ___

3 M S U

Apply rules 1 and 2, and you can place T and PQ:

1 P Q

2 T

3 M S U

T has to go in group 2, because U is not there. That means P has to go in group 1, and Q always goes with P.

Only K is left to place. they can go in any group.

A is **CORRECT.**

Game 4 - Piano Solos
Questions 19-23

Setup

This is a game where you can solve almost everything before starting. That's rare on the modern LSAT.

To do this, you must split the game into two scenarios. The third rule nearly forces you to make such a split.

Whenever a rule gives you two options, draw both of them. It lets you make extra deductions, and visualize the game more easily. This is a hidden feature of LSAT logic games.

But I'm getting ahead of myself. Let's start with the first rule. The third solo is traditional:

```
___ ___ ___ ___ ___
         T
```

You could make two rows to put both the performer and the type of music they play. I prefer to just put the type below the slots. It makes a smaller, simpler diagram which is easier to recopy.

Let's come back to the second rule in a minute. All we can do with it at the moment is try to draw it, which isn't very useful, since it's a non-standard rule.

It's perfectly ok to skip rules and come back later. I read everything before drawing precisely so that I can see which rules are simplest to draw first.

Rule 3 lets us make two scenarios.One where W performs a traditional piece, and one where Z performs a modern piece:

```
              W
___ ___ ___ ___ ___
         T   T

              Z
___ ___ ___ ___ ___
         T   M
```

Now we can add the second rule. It says there is one and *only* one group of two consecutive T's. You can't put more than two T's together, and it can only happen once.

In the first scenario, that has already happened. That means 2 and 5 must both be M:

```
              W
___ ___ ___ ___ ___
     M   T   T   M
```

In the second scenario, 2 must be T, and 1 must be M. It's the only way to put two T's together, but no more than two T's:

```
              Z
___ ___ ___ ___ ___
 M   T   T   M
```

Here's how I drew the fourth rule, that 2 and 5 must have different soloists:

```
              W
___ ___ ___ ___ ___
     M   T   T   M
      \_____+_____/

              Z
___ ___ ___ ___ ___
 M   T   T   M
      \_____+_____/
```

Lastly, W must perform a modern piece before the first traditional piece. In the first diagram, that means that the first piece is modern, and W goes first or second:

```
   W
  / \
              W
___ ___ ___ ___ ___
 M   M   T   T   M
      \_____+_____/
```

I made up this way of showing W can be 1 or 2. It's not a common rule. If you come across an uncommon rule, feel free to improvise.

In the second diagram, W must go first:

There is very little uncertainty in this game. All the rules are drawn directly on the diagram.

Main Diagram

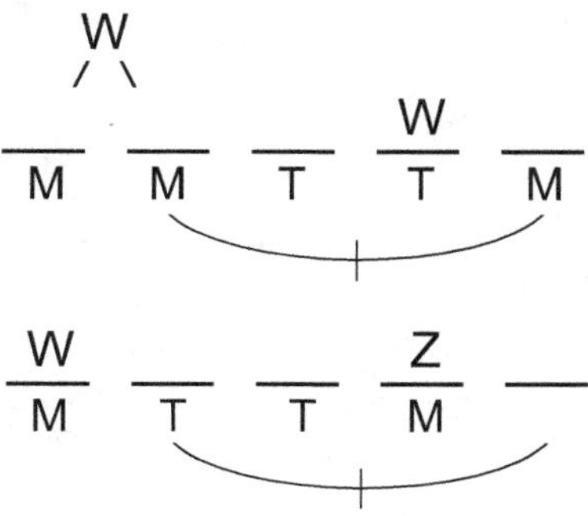

Question 19

You can use both diagrams from the setup to eliminate answers. Here they are again:

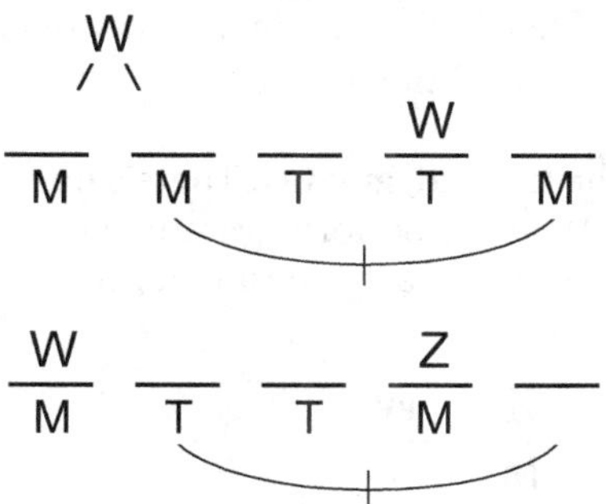

T can never be first, so **A** is wrong.

B has three T's in a row, which violates rule 2.

C is **CORRECT.** You can see it in the second diagram. Just make the final piece M.

D is wrong because it doesn't have two T's in a row. This violates rule 2.

E doesn't work on either diagram. In the first, T is fourth but not fifth. In the second, the fourth piece is M, not T.

Question 20

W doesn't have to perform *any* traditional pieces.
A is **CORRECT.**

You can prove this by making a diagram that doesn't have W performing any traditional pieces.

It's best to start at the low end, anyway. There's no obvious reason why W has to perform traditional pieces, so you might as well see if you can hit zero.

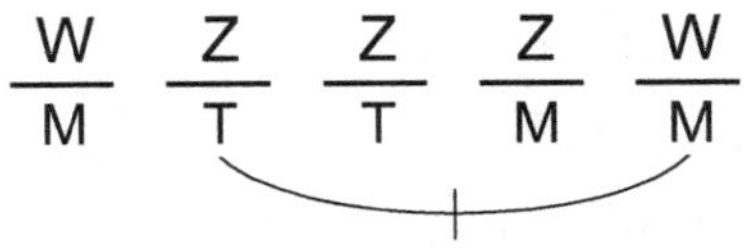

W	Z	Z	Z	W
M	T	T	M	M

This diagram obeys all the rules. I used the second scenario, because the first scenario has W performing a traditional piece.

Question 21

In both scenarios, W performs at least first, or second. So if the same pianist performs first and second, it must be W.

The fourth rule says that the player who performs second can't be the player who performs fifth.

So if W performs 2nd, then Z must perform 5th.

C is **CORRECT.**

Question 22

This is the second scenario. In the first scenario, the fifth piece was modern. Here's scenario two:

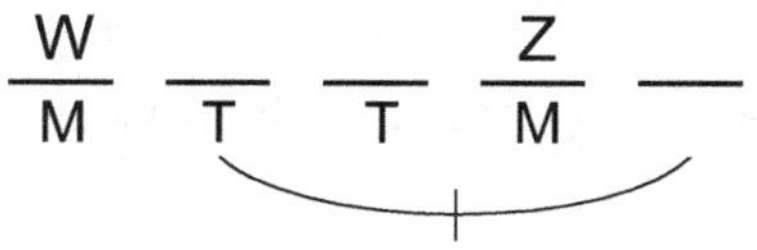

W			Z	
M	T	T	M	

Two players are placed. **B** is **CORRECT.**

Question 23

As with question 22, this has to be the second scenario. In the first scenario, the fifth piece was modern, not traditional.

Here's the second scenario, with W performing a traditional piece:

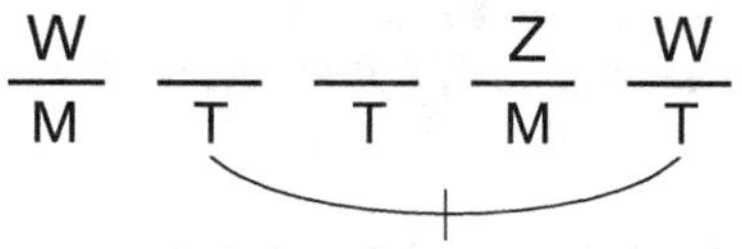

W			Z	W
M	T	T	M	T

As the line under the diagram reminds us, the second and fifth soloists must be different. So the second soloist is Z:

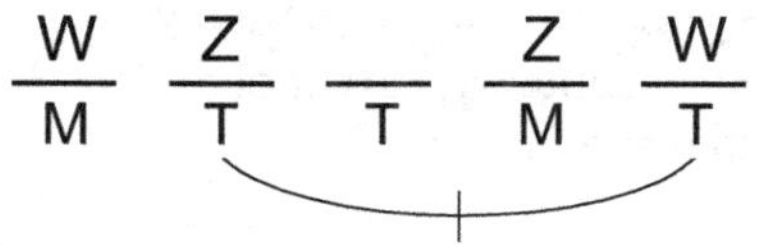

W	Z		Z	W
M	T	T	M	T

That's all we know. Everything is set except for the third soloist, which can be Z or W.

C is **CORRECT.**

Section IV - Logical Reasoning

Question 1

QUESTION TYPE: Flawed Reasoning

CONCLUSION: The results were rigged.

REASONING: The results said 80% of the population voted for the proposal. But everyone I know voted against it.

ANALYSIS: This is classic sample bias. Your friends are not representative of the population in general. They all have someone in common: they know you.

If you're a student, you probably mostly know young people. If you're left-wing or right-wing, then you probably hang out with people who are more left-wing or right-wing than average.

In fact, the fact that you're reading this book tells me that you're young, intelligent, motivated, ambitious. You're probably also uncertain about your near future and stressed out. All because I know you're taking the LSAT. Magic, right?

To get a true sense of the popularity of an idea, you must use a *random* sample.

A. CORRECT. A person's friends are not a random, representative sample.
B. This is code for circular reasoning. This argument isn't circular. The author does use evidence ('their friends voted against the proposal'). The problem is merely that their evidence sucks.
C. This is code for an ad hominem attack. The author didn't attack the character of the electoral officials who counted the votes.
D. The author never says how people should have voted.
E. The author doesn't say whether other people think the vote was rigged.

Question 2

QUESTION TYPE: Strengthen

CONCLUSION: We should regulate the information on the internet.

REASONING: We can't use information unless we can distinguish it from misinformation. The internet has much disinformation.

ANALYSIS: This sounds like a reasonable argument. There's one big problem though: the author didn't say that regulation helps distinguish between information and misinformation.

A. This weakens the argument by showing that regulation is likely to cause harm.
B. This shows that regulation won't help very much.
C. CORRECT. This at least shows that regulation helps solve the problem.
D. This tells us that the internet is unacceptable, because we can't distinguish good information from bad. But this doesn't show that regulation is the answer.
E. This tells us *not* to regulate.

Question 3

QUESTION TYPE: Necessary Assumption

CONCLUSION: The current president was right to ask Dr. Hines to speak, even though the president didn't consult members.

REASONING: A previous club president hired an accountant without consultation.

ANALYSIS: There are two problems here:

1. We don't know if the previous club president was right to hire the accountant.
2. Hiring a tax accountant may be different from getting a speaker. Maybe choice of speaker always requires consultation.

A. This doesn't show that the previous club president acted appropriately when he didn't consult.
B. Tempting, but it doesn't matter whether club members expected to be consulted. It matters whether it was *appropriate* not to consult them. As an analogy, I don't expect a totalitarian dictator to respect humans rights. But that doesn't make it *appropriate* for him not to respect human rights.
C. It doesn't matter what Dr. Hines did. We're concerned with the appropriateness of the request.
D. This *weakens* the argument by showing that inviting a speaker is a more serious matter.
E. **CORRECT.** If the previous president acted *inappropriately* then this is hardly a good argument.

Question 4

QUESTION TYPE: Weaken

CONCLUSION: The attack is groundless.

REASONING: Critics say our filter doesn't remove contaminants. But millions of people are satisfied with our filter.

ANALYSIS: It doesn't matter what users think. If I claim that Coca-Cola is unhealthy, it's irrelevant to point out that millions of people enjoy drinking it. It's still not a healthy drink.

Likewise, the chemical might satisfy customers because it looks nice, while being totally ineffective at removing chemicals from water.

A. It doesn't matter if the magazine evaluated taste. The study was only concerned with chemical removal. (Though better taste could explain why millions of people are satisfied with the product).
B. **CORRECT.** This shows that Filterator X owners can't help us decide whether it removes chemicals. They have no idea.
C. This doesn't show whether or not the filter helps remove those chemicals.
D. Why should it matter if consumers read this magazine? We care if the claims are true, not if the magazine is popular. For all we know this is the first issue that mentioned Filterator X, so there's no obvious impact on the views of Filterator X customers.
E. This could be either because of bias, or because the filters are terrible. This doesn't tell us anything.

Question 5

QUESTION TYPE: Main Point

CONCLUSION: The great artist was wrong to say that all great art imitates nature, OR great music is not always great art.

REASONING: Most great music doesn't imitate nature or anything at all.

ANALYSIS: This is a good example of how arguments don't need to explicitly state their conclusions.

The author's point is that the great artist was wrong. His evidence is a fact that contradicts the premise.

Artist's Claim: Great art → Imitates Nature
Author's evidence: Some great music does not imitate nature

Actually, I simplified that a bit. The right answer introduces a bit more nuance.

It's possible that great music is not always great art. If true, then it could be that the artist is correct, and any great music that doesn't imitate nature is not great art.

A. Nonsense. The author didn't say whether music is good or bad.
B. **CORRECT.** This is true. If great music is great art, then the artist is wrong, because great music doesn't always imitate nature. If the artist is right, then great music is sometimes not great art.
C. The author never mentioned great paintings or sculpture.
D. The author never said whether or not it's possible to imitate all of nature.
E. This would be true if the artist was correct, and if great music is necessarily correct.

Question 6

QUESTION TYPE: Weaken

CONCLUSION: Tamara says that many people feared ninjas.

REASONING: Many wealthy Japanese installed squeaky floorboards to warn against Ninjas.

ANALYSIS: To weaken Tamara's argument, we need to show that these wealthy Japanese were unrepresentative.

It's unlikely people would have paid to use ninjas against peasants. Probably their main targets were wealthy elites, who are only a small part of any population.

A. This would strengthen Tamara's argument by showing that poor Japanese also feared ninjas.
B. This shows that ninjas avoided the squeaky floor defense. It doesn't prove that few people feared ninjas.
C. **CORRECT.** This shows that the wealthy aren't a great example. They were a very small part of the population. And everyone knows that wealthy people often have different habits from poor people. So the wealthy are unlikely to be representative of the population at large.
D. Irrelevant. The stimulus is talking about what people thought during the Tokugawa period.
E. Same as D.

Question 7

QUESTION TYPE: Necessary Assumption

CONCLUSION: Moral agents need free will.

REASONING: You can't be a moral agent without wanting to conform to a principle.

ANALYSIS: The first sentence is irrelevant fluff. It isn't linked to the evidence or the conclusion.

Why? In this case, it's not a conditional statement that can be linked logically with the other claims. Consequences and motives aren't sufficient or necessary conditions for anything.

The problem with this argument is that the philosopher hasn't made a link between free will and wanting to conform to principles.

They need to assume that conforming to principles requires free will.

A. The consequences of actions are irrelevant fluff. They're not sufficient or necessary for anything.
B. CORRECT. If you can conform to principles without free will, then it's not clear why moral agents must desire to conform.
C. The first sentence is irrelevant to the argument. It doesn't introduce sufficient or necessary conditions. This answer just references something from the first sentence and then introduces a new concept which also isn't relevant, 'free'. Being free and having free will aren't the same thing.
D. This would mean, for example, that having a desire for chocolate chip cookies will make someone a moral agent. This answer is silly.
E. The moral worth of actions is only mentioned in the first sentence. It isn't a sufficient or necessary condition for anything. It's fluff that wasn't linked to the argument.

Question 8

QUESTION TYPE: Weaken

CONCLUSION: Publishing a scholarly journal must be more profitable now.

REASONING: Libraries pay more for individual journals, while the costs of publishing journals haven't increased.

ANALYSIS: This sounds very convincing. But there are at least two possible reasons profits wouldn't be 'much' higher.

1. Libraries subscribed to fewer journals once prices went up.
2. Libraries are only a small portion of journal subscribers, and prices for other subscribers haven't changed.

The second option is the right answer. Most subscribers are individuals, and they pay the same price as they did before.

I didn't think of the second reason before I saw it in the answers. I prephrased the first possibility. Prephrasing is very useful, but keep in mind there may be other options for the correct answer. Don't get hung up on a single prephrase.

A. This explains how universities can afford journals. It doesn't tell us anything about journal profits.
B. This doesn't matter. The university won't be using its sports budget to buy journals.
C. This tells us what happens if a journal is unprofitable. It doesn't tell us whether publishing journals is currently profitable.
D. CORRECT. This shows that journal prices haven't increased for most subscribers. Higher library prices surely increased profits, but these higher were only for a small portion of subscribers. The conclusion said that journals must be 'much more' profitable.
E. This is just a fact about journals. It doesn't tell us how profitable they are.

Question 9

QUESTION TYPE: Identify The Conclusion

CONCLUSION: Gurney is wrong to say that he hasn't received recognition because he is popular.

REASONING: Gurney probably hasn't received praise because his writing is flat.

ANALYSIS: This may be a good argument, we'd need more information to know if it was true.

In any case, the conclusion is that Gurney is wrong. The reason is that his writing is flat.

- **A. CORRECT.** The second sentence is the conclusion. 'Surely he is mistaken'. The argument backs this up by pointing out that his writing is flat.
- **B.** The author didn't say whether Gurney's books are literary achievements. They only wanted to explain why Gurney hasn't received praise.
- **C.** This is evidence for the conclusion. It shows an alternate reason why he hasn't received praise.
- **D.** This is Gurney's argument. The author disagrees, in the second sentence.
- **E.** Only Gurney said Gurney ought to receive praise. The author didn't say whether he should. He just offered an explanation for why he hasn't.

Question 10

QUESTION TYPE: Paradox

PARADOX: Lighting could create amino acids. Without a reducing atmosphere, amino acids break apart and can't form life.

At the time life formed, Earth did not have a reducing atmosphere.

ANALYSIS: First, it's important to read the scientific words carefully.

Reducing atmosphere: Has much hydrogen and little oxygen.

Earth's atmosphere when life formed: rich in oxygen and low in nitrogen.

So when life formed, Earth did *not* have a reducing atmosphere. This means amino acids could not have stuck together and formed life.

The right answer explains this by saying that a local reducing atmosphere protected the amino acids.

- **A. CORRECT.** This shows that there was a local reducing atmosphere in the area where life began.
- **B.** This doesn't explain how the amino acids formed life in a reducing atmosphere.
- **C.** This doesn't explain how life formed billions of years ago, when Earth had a reducing atmosphere.
- **D.** The lighting isn't the issue. We need to explain the reducing atmosphere. Though fewer lightning strikes make it *less* likely for life to form.
- **E.** That's nice. But once the amino acids survived the impact, they would encounter Earth's non-reducing atmosphere, and they would break apart.

Question 11

QUESTION TYPE: Principle - Strengthen

CONCLUSION: Paulsen shouldn't have gotten the criticism award.

REASONING: The award should go for criticism. Paulsen reviewed cars, which are utilitarian objects, not works of art. Objects that aren't art will not reveal truths about the culture around them.

ANALYSIS: This sounds like a good argument. But the author hasn't shown that writing can only be criticism if it talks about art. Maybe car reviews can be criticism.

We want to prove the author right. So we need to say something *should not* be criticism if it did some of the things Paulsen's writing did.

A. We don't know how Paulsen portrayed cars. Paulsen may not have claimed they were works of art.
B. **CORRECT.** Car reviews don't reveal truths, because only writing about art reveals truths. So Paulsen shouldn't get the award.
C. Paulsen may have written her reviews for the purpose of revealing truths. She would have failed, since cars aren't art, but she still would have had the right purpose.
D. We don't know whether Paulsen considers herself to be a critic.
E. We want to prove that Paulsen's writing is *not* criticism. This can't help with that. It's a sufficient condition. It doesn't say that something is not criticism if it doesn't reveal truths about a culture.

Question 12

QUESTION TYPE: Strengthen

CONCLUSION: Unlimited free shipping probably caused the increase in sales.

REASONING: Sales increased 25% around the time we offered unlimited free shipping.

ANALYSIS: The manager is making a causation-correlation error. If two things happen at the same time, that doesn't mean that one causes the other.

We can strengthen the manager's argument by eliminating alternate causes for the increase in sales, or by showing evidence that the free shipping did in fact cause the increase.

A. **CORRECT.** This shows that the sales increase is unusual in the industry. It wasn't industry-wide growth that caused the increase. This makes it more likely that free shipping was in fact the cause.
B. This weakens the argument. If customers didn't know about the free shipping, then it's unlikely it caused them to buy more.
C. That's nice for the company. Profits are fun. But this doesn't say that the change in shipping policy *caused* the profits. Sales went up, so it makes sense that profits went up.
D. Timing is irrelevant. If free shipping was important, then it would have had an impact even if the company was late to the game.
E. Same as D. If free shipping was important, then it would be expected to have an impact whether the company was early or late.

Also, this answer says 'most companies', whereas the company is a mail order company. So this doesn't necessarily tell us anything about other mail order companies.

Further, 'most companies' isn't relevant. We care about the companies which account for most sales, which could be only 1-3 companies. Who cares if 1,000 tiny, irrelevant companies don't offer free shipping, if amazon.com does?

Question 13

QUESTION TYPE: Parallel Reasoning

CONCLUSION: We shouldn't build nuclear power plants, even though they're unlikely to melt down.

REASONING: If a meltdown *did* occur, it would be catastrophic.

ANALYSIS: This is a reasonable argument. We shouldn't consider only the odds of something happening. We should also consider how big the impact would be if something bad happened.

You need to find a situation with low risk, but which has a big impact if anything does go wrong.

A. This is a good argument, but has a different structure. Here, the conclusion is that the odds of a climbing accident are actually quite high. In the stimulus, the author agreed that meltdowns are rare.
B. This doesn't discuss probability or impact. It may be good advice, but it's not a parallel argument.
C. This does mention small risk. But it doesn't talk about the high impact of a mistake. Instead, it just says there is little to gain from skydiving.
D. **CORRECT.** Low risk, but big impact if anything goes wrong. This argument is exactly parallel.
E. This talks about how easy it is to wear a seatbelt. It doesn't talk about what happens if you don't wear one.

Question 14

QUESTION TYPE: Principle

PRINCIPLE: Shows promise → Obligation to pursue research in a theoretical field

No Obligation → Doesn't show promise

ANALYSIS: I shortened the principle above. The full principle is that something must

'show promise to yield insight into the causes of practical problems that affect people's quality of life'

That's a mouthful. It's better to simplify such a statement, but keep in mind the full idea is a bit more complex than whatever you draw.

On this type of question, you need to do two things:

1. Figure out the sufficient and necessary condition, and the contrapositive.
2. Make sure the wording in the answer matches the concept in the stimulus. So, 'yielding insight into non-practical problems' wouldn't lead to any obligation.

You can only prove a necessary condition. So you need to find an answer that has one of the sufficient conditions from the 'PRINCIPLE' section, and that uses that condition to justify the necessary condition.

A. We don't know when it's correct to deny funding.
B. We have no idea if this is proper. It doesn't yield insight into practical problems.
C. This is administrative trivia. It has nothing to do with research aimed at practical problems.
D. This sounds wrong. Economic behavior is relevant to the practical problems of people's lives.
E. **CORRECT.** Disease is a practical problem. It sounds like the institute had an obligation to fund research in this theoretical field.

Question 15

QUESTION TYPE: Paradox

PARADOX: You get more carpal tunnel if you can't control your own work, even if you do the same amount of typing as workers who do have control.

ANALYSIS: The study made a very strict comparison. It compared workers who did similar amounts of typing. The only difference was how much control they had over their work.

Several wrong answers incorrectly compare workers who do different amounts of typing.

We need to find a reason that low control leads to more carpal tunnel. For example, maybe low control workers can't decide when to take breaks from typing.

The right answer instead shows that low control weakens nerves. Carpal tunnel is a nerve disease.

A. The study looked at workers who did similar amounts of typing.
B. **CORRECT.** Carpal tunnel is a nerve disorder. This shows that not having control increases your risk of this and other nerve diseases.
C. This doesn't explain why workers with little control get even more carpal tunnel.
D. The study compared only workers who typed a similar amount.
E. This adds to the confusion. If workers with the most control do *more* repetitive actions, then why do they get less carpal tunnel.

Question 16

QUESTION TYPE: Principle

PRINCIPLE: I'll write this as a logical statement:

Employee of telemarketing agency → Don't make people dislike your agency's clients.

APPLICATION: If someone someone says they don't want to buy, don't try to talk them into it.

ANALYSIS: The principle tells us exactly one thing that is wrong: making people dislike your clients.

The simple answer is that talking people into buying a client's product will make them dislike the client.

Remember that you're trying to support the application. So you must prove that employees should *never* try to talk someone into buying once they have refused.

If you care about such things, here's the correct answer turned into a logical statement:

Try to talk someone into it after they refuse → They will dislike your client

The principle says never to make someone dislike your client, so we can conclude you should never try to talk someone into buying.

A. This tells us something about a worker's judgment. But it doesn't tell us that the worker should never try to convince.
B. This doesn't help us prove that *all* employees ought to avoiding talking people into buying products.
C. **CORRECT.** This does it. No matter the circumstances, if you try to talk someone into buying a product after they have refused, they will dislike your client. And you should never make people dislike your client.
D. This weakens the application. It shows you might do no harm by trying to talk some people into buying.
E. This tells us what people are likely to do, but not whether we ought to convince them.

Question 17

QUESTION TYPE: Sufficient Assumption

CONCLUSION: Pluto is not a true planet.

REASONING: Pluto formed in orbit around Neptune.

ANALYSIS: You must prove that Pluto is not a planet. All we know about Pluto is that it formed in orbit around Neptune.

So the right answer must use that information. For example, we can assume that anything that formed in orbit around a planet can't itself be a planet.

Many answers point out that Pluto was once a moon. That isn't enough. Things can change. Those answers would need to say that something can't be a planet if it was once a moon.

A. Pluto was a moon when it was around Neptune. But it wouldn't be a moon once it left Neptune's orbit. So it wouldn't have been simultaneously a moon and a planet.
B. This is a necessary assumption. It proves that Pluto *could* be not a planet. But it doesn't prove that Pluto *is* not a planet.
C. This doesn't matter. It's like saying that if you never aged from the time you were 15 years old, you would still be a teenager. You did age, and Pluto did leave orbit. Things change.
D. This doesn't help us prove that Pluto isn't a planet. It's a fact about how we judge whether something is a planet, but it's not definitive.
E. **CORRECT.** Pluto didn't form in orbit exclusively around the sun. Therefore, it's not a planet.

Question 18

QUESTION TYPE: Paradox

PARADOX: It was easiest for the human brain to develop in coastal areas. But most brain development happened in savanna and woodland.

ANALYSIS: The stimulus showed an advantage for shore environments.

To solve the puzzle, you need to find an advantage for savanna and woodlands, or a disadvantage for shore areas.

The fact that a place has one advantage doesn't mean it's better. We need to know the full picture.

The right answer says it was hard to gather calories in shore areas. If you have to work hard then you need even more calories to eat.

Forests could offer an easier lifestyle and more calories even if they seem less abundant.

A. This is an interesting detail. But it doesn't change the fact that brain development was easiest on the coast.
B. Same as A.
C. That's nice. But the stimulus clearly says that, back then, shore areas offered even more abundant resources.
D. This helps explain why we don't know much. It doesn't help clarify the situation.
E. **CORRECT.** This shows that while there were more calories available in shore environments, it took more work to get them. So it was a wash.

Question 19

QUESTION TYPE: Point At Issue

ARGUMENTS: Editor Y says the picture is good. It has attractive composition, with blurred smoke in one corner.

Editor Z agrees it is pretty, but says it is a bad picture. The photograph makes no statement.

ANALYSIS: They disagree on whether the picture is good.

Note that Editor Y doesn't say whether the photograph makes a statement.

A. Editor Y doesn't say whether a photograph needs to make a statement.
B. Neither says whether attractiveness is a necessary condition for being a good photograph.
C. Editor Z agreed the photograph was pretty (which means the same as attractive).
D. **CORRECT.** Editor Y seems to agree that making a statement is not necessary - they didn't mention it, but said the photo is good.

Editor Z says a photograph needs to make a statement to be good.
E. Editor Z seems to agree that prettiness is the same as being attractive. Editor Y doesn't say. If anything, this might be a point they *agree* upon.

Question 20

QUESTION TYPE: Sufficient Assumption

CONCLUSION: We must market our programs more aggressively to keep quality.

REASONING: Without marketing, we can't increase enrollment. We will have to reduce spending if we can't increase enrollment.

ANALYSIS: This sounds like a good argument. But maybe the university can reduce spending without hurting quality. Here's the chain from the stimulus.

Evidence:

Quality ~~Reduce Spending~~ → Increase Enrollment → Marketing

Conclusion:

Quality → Marketing

There's an arrow missing between quality and not reducing spending. You need an arrow showing that not reducing spending is a necessary condition for quality:

'Quality → ~~Reduce Spending~~'

Sufficient Assumption questions are really simple. One element of the conclusion isn't linked to the rest of the evidence. You need a statement that links it. You may have to take the contrapositive to see how the right answer fits in the chain of logic.

A. Err....the president said that increasing enrollment would help the university keep quality. This weakens the argument.
B. Increase enrollment → ~~Reduce Spending~~. This doesn't help link quality to the rest of the evidence.
C. Marketing → Increase enrollment
Same as B.
D. **CORRECT.** This works:
Reduce Spending → ~~Quality~~,
contrapositive: Quality → ~~Reduce Spending~~
E. Marketing → ~~Reduce Spending~~
Same as B.

Question 21

QUESTION TYPE: Must Be True

FACTS:

1. If the city requires sorting, many residents will put recyclables in their regular garbage.
2. If residents put recyclables in their garbage, more recyclables will be buried in the landfill.
3. The sanitation department can't stay within its budget unless the city requires sorting.

ANALYSIS: It sounds like either more recyclables will end up in the landfill or the sanitation department will exceed its budget.

We have no idea what happens if the department exceeds its budget.

A. We don't know. We know many residents *won't* recycle. 'Many' could mean almost all residents (or even all). So maybe only 10% of residents will keep recycling after the change.
B. Who knows? Some residents might continue to recycle, but screw up and avoid sorting the recyclables they put out for pickup.
C. We have no idea how much landfills cost. There's no way to compare this to the cost of sorting.
D. **CORRECT.** If the sanitation department stayed within budget, it's because the city required sorting. Sorting would cause more recyclables to be sent to landfill.
E. Not necessarily true. We know the department will definitely exceed its budget without the sorting requirement. But it might exceed its budget even with sorting. Sorting was a necessary condition for meeting the budget, not a sufficient condition.

Question 22

QUESTION TYPE: Flawed Reasoning

CONCLUSION: The meerkat sentinels are altruistic and not entirely self-interested.

REASONING: The sentinels bark as they run for cover, alerting the other meerkats to the danger.

ANALYSIS: The argument said that meerkat sentinel behavior is *motivated* by altruism.

That means that when they bark, they do it *in order to* warn other meerkats.

But the argument hasn't proven why they bark. The sentinels might bark out of fear. The barks would have the *effect* of helping other meerkats, but that doesn't mean the barks are *intended* to help.

A. The fact that the sentinels give a warning does provide *some* support to the conclusion. The bark doesn't obviously help the sentinel. It helps other meerkats.
The only problem is that we don't know why they bark.
B. This is code for circular reasoning. But the argument does have some evidence of altruism: the sentinels bark.
C. **CORRECT.** The bark could just be a yelp of fear. The bark might not be *designed* to help other meerkats, even if it does have that *effect*.
D. The argument didn't say that sentinels are entirely altruistic. It just said they are motivated at least in part by altruism.
E. This is a different error. It's like saying 'Facebook will not survive ten years, because it hasn't been proven that it will survive ten years', without offering any evidence that Facebook will fail. Here, the author did offer *some* evidence that sentinels are altruistic.

Question 23

QUESTION TYPE: Point At Issue

ARGUMENTS: Alex says shrimp farmers damage the environment by making quick profits and abandoning farms.

Jolene says most owners try to keep their shrimp farms productive for many years, especially since properly built farms are expensive.

ANALYSIS: Jolene and Alex disagree on how long shrimp farm owners want to keep farming. Jolene thinks farmers need time to profit from shrimp farming.

A. Not quite. Jolene might agree that shrimp farmers *eventually* abandon farms. She just disagrees they do so quickly.
B. **CORRECT.** Jolene says properly built farms take a long time to build, and that most owners want to keep their farms running for a long time. She disagrees that shrimp farming produces a quick, easy profit.
C. Jolene might not go this far. Most economic activities damage the environment to some extent.
D. Jolene doesn't dispute this. She just says that farmers don't abandon farms all that quickly.
E. Jolene agrees that some farms do fail quickly. She might believe *those* owners were irresponsible in the way they abandoned their farms. But she thinks shrimp farmers in general are responsible.

Question 24

QUESTION TYPE: Flawed Parallel Reasoning

CONCLUSION: Lester must have gotten a poor performance evaluation.

REASONING: You can't have both poor performance and a raise. Lester didn't get a raise.

ANALYSIS: The evidence is that if you have one, you can't have the other.

The conclusion gets it backwards and says that if you *don't* have one you must have the other.

Evidence: ~~PE~~ or ~~R~~
Mistaken Interpretation: PE or R

This type of relationship is heavily tested on in-out grouping games in logic games. There is a big difference between not-both and either-or statements.

Not both is at least one of the two missing.
Either-or is at least one of the two present.

A. This is a good argument. They correctly use the evidence to show that since the neighbors have one they can't have the other.
B. This is a good argument. They've correctly shown that since the neighbors own, they don't rent.
C. This is a good argument. The premise says: no rent → own
D. **CORRECT.** The evidence says you can't have both. But that doesn't mean that if you don't have one then you have the other. Maybe a relative owns the house, for example.
Evidence: ~~own~~ OR ~~pay rent~~
Mistaken Interpretation: own OR pay rent
E. This is a good argument. Not own → Pay rent is the evidence.

Question 25

QUESTION TYPE: Flawed Reasoning

CONCLUSION: Lack of fiber causes colon cancer, and lots of fiber prevents it.

REASONING: There is an inverse correlation between fiber and colon cancer.

ANALYSIS: The argument has shown a correlation between colon cancer and lack of fiber. Without evidence, they've assumed that fiber prevents colon cancer.

There are a million other possible causes. Maybe people who eat fiber eat a healthier diet in general, and that is the cause.

The right answer says that foods high in fiber have other substances that fight cancer

---

A. This doesn't tell us whether fiber will help prevent colon cancer. It's just a fact about fiber consumption.
B. Other cancer is irrelevant. The conclusion was only about colon cancer.
C. This may be true, but it doesn't tell us whether fiber helps prevent colon cancer.
D. The argument hasn't even proven that fiber fights cancer. It's pointless to wonder if fiber in different foods has different effects on cancer.
E. **CORRECT.** This shows that other substances prevent cancer. It's not necessarily the fiber.

Question 26

QUESTION TYPE: Identify The Conclusion

CONCLUSION: It isn't true that chimpanzees must have had an early version of language.

REASONING: Humans didn't evolve from chimps. We evolved from a common ancestor. Evolution of language may have begun after the ancestor was extinct.

ANALYSIS: This is a good argument. If evolution of language happened after the common ancestor died, then it would be the direct ancestors of humans that evolved language. This is easiest to show with a diagram:

Common ancestor → chimp ancestor → chimps
Common ancestor → human ancestor → humans

If language evolution happened at the first stage, then chimps would have language. If language evolution happened at the second stage, then only humans would have language.

We don't know when language evolution occurred. So the conclusion is we can't say for sure whether chimps evolved some early version of language.

A. This is evidence supporting the conclusion that chimps may not have evolved language.
B. **CORRECT.** This is true, because humans didn't evolve from chimps.
C. We're not told what chimp communications are like.
D. The author never mentioned how smart chimps are. Maybe they outsmart us....
E. The author didn't even say that this is true. It's just *possible,* and that's why we can't say for sure whether language evolved in chimps.

Appendix: LR Questions By Type

Strengthen

Preptest 62

Section II, #2
Section II, #3
Section II, #16
Section IV, #3
Section IV, #22

Preptest 63

Section I, #11
Section I, #16
Section III, #21

Preptest 64

Section I, #17
Section I, #22
Section III, #9
Section III, #17
Section III, #24

Preptest 65

Section I, #1
Section I, #13
Section I, #19
Section IV, #15
Section IV, #22

Preptest 66

Section II, #3
Section II, #17
Section IV, #2
Section IV, #12

Weaken

Preptest 62

Section II, #22
Section IV, #5
Section IV, #14

Preptest 63

Section I, #2
Section I, #7
Section III, #9
Section III, #16

Preptest 64

Section I, #4
Section I, #8
Section I, #10
Section I, #13
Section III, #15

Preptest 65

Section I, #5
Section IV, #3
Section IV, #19

Preptest 66

Section II, #5
Section IV, #4
Section IV, #6
Section IV, #8

Sufficient Assumption

Preptest 62

Section II, #9
Section II, #15
Section II, #17
Section IV, #16
Section IV, #18

Preptest 63

Section I, #10
Section III, #17
Section III, #24

Preptest 64

Section I, #11
Section I, #23
Section III, #21
Section III, #26

Preptest 65

Section I, #16

Preptest 66

Section II, #6
Section II, #19
Section IV, #17
Section IV, #20

Parallel Reasoning

Preptest 62

Section IV, #25

Preptest 63

Section I, #21
Section III, #20

Preptest 64

Section I, #21
Section III, #25

Preptest 65

Section IV, #17

Preptest 66

Section II, #16
Section IV, #13

Flawed Parallel Reasoning

Preptest 62

Section II, #7
Section IV, #9

Preptest 63

Section I, #24
Section III, #25

Preptest 64

Section I, #9
Section III, #23

Preptest 65

Section I, #11
Section IV, #24

Preptest 66

Section II, #24
Section IV, #24

Necessary Assumption

Preptest 62

Section II, #12
Section II, #25
Section IV, #23

Preptest 63

Section I, #5
Section I, #19
Section III, #6
Section III, #11
Section III, #15

Preptest 64

Section I, #15
Section III, #12
Section III, #19

Preptest 65

Section I, #18
Section I, #21
Section IV, #2
Section IV, #13
Section IV, #20
Section IV, #23

Preptest 66

Section II, #2
Section II, #4
Section II, #10
Section IV, #3
Section IV, #7

Method Of Reasoning

Preptest 62

Section II, #14
Section IV, #21

Preptest 63

Section I, #17
Section III, #19

Preptest 64

Section I, #3

Preptest 65

Section IV, #16

Preptest 66

Section IV, #25

Must Be True

Preptest 62

Section II, #6
Section II, #19
Section IV, #6

Preptest 63

Section I, #6
Section I, #9
Section I, #20
Section III, #5

Preptest 64

Section I, #2
Section I, #18
Section I, #20

Preptest 65

Section I, #25
Section IV, #6

Preptest 66

Section II, #14
Section IV, #21

Must Be False

Preptest 62

Section II, #24

Most Strongly Supported

Preptest 62

Section II, #21
Section IV, #8
Section IV, #11

Preptest 63

Section I, #12
Section III, #3
Section III, #7
Section III, #13

Preptest 64

Section III, #22

Preptest 65

Section IV, #9

Preptest 66

Section II, #22

Paradox

Preptest 62

Section II, #4
Section II, #20
Section IV, #7
Section IV, #17
Section IV, #26

Preptest 63

Section I, #4
Section III, #8
Section III, #12
Section III, #26

Preptest 64

Section I, #6
Section III, #8
Section III, #13

Preptest 65

Section I, #12
Section IV, #1
Section IV, #10

Preptest 66

Section II, #23
Section IV, #10
Section IV, #15
Section IV, #18

Principle

Preptest 62

Section II, #1
Section II, #13
Section II, #18
Section II, #23
Section II, #26
Section IV, #2
Section IV, #15
Section IV, #20

Preptest 63

Section I, #15
Section I, #18
Section I, #22
Section III, #22
Section III, #23

Preptest 64

Section I, #12
Section I, #24
Section III, #2
Section III, #18
Section III, #20

Preptest 65

Section I, #6
Section I, #14
Section I, #24
Section IV, #5
Section IV, #18

Preptest 66

Section II, #7
Section II, #9
Section II, #12
Section IV, #11
Section IV, #14
Section IV, #16

Identify The Conclusion

Preptest 62

Section II, #10
Section IV, #1
Section IV, #12

Preptest 63

Section I, #8
Section I, #13
Section III, #10

Preptest 64

Section I, #1

Preptest 65

Section I, #2
Section I, #9
Section IV, #14

Preptest 66

Section II, #18
Section IV, #9
Section IV, #26

Main Point

Preptest 66

Section IV, #5

Point At Issue

Preptest 63

Section I, #14
Section III, #4

Preptest 64

Section III, #5
Section III, #7

Preptest 65

Section I, #23
Section IV, #4
Section IV, #25

Preptest 66

Section II, #20
Section IV, #19
Section IV, #23

Complete The Argument

Preptest 62

Section IV, #24

Preptest 63

Section I, #1

Preptest 64

Section III, #1
Section III, #3

Preptest 65

Section I, #4
Section I, #7

Role in Argument

Preptest 62

Section IV, #4

Preptest 63

Section III, #1

Preptest 64

Section I, #14
Section I, #25
Section III, #10
Section III, #16

Preptest 65

Section I, #10
Section I, #22
Section IV, #12
Section IV, #21

Argument Evaluation

Preptest 65

Section I, #3
Section IV, #7

Flawed Reasoning

Preptest 62

Section II, #5
Section II, #8
Section II, #11
Section IV, #10
Section IV, #13
Section IV, #19

Preptest 63

Section I, #3
Section I, #23
Section I, #25
Section III, #2
Section III, #14
Section III, #18

Preptest 64

Section I, #5
Section I, #7
Section I, #16
Section I, #19
Section III, #4
Section III, #6
Section III, #11
Section III, #14

Preptest 65

Section I, #8
Section I, #15
Section I, #17
Section I, #20
Section IV, #8
Section IV, #11
Section IV, #26

Preptest 66

Section II, #1
Section II, #8
Section II, #11
Section II, #13
Section II, #15
Section II, #21
Section IV, #1
Section IV, #22
Section IV, #25

Thank You

First of all, thank you for buying this book. Writing these explanations has been the most satisfying work I have ever done. I sincerely hope they have been helpful to you, and I wish you success on the LSAT and as a lawyer.

If you left an Amazon review, you get an extra special thank you! I truly appreciate it. You're helping others discover LSAT Hacks.

Thanks also to Anu Panil, who drew the diagrams for the logic games. Anu, thank you for making sense of the scribbles and scans I sent you. You are surely ready to master logic games after all the work you did.

Thanks to Alison Rayner, who helped me with the layout and designed the cover. If this book looks nice, she deserves credit. Alison caught many mistakes I would never have found by myself (any that remain are my own, of course).

Thanks to Ludovic Glorieux, who put up with me constantly asking him if a design change looked good or bad.

Finally, thanks to my parents, who remained broadly supportive despite me being crazy enough to leave law school to teach the LSAT. I love you guys.

About The Author

Graeme Blake lives in Montreal Canada. He first took the LSAT in June 2007, and scored a 177. It was love at first sight. He taught the LSAT for Testmasters for a couple of years before going to the University of Toronto for law school.

Upon discovering that law was not for him, Graeme began working as an independent LSAT tutor. He teaches LSAT courses in Montreal for Ivy Global and tutors students from all around the world using Skype.

He publishes a series of LSAT guides and explanations under the title LSAT Hacks. Versions of these explanations can be found at LSAT Blog, Cambridge LSAT, as well as amazon.com.

Graeme is also the moderator of www.reddit.com/r/LSAT, Reddit's LSAT forum. He worked for a time with 7Sage LSAT.

Graeme finds it unusual to write in the third person to describe himself, but he recognizes the importance of upholding publishing traditions. He wonders if many people read about the author pages.

You can find him at http://lsathacks.com and www.reddit.com/r/LSAT.

Graeme encourages you to get in touch by email, his address is graeme@lsathacks.com. Or you can call 514-612-1526. He's happy to hear feedback or give advice.

Further Reading

I hope you liked this book. If you did, I'd be very grateful if you took two minutes to review it on amazon. People judge a book by its reviews, and if you review this book you'll help other LSAT students discover it.

Ok, so you've written a review and want to know what to do next.

The most important LSAT books are the preptests themselves. Many students think they have to read every strategy guide under the sun, but you'll learn the most simply from doing real LSAT questions and analyzing your mistakes.

At the time of writing, there are 72 official LSATs. The most recent ones are best, but if you've got a while to study I recommend doing every test from 19 or from 29 onwards.

This series (LSAT Hacks) is a bit different from other LSAT prep books. This book is not a strategy guide.

Instead, my goal is to let you do what my own students get to do when they take lessons with me: review their work with the help of an expert.

These explanations show you a better way to approach questions, and exactly why answers are right or wrong.

If you found this book useful, here's the list of other books in the series:

(Note – the series was formerly titled "Hacking the LSAT" so the older books still have that title until I update them)

- Hacking The LSAT: Full Explanations For LSATs 29-38, Volume I
- Hacking The LSAT: Full Explanations For LSATs 29-38, Volume II
- LSAT 62 Explanations (Hacking the LSAT Series)
- LSAT 63 Explanations (Hacking the LSAT Series)
- LSAT 64 Explanations (Hacking The LSAT Series)
- LSAT 65 Explanations (Hacking The LSAT Series)
- LSAT 66 Explanations (Hacking The LSAT Series)
- LSAT 67 Explanations (Hacking The LSAT Series)
- LSAT 68 Explanations (Hacking The LSAT Series)
- LSAT 69 Explanations (Hacking The LSAT Series)
- LSAT 70 Explanations (Hacking The LSAT Series)
- LSAT 71 Explanations (Hacking The LSAT Series)
- LSAT 72 Explanations (LSAT Hacks)
- Explanations for 10 Actual, Official LSAT Preptests, Volume I: Preptests 62-66 (LSAT Hacks Series)
- Explanations for 10 Actual, Official LSAT Preptests, Volume II: Preptests 67-71 (LSAT Hacks Series)

Except for LSAT 72, the single volume books cover the same preptests that are covered in this book.

If you *are* looking for strategy guides, try Manhattan LSAT or Powerscore. Unlike other companies, they use real LSAT questions in their books.

I've written a longer piece on LSAT books on Reddit. It includes links to the best LSAT books and preptests. If you're serious about the LSAT and want the best materials, I strongly recommend you read it:

http://redd.it/uf4uh

(this is a shortlink that takes you to the correct page)

Free LSAT Email Course

This book is just the beginning. It teaches you how to solve individual questions, but it's not designed to give you overall strategies for each section.

There's so much to learn about the LSAT. As a start, I've made a free, five day email course. Each day I'll send you an email teaching you what I know about a subject.

LSAT Email Course Overview

- Intro to the LSAT
- Logical Reasoning
- Logic Games
- Reading Comprehension
- How to study

What people say about the free LSAT course

These have been awesome. More please!!! - **Cailie**

Your emails are tremendously helpful. - **Matt**

Thanks for the tips! They were very helpful, and even make you feel like you studied a bit. Great insight and would love more! - **Haj**

Sign up for the free LSAT email course here

http://lsathacks.com/email-course/

p.s. I've had people say this free email course is more useful than an entire Kaplan course they took. It's 100% free. Good luck - Graeme

CPSIA information can be obtained
at www.ICGtesting.com
Printed in the USA
BVHW01s1019201018
530770BV00018B/290/P